EU COUNTER-TERRORISM LAW

EU Counter-Terrorism Law: Pre-emption and the Rule of Law is a detailed study of EU action to combat terrorism since 11 September 2001 and the implications that action has had for the EU legal order. It critically examines EU counter-terrorism measures to ascertain how rule of law principles have been affected in the 'war on terrorism'. The book opens with a critical examination of the rule of law in the EU legal order and provides an overview of the 'war on terrorism' before analysing five key facets of EU counter-terrorism: the common European definition of terrorism along with related offences contained in the Framework Decision on Combating Terrorism; the EU's anti-money-laundering and counter-terrorist finance laws; UN and EU targeted asset-freezing sanctions; the EU's data retention measures such as the Data Retention Directive and the Passenger Name Records agreements; and the European Arrest Warrant and European Evidence Warrant. The book argues that EU counter-terrorism is weakening the rule of law and bypassing safeguards in favour of a system emphasising coercive control over individual autonomy. It concludes by examining the prospects for the future as the EU becomes a more powerful security actor following the Lisbon Treaty and the adoption of the Stockholm Programme.

Volume 31 in the series Modern Studies in European Law

Modern Studies in European Law

Recent titles in this series:

Unfair Contract Terms in European Law: A Study in
Comparative and EC Law *Paolisa Nebbia*

Energy Security: The External Legal Relations of the European Union with Major Oil and
Gas Supplying Countries *Sanam S Haghighi*

EU Criminal Law *Valsamis Mitsilegas*

Effective Judicial Protection and the Environmental Impact Assessment Directive in
Ireland *Áine Ryall*

Network-Based Governance in EC Law: The Example of EC Competition and EC
Communications Law *Maartje de Visser*

Legitimacy in EU Cartel Control *Ingeborg Simonsson*

Mixed Agreements Revisited: The EU and its Member States in the World *Edited by
Christophe Hillion and Panos Koutrakos*

Reflexive Governance: Redefining the Public Interest in a Pluralistic World *Edited by
Olivier De Schutter and Jacques Lenoble*

The Impact of EU Law on Minority Rights *Tawhida Ahmed*

Direct Investment, National Champions and EU Treaty Freedoms: From Maastricht to
Lisbon *Frank S Benyon*

The Cyprus Issue: The Four Freedoms in a Member State under Siege *Nikos Skoutaris*

The European Union and Global Emergencies: A Law and Policy Analysis
Edited by Antonis Antoniadis, Robert Schütze and Eleanor Spaventa

Public Liability in EU Law: *Brasserie, Bergaderm* and Beyond
Pekka Aalto

Professional Services in the EU Internal Market: Quality Regulation and Self-Regulation
Tinne Heremans

Environmental Integration in the EU's External Relations: Beyond Multilateral
Dimensions *Gracia Marín Durán and Elisa Morgera*

The Constitutional Dimension of European Criminal Law
Ester Herlin-Karnell

**For the complete list of titles in this series,
see 'Modern Studies in European Law' link at
www.hartpub.co.uk/books/series.asp**

EU Counter-Terrorism Law

Pre-Emption and the Rule of Law

Cian C Murphy

·HART·
PUBLISHING

OXFORD AND PORTLAND, OREGON

2012

Published in the United Kingdom by Hart Publishing Ltd
16C Worcester Place, Oxford, OX1 2JW
Telephone: +44 (0)1865 517530
Fax: +44 (0)1865 510710
E-mail: mail@hartpub.co.uk
Website: http://www.hartpub.co.uk

Published in North America (US and Canada) by
Hart Publishing
c/o International Specialized Book Services
920 NE 58th Avenue, Suite 300
Portland, OR 97213-3786
USA
Tel: +1 503 287 3093 or toll-free: (1) 800 944 6190
Fax: +1 503 280 8832
E-mail: orders@isbs.com
Website: http://www.isbs.com

British Library Cataloguing in Publication Data
Data Available

ISBN: 978-1-84946-135-1

Typeset by Compuscript Ltd, Shannon
Printed and bound in Great Britain by
TJ International Ltd, Padstow, Cornwall

do m'athair agus mo mháthair
le grá

Table of Contents

Acknowledgements

This book is the revised and updated product of my doctoral research. It would never have begun, let alone been completed, without the support of my supervisor, Piet Eeckhout. I am also indebted to Penny Green who served as my second supervisor during my final year. Piet and Penny have together guided me into life as an academic and I am fortunate to count them as friends and colleagues. My research was supported by a National University of Ireland Travelling Studentship, an Arts and Humanities Research Council Doctoral Award and a Modern Law Review Scholarship. I am grateful to these institutions for their generous support and in particular to Noirín Moynihan and Karyn O'Brien at the NUI for their patience. My doctoral examiners, Takis Tridimas and Miguel Maduro, made the examination process a pleasure and have provided wonderful support over the past two years. Participants at the EUI High Level Policy Seminar in March 2011 allowed me to test the conclusions of this research—I am grateful to Miguel Maduro and Martin Scheinin for the invitation and to Deirdre Curtin, Kent Roach, Gabor Rona, and Kim Lane Scheppele for the lively debate (and snow clowns). Diego Acosta, Stephen Coutts, Piet Eeckhout, Marta Iljadica, Jan Oster, Eloise Scotford and Rachael Walsh each read draft chapters and the book is much improved as a result. Two exceptional scholars provided invaluable research assistance as I updated the manuscript. Sofia Marques da Silva helped on counter-terrorist finance and data surveillance and Mike Tucker assisted on European warrants. Richard Hart is a true gentleman who has supported each book proposal I've sent him with enthusiasm and provided much sage advice. I am grateful to him and to everyone else at Hart Publishing for producing such an attractive volume. Any errors, of course, are my own.

I am grateful for the support of colleagues at King's and elsewhere. I owe particular thanks to Tanya Aplin, David Anderson, Andrea Biondi, Robert Blackburn, Ben Bowling, Fiona de Londras, Sionaidh Douglas-Scott, Nick Hatzis, Jeremy Horder, Francis Jacobs, Annette Lee, Tim Macklem, Thomas MacManus, Susan Marks, Aileen McColgan, Caroline Morris, Valsamis Mitsilegas, Susan Nash, Dawn Oliver, Federico Ortino, DO Richards, Sandy Steel, Alex Türk, Dan Wilsher, Lorna Woods and the entire Human Rights in Ireland team. I am also thankful for the Melbourne House gang who made doctoral life bearable and the lunchtime posse at Chapters and Tom's who get me through the working day. At home, my grandparents, Thomas and Kathleen Quilligan and Clare (and the late John) Murphy fill my stomach whenever I turn up unannounced. Tom Hinchy, David Cronin and Rory Conboye have the misfortune of knowing me for far too long but put up with me all the same. The same is true of my former partners in crime, Stephen Coutts and Noel McGrath. My sisters, Eimear and Grace, drive me insane half the time and keep me sane the rest of the time. Sarah Deeny has endured this book being written and rewritten and continues to offer love and support. The last and greatest thanks are owed to my parents, Christy and Eileen, who saw me through two decades of education. This book is as much the product of their efforts as it is mine and so is dedicated, *le grá*, to them.

CM
London, 15 September 2011

Table of Cases

European Union

Alphabetical

Case Number

European Court of Human Rights

EU Member States

Bulgaria

Cyprus

Czech Republic

Germany

Poland

Part I

Terrorism, Pre-Emption and the EU Rule of Law

Introduction

September 11, Counter-Terrorism and the Rule of Law

> Anything can happen, the tallest towers
> Be overturned, those in high places daunted...
> Ground gives. The heaven's weight
> Lifts up off Atlas like a kettle lid.
> Capstones shift. Nothing resettles right.[*]

A DECADE HAS passed since the attacks in New York and Washington DC on 11 September 2001 claimed the lives of 2,973 victims and 19 hijackers. The response to those events has dramatically reshaped the relationship between states and individuals across the globe and nothing has resettled right. In the United States (US) the USA PATRIOT Act has extended the power of the state to conduct surveillance of its citizens.[1] In the United Kingdom (UK) the time an individual may be detained without charge has increased from 7 to 28 days, while some individuals are placed under indefinite house arrest.[2] In Australia legislation has introduced new criminal offences and new powers for intelligence agencies.[3] Much of the action by states and international organisations in the 'war on terror' has been criticised because of its effect on human rights and the rule of law.[4] The trend in both the US and UK has been towards pre-emptive intervention that attempts to eliminate threats to national security before they arise. Building on twentieth-century ideas of risk and actuarial justice, these trends undermine traditional legal protections by shifting the target of law enforcement from acts already committed to action that

---

[*] S Heaney, 'Anything Can Happen: After Horace, Odes, I, 34', *District and Circle* (London, Faber, 2006).

[1] Uniting and Strengthening America by Providing Appropriate Tools Required to Intercept and Obstruct Terrorism Act 2001. D Cole and J Lobel, *Less Safe, Less Free: Why America Is Losing the War on Terror* (New York, The New Press, 2007) 31–32.

[2] Prevention of Terrorism Act 2005, Terrorism Act 2006. For discussion see C Walker, *Blackstone's Guide to the Anti-Terrorism Legislation*, 2nd edn (Oxford, Oxford University Press, 2009); C Walker, *Terrorism and the Law* (Oxford, Oxford University Press, 2011).

[3] J McCulloch and S Pickering, 'Pre-Crime and Counter-Terrorism: Imagining Future Crime in the "War on Terror"' (2009) 49 *British Journal of Criminology* 628.

[4] Ibid.

may be committed in the future.[5] The adoption of new counter-terrorism legislation around the world has given rise to several libraries' worth of popular and scholarly literature.[6] However, amidst this proliferation of law and literature, there has been no sustained examination of EU counter-terrorism action. For present purposes, existing literature on EU counter-terrorism action may be divided into two broad categories: non-legal and legal. First, scholars in diverse disciplines including philosophy, criminology and politics have attempted to provide an overview of post-September 11, 2001 counter-terrorism action and have criticised the practical effects of EU law and policy.[7] Second, legal scholars have described and critiqued various discrete measures adopted by the European Union (EU), including the Framework Decision on Combating Terrorism, the European Arrest Warrant and targeted asset-freezing sanctions.[8] The latter works tend to focus strictly on the legal developments and implications for EU law. However, to adequately understand the diffuse effects of the 'war on terror' on the EU legal system it is necessary to draw on both legal and non-legal literature and develop a critique of EU counter-terrorism action that is rooted in the wider academic debate.

If the 'war on terror' provides the contemporary backdrop for this book then the rule of law is the legal concept at its core. The rule of law is an essentially contested concept[9] which we most often hear of when it is being flaunted by outlaws or violated by states. This is because it is a political concept which comes to the fore when it is 'under stress' and is most valued in places where it has been ignored in the past.[10] In such circumstances, opposing ideologies may view the principle as either a luxury or an indispensible necessity. The polarisation of opinions on the meaning and usefulness of the rule of law has been visible on both sides of the Atlantic since 11 September 2001. The actions of governments across the world have been criticised for violating the principle while some of those governments have attempted to evade such criticism by claiming that the 'rules of the game' have changed.[11] While some actions by governments have appeared unlawful others seem to exploit gaps in legal protection and cannot easily be called illegal. The relationship between the war and the rule of law is therefore a complex one in which both terrorism and action taken to combat it can reshape legal principles in new and challenging ways.

---

[5]   Cole and Lobel, n 1 above, p 1.

[6]   M Breen Smyth, J Gunning, R Jackson, G Kassimeris, P Robinson, 'Critical Terrorism Studies: An Introduction' (2008) 1 *Critical Studies on Terrorism* 1, 1.

[7]   See for some useful examples: L Amoore and M de Goede, *Risk and the War on Terror* (London, Routledge, 2008); JP Sterba (ed), *Terrorism and International Justice* (Oxford, Oxford University Press, 2003); P Scraton (ed), *Beyond September 11: An Anthology of Dissent* (London, Pluto Press, 2002); T Rockmore, J Margolis and AT Marsoobian (eds), *The Philosophical Challenge of September 11* (London, Wiley-Blackwell, 2004).

[8]   See, eg: E Dumitriu, 'The EU's Definition of Terrorism: The Council Framework Decision on Combating Terrorism' (2004) 5 *German Law Journal* 585.

[9]   WB Gallie 'Essentially Contested Concepts' (1956) 56 *Proceedings of the Aristotelian Society* 167–98.

[10]   A Marmor, 'The Rule of Law and its Limits' (2004) 23 *Law and Philosophy* 1.

[11]   T Blair, PM Press Conference, 5 August 2005.

I. TERRORISM AND THE RULE OF LAW

Terrorism poses several challenges to the rule of law, most notably through the action taken by states in response to it. However, the first challenge to the rule of law is posed by the act of political violence itself. For Montesquieu the rule of law exists 'in order to avoid ... constant fear created by the threats of violence and the actual cruelties of the holders of military power'.[12] On this basis, those who engage in terrorism operate contrary to the rule of law—as do all those who knowingly violate the criminal law. However, unlike most ordinary criminals, those who engage in *political* violence seek to fundamentally undermine the state and its legal order. While this threat can in some circumstances be real—such as the effective control the Provisional Irish Republican Army held over certain parts of Derry and Belfast in Ireland during the 'Troubles'[13]—it seems unlikely that the modern terrorism could cause states in Europe or North America to collapse. As Lord Hoffmann defiantly declared in the Belmarsh case, 'there is no doubt that we shall survive Al-Qaeda'.[14] As such, while terrorism is a rejection of the rule of law, the real threat for liberal democracies often comes from the state's response to the violence and not the violence itself.

The problem of response begins with the problem of definition. 'Terrorism' is, like the rule of law, a contested concept. Fortunately, when examining counter-terrorism, which is the state's response to what it perceives as terrorism, it is not necessary to venture too far into the debate on the definition of terrorism itself. It is sufficient to note that states, international organisations, and especially those involved in scholarly discourse, have failed to agree a definition of that which they seek to combat.[15] The principal problem is that any definition of terrorism is considered pejorative. The link between 'terror' and 'political violence' can be traced to Robespierre and the Reign of Terror in the French Revolution. Robespierre described terror as 'nothing else than swift, severe, indomitable justice; it flows, then, from virtue'.[16] However, moral claims made by Robespierre were swiftly rebutted by Edmund Burke, who referred to the Jacobins as 'those Hell-hounds called terrorists'.[17] Ever since, the idea of 'terrorism' has been morally loaded, giving rise to the tired adage that one man's terrorist is another man's freedom fighter.[18] The Thatcher government in the UK offers a clear example of a state

---

[12] Baron Charles de Montesquieu, quoted in J Skhlar, 'Political Theory and the Rule of Law' in AC Hutchinson and P Monahan (eds), *The Rule of Law: Ideal or Ideology* (Toronto, Carswell, 1987) 5.

[13] D McKittrick and D McVea, *Making Sense of the Troubles* (London, Penguin, 2001).

[14] *A v Secretary of State for the Home Department* [2004] UKHL 56 [96].

[15] B Saul, *Defining Terrorism in International Law* (Oxford, Oxford University Press, 2006).

[16] For a discussion of the origins of the term see the thoughts of Jacques Derrida in G Borradori (ed), *Philosophy in a Time of Terror: Dialogues with Jürgen Habermas and Jacques Derrida* (Chicago, University of Chicago Press, 2003) 102–03. For a useful perspective from cultural theory see T Eagleton, *Holy Terror* (Oxford, Oxford University Press, 2005).

[17] E Burke, *Letters on a Regicide Peace* (1796).

[18] C Gearty, 'Terrorism and Morality' (2003) *European Human Rights Law Review* 377. For an excellent exposition of the struggle over the use of the language in 'terror' in public debate see S Poole, *Unspeak* (London, Little Brown, 2006).

attempting to gain advantage in conflicts through the use of language in relation to political violence. In the 1980s, Irish Republican prisoners in the Maze Prison sought special status as recognition that they were not ordinary inmates but rather political internees. Prime Minister Margaret Thatcher responded that

> There is no such thing as political murder, political bombing or political violence. There is only criminal murder, criminal bombing and criminal violence. We will not compromise on this. There will be no political status.[19]

By denying the prisoners' claim to political status, she sought to deny the existence of a political dispute and to reduce the conflict to a simple case of a state enforcing its criminal law. While Thatcher prevailed at the time, former internees are now in government in Northern Ireland. In a similar vein, the UK Conservative Party recently issued an apology for Margaret Thatcher's branding of Nelson Mandela as a terrorist.[20] Defining 'terrorism' by reference to the moral legitimacy of the actor's cause is not a sound basis for law which requires general rules and equal application. A morally subjective approach to the definition of a crime would undermine the principle of legal certainty that is at the heart of the rule of law.[21] It is for this reason that the international community has historically avoided defining terrorism per se, focusing instead on certain actions that may be carried out for political ends, such as hijacking an airplane.[22] Indeed, so problematic is the term from the both legal and philosophical perspectives that some have called for it to be abandoned altogether.[23]

The problem of defining terrorism is compounded by the state's tendency to overreact to it. The case reports of the European Court of Human Rights provide a plethora of examples of states that have strayed from fundamental legal principles in their attempts to respond to the real or perceived threat of political violence.[24] Indeed, the very first case before the Court concerned the anticipation of a threat to the integrity of the Irish state.[25] Much of the Court's law on the right to life, prohibition against torture and inhuman or degrading treatment and right to personal liberty has flowed from such cases. Rights violations by the Irish and British states in response to Republican and Loyalist violence, by the Spanish state in response to Basque separatists and by Turkey in relation to the Kurdish minority have all demonstrated the tendency of ostensibly liberal states to overreact to challenges to state authority. Violations of the European Convention on Human

---

[19] M Thatcher, 'Speech in Belfast', 5 March 1981, available at www.margaretthatcher.org, last accessed 5 May 2010.

[20] 'Cameron: We Were Wrong to Call Mandela a Terrorist', *Independent* (26 August 2006).

[21] All definitions of the rule of law include some element of legal certainty. See, for an example of a narrow definition that nonetheless includes legal certainty, J Raz, 'The Rule of Law and its Virtue' (1977) 93 *Law Quarterly Review* 195.

[22] Saul, n 15 above, p 129.

[23] C Gearty, 'Terrorism and Morality' (2003) *European Human Rights Law Review* 377.

[24] S Sottiaux, *Terrorism and the Limitation of Human Rights: The ECHR and the US Constitution* (Oxford, Hart Publishing, 2008).

[25] *Lawless v Ireland* (1960) 1 EHRR 1.

Rights are particularly noteworthy as the Convention contains clear limitations on rights and the facility to derogate from most rights in times of emergency.[26]

Despite the problems for the rule of law caused by both the difficulty of definition and the tendency to overreact, perhaps the greatest challenge posed by terrorism and counter-terrorism to liberal democracies is its effect on political discourse. Most definitions of terrorism view the phenomenon as a form of violent communication.[27] The purpose of the violence is not merely the immediate harm caused, but the message sent by the act to the wider population and the state apparatus. Mutua notes that '[t]he broad and vague use of the term "terrorist" ... has had a chilling effect on legitimate debate and differences on serious issues both in the academe and in popular public and political discourses'.[28] The fear caused by political violence polarises politics and undermines rational discussion.

This polarised discourse is most clearly demonstrated by the chimera of 'balancing liberty and security' or, put more bluntly, by asking whose human rights come first.[29] It is in the tension between what is just and what is necessary that the true problems of legal philosophy are revealed.[30] As terrorism damages the fragile consensus on divisive philosophical issues, it raises the question of what a just society can legitimately do in response to actions that reject that society's very foundational values. In the aftermath of the September 11 attacks in New York and Washington DC, that question came to the fore and may well be the defining philosophical challenge of the twenty-first century so far.

II. A 'WAR ON TERROR'

The 'war on terror' was declared by US President George W Bush in the aftermath of the attacks on 11 September 2001. While many states have overreacted to terrorism, the reaction of the United States following the 2001 attacks has been singular. It was not the first time in history that the phrase has been, but it may be the most significant.[31] The declaration of has shaped legal, political and cultural

---

[26] CA Gearty, *Principles of Human Rights Adjudication* (Oxford, Oxford University Press, 2003) 40–41.

[27] AP Schmid, 'Terrorism: The Definitional Problem' (2004) 36 *Case Western Reserve Journal of International Law* 375, 382.

[28] M Matua, 'Terrorism and Human Rights: Power, Culture, and Subordination' (2002) 8 *Buffalo Human Rights Law Review* 1, 10.

[29] T Blair, 'Labour Party Conference Speech 2005', *Guardian* (27 September 2005).

[30] F Neumann, *The Rule of Law: Political Theory and the Legal System in Modern Society* (Leamington Spa, Berg Publishers, 1986) 12.

[31] The New York Times records several pre-2001 uses of the phrase, including: 'The War on Terrorism: European Measures for its Extermination', *New York Times* (2 April 1881) in relation to Russian Anarchists; 'British Arrest Jewish Mayors', *New York Times* (5 August 1947), a story relating to violence in Palestine that made reference to the 'British war on terrorism' and 'Congress; The War on Terrorism, from Tripoli to Belfast', *New York Times* (30 April 1986), in relation to Irish republican links to Libya.

debate ever since.[32] Despite its initial popularity, the decision to declare war has been described as 'a serious normative and pragmatic error'.[33] Normatively the declaration gave the status of soldiers to mere criminals, and pragmatically, it is a war that cannot be won.[34] In some respects the declaration could be considered a mere rhetorical flourish that was deemed a necessary response to the sheer scale of the violence.[35] The respected US commentator, Phillip Bobbit, has since claimed that the US is at the beginning of the 'wars against terror'; a prophesy that threatens to cement a seemingly perpetual war in the public's collective imagination.[36]

The declaration of 'war' did have certain benefits from the Bush administration's point of view. A war allows the US President to 'invoke his special mystique as Commander in Chief' and thus may provide the 'rhetorical cover' for acts of 'questionable legality'.[37] Most pertinently, the 'war' has facilitated an important shift in global counter-terrorism—from a traditional criminal justice approach to one that is 'pre-emptive':

> [T]he impact of 9/11, of the London bombings, and the continuing threat of catastrophic risk has significantly increased the pressure on governments to think and act pre-emptively. The trajectory towards anticipatory endeavour, risk assessment and intelligence gathering is accelerating.[38]

After 11 September 2001, the Bush government developed various doctrines based on pre-empting terrorist attacks before they occur. These new doctrines are evident in both the external and internal counter-terrorism efforts of the US.[39] Externally, the US Security Strategy trumpeted the need for pre-emptive war:

> The greater the threat, the greater is the risk of inaction—and the more compelling the case for taking anticipatory action to defend ourselves, even if uncertainty remains as to the time and place of the enemy's attack. To forestall or prevent such hostile acts by our adversaries, the United States will, if necessary, act pre-emptively.[40]

Internally, the USA PATRIOT Act 2001 allowed law enforcement officers broad powers justified in terms of preventing a further attack on US soil.[41] Perhaps the most memorable image of the pre-emptive approach to counter-terrorism

---

[32] P Sands, *Lawless World: Making and Breaking Global Rules* (London, Penguin, 2005) 153.

[33] J Habermas, *The Divided West* (London, Polity Press, 2006) 14–15.

[34] Ibid.

[35] L Richardson, *What Terrorists Want: Understanding the Terrorist Threat* (London, John Murray, 2006) 208.

[36] P Bobbit, *Terror and Consent: The Wars for the Twenty-First Century* (London, Allen Lane, 2008).

[37] B Ackerman, 'This is Not a War' (2004) 113 *Yale Law Journal* 1870, 1871.

[38] L Zedner, 'Pre-Crime and post-Criminology?' (2007) 11 *Theoretical Criminology* 261, 264.

[39] The 'paradigm of prevention' was introduced by former US Attorney General John Ashcroft. See: J Ashcroft, 'Speech to the Council on Foreign Relations', 10 February 2003.

[40] The White House, 'The National Security Strategy of the United States', September 2002, available at http://georgewbush-whitehouse.archives.gov/nsc/nss/2002/index.html. For the case in favour of pre-emptive war, see: AD Sofaer, 'On the Necessity of Pre-emption' (2003) 14 *European Journal of International Law* 209.

[41] Cole and Lobel, n 1 above, p 31.

has been the indefinite detention without trial of 'enemy combatants' at the military base in Guantánamo Bay and more recently at Bagram Airbase.[42] The Bush administration's aim was made clear by former US Attorney General John Ashcroft: 'our single objective is to prevent terrorist attacks by taking suspected terrorists off the street'.[43]

In taking a pre-emptive approach, the Bush administration reflected the risk society thinking that had become increasingly influential in criminal justice in the latter half of the twentieth century. A punitive turn and new thinking on crime prevention caused institutional cultures to shift more and more towards coercion and control.[44] While use of the criminal sanction was increasing, other forms of social control were also being developed: aimed at regulating the risks of modern life. This led to the rise of a mode of governance known as the 'risk society'.[45] Risks are 'consequences that relate to the threatening forces of modernization and to its globalization of doubt'.[46] Such risks might include damage to property from climate change, threats to public health from pandemics, and the dangers posed by global economic uncertainty. In recent decades, the threat of crime has increasingly been seen as such a risk. In the risk society, criminal behaviour is taken to be an ordinary part of life: 'a contingency for which there are risk technologies to help spread the loss and prevent recurrence ... a technical problem that requires an administrative solution'.[47]

If this is how crime is understood then the goal of the criminal justice system 'is not to eliminate crime but, accepting the "normalization" of crime, to make tolerable the twin burdens of crime and control through systemic co-ordination'.[48] Therefore criminal justice is superseded by 'actuarial justice'.[49] Actuarial justice is

> concerned with techniques for identifying, classifying and managing groups assorted by levels of dangerousness. It takes crime for granted. It accepts deviance as normal ... Thus its aim is not to intervene in individuals' lives for the purpose of ascertaining responsibility, making the guilty 'pay for their crime' or changing them. *Rather it seeks to regulate groups as part of a strategy of managing danger.*[50]

---

[42] K Greenberg, *The Least Worst Place: How Guantanamo Became the World's Most Notorious Prison* (Oxford, Oxford University Press, 2009).

[43] J Ashcroft, 'Prepared remarks for US Mayors' Conference', October 25 2001, available: www.justice.gov/archive/ag/speeches/2001/agcrisisremarks10_25.htm.

[44] D Garland, *The Culture of Control: Crime and Social Order in Contemporary Society* (Chicago, University of Chicago Press, 2001).

[45] U Beck, *Risk Society: Towards a New Modernity* (London, Sage Publications, 1992).

[46] Ibid, p 22.

[47] RV Ericson and KD Haggerty, *Policing the Risk Society* (Oxford, Clarendon Press, 1997) 40.

[48] I Brownlee, 'New Labour: New Penology? Punitive Rhetoric and the Limits of Managerialism in Criminal Justice Policy' (1998) 25 *Journal of Law and Society* 313, 324.

[49] M Feeley and J Simon, 'The New Penology: Notes on the Emerging Strategy of Corrections and Its Implications' (1992) 30 *Criminology* 449; M Feeley and J Simon, 'Actuarial Justice: The Emerging New Criminal Law' in D Nelken (ed), *The Futures of Criminology* (London, Sage Publishing, 1994).

[50] Feeley and Simon, 'Actuarial Justice', n 49 above, p 174 (emphasis added).

The final point is particularly important in the context of counter-terrorism. In the past the concept of 'dangerousness'[51] was to justify the preventive detention of those considered a threat to public safety.[52] Despite the precedent's resonance, determinations of dangerousness were primarily concerned with the characteristics of particular individuals.[53] Actuarial justice goes further by basing decisions in statistical analysis rather than individual judgments. It grounds its logic in the likelihood of criminality in those with particular traits rather than a prediction of outcomes in individual cases.[54] Feeley and Simon offer three characteristics of such an approach: the whole population is the target of power; that power is aimed at prevention and risk minimisation; and justice is viewed as the rationality of the system of control.[55] The primary goal is not deterring the public from committing crime, or seeking retribution against, or rehabilitation of, those who have broken the law. Rather it is to manage dangerous persons through incapacitation: curtailing their ability to interact with and harm the law-abiding majority. To achieve this objective, criminal law must be viewed as 'only one of a range of formal and informal forms of social control from which one has to chose in a rational way, unhampered by moral considerations'.[56] Even before 11 September 2001, courts were 'rethinking the values of constitutional criminal jurisprudence from an orientation deeply informed by actuarial justice'.[57]

The resonance of post-September 11, 2001 action by the US government with risk society thinking is clear, both in terms of the targets of the action ('*suspected* terrorists') and the action itself (incapacitation). Thus, individuals captured overseas have been subject to indefinite detention in Guantánamo Bay and latterly Bagram Airbase. Political organisations have had their assets frozen in accordance with 'material support' legislation. Iraq was invaded ostensibly to pre-empt any use of weapons of mass destruction by Saddam Hussein. However, despite the superficial similarities, recent counter-terrorism efforts are not as compatible with an actuarial approach as they may seem. Two central differences exist. The first difference is caused by the incalculability of the threat. The risk society treats crime as predictable. On the other hand, 'the war on terror recognizes that the sheer uncertainty and randomness of terrorist attack renders conventional

---

[51] Dangerousness is '*a pathological attribute of character: a propensity to inflict harm on others in disregard or defiance of the usual social and legal constraints ...*'. See J Floud and W Young, *Dangerousness and Criminal Justice* (London, Heinemann, 1981) 20.

[52] Ibid; N Walker, 'Unscientific, Unwise, Unprofitable or Unjust? The Anti-Protectionist Arguments' (1982) 22 *British Journal of Criminology* 276.

[53] J Steele, *Risks and Legal Theory* (Oxford, Hart Publishing, 2004), 43.

[54] E Silver and LL Miller, 'A Cautionary Note on the Use of Actuarial Risk Assessment Tools for Social Control' (2002) 48 *Crime Delinquency* 138, 139–43.

[55] Feeley and Simon, 'Actuarial Justice', n 50 above, p 177.

[56] I Brownlee, 'New Labour: New Penology? Punitive Rhetoric and the Limits of Managerialism in Criminal Justice Policy' (1998) 25 *Journal of Law and Society* 313, 323.

[57] Feeley and Simon, 'Actuarial Justice', n 50 above, p 180.

risk assessment techniques inadequate'.[58] Former US Defence Secretary Donald Rumsfeld has referred to the 'unknown unknowns'—those threats that we do not even know that we do not know about.[59] In the face of these unknowns, government agencies have taken to imagining potential future attacks: replacing the statistical basis of actuarial justice with a worst case scenario hypothesis.[60] Any action based on such an exercise can only be justified by reference to a possible future rather than one that is statistically probable.

The second difference between actuarialism and post-September 11 counter-terrorism lies in the attitude to the harm. Actuarial justice operates on the basis of crime as an everyday occurrence to be regulated and managed (but, implicitly, never eradicated). On the other hand, the Bush administration sought to prevent all terrorist attacks regardless of their likelihood. This 'One Percent Doctrine' was described by former Vice President Dick Cheney: 'If there's a 1% chance that Pakistani scientists are helping al-Qaeda build or develop a nuclear weapon, we have to treat it as a certainty in terms of our response'.[61] While a traditional risk society accepts a certain level of violence, post-September 11 counter-terrorism does not. The acceptable level of risk is zero.

The difference between pre- and post-September 11 approaches to criminal justice and counter-terrorism in particular is captured in the use of the term 'pre-emption' rather than 'prevention'. Both preventive and pre-emptive approaches aim to avoid harm by incapacitating dangerous groups and individuals. However, since the al-Qaeda attacks, as the risk is considered incalculable, the potential damage catastrophic, and any harm intolerable, measured action based on prudential assessments is impossible. It is at this point that the approach shifts from prevention to pre-emption. Thus it can be said that 'prevention takes place when, for example, someone knows a house will catch fire today and tries to prevent it happening—even if that includes infringing property rights. [Pre-emption] would mean that one occupies the house, arguing that a fire could break out any time'.[62] In this example, pre-emption entails a greater intervention without concrete evidence of harm. The same tendencies can be observed in post-September 11 counter-terrorism action. Cole and Lobel note that while 'preventive strategies have become increasingly common in ordinary criminal law enforcement as well ... the Bush administration's preventive paradigm is qualitatively more extreme'.[63]

---

[58] M de Goede, 'The Politics of Preemption and the War on Terror in Europe' (2008) 14 *European Journal of International Relations* 161, 164.

[59] D Rumsfeld, 'Briefing to the US Department of Defence', 12 February 2002.

[60] M de Goede, 'Beyond Risk: Premediation and the Post-9/11 Security Imagination' (2008) 39 *Security Dialogue* 155, 158.

[61] R Suskind, *The One Percent Doctrine: Deep Inside America's Pursuit of its Enemies since 9/11* (New York, Simon & Schuster, 2006).

[62] O Kessler, 'Is Risk Changing the Politics of Legal Argumentation?' (2008) 21 *Leiden Journal of International Law* 863, fn 7. Kessler uses the example to highlight the difference between prevention and precaution, but it is equally applicable to the difference between prevention and pre-emption.

[63] Cole and Lobel, n 1 above, p 267.

A pre-emptive strategy is an enabler of government action. Pre-emption facilitates authoritarian counter-terrorism action because it demands that action be taken against an unknown threat and so consigns traditional ideas of prevention and deterrence to obsolescence.[64] For the state governed through pre-emptive counter-terrorism, the ideal situation is not the normalisation of violence, but the normalisation of the threat of violence. Whereas a successful attack may undermine the public's confidence in government's ability to fulfil its role as public protector, an ongoing sense of threat creates a political environment where anything is possible. To justify the extreme measures adopted following 11 September 2001, the Bush administration resorted to the flawed strategy of a 'war on terror', divisive political tactics, and the cultivation of an atmosphere of fear. Following the attacks, President Bush claimed 'every nation, in every region, now has a decision to make. Either you are with us, or you are with the terrorists'.[65] Statements such as these can be effective in coercing support from allies, quelling internal dissent, and engendering an Us/Them mentality amongst the population.[66] While this book does not examine US counter-terrorism in detail it is useful to draw out the key characteristics of post-September 11 counter-terrorism in that jurisdiction. The profound effect US policy has had on global counter-terrorism as well as the evident shift towards pre-emption that has taken place makes the US the paradigmatic example of action in this policy field in the past decade.

Pre-emptive measures go beyond risk society thinking, challenging legal principles and reshaping criminal justice. Three changes are evident. First, control of coercive power is shifted away from the criminal justice process and towards executive, administrators and private actors. When such mechanisms are employed for pre-emptive counter-terrorism, legal accountability is difficult, as executive organs of state are given much discretion in relation to national security matters. Second, just as the exercise of coercive power changes, so too does its target. In the absence of clear information on who poses a threat, the net is cast widely to catch all potential perpetrators. One CIA (Central Intelligence Agency) operative noted that the question asked is not 'whether the men could be linked to a crime, [but the] broader issue of whether the men posed a danger'.[67] Criminal offences are drafted more broadly to catch behaviour that may not cause harm but may offer support or encouragement to those that do seek to cause harm.[68] The third and final area of change relates to the nature of the action taken. Despite broadly drafted criminal statutes, many 'suspected terrorists' are not prosecuted.

---

[64] de Goede, n 60 above, p 162.

[65] GW Bush, *Address to a Joint Session of Congress and the American People*, 20 September 2001.

[66] The US/Them distinction is a cornerstone of the political philosophy of Carl Schmitt. See: C Schmitt, *The Concept of the Political* (Chicago, Chicago University Press, 2007).

[67] Quoted in M de Goede, 'Beyond Risk: Premediation and the Post-9/11 Security Imagination' (2008) *Security Dialogue* 155, 163.

[68] Eg, 'material support' laws under the USA PATRIOT Act. For a discussion, see: D Cole, 'Terror Financing, Guilt by Association and the Paradigm of Prevention in the 'War on Terror' in A Bianchi and A Keller (eds), *Counterterrorism: Democracy's Challenge* (Oxford, Hart Publishing, 2008).

In the absence of criminal prosecutions, control takes the form of incapacitation: preventive detention or the freezing of financial assets. Such severe measures blur the distinction between criminal, civil and administrative law enforcement. The general public, and 'suspect populations' in particular, find themselves subject to pervasive surveillance.[69] Once this Pandora's Box has been opened, it is not easily closed—as demonstrated by the legal difficulties experienced by the Obama administration in closing Guantánamo Bay.[70] In the midst of the developing pre-emptive approach to counter-terrorism, rule of law principles are being challenged and reshaped.[71]

III. METHODOLOGY AND A FRAMEWORK FOR ANALYSIS

Despite the ubiquity of the rule of law in post-September 11 writings there remains an inherent methodological danger in its use—and that danger is that the criticism might slide towards vague denunciations of unsatisfactory law. This tension is a perhaps inevitable consequence of reliance on a concept such as the rule of law. In this book the rule of law is seen as a politico-legal ideal to which constitutional systems, and the EU in particular, aspire. But it is also seen as an umbrella term for a collection of legal principles, which, if upheld, lead to a better legal system and one that is more respectful of the inherent dignity of its subjects. This latter understanding of the rule of law means that the counter-terrorism measures assessed are criticised both for their doctrinal failings (a lack of legal certainty or the bestowing of wide discretion on executive and administrative actors) but also, in a 'law in context' manner, for the negative impact they have had on European populations. These developments are considered to be indicative of a trend in governance towards the 'pre-emptive'—a term which in the present context springs from criminology but which has analogous counterparts in other areas of study of law and regulation. The approach taken in this book is to argue that the cumulative effect of these legal and socio-legal failings of EU counter-terrorism law, which is pre-emptive in nature, amounts to a failure by the EU to live up to the politico-legal ideal of the rule of law.

The book is divided into three parts. Part One presents the historical and theoretical background for the study and consists of this Introduction and the first two chapters. Chapter One analyses the development of EU counter-terrorism and in particular the 'Action Plan Against Terrorism', a forty page document of policies and legislative proposals aimed at securing Europe from terrorism. Chapter Two traces the development of the EU rule of law which is described as having two

---

[69] Paddy Hillyard's work on the construction of a 'suspect community' in the UK under the Prevention of Terrorism Acts foreshadowed much of this thought: P Hillyard, *Suspect Community: People's Experience of the Prevention of Terrorism Acts in Britain* (London, Pluto Press, 1993).

[70] D Cole, 'Closing Guantánamo: The problem of preventive detention', *Boston Review* (January/February 2009), available at: www.bostonreview.net/BR34.1/cole.php.

[71] Cole and Lobel, n 1 above, p 33.

aspects: a constitutive aspect and a safeguarding aspect.[72] The conception of the EU rule of law developed here is based on the work of Armin von Bogdandy.[73] It considers the rule of law as being concerned with both constituting the legal order and the safeguarding of individuals within that order. This conception is used for several reasons. First, it incorporates both the views of those who consider the principle as enforcing state power and those who claim it protects individual autonomy. Second, it is sufficiently flexible to incorporate an evolving set of rules under its safeguarding aspect. The particular usefulness of von Bogdandy's conception though is that it provides the intellectual tools to bridge the gap between the politico-legal ideal of the rule of law and the second understanding of the concept as a collection of legal rules and values about the nature of the law and its application. As such, it is suitable tool for use in a study faced with the methodological problems that have already been discussed.

In unpacking the concept, Chapter Two begins with a consideration of the community of law in the EU, describing the development of an international rule of law in Europe, and illustrating the manner in which the European Court of Justice (ECJ) ensured that European law was enforced. Having addressed the constitutive aspect of the rule of law, the focus switches to the principles that make up its safeguarding aspect. Here, it draws on the jurisprudence of the ECJ and the European Court of Human Rights (ECtHR) in elucidating the principles that must be upheld. Part One concludes by outlining the trends towards pre-emptive counter-terrorism in EU action and the manner in which the EU rule of law is vulnerable to being eroded by a pre-emptive approach.

Part Two contains an analysis of five areas of EU counter-terrorism action. Europe is no stranger to terrorism. It was an Anglo-Irish philosopher's condemnation of a French revolutionary that first wedded the concepts of political violence and terror. In the twentieth century—apart from the many acts of states in the two World Wars and afterwards that might be labelled 'terrorism'—a wide range of transformational and ethno-nationalist groups used violence as a means to further their political ends.[74] This history has led to counter-terrorism efforts by several European states at national level and sporadic attempts at co-operation at international level. It is thus hardly surprising that the EU became involved in counter-terrorism after 11 September 2001 and increasingly so following the attacks in Madrid and London in 2004 and 2005 respectively. As a result of the EU's action in this field, counter-terrorism action in Europe can now be described as taking place in one of three types of legal system: national, European Union or international. The distinction is not a clear one. EU Member States may pursue

---

[72] Ibid.

[73] A von Bogdandy, 'Constitutional Principles' in A von Bogdandy and J Bast (eds), *Principles of European Constitutional Law*, 1st edn (Oxford, Hart Publishing, 2006) 15–18. Note also the updated chapter: A von Bogdandy, 'Founding Principles' in A von Bogdandy and J Bast (eds), *Principles of European Constitutional Law*, rev 2nd edn (Oxford, Hart Publishing, 2009) 28–33.

[74] L Richardson, *What Terrorists Want: Understanding the Terrorist Threat* (London, John Murray, 2006) 40–56.

national policies through EU law-making institutions or international treaties. Similarly, any EU law adopted as part of counter-terrorism action relies on the Member States to enforce it. The interaction between national, international and EU counter-terrorism policies reflects a wider migration of legal rules in this field since 11 September 2001.

Nonetheless, it is possible to identify legislation adopted at EU level and to study it as 'EU counter-terrorism'. Such measures are the subject of the analysis in this book. The objective of the analysis is to determine whether or not the adoption of the measures, their transposition into national law and subsequent enforcement has affected the rule of law in the EU. These measures all feature in the EU Action Plan and they facilitate an examination of different aspects of EU counter-terrorism action. The measures in question are the Framework Decision on Combating Terrorism (as amended); the Anti-Money-Laundering Directives; targeted asset-freezing sanctions; the Passenger Name Record Agreements and the Data Retention Directive; and the European Arrest and Evidence Warrants.

Part Three draws together the discussion and addresses the core question of how the 'war on terror' has affected the EU's commitment to the rule of law. Chapter Eight addresses the state of the rule of law in the EU today and how it is being reshaped by pre-emptive counter-terrorism. It brings together the various strands of thought from Part Two: the nature of EU counter-terrorism action and the effect on the rule of law. The conclusions suggest that the EU rule of law is being reconfigured to the detriment of both the EU legal order and those individuals subject to EU law. These developments are made all the more disturbing as they come at a time when EU law is playing an increasing role in criminal justice in Europe. The Epilogue looks to the future under the Lisbon Treaty, the Stockholm Programme and the newly-updated Council Action Plan against Terrorism. It asks whether the EU can develop more rule of law compliant counter-terrorism in the post-'war on terror' world.

1

European Counter-Terrorism Action

US POLITICIANS, LAW enforcement officials and even academics have been the vanguard of the 'war on terror'. As a result it is not surprising that the pre-emptive turn in counter-terrorism is strongly associated with the Bush administration.[1] Pre-emption has become a key theme of contemporary criminal justice whereby intrusive state action is justified by a risk calculation based on unpredictable and unacceptable harms. Although the EU has only recently developed a role in the fields of internal and external security, it relies on the logic of risk in other policy areas, most notably in public health and environmental protection.[2] The 'precautionary principle' is a general principle of EU law which 'posits that it may be warranted to undertake regulatory action to protect health or the environment in the absence of conclusive evidence of harm'.[3] The principle has a Treaty basis in Article 191(2) TFEU (Treaty on the Functioning of the European Union) which declares that Union policy on the environment shall be based on precaution. However, despite the EU being 'one of the biggest proponents of the [precautionary principle] on the international chessboard', the principle is not defined under EU law.[4] Furthermore, the relationship between precaution and democratic decision-making remains controversial. The benefits of a risk-based approach are contested even when applied to environmental protection or public health.[5] Their application to crime can significantly undermine the foundation of the criminal justice system. Despite the difficulty of predicting human behaviour and designing state intervention on the basis of such predictions, the twenty-first century is 'an era of precaution that has significant and worrisome

---

[1] Note, however, critiques of the Obama administration that argue that some of the worst Bush policies have not yet been abandoned. See, eg: D Jenkins, 'The Closure of Guantanamo Bay: What Next for the Detainees?' (2010) *Public Law* 46.

[2] K Ladeur, 'The Introduction of the Precautionary Principle into EU Law: A Pyrrhic Victory for Environmental and Public Health Law? Decision-Making Under Conditions of Complexity in Multi-level Political Systems' (2003) 40 *Common Market Law Review* 1455.

[3] V Heyvaert, 'Facing The Consequences of the Precautionary Principle in European Community Law' (2006) 31 *European Law Review* 185.

[4] A Khoury, 'Is it Time for an EU Definition of the Precautionary Principle?' (2010) 21 *King's Law Journal* 133, 141.

[5] C Sunstein, *Laws of Fear: Beyond the Precautionary Principle* (Cambridge, Cambridge University Press, 2005).

implications for the criminal law'.[6] When dealing with counter-terrorism, where the risk of harm is seen as simultaneously unknowable and utterly unacceptable, the state response can be 'to call for *pre*-cautious, pre-emptive measures' that seek to submit individuals and groups to a regime of coercive state control.[7] Of course, the presence of the precautionary principle in EU law does not necessarily mean that the EU will develop pre-emptive counter-terrorism. However, its existence is evidence that the EU legal order is at least open to the incorporation of actuarial approaches to social regulation.

I. EUROPEAN COUNTER-TERRORISM BEFORE 11 SEPTEMBER 2001

Terrorism in Europe has historically been considered either a national or an international problem and action was pursued at those levels. Threat perceptions varied (and indeed continue to vary) across the continent.[8] Therefore, European counter-terrorism action has traditionally been pursued through the Member States' criminal justice system as each state acted in accordance with its own security interests. Whereas some states—such as the United Kingdom—had adopted specific counter-terrorism legislation as long ago as the 1960s, others dealt with such violence through their ordinary criminal justice systems. A 2004 European Commission Staff Working Paper claimed that in the 'majority' of EU Member States 'terrorist actions were just punished as common offences' prior to 11 September 2001.[9] At international level, European counter-terrorism co-operation before 2001 is characterised by little success in formal fora coupled with the development of informal networks of security and law enforcement agencies.

Early European attempts at co-operation were unsuccessful. In 1934 two Conventions were drafted following the assassination of King Alexander of Yugoslavia: a Convention for the Prevention and Punishment of Terrorism and a Convention for the Creation of an International Criminal Court. Neither came into effect.[10] The first successful attempt at drafting a European-wide counter-terrorism treaty was achieved by the Council of Europe in 1977. However, despite being modest in its scope, the European Convention on the Suppression of Terrorism (Terrorism Convention) enjoyed only limited success. The Convention

---

[6] L Zedner, 'Fixing the Future? The Pre-emption Turn in Criminal Justice' in B McSherry, A Norrie and S Bronitt (eds), *Regulating Deviance: The Redirection of Criminalisation and the Futures of Criminal Law* (Oxford, Hart Publishing, 2009) 35.

[7] Ibid, p 57.

[8] C Eckes, *EU Counter-Terrorist Policies and Fundamental Rights: The Case of Individual Sanctions* (Oxford, Oxford University Press, 2009) 64.

[9] Commission (EC), Commission Staff Working Document Annex to the Report from the Commission based on Art 11 of the Council Framework Decision of 13 June 2002 on combating terrorism SEC (2004) 688 (Brussels, 8 June 2004) 4.

[10] MC Wood, 'The European Convention on the Suppression of Terrorism' (1981) 1 *Yearbook of European Law* 307, 311. See also B Saul, 'The Legal Response of the League of Nations to Terrorism' (2006) *Journal of International Criminal Justice* 78.

sought to establish an *aut dedere aut punire* ('prosecute or extradite') principle in respect of those suspected of agreed terrorist offences set out in Article 1.[11] The Convention's most prominent limitation was the power to refuse to extradite when a person will be prosecuted, punished or dealt with prejudicially due to his race, religion, nationality or political opinion.[12] While *non-refoulement* strengthened national control over extradition, it highlighted the signatories' lack of trust in each others' criminal justice systems and undermined the effectiveness of the Convention as a regional co-operation mechanism. A further perceived drawback was that a number of states attached reservations and qualifications to their signature. These difficulties arise as there are important constitutional questions in extradition law, with some states, such as France and Ireland, upholding a right to seek political asylum on their soil.[13] The EU's success in overcoming these difficulties thirty years later with the adoption of the European Arrest Warrant required the unprecedented catalyst of the 11 September attacks.[14]

Though the Terrorism Convention attempted to co-ordinate European efforts, it was more successful in highlighting the lack of political will to co-operate in this sphere. A year later the Dublin Convention was agreed, which directly related to the Terrorism Convention. Its aim was to use the links of trust and co-operation developed within the European Community to secure the objectives of the earlier agreement. By attempting to dissuade states from entering reservations to the Terrorism Convention, the Dublin Convention was more ambitious than the earlier agreement, but only marginally more successful at overcoming the states' reluctance to yield control. Again, the political sensitivities of the states trumped their willingness to co-operate at the European level.[15] While many European states had experienced some form of political violence, few were willing to cede control over internal security to supra- or international institutions. The strong associations of sovereignty and security ensured that while terrorism was an international problem, counter-terrorism largely remained a domestic undertaking.

This reticence to relinquish control persisted despite an increased desire to co-operate at EU level. Notwithstanding the slow progress in the field, Member State governments believe that the free movement of goods, services and people

---

[11] These offences are those set out by the Convention for the Suppression of Unlawful Seizure of Aircraft 1970, the Convention for the Suppression of Unlawful Acts against the Safety of Civil Aviation 1971, or 'a serious offence involving an attack against the life, physical integrity or liberty of internationally protected persons, including diplomatic agents' or 'an offence involving kidnapping, the taking of a hostage or serious unlawful detention' or 'an offence involving the use of a bomb, grenade, rocket, automatic firearm or letter or parcel bomb if this use endangers persons' or 'an attempt to commit any of the foregoing offences or participation as an accomplice of a person who commits or attempts to commit such an offence'.

[12] Arts 5, 8(2) Terrorism Convention; see: Wood, n 10 above, p 314.

[13] Wood, n 10 above, p 311.

[14] Council Framework Decision of 13 June 2002 on the European arrest warrant and the surrender procedures between Member States (2002/584/JHA).

[15] Wood, n 10 above, pp 324–27; see also: D Freestone, 'The EEC Treaty and Common Action on Terrorism' (1984) 4 *Yearbook of European Law* 207, 207.

in Europe has been joined by the free movement of crime.[16] In response, informal bilateral and multilateral networks of law enforcement officials have thrived, not least because of the need to address political violence.[17] During its early stages, co-operation was informal and bottom-up. Formed in 1971 by the security agencies of six European states, the Club de Berne remains one of the most loosely arranged of the informal networks in place.[18] Under its auspices, the heads of national security services meet twice annually to discuss matters of mutual concern.[19] Little information on the Club or its activities is available in the public domain. The Police Working Group on Terrorism was established in 1979 by Germany, Italy, the UK and other European states to pool their thinking in dealing with different political extremist groups (eg Irish Republican, Middle-Eastern and Communist groups). It is operational in focus, working at 'about the level of the Head of the Metropolitan Police Special Branch'.[20] The Working Group meets twice annually and works on an informal basis. It allows intelligence exchange and officer secondment, hosts seminars and facilitates the passing of information between forces.[21] As collaborations of operational figures rather than legislators, Club de Berne and the Working Group involve neither democratic accountability nor compliance with rule of law principles. Den Boer et al note that in contrast with such networks in other policy areas, transnational counter-terrorism security networks tend to exclude civil society groups (due to concerns about secrecy) and as such lack social legitimacy.[22]

While transnational networks were working quietly in the background, attempts at formalised European security co-operation foundered before the adoption of the Treaty on European Union. Until the agreement of that Treaty discussion of counter-terrorism efforts was considered too politically sensitive for supranational institutions such as the European Commission and European Parliament. As a result, the TREVI group was established in 1976 under European Political Co-operation, the more informal predecessor to the EU's Common Foreign and Security Policy (CFSP).[23] TREVI Working Group I sought 'to inform strategy and tactics in countering terrorist groups which operate internationally' and to examine

[16] V Mitsilegas, *EU Criminal Law* (Oxford, Hart Publishing, 2009) 6–7.

[17] J Benyon, 'Policing the European Union: The Changing Basis of Co-operation on Law Enforcement' (1994) 70 *International Affairs* 497.

[18] RJ Aldrich, 'Transatlantic Intelligence and Security Co-operation' (2004) 80 *International Affairs* 731, 738. Lander cites its establishment as 'in the 1960s': S Lander, 'International Intelligence Co-operation: An Inside Perspective' (2004) 17 *Cambridge Review of International Affairs* 481, 489.

[19] Aldrich, n 18 above, p 738.

[20] House of Lords EU Select Committee, *Select Committee on the European Union Fifth Report* (London, TSO, 2005), [49]. According to Bunyan, the impetus for the group was the shooting of Sir Richard Dykes, UK ambassador to the Netherlands. See: T Bunyan, 'Trevi, Europol and the European State' in *Statewatching the New Europe* (London, StateWatch, 1993) 4.

[21] Benyon, n 17 above, pp 511–12.

[22] M Den Boer, C Hillebrand and A Nolke, 'Legitimacy under Pressure: The European Web of Counter-Terrorism Networks' (2008) 46 *Journal of Common Market Studies* 101, 119.

[23] Monar claims that TREVI stood officially for 'Terrorisme, radicalisme et violence international' but its real background seems to have been a play on words linked to the name of the Dutch minister

ways in which 'co-operation may be needed'.[24] The Working Group was an informal intergovernmental forum for discussion that was only loosely linked to the EU and its more formalised structures of governance. The exclusion of TREVI from the institutions until the Treaty on European Union was 'a deliberate choice due to sensitivities about sovereignty and problems of a practical and ideological nature'.[25] Even after the adoption of the EU Treaty the role of the European Parliament and European Commission was severely limited as Member State governments sought to retain control of the security agenda. Not all early attempts at EU counter-terrorism were led by national governments and law enforcement. The European Parliament engaged in a number of unsuccessful initiatives. One Member of the European Parliament went so far as to propose a European Criminal Court; directives on the suppression of terrorism; and common extradition rules across Europe.[26] Though the Parliament itself was less ambitious, it did call for co-operation in counter-terrorism action. Certainly, inter-institutional politics played some part in this move: the Parliament was excluded from European Political Co-operation and TREVI discussions, whereas any formal action would require it to be at least consulted.[27] It was ambitious of the European Parliament to suggest that formal counter-terrorism co-operation could be pursued using the (more integrated) supranational approach. When the time came to formalise co-operation, the supranational method was still seen as too far removed from Member State control for the sensitive field of national security.

A formal role for the EU in internal and external security was agreed in 1992 in the Treaty on European Union (TEU). The Treaty established the EU, adding two more 'pillars' to the first pillar (the existing European Community). The second pillar, Common Foreign and Security Policy, provided mechanisms for co-ordinating external security policy. The third pillar, Justice and Home Affairs (JHA)—and later Police and Judicial Co-operation in Criminal Matters (PJCCM)—set out EU competences for internal security matters. Scattered throughout the three pillars were various competences that could be used for counter-terrorism. First, counter-terrorism action was possible in the first pillar where that action relates to a competence or objective under that pillar. While 'terrorism' was not mentioned explicitly in the Treaty provisions on the second pillar, the objective 'to strengthen the security of the Union in all ways' had potential application.[28] Monar sketched

---

Fonteijn (Dutch 'fountain') who chaired the meeting which established TREVI and a dinner the ministers had close to the Trevi Fountain in Rome.

See: J Monar, 'Common Threat and Common Response? The European Union's Counter-Terrorism Strategy and its Problems' (2007) 42 *Government and Opposition* 292, 292.

[24]   Bunyan, n 20 above, p 2.

[25]   P deHert, 'Division of Competencies between National and European Levels with regard to Justice and Home Affairs' in J Apap (ed), *Justice and Home Affairs in the EU: Liberty and Security Issues after Enlargement* (Cheltenham, Edward Elgar Publishing, 2004) 69.

[26]   Freestone, n 15 above, p 207.

[27]   Freestone, n 15 above, p 211.

[28]   Art 11(1) EU(N). EU(N) is used in this book to refer to the EU Treaty under the Nice Treaty (ie before the Lisbon Treaty).

the third pillar counter-terrorism competences as follows: police co-operation,[29] Europol development,[30] judicial co-operation,[31] criminal law harmonisation[32] and external activities.[33] Prior to the coming into force of the Lisbon Treaty, the EU's first pillar was much more integrated than the second and third pillars. The status of these competences has evolved since the 11 September 2001 attacks—most recently due to the ratification and entry into force of the Lisbon Treaty. The first and third pillars have now been merged—though transitional measures will remain in place until 2015. Despite some developments towards a greater EU role in foreign affairs, the Common Foreign and Security Policy remains outside the ordinary law-making processes. As a result, EU counter-terrorism action has to address the question of which pillar should be used, a question that impacts directly on the effectiveness and the uniformity of the law.[34]

In addition to the formal Treaty provisions, the EU also established a number of organisations concerned with police and judicial co-operation and immigration enforcement. Mitsilegas describes the development of Europol (the European Police Office) as 'emblematic' of co-operation in this field.[35] Europol was established by the Europol Convention in 1995 and became a formal EU agency in January 2010. However, its purpose, powers and mode of operation remain the subject of debate amongst the Member States.[36] Eurojust mimicked Europol in establishing a European judicial office. However, neither Europol nor Eurojust has a direct operational role—their mandates focus on co-ordinating national police and justice agents rather than operational policing and prosecution.[37] Another group, the Police Chief's Task Force, was established following the Tampere European Council and operates at a more senior level than the Police Working Group on Terrorism.[38] The Task Force met for the first time in April 2000.[39] The aim of the Task Force is to bridge the gap between Europol intelligence and action by domestic police services. It is based solely on the Tampere recommendation, and the absence of a stronger legal basis has exposed it to criticism.[40]

---

[29] Art 30(1) EU(N).

[30] Art 30(2) EU(N).

[31] Art 31(a)–(d) EU(N).

[32] Art 31(e) EU(N).

[33] Art 38 EU(N) in association with Art 24 EU(N). See: J Monar, 'The EU's Approach Post-September 11: Global Terrorism as a Multidimensional Law Enforcement Challenge' (2007) 20 *Cambridge Review of International Affairs* 267, 272.

[34] Monar, 'Common Threat and Common Response?', n 23 above, p 294.

[35] V Mitsilegas, *EU Criminal Law* (Oxford, Hart Publishing, 2009) 161–63.

[36] Ibid.

[37] S Peers, *EU Justice and Home Affairs Law*, 2nd edn (Oxford, Oxford University Press, 2006) 487–89, 536–39.

[38] L Lugna, 'Insitutional Framework of the European Union Counter-Terrorism Policy Setting' (2006) 8 *Baltic Security and Defence Review* 101, 116.

[39] D Zimmerman, 'The European Union and Post-9/11 Counterterrorism: A Reappraisal' (2006) 29 *Studies in Conflict & Terrorism* 123, fn 21.

[40] T Bunyan, *The EU's Police Chief Task Force (PCTF) and Police Chiefs Committee* (London, StateWatch, 2006).

As de Boer and Monar note, 'several strata of counter-terrorism activities were already in place within the EU before September 11 [2001]'.[41] Despite the various ad hoc attempts at co-operation, before 11 September 2001, terrorism was not at the forefront of the European security agenda. While the 11 September 2001 attacks had been foreshadowed by earlier attacks on the World Trade Centre itself, by the bombing of the USS Cole, and by attacks on US embassies in Dar es Salaaam and Nairobi, in Europe the trends was one of decreasing rather than increasing violence.[42] A 2000 *International and Comparative Law Quarterly* report on Justice and Home Affairs made no mention of terrorism.[43] Thus, although the building blocks were in place, the structures were not, by and large, being used.

II. EUROPE AND SEPTEMBER 11 2001

September 11 2001 had almost as profound an effect on the European side of the Atlantic as it did on the American. The immediate reaction in Europe was one of shock and solidarity with the United States. A *Le Monde* editorial in the days following the attack carried the headline 'Nous sommes tous Américains'.[44] The European Council's Extraordinary Meeting concluded that it was 'totally supportive of the American people in the face of the deadly terrorist attacks'.[45] Europe's solidarity may have been partly built on a shared sense of victimhood: 67 Britons died in the attack, along with 11 Germans, 10 Italians, 6 Irish, 5 Portuguese, 3 French and several other Europeans. It may also have been built on a sense of empathy as the US experienced the sort of violence that many European states had endured in the twentieth century—albeit on a different scale.

The international community's immediate reaction to September 11 came in the form of a UN Security Council resolution. Resolution 1373 was agreed unanimously on 28 September 2001 by a Council which included France, Ireland and the UK (as well as fellow European state Norway). The resolution has been referred to as 'exercising an unprecedented global legislative sweep' as it requires all states to adopt legislation making criminal certain acts of terrorism.[46] Its provisions call on states to prevent and suppress the financing of terrorism, to refrain from providing support to terrorists, to implement effective border controls to prevent the movement of

---

[41] M Den Boer and J Monar, 'Keynoted Article: 11 September and the Challenge of Global Terrorism to the EU as a Security Actor' in G Edwards and G Wiessala (eds), *The European Union: Annual Review of the EU 2001/2002* (Oxford, Blackwell, 2002) 21.

[42] In 1998 the Good Friday Agreement in Ireland followed a period in which the IRA had established a ceasefire. The other major violent political group, ETA in Spain, declared ceasefires in both 1996 and 1998.

[43] S Peers, 'Current Developments: EC Law II Justice and Home Affairs' (2000) 49 *International and Comparative Law Quarterly* 222.

[44] 'Nous sommes tous Américains', *Le Monde* (13 September 2001).

[45] European Council, 'Conclusions and Plan of Action of the Extraordinary European Council Meeting of 21 September 2001' SN140/01.

[46] EJ Flynn, 'The Security Council's Counter-terrorism Committee and Human Rights' (2007) *Human Rights Law Review* 371, 376.

terrorists and to co-operate with each other including through the exchange of information. The resolution declares that there is a 'close connection' between terrorism and crimes such as the trafficking of drugs and arms, transnational organised crime and money-laundering. The resolution has been described as an example of 'hegemonic' international law due to its broad-reaching effects.[47]

In addition to the legal action, the US launched a military campaign against the Taleban and Al-Qaeda in Afghanistan. Most European Member States offered some form of support to the US-led Operation Enduring Freedom to depose the Taleban. Despite this initial sense of solidarity, as the wide scope of the Bush administration's response to the attacks became clear, European governments took different views on whether or not, and to what extent, they should co-operate. Perhaps the greatest divider of opinion was the subsequent invasion of Iraq in 2003. The invasion, on (at best) dubious legal and moral grounds polarised public opinion in Europe and divided governments on the correct course of action. In European civil society, many hoped for a counter-narrative to the Bush administration's pre-emptive strategies. Habermas and Derrida called upon Europeans to seize this opportunity to foster a public space in constructive opposition to the Washington establishment.[48] They argued that

> Just as little should we forget February 15, 2003, the day on which the masses of demonstrators in London, Rome, Madrid, Barcelona, Berlin, and Paris responded to [certain European governments' support for the war in Iraq]. The simultaneity of these overpowering demonstrations—the largest since the end of World War II—may go down in future history books as a signal for the birth of a European public.[49]

However, the Iraq War and the 'war on terror' in general was to evidence key divisions between European governments and give lie to the idea that Europe had a Common Foreign and Security Policy.[50] In some respects, a counter-narrative may indeed be identified—if not in individual Member States then certainly at European level. Jackson notes that the EU's

> rejection of a war-based framework in favour of a law-based approach, its recognition of the dangers associated with the language of 'Islamic terrorism' and its recognition of the need to deal with root causes suggest that genuine discursive change is possible.[51]

On the other hand, the EU might not be as virtuous as it first seems. While the EU did not (and could not) resort to military force, as a whole Europe responded to September 11 with a range of new laws. Thus, in place of military force there

---

[47] JE Alvarez 'Hegemonic International Law Revisited' (2003) *American Journal of International Law* 873.

[48] J Habermas, 'February 15, or: What Binds Europeans' in *The Divided West* (Cambridge, Polity Press, 2006); G Borradori (ed), *Philosophy in a Time of Terror: Dialogues with Jürgen Habermas and Jacques Derrida* (Chicago, University of Chicago Press, 2003).

[49] Habermas, 'February 15', n 48 above, p 40.

[50] J Peterson, 'Europe, America and 11 September' (2002) 13 *Irish Studies in International Affairs* 1.

[51] R Jackson 'An Analysis of EU Counterterrorism Discourse post-September 11' (2007) 20 *Cambridge Review of International Affairs* 233, 245.

has been the force of law.[52] It is clear from the wide range of critical literature that this is the case for the national law of EU Member States.[53] The legislation that has flown from the spring of UN Security Council resolution 1373 clearly evidences a trend identified in the resolution itself—the 'weaponisation of law'.[54] Indeed, the extent to which law was a tool of those persecuting the war on terror is perhaps too easily overlooked. Much of the debate surrounding the Iraq war centred on the legality of the invasion and consequentially on the terms of UN Security Council resolution 1441.[55] The use of torture by the US and its allies was based on a series of legal memoranda which—although exhibiting a poor standard of professional work—nonetheless relied on legal arguments to make their case.[56] Thus, it is worth recalling that lawyer's role can be 'to convert words on paper into instruments of power. And depending where the power is, the law will mean different things'.[57]

After 11 September 2001, in the US and many other states across the world, power lay with executive actors: governments, intelligence agencies and law enforcement officers who used their powers in the name of national security. Legal principles wilted in the face of the overwhelming will to act. Some scholars have sought to reclassify this form of law—that corrodes the very principles on which a legal system is based—as 'counter-law' or 'law-against-law'.[58] Despite the attractiveness of this idea it cannot be denied that many of the rights infringements in the 'war on terror' have had a legislative basis.

The British case is a useful example of the post September 11 approach in Europe. In response to the attacks, the UK, which in 2000 had adopted legislation to consolidate its counter-terrorism law, promulgated the Anti-Terrorism, Crime and Security Act 2001.[59] The Act was much-criticised, in particular because it provided for Britain to derogate from the European Convention on Human Rights: the only state to do so in response to the 11 September attacks.[60] Part IV of the Act provided for the internment of those non-citizens suspected of (but not necessarily

---

[52] M de Goede, 'The Politics of Preemption and the War on Terror in Europe' (2008) 14 *European Journal of International Relations* 161, 180.

[53] See for a wide variety of examples: L Fekete 'Anti-terrorism and Civil Liberties: Country Summaries', *European Race Bulletin* (London, Institute of Race Relations, Autumn 2007) 11.

[54] D Kennedy, *Of War and Law* (Princeton, Princeton University Press, 2006) 37.

[55] P Sands, *Lawless World: Making and Breaking Global Rules* (London, Penguin, 2006) 174–204.

[56] KJ Greenburg and J Dratel (eds), *The Torture Papers: The Road to Abu Ghraib* (Cambridge, Cambridge University Press, 2005).

[57] PR Mitchell and J Schoeffel (eds), *Understanding Power: The Indispensible Chomsky* (New York, The New Press, 2002) 347.

[58] RV Ericson, 'The State of Preemption: Managing Terrorism Through Counter Law' in L Amoore and M de Goede (eds), *Risk and the War on Terror* (Abingdon, Routledge, 2008) 57–76. Ericson notes that 'Counter law I is law against law. New laws are enacted and new uses of existing law are invented to erode or eliminate traditional principles, standards, and procedures of criminal law that get in the way of pre-empting imagined sources of harm' (ibid, p 57).

[59] Terrorism Act 2000; Anti-Terrorism, Crime and Security Act 2001.

[60] A Tomkins, 'Legislating against Terror: The Anti-terrorism, Crime and Security Act 2001' (2002) *Public Law* 205.

convicted of) activity related to terrorism who could not be deported as they would face torture in their states of nationality. This part of the Act was eventually found in violation of the European Convention on Human Rights (ECHR) by the House of Lords.[61] In response, Parliament enacted the Prevention of Terrorism Act 2005 which allowed those suspected of terrorism (irrespective of nationality) to be made subject to 'control orders' which amounted in some instances to house arrest. This regime, though attracting judicial, academic and popular criticism, remained in force.[62] Further legislation was adopted in the UK following the bombings in London on 7 July 2005 (Terrorism Act 2006) and the attempted attacks in August 2007 (Counter-Terrorism Act 2008).[63] The control orders saga in particular is indicative of both the pre-emptive nature of UK counter-terrorism action and the corrosive effect such action can have on the rule of law. The action was pre-emptive as the imposition of a control order is based on suspicion that those individuals subject to the regime may be involved—in the past, present or future—in political violence. The corrosive nature of the pre-emption can be demonstrated by the way in which the regime was crafted to fit within a dubious loophole in ECHR protection inadvertently created by three Italian cases before the Strasbourg Court.[64] By being ostensibly temporary and not punitive, control orders may be subject to a more lenient form of scrutiny under the Convention system. However, the effect is that some individuals have been subject to serious infringements of their personal liberty for almost a decade without having been convicted of any criminal offence. It is noteworthy that the abandonment of control orders has come about not because of the findings of a court but because of a change in government which has prompted new legislation.

While Britain's action has been some of the most draconian in Europe, it is not the only Member State to legislate in response to actual or anticipated violence. A 2007 Report by the Institute of Race Relations in London critiqued law and policy in several EU Member States, including Austria, Cyprus, Denmark, France, Finland, Germany, Greece, Italy, the Netherlands, Norway, Spain, Sweden and the UK.[65] The pre-emptive approach to counter-terrorism is not limited to states in the common law tradition. In France, existing legislation has been used to pursue a strategy of 'preventive judicial neutralization'.[66] Human Rights Watch has criticised French action noting that 'France has refined a preemptive criminal justice approach to countering terrorism' and warning that 'too much flexibility in the

---

[61] *A v Secretary of State for the Home Department* [2004] UKHL 56.

[62] C Walker, 'The Threat of Terrorism and the Fate of Control Orders' (2010) *Public Law* 4.

[63] A detailed consideration of this legislation is beyond the scope of the present work. See C Walker, *Blackstone's Guide to the Anti-Terrorism Legislation*, 2nd edn (Oxford, Oxford University Press, 2009).

[64] KD Ewing and JC Tham, 'The Continuing Futility of the Human Rights Act' (2008) *Public Law* 668. See further the discussion in section IV of this chapter.

[65] L Fekete, 'Anti-terrorism and Civil Liberties: Country Summaries', *European Race Bulletin* (London, Institute of Race Relations, Autumn 2007) 11.

[66] Human Rights Watch, *Pre-empting Justice: Counter-Terrorism Laws and Procedures in France* (Paris, Human Rights Watch, 2008) 11.

system will stretch the rule of law to the breaking point'.[67] Indeed, pre-emptive domestic action to counter terrorism has led to the erosion of rights across Europe—in particular through the disproportionate use of police and security services powers against minority communities.[68]

With Member State governments highly active on the domestic front it was almost inevitable that they would also seek to co-operate in the wider European context. The Council of Europe adopted a Protocol to the 1977 Terrorism Convention and agreed two further Conventions relevant to terrorism.[69] In the aftermath of the September 11 attacks, the Council of Europe's Multidisciplinary Group on International Action against Terrorism examined the 1977 Terrorism Convention with a view to 'updating' its provisions. The outcome of these deliberations was a Protocol amending the Convention.[70] It provided for a wider list of offences—incorporating all extant UN conventions on terrorism—to fall outside the list of 'political offences' for the purpose of extradition. The Protocol therefore made it easier to obtain the extradition of an individual suspected of terrorism offences within Europe. The Protocol also introduced a simplified amendment procedure and allowed observers to the Council of Europe to accede to the Convention. It has been signed by 46 states, 30 of which have also ratified it.

The principal post-September 11 Council of Europe action is the Convention on the Prevention of Terrorism. The Convention did not create new terrorism offences, but instead made reference to existing international treaties. It then sought to make criminal a wide range of inchoate behaviour including the provocation of terrorism, recruitment for terrorism and training for terrorism. Notably, the Convention does not require any act of terrorism to take place for an offence to be committed. This is indicative of its general approach, which aims not just to punish those who commit attacks, but also to attempt to diminish the potential for any terrorism to take place. The provocation offence targets speech that 'causes a danger' that an offence may be committed. In this way the Convention evidences at international level the sort of pre-emptive approach already identified at national level. It has been signed by 43 states (including all EU Member States except the Czech Republic) and ratified by 24 states. It has also had an impact on EU law as some of its provisions have been replicated in the Framework Decision amending the Framework Decision on Combating Terrorism.[71]

Another terrorism-related Convention adopted in 2005 is the Convention on Laundering, Search, Seizure and Confiscation of the Proceeds from Crime and on

---

[67]   Ibid, p 1.

[68]   L Fekete 'Anti-terrorism and Human Rights' (2004) 47 *European Race Bulletin*.

[69]   For commentary see: A Hunt, 'The Council of Europe Convention on the Prevention of Terrorism' (2006) 12 *European Public Law* 603; E Chadwick, 'The 2005 Terrorism Convention: A Flexible Step Too Far?' (2007) 16 *Nottingham Law Journal* 29.

[70]   Protocol amending the European Convention on the Suppression of Terrorism CETS No 190.

[71]   Council Framework Decision 2008/919/JHA of 28 November 2008 amending Framework Decision 2002/475/JHA on combating terrorism. This framework decision and the parent legislation are both analysed in Chapter 3.

the Financing of Terrorism (Financing Convention). That Convention also echoes a wider post-September 11 trend in acting against legal as well as illegal sources of funds based on a new understanding that the former is as likely to be used to fund terrorism as the latter. To date it has attracted 33 signatures (including that of the EU itself) and 20 ratifications. As with the Convention on the Prevention of Terrorism, the Financing Convention has influenced EU law. It significantly builds on the Council of Europe's 1990 Convention and seeks to establish a broad system of financial surveillance. As such, it fits well within a pre-emptive approach to counter-terrorism.

III. THE EU IN THE 'WAR ON TERROR'

While EU Member States have not engaged in military action on the same scale as the US, the pace of legal and administrative policy developments at national level has been breath-taking. The same is true at EU level. An *International and Comparative Law Quarterly* report on EU counter-terrorism action in 2003 was over twice as long as the journal's 2000 Justice and Home Affairs report.[72] Some of the measures that have been adopted since 2001 were drafted prior to the Al-Qaeda attacks, but lacked sufficient political support to be adopted—such as the European Arrest Warrant, which has been an aspiration of the European Council since 1999.[73] Others, such as the Data Retention Directive, have been devised in response to the perceived needs of law enforcement agencies in the post-September 11 world.[74]

The new political climate has had a constitutional impact in the EU: the Constitutional Treaty would have provided a new basis for counter-terrorism co-operation through a 'solidarity clause'.[75] The clause has its origins in a European Council statement issued following the Madrid bombings.[76] The Lisbon Treaty retains the clause as Article 222 TFEU. Immediately after the New York and Washington attacks, the EU was concerned with other efforts.[77] An Extraordinary European Council meeting on 21 September 2001 adopted a counter-terrorism policy document: an 'Action Plan'.[78] The initial Action Plan

---

[72] S Peers 'EU Responses to Terrorism' (2003) 52 *International and Comparative Law Quarterly* 227.

[73] M Deflem 'Europol and the Policing of International Terrorism: Counter-Terrorism in a Global Perspective' (2006) 23 *Justice Quarterly* 336, 340–41.

[74] The Data Retention Directive is analysed in Chapter Six.

[75] Art I-43 Constitutional Treaty.

[76] European Council, 'Declaration of the European Council on Combating Terrorism' (25 March 2004).

[77] For a useful historical overview of EU policy-making activity in the wake of the September 11 attacks, see: R Bossong 'The Action Plan on Combating Terrorism: A Flawed Instrument of EU Security Governance' (2008) 46 *Journal of Common Market Studies* 27.

[78] European Council, 'Conclusions and Plan of Action of the Extraordinary European Council Meeting of 21 September 2001' SN140/01.

has undergone several revisions since 2001. The most recent consolidated edition was released on 9 March 2007 and ran to almost 40 pages.[79] In November 2009 a Report from the Counter-Terrorism Co-ordinator to the Council on the EU's activities contained an 'overall update' on the Action Plan that was considerably shorter.[80] In November 2010, the Council published a further report and update of the Action Plan.[81] The total list of EU counter-terrorism measures, both legal and non-legal, has been estimated at over 200.[82] The Action Plan has been much discussed in security studies. Opinions vary, with some claiming that the Action Plan provides the EU with the means to be an effective actor in international security.[83] Others take a more negative view, opining that it may be more of a 'paper tiger' than a real one.[84] One of its perceived benefits is that it sets out a long-term strategy, removing the power of the rotating Council presidency to steer counter-terrorism policy.[85] However, the Action Plan 'has mostly been treated as a useful, if perhaps somewhat unwieldy summary' of EU counter-terrorism initiatives.[86] This perception of the Plan, as an 'unwieldy summary', has been strengthened in light of the recent use of annual updates rather than consolidated documents. Policy items appear and disappear in different plans making the task of mapping out the EUs priorities in this area a labyrinthine one. Regardless of the Action Plan's success, failure, or coherence, counter-terrorism strategy has provided a focal point for the development of an EU role in security and a policy space in which EU criminal law is being pioneered.

The Action Plan is divided into four strands: prevent, protect, pursue and respond. The first strand seeks to 'prevent people turning to terrorism by tackling the factors or root causes which can lead to radicalisation and recruitment in Europe and internationally'.[87] In the 2010 edition of the Action Plan, these aims are set out in five policy areas: seeking to disrupt recruitment networks (1.1), ensuring 'the voices of mainstream opinion prevail' (1.2), promoting democracy and security (1.3), assessment and analysis (1.4) and prevention of chemical, biological, radiological and nuclear (CBRN) risks. There are research projects, seminars, training programmes (for everyone from police to imams), political dialogues and 'diplomatic steps' in this strand. Perhaps the most ambitious element in this strand in recent years was point 1.3.3 of the 2007 Action Plan: 'Promote good governance, democracy, education and economic prosperity outside the EU'. This

---

[79] European Council, 'EU Action Plan on combating terrorism' (Brussels, 9 March 2007).

[80] European Council, 'EU Action Plan on combating terrorism' (Brussels, 26 November 2009).

[81] European Council, 'EU Action Plan on combating terrorism' (Brussels, 15 November 2010).

[82] Monar, 'Common Threat and Common Response?', n 23 above, p 303.

[83] D Dubois, 'The Attacks of 11 September: EU–US Co-operation Against Terrorism in the Field of Justice and Home Affairs' (2002) 7 *European Foreign Affairs Review* 317.

[84] O Bures, 'EU Counterterrorism Policy: A Paper Tiger?' (2006) 18 *Terrorism and Political Violence* 57.

[85] Ibid, p 60.

[86] Bossong, n 77 above, p 28.

[87] European Commission website: ec.europa.eu/justice_home/fsj/terrorism/strategies/fsj_terrorism_strategies_counter_en.htm, last accessed 12 September 2009.

is not simply counter-terrorism strategy; it is an entire foreign policy objective. It was not mentioned in the 2009 or 2010 updates. A closer examination makes clear that these measures are first and foremost about 'counter-radicalisation'. This is not unproblematic from the point of view of human rights and the rule of law: efforts to 'ensure that voices of mainstream opinion prevail' raise concerns about the boundaries of acceptable political discussion and the role of the state in regulating those boundaries.[88] The UK is described as a leading Member State in relation to two projects under this strand. British leadership is noteworthy as the UK has been heavily criticised for the effect of its domestic counter-terrorism on Muslim communities.[89] Such efforts certainly fit within a pre-emptive approach. The only legal aspect of the first strand is the obligation to criminalise incitement to violence (1.1.3). The obligation stems from international law: both UN Security Council resolution 1624, and the Council of Europe Convention on the Prevention of Terrorism require it. The EU legislated on the matter in December 2008, with the amendment of the Framework Decision on Combating Terrorism.

The second strand aims to 'protect citizens and infrastructure and reduce our vulnerability to attack, including through improved security of borders, transport and critical infrastructure'. In the 2010 Action Plan, the elements of this strand were: protection of critical infrastructure (2.1), CBRN preparedness (2.2), and border control. Transport security, concerned with airports, aircraft, ships and ports, including staff screening, and baggage and cargo security, was a separate point in previous Action Plans but now appears to be considered part of border control. Outside of the Pursue section of the Action Plan, Protect has the greatest number of legal measures. These feature in particular in relation to border control. This policy area deals with Schengen issues such as information systems, biometrics and passenger name records. Security co-operation through the Schengen system predates the New York and Washington attacks, and many of the concerns relating to the surveillance that are raised in this study resonate with critiques of Schengen policies. Analysing the development of the Schengen Information System and the complementary SIRENE system, Mathiesen argued that the Schengen process' goal 'is to be found at the cross point between the shutting out of aliens and the protection of vaguely defined public order and state security'.[90]

There is obvious overlap here between the trends in immigration and asylum policy and those in counter-terrorism policy.[91] In the 2007 Action Plan item 2.5.8 of the 'Protect' strand required the 'effective risk analysis of the EU external border' and 'discussion of the contribution which border security makes to the [counter-terrorism]

---

[88] See generally, W Sadurski (ed), *Political Rights Under Stress in 21st Century Europe* (Oxford, Oxford University Press, 2006).

[89] G Peirce, 'Was It Like This for the Irish?' (2008) 30(7) *London Review of Books* 3.

[90] T Mathiesen, 'On the Globalisation of Control: Towards an Integrated Surveillance System in Europe' in P Green and A Rutherford (eds), *Criminal Policy in Transition* (Oxford, Hart Publishing, 2000) 175.

[91] In the US context, see D Cole, *Enemy Aliens* (New York, The New Press, 2003).

effort'. The use of immigration law and procedures often allows state intervention based on lower standards of proof than criminal justice.[92] As such, immigration control has become a tool of counter-terrorism action—even in the absence of proof that non-citizens are in any way more likely to commit offences than state citizens. The bombings in London on 7 July 2005 and the attempted bombing in Times Square, New York, in May 2010 were carried out by British and American citizens respectively. Despite this, the 'war on terror' has proven a harsh landscape for migrants to navigate.[93]

The third strand of the Action Plan is its legislative core and the central focus of this study. Its aim is to:

> Pursue and investigate terrorists across Europe … to continue and increase our efforts to uncover terrorist networks, to impede communication, travel and planning activities of terrorists and their supporters; to cut off funding and access to attack materials and to file them in court.

This description is peppered with the language of pre-emption. Indeed, surprisingly for a section dealing with the pursuit of those who perpetrate attacks, bringing terrorists before courts features at the end of the description. This clause, which was previously termed 'to bring terrorists to justice' appears almost as an afterthought. The Pursue section of the plan appears to have most suffered from fragmentation due to being annually updated. For example, section 3.0 of the 2007 Action Plan related to the Framework Decision on Combating Terrorism, which establishes an EU definition of terrorism, provides for liability for those involved in 'terrorist groups' and sets out minimum penalties for terrorist offences. It is entirely omitted from the 2010 Action Plan. In a recent edition, there are three items in this section: information gathering (3.1); terrorist financing (3.3) and international dimension (3.4). Separate items on police and judicial co-operation have been excluded from this most recent update. Many key legislative developments in EU counter-terrorism are referenced in the report on this section, including the Framework Decision on Combating Terrorism (as amended) and legislation relating to terrorist financing and data retention and information exchange. The Pursue section of the Action Plan has therefore been the strand of greatest relevance for legal scholarship.

The final strand is concerned with responding to terrorist attacks. This part of the Action Plan is almost entirely removed from the legal sphere. A 2007 Council Factsheet describes the objective as: 'to prepare ourselves, in the spirit of solidarity, to manage and minimise the consequences of a terrorist attack'.[94] There are obvious echoes of the solidarity clause in this objective. The 2010 Action Plan items include civilian rapid response (4.1), military rapid response (4.2), response

---

[92]   K Roach, 'The Criminal Law and Terrorism' in VV Ramraj, M Hor and K Roach (eds), *Global Anti-Terrorism Law and Policy* (Cambridge, Cambridge University Press, 2005).

[93]   V Türk, 'Forced Migration and Security' (2003) 15 *International Journal of Refugee Law* 113.

[94]   EU Council Secretariat, *The European Union and the fight against terrorism*, Brussels, March 9 2007, p 4.

to CBRN incidents (4.3) and assistance to victims (4.4). What little law there has been in this strand featured in item 4.1 of the 2007 Action Plan, which referred to a Council Decision on a Community mechanism in civil protection assistance and a proposal for a Council regulation on a Rapid Response and Preparedness Instrument. The low level of legal action is noteworthy in one respect: 4.1.3 commits the Union to 'protect minority communities which may be at risk of a backlash in the event of a major attack'. However, the action under this point is limited to 'continued monitoring' of racial violence and discrimination. Monitoring would do little to protect those communities in the event of an attack and the item fails to mention that a joint action was adopted in this area as early as 1996 and a Framework Decision was agreed in December 2008.[95] Given the all-inclusive nature of the Action Plan, the absence of a reference to the legislation is a peculiar oversight. In the 2010 edition of the Action Plan the action remains limited to monitoring—this time by the newly established EU Fundamental Rights Agency.

Also of thematic relevance was item 4.1.4 of the 2007 Council Action Plan. It sought to improve the ability of the Member States 'to use a risk based approach to develop their capabilities to respond to national emergencies and those of their neighbours in a spirit of solidarity'. The item was noteworthy on two counts. First, the invocation of the 'spirit of solidarity' echoes the 2005 Declaration and the solidarity clause in the Lisbon Treaty. Second, and most pertinently, it advocates a risk based approach. The 'competent body' for this item is the Council, and the item is described as 'ongoing'. The only action that is listed is the holding of two workshops on 'the assessment of risks deriving from terrorism and other threats' that were held in London in 2005. As with the counter-radicalisation elements discussed above, item 4.1.4 indicated the logic of risk has influenced EU counter-terrorism.[96]

The questionable efficacy of an Action Plan as a tool of counter-terrorism policy has already been raised.[97] The EU also has its own Counter-Terrorism Co-ordinator. The office was proposed by the Irish presidency of the EU following the March 2004 bombings in Madrid. The office of Co-ordinator—which exercises no formal power—was held by Gijs de Vries for three years. It was unoccupied until September 2007 when Gilles de Kerchove was appointed. The EU's efforts to strengthen its counter-terrorism role have been less than entirely successful as a number of actors continue to prefer to operate outside EU institutions using bilateral and multilateral informal networks. This is despite 'long-standing co-ordination, competence and accountability problems in this "crowded policy space".[98] Since 11 September 2001, the Club de Berne has

---

[95] Joint action/96/443/JHA of 15 July 1996 adopted by the Council on the basis of Art K.3 of the Treaty on European Union, concerning action to combat racism and xenophobia; Council Framework Decision 2008/913/JHA of 28 November 2008 on combating certain forms and expressions of racism and xenophobia by means of criminal law.

[96] The most recent versions of the Action Plan, published in November 2009 and 2010, do not contain item 4.1.4.

[97] Bossong, n 77 above, p 40.

[98] Ibid.

established the Counterterrorism Group, which includes Club members, all other EU Member States, Switzerland, Norway, and (with observer status) the US.[99] The chair of the Counterterrorism Group rotates with the presidency of the EU, and it submits intelligence to 'some high-level EU committees'.[100] It 'remains, however, a manifestation of inter-governmental co-operation, not of the European Union'.[101] In addition, because of their frustration with the pace of progress in the EU, the five largest Member States (France, Germany, Italy, Spain and the UK) engage in informal discussions regarding internal security. Poland joined this group following its accession to the EU in 2003. Representing over three-quarters of the EU's population, the group's decisions are likely to have a significant impact on EU policy. Den Boer et al note that 'the group is allegedly working to conclude a series of bilateral agreements which should then form the basis of future EU-wide laws and measures'.[102] The persistence of informal networks notwithstanding formal EU competences for counter-terrorism raises concerns about the transparency of European policy-making processes.

A number of recurring trends are evident in European counter-terrorism both before and after 11 September 2001: a jealous guarding of counter-terrorism competence by national government and law enforcement and a preference for informal professional networks rather formal co-operation. While EU action has been limited by this reluctance to cede control it has still been possible for the Union to play a role in European counter-terrorism. However, the central mechanism for doing so, the Action Plan, is a confused document. The European law that emerges from this policy milieu might be expected to pose problems for a principle such as the rule of law which requires—at its core—legal certainty and legal accountability.

---

[99] Aldrich, n 18 above, p 739. The ten states that joined the EU on 1 May 2004 also joined the Counter-Terrorism Group on that date. Deflem describes the group as an informal gathering of the heads of security and intelligence services ... the [Counter-Terrorism Group] provides for co-operation in terrorism matters on the basis of an extra-legal memorandum of understanding. Focusing specifically on Islamic extremist terrorism, the Group meets regularly to facilitate operational co-operation among the EU's police and intelligence agencies.

See: Deflem, n 73 above, p 341.

[100] Aldrich, n 18 above, p 739.

[101] Lander, n 18 above, p 489.

[102] M Den Boer, C Hillebrand and A Nolke, 'Legitimacy under Pressure: The European Web of Counter-Terrorism Networks' (2008) 46(1) *Journal of Common Market Studies* 101, 117.

2

The EU Rule of Law

T HE RULE OF law underwent something of a renaissance in the latter half of the twentieth century.[1] The abuses of World War II brought the need for safeguards against state power to the fore once more. The most obvious beneficiary of the reaction to the war was the human rights movement. However, the rule of law also grew in importance—in particular in Europe. The concept is often invoked but is under-theorised in EU law. In the European context it appears in the Preambles to the European Convention on Human Rights (ECHR) and the European Charter of Fundamental Rights (EU Charter). The Copenhagen criteria, which set out the standards to be met by new members of the EU, also include adherence to the rule of law.[2] Unlike in many treaties and conventions, the rule of law is mentioned in the substantive text of the EU Treaty rather than in the Preamble. Thus Article 2 TEU provides that the EU is 'founded on the principles of liberty, democracy, respect for human rights and fundamental freedoms, and the rule of law' and states that these principles are 'common to the Member States'.[3] Advocate General Maduro has described this clause as expressing 'the respect due to national constitutional values'.[4] As a general provision of the Treaty on European Union this principle applies to all of the Union's activities. One might fairly expect Article 6 TEU to be of real normative value in European jurisprudence. However, the EU Treaty does not elaborate on the nature of the EU rule of law, an omission that must be remedied if it is to be the subject of sustained analysis.[5]

---

[1] See generally: BZ Tamanaha, *On the Rule of Law: History, Politics, Theory* (Cambridge, Cambridge University Press, 2006) 7. For a useful recent discussion in the Anglo-American context see T Bingham, *The Rule of Law* (London, Allen Lane, 2010). For a historical overview see J Rose, 'The Rule of Law in the Western World: An Overview' (2004) 35 *Journal of Social Philosophy* 457. For critical analysis see D Dyzenhaus (ed), *Recrafting the Rule of Law: The Limits of Legal Order* (Oxford, Hart Publishing, 1999).

[2] European Council, Presidency Conclusions Copenhagen European Council, 21–22 June 1993.

[3] Art 6 TEU.

[4] Case C-127/07 *Arcelor* [2008] ECR I-9895, para 16.

[5] Note that the Treaties do set out some aspects of the rule of law, eg Art 19(1) EU which sets out the ECJ's role in the legal order. The most thorough treatment the idea has received in the EU context is L Pech, *The Rule of Law as a Constitutional Principle of the European Union*, Jean Monnet Working Paper 04/09 (New York, NYU School of Law, 2009).

I. DEFINING THE RULE OF LAW IN THE EU

Defining the content or role of the rule of law in any given jurisdiction is a difficult task. The concept is inherently contested and different theories afford it different content. In politics, and especially for governments, the rule of law may sometimes be reduced to the idea of obedience to the law. Individuals and civil society groups invoke the rule of law as a principle constraining government action and protecting individual freedom. In the academy there is little agreement as to the concept's content and even its usefulness.[6] Faced with this ambiguity, one could almost be forgiven for giving up on the concept as an empty vessel, of little use except for making noise. However, the rule of law is strongly associated with modern liberal democracy, with compliance seen as a benchmark of good government. Any failure to properly articulate what is meant by the concept prevents it being a useful tool for the evaluation of government action such as counter-terrorism. Instead, its legitimising power could be used to give a veneer of validity to dubious practices. It is therefore important that the rule of law is not left to abuse and that its meaning is clearly articulated whenever it is invoked.[7]

In legal scholarship we can say that any particular definition of the rule of law exists on a continuum between formalism and substantivism—a continuum that is open-ended.[8] In general scholars tend to view the rule of law as related to the protection of individual freedom and therefore incorporate various principles such as legal certainty, the right to judicial review and the protection of human rights in their conceptions.[9] If the definition is extremely formalistic then the rule of law becomes little more than the idea of rule by law.[10] The more substantive content the concept is said to contain the more it becomes a full theory of justice,[11] but also the more scope that is created for diverging definitions.

---

[6] See: AC Hutchinson and P Monahan (eds), *The Rule of Law: Ideal or Ideology* (Toronto, Carswell, 1987; P Costa and D Zola (eds), *The Rule of Law: History, Theory and Criticism* (Netherlands, Springer, 2010).

[7] Pech, n 5 above, p 45.

[8] While Craig argues that all conceptions must be either strictly formal or substantive his analysis is predicated on the assumption that it is possible to strictly define what constitutes 'substantive' content. However, all conceptions of the rule of law that go beyond mere obedience to the law necessarily include some moral content. Thus the difference between Raz and Dworkin is one of degree. Pech comes to this conclusion in relation to the EU based on an examination of how the European Court of Justice has used the idea in its case law. P Craig, 'Formal and Substantive Conceptions of the Rule of Law' (1997) *Public Law* (1997) 467; Pech, n 5 above, p 52. See also N Barber, 'Must Legalistic Conceptions of the Rule of Law Have a Social Dimension' (2004) 17 *Ratio Juris* 474.

[9] Craig, 'Formal and Substantive', n 8 above. For classic examples of formal and substantive theories of the rule of law see J Raz, *The Authority of Law* (Oxford, Oxford University Press, 1979) and also, by the same author, 'The Rule of Law and its Virtue' (1977) 93 *Law Quarterly* Review 195; R Dworkin, *Law's Empire* (Harvard, Harvard University Press, 1986). For a discussion of the degree of substantive content in the rule of law see M Neumann, *The Rule of Law: Politicizing Ethics* (Aldershot, Ashgate Publishing, 2002).

[10] Tamanaha, n 1 above, p 92.

[11] Craig, 'Formal and Substantive', n 8 above, p 479.

The focus in this book is not on the rule of law as an abstract politico-legal concept but as a legal principle and political ideal in the context of the EU legal system. To discover the content of the rule of law in a particular legal system it is necessary to consider the broad constitutional framework. The rule of law can be said to represent the common values that underpin theories of justice based in the constitution. On this basis it is a dynamic concept which can evolve as the constitution does. Ultimately the extent—and nature—of the substantive content in the rule of law depends on how much work the concept is expected to do in the constitutional framework. Within the EU the rule of law is required to do much work indeed. Several Member States have a rule of law concept in their national constitutions. In English jurisprudence the classic, if outdated, statement of the principle is found in the work of Albert Venn Dicey. The German legal system is based on the concept of the *Rechtsstaat* while French law has *État de droit*.[12] The EU concept of the rule of law is a unique one which draws on Member State law but remains an autonomous concept.[13]

Though each institution of state can play a part in upholding the rule of law it is in courts that legal disputes are resolved and therefore it is ultimately the judiciary who must uphold the principle. The European Court of Justice has used the rule of law to assert the need for respect for EU law and it has been a key tool in the construction of the European legal order. The Court has also used it to strengthen its own position within the EU legal order and to develop legal accountability for action by the EU and its Member States when implementing EU law. The EU rule of law is therefore concerned with the effective enforcement of the law but also with safeguards for individual freedom.[14] It is a sufficiently flexible concept for a study that examines how the rule of law may evolve, or be eroded, as a result of government action. The EU rule of law can be said to have two roles: one addresses the citizen and demands that legal order be respected while the other addresses the government and requires that individual freedom be protected. It is concerned with constituting but also safeguarding the exercise of power in the EU legal order.

The constitutive role of the rule of law relates to the means by which the community is governed: through law. The law regulates social relationships and therefore effective enforcement of the law is 'constitutive for the rule of law'.[15] Most legal systems are not just communities of law, but also communities of coercion.[16] The EU does not constitute a community of coercion as actual

---

[12] Pech, n 5 above, p 22.

[13] Pech, n 5 above, p 48.

[14] The greatest intellectual debt owed by this approach is to the recent work of Armin von Bogdandy on this subject. A von Bogdandy, 'Constitutional Principles' in A von Bogdandy and J Bast (eds), *Principles of European Constitutional Law*, 1st edn (Oxford, Hart Publishing, 2006) 15–18. Note also the updated chapter: A von Bogdandy, 'Founding Principles' in A von Bogdandy and J Bast (eds), *Principles of European Constitutional Law*, rev 2nd edn (Oxford, Hart Publishing, 2009) 28–33.

[15] von Bogdandy, 'Constitutional Principles', n 14 above, p 15.

[16] von Bogdandy, 'Constitutional Principles', n 14 above, p 16.

coercive force is retained by the Member States. EU institutions secured the EU community of law without resort to coercion through reliance on legal doctrines and procedures. The safeguarding role of the rule of law protects individuals and contains principles that 'aim at the rational exercise of public power and protect qualified interests of its subjects'.[17] This is what is ordinarily understood by the rule of law. The precise content of this side of the rule of law is contested even within the context of a particular legal system such as the EU. There are several sources of principles that may form part of this role including the ECHR and the common constitutional traditions of the Member States. Both aspects of the rule of law help to legitimate the EU as a governmental entity—the constitutive role legitimises the EU as power is granted by law and the safeguarding role legitimates the EU as power is exercised in a manner that is respectful of European ideas of individual freedom.[18]

II. THE CONSTITUTIVE ROLE OF THE RULE OF LAW

The constitutive role of the rule of law reflects that the EU is a community of law which uses rules to govern social relationships.[19] A legal order's powers to legislate and to enforce its law usually flow from the same source and so the community of law is underpinned by a community of coercion.[20] The community of coercion can be equated with the Weberian idea of the 'community that successfully claims a monopoly of the legitimate use of physical force within a given territory'.[21] The community of coercion ensures the effectiveness of the community of law. If the law is not enforced it might even fail to be 'law'. It might therefore be argued that without coercion the community of law cannot exist and any separation of the communities of law and coercion is somewhat false. However, the EU is the result of successive international treaties between sovereign states that continue to claim coercive control over their respective territories. As the EU is only a community of law, and not a community of coercion, the actual enforcement of its legal system cannot be assumed. The constitutive role of the rule of law is thus the 'first condition for an actual rule of law'.[22] The extent to which EU law is enforced must be considered to establish whether there is, in fact, an EU rule of law.

---

[17] von Bogdandy, 'Constitutional Principles', n 14 above, p 17.

[18] M Maduro, *We the Court: The European Court of Justice and the European Economic Constitution* (Oxford, Hart Publishing, 1998) 27–30.

[19] von Bogdandy, 'Constitutional Principles', n 14 above, p 15.

[20] Here, von Bogdandy draws on the work of W Hallstein, *Die Europäische Gemeinschaft*, 5th edn (Düsseldorf, Econ, 1979). In an earlier version of the 'Constitutional Principles' essay, von Bogdandy uses the translation 'community of compulsion' to refer to Hallstein's idea. Here, coercion is used as it chimes more clearly with the language of state power, and as, one assumes, von Bogdandy decided it the more appropriate of the two terms. See A von Bogdandy, *Doctrine of Principles*, Jean Monnet Working Paper 9/03 (New York, NYU School of Law, 2003) 19.

[21] M Weber, *Politics as a Vocation*, Lecture to Munich University, January 1919.

[22] von Bogdandy, 'Constitutional Principles', n 14 above, p 29.

A. Establishing the European Legal Order

Many jurists have traced the development of an 'international rule of law' in Europe.[23] The development of the EU into the quasi-federal entity it is today was not inevitable. Rather, it was the result of choices by national and supranational institutions.[24] The role of the ECJ in particular has been central. Law requires an adjudicative body to settle disputes as to its meaning and in the EU that task falls to the ECJ.[25] The Court must ensure 'that in the interpretation and application of the Treaties the law is observed'.[26] The ECJ has used its role as interpreter and adjudicator to facilitate legal integration by ensuring that EU law is respected by the Member States. Its careful use of the preliminary rulings procedure has empowered private actors to ensure national compliance with EU law helping it to become embedded in Member States' legal systems.[27] The choice by Member State institutions to comply with the rulings of the ECJ was also important for this process. Thus, as the internal market was being completed so too was the legal system that regulates it. Other systems of international law may have 'a weak rule of law, which in turn undermines the influence and authority of the legal process, the independence of judges, and respect for legal rules'.[28] An effective legal system is one which establishes 'a virtuous circle, building respect for the law'.[29] It is the strong enforcement of EU law that sets it apart from other international systems.[30] The ECJ's adjudication ensured that despite the absence of actual coercive force, EU law was enforced throughout the Member States and a community of law was secured.

The limited but relatively coherent community of law was expanded following the formation of the EU by the Maastricht Treaty in 1992. The EU was founded upon the internal market which constituted the then first pillar of the EU. The Maastricht Treaty added the Common Foreign and Security Policy and Justice and Home Affairs as the second and third pillars respectively. Thus, the establishment of the EU was a result of functional spill-over that had already resulted in some European action outside of the internal market. The pillar structure resulted from a desire to 'formalize multilateral co-operation and create law-making procedures in highly sensitive areas, but without making the larger transfer of

---

[23] K Alter, *Establishing the Supremacy of European Law: The Making of an International Rule of Law In Europe* (Oxford, Oxford University Press, 2001). See also M Maduro, *We the Court: The European Court of Justice and the European Economic Constitution* (Oxford, Hart Publishing, 1998) and JHH Weiler, *The Constitution of Europe 'Do the New Clothes Have an Emperor?' and Other Essays on European Integration* (Cambridge, Cambridge University Press, 1999).

[24] Alter, n 23 above, p 16.

[25] von Bogdandy, 'Constitutional Principles', n 14 above, p 17.

[26] Art 19 EU (ex Art 220 EC).

[27] Alter, n 23 above, pp 218–20.

[28] Alter, n 23 above, p 217.

[29] Ibid.

[30] Weiler, n 23 above, pp 28–29.

national autonomy'.[31] The three pillars were asymmetrical. In terms of the degree of co-operation at international level, the second and third pillars varied greatly, both from the first pillar and each other. Sitting atop the pillars were the various EU institutions which were common to all pillars albeit with different powers in each. The adoption of the Lisbon Treaty has ended this complex institutional structure while retaining certain idiosyncrasies.[32] Whether or not the EU will continue to evolve towards a unified supranational legal system will depend not just on further legal advances but also the political will to create that system. Regardless of future developments as to the scope of EU powers, the operation of the EU legal order remains reliant on the rule of law's constitutive role. Key facets of the constitutional order—such as the principle of conferred powers and judicial application of the law—remain central to the effectiveness of EU law.

B. Conferral of Power and EU Legislation

In addition to being central to the establishment of the legal order the rule of law also requires that power is exercised in accordance with legal rules. The constitutive role of the rule of law is central to EU governance insofar as it is through the treaties, the de facto EU constitution, that the EU is governed. The EU operates on the basis of limited or conferred powers granted to the Union and its institutions by the Member States. For the EU to adopt a legislative act, it must possess the required power and use the correct legal basis to do so.[33] The absence of a valid basis for an EU instrument in the treaties is grounds for annulment of the instrument by the ECJ. The use of an incorrect legal basis also provides grounds for annulment. The question of legal basis has been the cause of much inter-institutional litigation as different institutions have different roles depending on which legal basis is used. EU action must also respect the principles of subsidiarity and proportionality—though these are rarely the basis of a successful challenge to the lawfulness of EU legislation.[34] After the Lisbon Treaty the EU has the power to adopt legislative actions with the 'ordinary legislative procedure' involving an equal power for the Council and the European Parliament. Nonetheless there remain different powers to act in different policy fields and inter-institutional litigation continues.[35] Thus, while the EU rule of law cannot be reduced to the principle of conferred powers it is this principle that is at the core of the rule of law's constitutive role.[36]

---

[31] E Denza, *The Intergovernmental Pillars of the European Union* (Oxford, Oxford University Press, 2002) 3.

[32] P Craig, *The Lisbon Treaty: Law, Politics and Treaty Reform* (Oxford, Oxford University Press, 2010).

[33] See S Douglas-Scott, *Constitutional Law of the European Union* (Harlow, Longman, 2002), ch 4.

[34] See Protocol on the Application of the Principles of Subsidiarity and Proportionality OJ C310/207 (16 December 2004).

[35] Case C-130/10 *European Parliament v. Council of the European Union* [2010] OJ C 134.

[36] Pech, n 5 above, p 10.

The legislation and other legal acts examined in this book relate to EU counter-terrorism. The three key types of legislative instrument that have been used for counter-terrorism are directives, regulations and framework decisions.[37] Directives and regulations were first devised as legislative instruments used for the governance of the internal market. The key difference between the two remains the need for directives to be transposed into national law while regulations are directly applicable in national legal systems. The debate on whether or not these instruments could also be used for the purpose of criminal law and criminal justice predates the formation of the EU. For example, when drafting the first Anti-Money-Laundering Directive, the Council was concerned that they lacked the necessary legal power. To avoid a difficult debate on power over criminal justice they used a legislative formula requiring that certain actions 'shall be prohibited'.[38] Two key decisions of the ECJ confirmed that the EU could require Member States to adopt criminal sanctions for breaches of EU law—at least in the limited field of environmental law.[39] The judicial development of the law in this area has been confirmed by the Lisbon Treaty which provides an explicit power to impose criminal sanctions for breaches of EU law.[40] Internal market powers can also be used to adopt legislation for counter-terrorism action where that action affects aspects of the internal market. Examples of such legislation include targeted asset-freezing sanctions and data retention laws which involve several regulations and a directive.[41]

When the Member States decided to provide the EU with the specific power to adopt legislation to co-ordinate criminal justice they were reluctant to afford the Union the same power it had over the internal market. As a result, between the coming into force of the Amsterdam and Lisbon Treaties, the EU Treaty established 'framework decisions' to be used to co-ordinate criminal justice. Framework decisions were used for two of the EU's most important counter-terrorism actions. They sought to facilitate the 'approximation of the laws and regulations of the Member States'. Although binding on the Member States they leave 'the choice of form and methods' to national authorities.[42] The Treaty stated that framework

---

[37] Other measures, such as common positions and decisions, will also be encountered throughout this work. What constitutes legislation under EU law remains the subject of debate. See AH Türk, *The Concept of Legislation in European Community Law: A Comparative Perspective* (Netherlands, Kluwer Law International, 2006).

[38] V Mitsilegas and B Gilmore, 'The EU Legislative Framework Against Money Laundering and Terrorist Finance: A Critical Analysis in the Light of Evolving Global Standards' (2007) 56 *International and Comparative Law Quarterly* 119, 136.

[39] C-176/03 *Commission v Council* [2005] ECR I-7879 (hereafter, *Environmental Crimes*); C-440/05 *Commission v Council* [2007] ECR I-9097 (hereafter, *Ship Source Pollution*). Opinion Advocate General Mazak *Ship Source Pollution*. See para 102:

the Community legislature has the power to adopt measures providing for the imposition of criminal penalties where it considers such penalties necessary in order to ensure that the rules which it lays down are fully effective and on condition that criminal measures are essential for combating serious offences in the area concerned.

[40] Art 83 TFEU.

[41] See below: chs 4 and 6 respectively.

[42] Art 34 EU(N).

decisions 'shall not entail direct effect'. They are therefore only enforced in the Member States if national implementing legislation is enacted. Furthermore, they are for approximation rather than harmonisation of the law. As legislative instruments, framework decisions are therefore less effective than directives.[43] The framework decisions that were adopted cast doubt on the suitability of 'approximation' of criminal law as a means to establish an EU community of law in the field of criminal justice. Indeed, the very text of the Treaty attempted to limit the effectiveness of the framework decision as a legislative instrument. These differences were both causes and symptoms of the weak community of law outside of the internal market prior to the coming into force of the Lisbon Treaty. Outside of the first pillar the doctrines and processes that are central to the rule of law's constitutive role were absent. As a result the legal order remains fragmented.

C. The Enforcement of EU Law

While the constitutive role of the rule of law relates in part to the EU's legislative power that legislation must be enforced for the rule of law to be upheld. The early judgments of the ECJ established the principles of supremacy and direct effect and later a law of remedies.[44] A legal system requires its rules to be subject to interpretation and application by a court to ensure compliance. This sets up the 'virtuous circle' that reinforces the community of law. These principles were used to ensure that EU law was enforced and thus have been key to securing the community of law in the former first pillar. EU action is undeniably effective in this field. However, enforcement of EU law outside the first pillar—and thus the effectiveness of the EU as an actor in criminal justice—remains problematic.

Under the pre-Lisbon Treaty framework, the ECJ had no jurisdiction in the Common Foreign and Security Policy, and had limited jurisdiction in the field of Justice and Home Affairs.[45] The Court had jurisdiction to give preliminary rulings on the 'validity and interpretation' of framework decisions but that jurisdiction was limited in two ways. First, the Court could not review the 'validity or proportionality' of law enforcement operations. Second, the power to refer cases was only extended to courts in Member States that accept the ECJ's jurisdiction by declaration.[46] The absence of jurisdiction clearly limits the development of a

---

[43] For a discussion see S Peers, *EU Justice and Home Affairs Law*, 3rd edn (Oxford, Oxford University Press, 2011) 29–30.

[44] Case 26/62 *Van Gend en Loos* [1963] ECR 1; Case 6/64 *Costa v ENEL* [1964] ECR 585; Case C-6/90 *Francovich* [1991] ECR I-5357.

[45] See Arts 35 & 46(b) EU(N).

[46] Of the Member States 2 permitted only their courts of last instance to refer cases (Spain and Hungary), a further 12 permitted any court to refer (Austria, Belgium, Czech Republic, Finland, France, Germany, Greece, Italy, Luxembourg (Netherlands, Portugal, Sweden), and the remaining 13 Member States did not accept the jurisdiction of the Court in such matters (Bulgaria, Cyprus, Denmark, Estonia, Ireland, Latvia, Lithuania, Malta, Poland, Romania, Slovakia, Slovenia, United Kingdom). See [2005] OJ L327/19 (14 December 2005).

community of law in EU action in this policy field. Therefore, the 'virtuous circle' that upholds the rule of law was not established.[47] A further, related, limitation on the development of a strong community of law arises from the restriction of constitutional principles such as supremacy and direct effect to the former first pillar.[48] Without these doctrines and procedures to ensure the enforcement of EU law, the community of law was entirely dependent on national executives, legislatures and judiciaries implementing and enforcing the law. This study demonstrates that framework decisions adopted to counter terrorism indicate the limitations of that approach to building an effective legal order.

The Lisbon Treaty extended the ECJ's jurisdiction over security and criminal justice.[49] In principle, judicial review is extended to all EU justice and home affairs as the third pillar has been merged with the first. However, this development is subject to three limitations which are 'material, temporal and geographic'.[50] Materially, the exclusion of the ECJ's jurisdiction over operational matters is continued. Thus, the ECJ has no jurisdiction to review actions carried out by national law enforcement authorities pursuant to EU law. While national courts and the European Court of Human Rights can perform this role the exclusion of operational matters from its jurisdiction is a significant limitation on the ECJ's ability to preserve rule of law principles as the EU increases its role in criminal justice. Temporally, the ECJ's pre-Lisbon Treaty jurisdiction over existing third pillar legislation continues until 2015. Geographically, the Lisbon Treaty continues British and Irish opt-outs in police and judicial co-operation with the two Member States having the power to opt-in to instruments on a case-by-case basis.

In summation, although the rule of law plays a constitutive role in the EU that role is variable depending on the power used to act. The key doctrines and procedures that ensure the effective enforcement of EU law have been largely absent in EU policy fields outside the internal market. The establishment of the EU at Maastricht can be seen as entailing an anti-constitutional backlash against the court's progressive development of the EU rule of law.[51] While September 11 2001 has invigorated EU counter-terrorism, the action taken in this field has demonstrated the limitations of the pre-Lisbon Treaty constitutional framework. Furthermore, the restriction of the rule of law's constitutive role at Maastricht was only partly remedied at Lisbon. In particular, the ECJ's jurisdiction will remain restricted for much of the duration of the Stockholm Programme.

---

[47] Alter, n 23 above, 217.

[48] While there has been some discussion of supremacy evidence of the principle's establishment in the third pillar remained unconvincing. See D Leczykiewicz, 'Constitutional Conflicts and the Third Pillar' (2008) 33 *European Law Review* 230.

[49] Art 19 EU.

[50] E Sanfrutos-Cano 'The End of the Pillars? A Single EU Legal Order after Lisbon' in CC Murphy and P Green (eds), *Law and Outsiders: Norms, Processes and 'Othering' in the 21st Century* (Oxford, Hart Publishing, 2011).

[51] Weiler, n 23 above, 233.

III. THE SAFEGUARDING ROLE OF THE RULE OF LAW

The constitutive role of the rule of law ensures that the EU is an effective legal system. However, it is the other role that most readily comes to mind when the rule of law is invoked. The rule of law has a safeguarding role in the EU legal order—ensuring that insofar as the Union is governed through law that law is respectful of individual freedom. The principles that are involved in safeguarding individuals are the subject of several scholarly treatises.[52] All theories tend to start with the idea of a certain, clear and accessible system of rule—commonly referred to as the principle of legality. This principle is an aspect of the EU rule of law in both criminal and civil matters. Theories tend to diverge beyond this agreed starting point. Today, many of the legal principles and legal rules that are said to be part of the rule of law have become subsumed within human rights. It is this latter concept—of human rights—which has come to dominate popular, political and legal discourses on how state interferences with individual freedom can best be limited. The rule of law does not itself operate as a rule of law within the EU and a breach of the rule of law cannot, of itself, form the basis of a legal action.[53] To appreciate the nature of the rule of law's safeguarding role in the EU it is necessary to consider how that role developed and to examine, in particular, the development of the Court's human rights jurisprudence.

A. Rights and the European Union

Due to the Union's origins in economic co-operation, and the existence of the Council of Europe, human rights were once entirely absent from EU law. However, the growth of the European institutions' powers and the need for appropriate safeguards caused national courts to force the ECJ to consider its position on the matter.[54] In *Internationale Handelsgesellschaft* the Court declared that respect for human rights is 'an integral part of the general principles of law protected by the Court of Justice'. It stated that while protection was 'inspired by the constitutional traditions common to the Member States', it must be ensured within the European legal order itself.[55]

Following this decision, the Court proceeded to conduct human rights-based reviews with growing enthusiasm.[56] The ECJ used the common constitutional traditions of the Member States, as well as their common membership of the ECHR, to imbue European law with a human rights conscience. In *Opinion 2/94*,

---

[52] See Raz, *The Authority of Law* and 'The Rule of Law', n 9 above; Dworkin, n 9 above, for key examples.

[53] Pech, n 5 above, p 58.

[54] *Solange I* [1974] 2 CMLR 540.

[55] Case C-11/70 *Internationale Handelsgesellschaft* [1970] ECR 1125, 1134.

[56] A von Bogdandy, 'The European Union as a Human Rights Organisation? Human Rights and the Core of the European Union' (2000) 37 *Common Market Law Review* 1307–38.

the Court reiterated that fundamental rights are 'an integral part of the general principles of law whose observance the Court ensures' and that 'respect for human rights is therefore a condition of the lawfulness of Community acts.'[57] This human rights conscience has recently reached its zenith with the coming into force of the Lisbon Treaty. The Treaty has given legal effect to the European Charter of Fundamental Rights and provides for the accession of the EU to the ECHR.[58]

Despite the undeniable importance of human rights in the EU, the question here is whether a particular level of human rights protection is required by the rule of law. It is difficult to ascertain the precise relationship between human rights and the EU rule of law. One might argue that the EU idea of the rule of law is so broad that any breach of human rights amounts to a breach of the rule of law. EU legislative acts can be annulled for breach of human rights. On the other hand including protection of human rights within the rule of law would render the concept quite broad indeed and potentially stripping it of any real meaning. This therefore returns to the question of how much work the concept must do in the EU legal order.

B. Rights and the Rule of Law

While human rights are an essential part of EU law there are several reasons not to consider a particular level of human rights protection as a substantive element of the EU rule of law. The first difficulty with such an approach lies in the loss of the neutrality of the rule of law. Human rights provide 'the words-based platform for the communication of a particular ethical perspective on the world'.[59] The greater the substantive content in the rule of law the greater the risk that the concept's broad acceptance would be undermined. On the other hand, the conception of the rule of law used in the EU is patently not neutral and is linked, in the treaties and in judgments of the Court, to other values such as human rights and democracy.[60] Thus a concern for neutrality would be an insufficient reason for rejecting substantive human rights protection as part of the EU rule of law.

A more compelling reason is the risk of fixing the rule of law based on a particular historical interpretation of human rights. If the rule of law is to remain a dynamic concept it must be capable of development. Of course, there is no guarantee that any development of the rule of law will leave individuals in a better position. The rule of law might be eroded just as easily as it might be evolved. However the potential for erosion reflects the idea that the rule of law is a value

---

[57] *Opinion 2/94* [1996] ECR I-1763.

[58] D Anderson and CC Murphy, 'The Charter of Fundamental Rights' in A Biondi, P Eeckhout and S Ripley, *EU Law after Lisbon* (Oxford, Oxford University Press, 2011). See also, in the same volume, G Gaja, 'Accession to the ECHR'.

[59] C Gearty, 'Can Human Rights Survive? A Symposium on the 2005 Hamlyn Lectures' (2007) *Public Law* 209, 228.

[60] Pech, n 5 above, pp 54–55.

that legal systems may have to a greater or lesser degree and in different qualities. As a legal value it must be open to development and incorporating within it a substantive level of rights protection might impede that development. Nonetheless the idea of human rights is also a dynamic one. As such linking the rule of law to human rights does not necessarily risk the concept atrophying. One could consider a particular level of rights protection to be linked to a particular understanding of the rule of law with the two concepts waxing and waning together.

Perhaps the strongest reason not to equate a particular level of human rights protection with the rule of law is the risk of conflating an individual breach of rights with a systematic failure in legal protection. If every unlawful interference with human rights is considered to be a violation of the rule of law then there is a risk that critical commentary would tend towards hysteria. A failure to protect a suspect's rights in a criminal trial is a violation of those rights which should be remedied by the legal system. It should not be considered, of itself, a breach of the rule of law. If the violation of human rights goes without remedy, and such violations become commonplace, then the system of protection has indeed failed and so the rule of law has been eroded.

It is therefore most accurate to claim that the safeguarding role of the EU rule of law requires accountability processes that are capable of considering the lawfulness of legislative action and that include vindicating human rights. This claim has the support of the ECJ's case law which consistently upholds the right to have EU action reviewed by a court of law.[61] In *Les Verts* the European Green Party sought to challenge the internal regulation of the European Parliament. The Treaty did not then include the Parliament as an institution whose acts could be subject to legal challenge. Nevertheless, the ECJ held that the European legal order is based on the rule of law and therefore 'neither its Member States nor its institutions can avoid a review of the question whether the measures adopted by them are in conformity with the basic constitutional charter, the Treaty'.[62] The Court upheld the applicants' right to judicial review of the Parliament's regulatory measure.

Since the decision in *Les Verts*, the ECJ has developed a rich jurisprudence on the right to hold the EU's exercise of power accountable before the courts. It is this accountability process—rather than the substantive outcome of the proceedings—which is the key to the rule of law's safeguarding role. This is best illustrated with an example. In *Schmidberger* the ECJ had to consider the relationship between the right to protest and the fundamental freedoms of the internal market.[63] The Court found for the protesters. Had the Court decided against the protesters its judgment would not necessarily have been an erosion of the rule of law—merely a restriction of the right to protest. However, the court would act contrary to the rule of law if it refused to assess the human rights arguments at all or if its protection of those

---

[61] Case C-294/83 *Parti Ecologiste 'Les Verts'* [1986] ECR 1339.
[62] Ibid, para 23.
[63] Case C-112/00 *Schmidberger* [2003] ECR I-5659.

rights was merely illusory. As former Advocate General Francis Jacobs describes it, the basic requirement involves 'the right to a fair trial, the availability of effective remedies; and also the idea that all exercise of power is ... subject to review of courts'.[64] It is therefore the availability of human rights review rather than the precise level of human rights protection that is required by the rule of law.

C. The Level of Protection in the EU

Notwithstanding the emphasis on the availability of human rights protection it remains necessary to consider the level of rights protection. The extent to which the courts will examine human rights issues in the field of security is determinative of how robust the rule of law protection is in practice. If the courts become too deferential to the executive or legislature then the rule of law, though ostensibly upheld, will be effectively eroded. Thus even though a particular level of human rights protection may not be mandated by the rule of law a systematic lowering of the level of protection would represent an erosion of the rule of law. This position blurs the line between the idea of the rule of law and the values that it seeks to protect. However, that may be an inevitable consequence of the inextricable linking of the principle with the other values in Article 6 TEU.[65] The list of rights the ECJ will seek to protect is a long one. In addition to the ECHR and EU Charter the Court has also developed general principles of EU law based on the Member States' constitutions.[66]

The rights involved in any particular case will of course depend on the law under examination. European counter-terrorism is pursued in large part through criminal justice. However, the historic absence of an EU criminal law, the ECJ's limited role to date outside of the internal market, and the continuing dominance of the Member States in this sphere means there is little ECJ jurisprudence on criminal justice. This restricts the extent to which existing case law can guide a study of EU counter-terrorism. Nonetheless, in *Pupino*, the Court noted that EU criminal law must be interpreted so that 'fundamental rights, including in particular the right to a fair trial as set out in Article 6 of the Convention and interpreted by the European Court of Human Rights, are respected'.[67] Indeed, there is a co-operative relationship between the EU and ECHR legal systems that has seen an evolution of rights protection in recent years with the case law of the two courts complementing each other to raise the standard of protection.[68]

---

[64] FG Jacobs, *The Sovereignty of Law: The European Way* (Cambridge, Cambridge University Press, 2007) 62.

[65] Pech, n 5 above, 52.

[66] T Tridimas, *The General Principles of EU Law*, 2nd edn (Oxford, Oxford University Press, 2007).

[67] C-105/03 *Criminal Proceedings against Maria Pupino* [2005] ECR I-5285, para 59.

[68] S Douglas-Scott 'A Tale of Two Courts: Luxembourg, Strasbourg and the Growing European Human Rights Acquis' (2006) 43 *Common Market Law Review* 619.

The Convention deals extensively with criminal justice. It contains a well-developed right to personal liberty, the right to a fair trial and the principle of legality in criminal law.[69] These three rights have also been recognised in EU law. The principle of legality is an illustrative example and an appropriate one as it is at the core of the rule of law. In *Kirk* the ECJ held that a regulation may not retrospectively validate penalties for an act that was not punishable at the time of its commission.[70] Retrospectivity of criminal penalties would be in breach of the principle of legality in criminal law which 'takes its place among the general principles of law whose observance is ensured by the Court of Justice'.[71] In a similar vein, a directive cannot, without implementation, 'have the effect of determining or aggravating the liability in criminal law of persons who act in contravention of the provisions of that directive'.[72] This rule has a number of corollaries. The obligation to interpret national law consistently with EU law cannot of itself determine or aggravate criminal liability.[73] Where a directive requires national law to be set aside for incompatibility, an individual cannot be subject to the previous, harsher penalties.[74] Furthermore, authorities should retrospectively apply less severe penalties, a principle which goes further than the protection previously provided by the ECHR.[75] The principle of legality in criminal law can now be found in Article 49 of the EU Charter.[76] The European Court of Human Rights has drawn on the Charter to develop its own case law on the principle of legality and the Convention system now emulates the EU in providing for the retrospective application of less severe penalties.[77] European standards of protection in criminal justice are therefore evolving through the cross-pollination of European laws.[78]

Rights other than those explicitly linked to criminal justice can also be engaged by counter-terrorism action. Action by the EU since 11 September 2001 has rendered criminal behaviour that was previously considered lawful. The Council of Europe's Directorate General of Human Rights and Legal Affairs notes that the Convention prevents 'the prohibition of the criminalisation of the lawful exercise of Convention rights'.[79] However, neither EU law nor the ECHR offers any clear guidance as to what may or may not be designated criminal. Any criminalisation must pursue a legitimate aim, be prescribed by law, and be 'necessary in a

---

[69] Arts 5, 6 and 7 ECHR respectively.

[70] Case 63/83 *Kirk* [1984] ECR 2689.

[71] Ibid [21–22].

[72] 14/86 *Pretore di Salo v Persons Unknown* [1987] ECR 2545.

[73] 80/86 *Kolpinghuis Nijmegen BV* [1987] ECR 3969; C-168/95 *Criminal Proceedings Against Luciano Arcaro* [1996] ECR 4705.

[74] C-387/02, C-391/02, C-403/02 *Berlusconi and Others* [2005] ECR I–3565 [69]; Opinion of Advocate General Kokott *Berlusconi* [157].

[75] C-295/02 *Gerken* [2004] *ECR* I-6369.

[76] C-105/03 *Criminal Proceedings against Maria Pupino* [2005] ECR I-5285 [44].

[77] *Scoppola v Italy (No 2)* Judgment of the Court (Grand Chamber) 17 September 2009.

[78] See Douglas-Scott, n 68 above, and Anderson and Murphy, n 58 above, for examples.

[79] Directorate General of Human Rights and Legal Affairs *Fair Trial in Criminal Cases*, available at <www.coehelp.org/mod/resource/view.php?inpopup=true&id=1206>, last accessed 4 April 2011.

democratic society'. The Convention therefore affords significant discretion to criminalise behaviour. The rule of law can also be impacted upon by policies which seek to counter terrorism through civil and administrative law. The principle of legality is found in the requirement that interferences with other rights be 'prescribed by law'.[80] This broader principle of legality offers some protection for individuals—though it is a lower level of protection than in the field of criminal law.[81] The wide range substantive rights that might be affected by EU counter-terrorism include freedom of expression (incitement to terrorism offences), freedom of assembly (proscription of terrorist groups), the right to privacy (data retention laws) and the right to property (targeted asset-freezing sanctions). The rule of law's safeguarding role requires a system of judicial oversight that can review the lawfulness of this action—in particular in relation to breaches of human rights. Such a system is essential if individuals are to be protected from EU action in the field of counter-terrorism.

IV. COURTS, PRE-EMPTION AND THE RULE OF LAW

The erosion of established legal principles is one of the key effects of a pre-emptive approach to counter-terrorism. Focused on control, pre-emptive counter-terrorism undermines the idea that political violence is addressed through clearly-defined norms enforced by prescribed sanctions. Instead, 'control becomes a matter of state will and bureaucratic determination rather than the juridical allocation of rights and responsibilities'.[82] The scope of criminal law is broadened to catch behaviour that was previously considered legal. Civil law is deployed in a more coercive and intrusive manner with administrative sanctions used to control behaviour. The overall effect is to weaken the coherence and symbolic power of the criminal law and turn civil law into a potent tool of counter-terrorism. This threatens both the constitutive and safeguarding roles of the rule of law to the detriment of the legal system and those subject to it.

Throughout this examination of the rule of law the focus has, by and large, been on courts. Yet each institution has a role to play in upholding the rule of law. The legislature can ensure that it acts on an appropriate basis in the treaties, that it legislates with clarity and precision, and that it provides for systems of accountability when it affords power to the executive. The executive can use its power

---

[80] Art 8 ECHR uses the language 'in accordance with law' while Arts 9–11 use 'prescribed by law'. However nothing turns on the distinction and the latter is used here to refer to the general principle. Note also the requirement in Art 5 ECHR that any deprivation of liberty be 'in accordance with a procedure prescribed by law'. See: S Greer, *The European Convention on Human Rights: Achievements, Problems and Prospects* (Cambridge, Cambridge University Press, 2006) 201–03.

[81] CC Murphy, 'The Principle of Legality in Criminal Law under the European Convention on Human Rights' (2010) *European Human Rights Law Review* 192.

[82] A Norrie, 'Citizenship, Authoritarianism and the Changing Shape of the Criminal Law' in B McSherry, A Norrie and S Bronitt (eds), *Regulating Deviance: The Redirection of Criminalisation and the Futures of Criminal Law* (Oxford, Hart Publishing, 2009) 31–32.

judiciously and in accordance with the empowering legislation and can make an effort to comply with rule of law principles. However, assessing whether or not the other two organs of government have satisfactorily upheld rule of law values remains the task of the courts. Both the constitutive and the safeguarding roles of the rule of law require the courts to assess whether or not EU counter-terrorism action complies with the fundamental principles of the legal order.

Despite the ECJ's strong record there remain reasons to be cautious about its ability to uphold the rule of law. First, the Court's jurisdiction remains limited and will continue to exclude operational matters even after the Lisbon Treaty's transitional provisions expire. Although national courts and the European Court of Human Rights can review operational matters the system of accountability remains fragmented. Second, courts often defer to the executive and legislative branches on questions of national security.[83] Prior to 11 September 2001 there was no indication as to the ECJ's stance on the role of the judiciary in the field of national security. The matter simply had not arisen in the EU legal system. However, as the EU legislates in this field the question is increasingly pertinent. Third, if carefully crafted, pre-emptive counter-terrorism offers the opportunity for the EU to exert control with human rights law legitimating instead of constraining action.[84] For example, UK control orders were designed to comply with three judgments of the ECtHR on preventive action against organised crime in Italy.[85] Despite the apparent compliance with human rights law the system was found to breach human rights in several cases as individuals were subject to de facto house arrest based on mere suspicion. The greatest danger is posed to the rule of law when law is used to construct a 'jurisprudential black hole'.[86] If any of these potential problems manifest themselves in practice they could significantly curtail the Court's ability to uphold the rule of law. The position of the ECJ is vital to the EU rule of law. If it is undermined then the potential for eroding the rule of law would be very great indeed.

[83] F De Londras and F Davis, 'Controlling the Executive in Times of Terrorism: Competing Perspectives on Effective Oversight Mechanisms' (2010) 30 *Oxford Journal of Legal Studies* 19.

[84] On this, see S Marks, 'Comment on a Paper by Joseph Raz: Human Rights in the New World Order' *ISCI Working Paper 2/2010*, available: www.statecrime.org.

[85] See: KD Ewing and JC Tham, 'The Continuing Futility of the Human Rights Act' (2008) *Public Law* 668.

[86] A Ashworth, 'Criminal Law, Human Rights and Preventative Justice' in B McSherry, A Norrie and S Bronitt (eds), *Regulating Deviance: The Redirection of Criminalisation and the Futures of Criminal Law* (Oxford, Hart Publishing, 2009) 100.

Part II

EU Counter-Terrorism Action

3

Criminalising 'Terrorism' in EU Law

I F 'TERRORISM' IS a form of political communication using violence then the definition of terrorism in criminal law draws the boundaries of acceptable political action within a polity. The Framework Decision on Combating Terrorism (FDCT) offers the first comprehensive European definition of terrorism and is the central plank of EU counter-terrorism action. However, it may also be the paradigmatic example of the deficiencies of the framework decision as a legislative instrument. Framework decisions are designed to 'approximate' rather than 'harmonise' Member State criminal law, and the FDCT has resulted in broad legal rules that run contrary to the principle of legality. Implementation of the framework decision by Member States has been poor and has not resulted in a de facto single definition of terrorism across the EU but rather a range of definitions which have the framework decision as their inspiration. This poses a serious question about the usefulness of the framework decision and the nature of the criminal law that it can produce. The framework decision does not appear to be used as the basis for special co-operation between the Member States or for safeguarding powers granted to law enforcement authorities. In 2008 the framework decision was amended in light of developments in global counter-terrorism to provide for further offences. The law, as amended, contributes to the EU's preemptive counter-terrorism as it empowers Member States to take action against a wide variety of individuals and organisations whose behaviour often stops short of causing harm itself.

I. THE POLITICS AND PHILOSOPHY OF CRIMINALISING TERRORISM

The significance of agreeing an EU definition of terrorism can be demonstrated by contrasting the framework decision with the Council of Europe's 1977 Convention on the Suppression of Terrorism. That Treaty did not provide a definition but instead specified a list of offences to be subject to the 'prosecute or extradite' principle.[1] The more recent 2005 Council of Europe Convention on the Prevention of Terrorism also used a list based approach.[2] The United Nations (UN), with an even larger

---

[1] Council of Europe, Convention on the Suppression of Terrorism, 27 January 1977.
[2] Council of Europe, Convention on the Prevention of Terrorism, 16 May 2005. Art 1(1) provides that 'for the purposes of this Convention, "terrorist offence" means any of the offences within the

membership, has had similar difficulty in agreeing a definition.[3] With a single recent exception, the UN has also taken the approach of targeting certain particular acts rather than categorically defining 'terrorism'.[4] By and large, the difficulty of defining terrorism in international law can be attributed to the term's stigmatising effect. Any objective definition would likely include an individual or group whose actions are or were viewed as legitimate by some members of the international community.[5] In a nutshell, members of the UN General Assembly may recognise that political violence can sometimes be legitimate, but never when it is directed at them. Definitional paralysis is the predictable outcome.[6] A draft comprehensive Convention on International Terrorism, under discussion since 1996, remains mired in disagreement.[7]

The failure to agree a definition is not limited to international relations. Even (or perhaps especially) in academic debate, achieving a universally agreed-upon definition of terrorism has proven impossible. Schmid and Jongman surveyed a section of the academy to ascertain whether there was an agreed definition of terrorism. They then combined all of the responses to produce a broad statement that captures all the definitions of terrorism submitted to them. The result was the following:

> an anxiety-inspiring method of repeated violent action, employed by (semi-) clandestine, individual, group, or state actors, for idiosyncratic, criminal, or political reasons,

scope of and as defined in one of the treaties listed in the Appendix'. The Appendix refers to ten international Conventions aimed at particular offences.

[3] A report by the UN Secretary General's High Level Panel on Threats, Challenges and Change noted that a definition of terrorism includes

any action, in addition to actions already specified by the existing conventions on aspects of terrorism, the Geneva Conventions and Security Council resolution 1566 (2004), that is intended to cause death or serious bodily harm to civilians or non-combatants, when the purpose of such act, by its nature or context, is to intimidate a population, or to compel a Government or an international organization to do or to abstain from doing any act.

However, no agreement has yet been reached on a uniform international definition. See UN High Level Panel, *A More Secure World: Our Shared Responsibility* (New York, UN Department of Public Information, 2004) 52.

[4] 1963 Convention on Offences and Certain Other Acts Committed On Board Aircraft; 1970 Convention for the Suppression of Unlawful Seizure of Aircraft; 1971 Convention for the Suppression of Unlawful Acts against the Safety of Civil Aviation; 1973 Convention on the Prevention and Publishment of Crimes against Internationally Protected Persons; 1979 International Convention against the Taking of Hostages; 1980 Convention on the Physical Protection of Nuclear Material; 1988 Protocol for the Suppression of Unlawful Acts of Violence at Airports Serving International Civil Aviation; 1988 Convention for the Suppression of Unlawful Acts against the Safety of Maritime Navigation; 1988 Protocol for the Suppression of Unlawful Acts against the Safety of Fixed Platforms Located on the Continental Shelf; 1991 Convention on the Marking of Plastic Explosives for the Purposes of Detection; 1997 International Convention for the Suppression of Terrorist Bombings; 1999 International Convention for the Suppression of the Financing of Terrorism; 2005 International Convention for the Suppression of Acts of Nuclear Terrorism.

[5] N Chomsky, 'International Terrorism: Image and Reality' in A George (ed), *Western State Terrorism* (Oxford, Polity Press, 1991).

[6] Note though that Cassese claims that contrary to the claim made in most academic scholarship, there is a 'generally accepted' definition of terrorism in times of peace in customary international law. See A Cassese, 'The Multifaceted Criminal Notion of Terrorism in International Law' (2006) *Journal of International Criminal Justice* 933.

[7] B Saul, *Defining Terrorism in International Law* (Oxford, Oxford University Press, 2006) 184–90.

whereby—in contrast to assassination—the direct targets of violence are generally chosen randomly (targets of opportunity) or selectively (representative or symbolic targets) from a target population, and serve as message generators. Threat- and violence-based communication processes between terrorist (organisation), (imperilled) victims and main targets are used to manipulate the main target (audience(s)), turning it into a target of terror, target of demands, or a target of attention, depending on whether intimidation, coercion or propaganda is primarily sought.[8]

Schmid and Jongman's aggregation certainly captures the essential aspects of all definitions of terrorism. It is a lowest common denominator which will include aspects of political violence that some parties to the debate would exclude. However, it is useful only as a sketch of the broad phenomenon and has no place on statute books. The formulation is so broad that even if political agreement were possible, it would not be desirable to use it as the basis for criminal legislation. Nonetheless, the definition is useful in that it draws attention to the three key elements of any definition: the action taken; the motivation for the action; and the actor involved. In the past, international counter-terrorism efforts focused on the action taken—which is sometimes referred to as the objective aspect of the definition. While this in itself is the subject of contest and controversy,[9] it is in asking who, and in particular why, that the difficulty of agreeing a definition truly becomes clear. Although attempts to address the latter aspects in the draft comprehensive Convention on International Terrorism have borne some fruit, disputes over exemptions on the actor and the motivation behind the act remain at the heart of persisting disagreements.[10]

If criminalising 'terrorism'—and by necessity defining it—is seemingly impossible, it is worth considering why the EU has attempted to do so. Saul outlines three policy rationales for criminalisation: that terrorism undermines individual human rights; the State and political discourse; and international relations.[11] This may well be correct but these aims could be met by the criminalisation of individual actions. One possibility is that the adoption of a common definition is significant for transatlantic co-operation.[12] However, transatlantic solidarity is an insufficient explanation for the EU measure as US legislation and law enforcement agencies themselves deploy multiple definitions.[13] Another possible reason is that a definition is useful to acknowledge the perceived increase in contemporary

---

[8] See discussion in AP Schmid, 'Terrorism: The Definitional Problem' (2004) 36 *Case Western Reserve Journal of International Law* 375, 382.

[9] Eg, questions concerning whether the action be limited to attacks on civilians, or whether attacks on the military and/or state apparatus also count as terrorism; whether damage to property should be included, and if so what level of seriousness is required to be caught by the definition.

[10] Saul, *Defining Terrorism*, n 7 above, pp 184–90.

[11] B Saul, 'International Terrorism as a European Crime: The Policy Rationale for Criminalization' (2003) 11 *European Journal of Crime, Criminal Law and Criminal Justice* 323, 326.

[12] D Dubois, 'The Attacks of 11 September: EU–US Co-operation Against Terrorism in the Field of Justice and Home Affairs' (2002) 7 *European Foreign Affairs Review* 317, 326.

[13] B Hoffmann, *Inside Terrorism*, rev and expanded edn (Columbia, Columbia University Press, 2006) p 31.

terrorism and therefore to deploy the symbolic power of the criminal law against it.[14] This suggests that the purpose of a definition is largely declaratory: either to express solidarity with allies or to stigmatise opponents. While the political benefits of a legal definition are not insignificant, they do not provide a convincing rationale for the adoption, at EU level, of a comprehensive legal measure.

A different approach is to consider the definition of terrorism as part of a crime prevention strategy rather than a means to punish wrong-doing after it has occurred. Traditional criminal law is aimed at punishment after a crime has been committed. Modern counter-terrorism places greater emphasis on prevention of attacks rather than pursuit of perpetrators.[15] Therefore, one could argue that the role of the definition of terrorism is to identify those persons who are likely to commit such acts and authorise greater investigative powers to be used against them: disrupting their activities rather than responding after an attack.[16] If preventive powers are to be used against those suspected of terrorism, a definition of terrorism could be used to ring-fence those powers, avoiding their transfer into ordinary criminal justice. Of course, due to the pejorative nature of the term, a definition of terrorism not only identifies those to be targeted, it also provides a justification for the deployment of extraordinary measures. Those whose actions fall within the definition are thereby considered to fall outside the limits of acceptable political action. The definition of terrorism is thus 'justificatory': a rhetorical, political and legal basis for government actions taken to prevent political violence.[17] When justifying the US preventive detention programme at Guantánamo Bay, former Defence Secretary Donald Rumsfeld described the detainees as the 'worst of the worst'. As such, the Secretary argued, the otherwise indefensible detention was not only justifiable, it was necessary.[18] Rumsfeld's logic is an illuminating example of post-September 11 government reasoning. The European Commission, in its Second Evaluation Report on Member State implementation, noted that a common definition 'constitutes the basis on which all other provisions in the Framework Decision are built and allows for the use of law enforcement co-operation instruments'.[19] The report thus foreshadows other counter-terrorism measures to come. Criminalising 'terrorism' might therefore serve to outlaw political violence itself; to delineate those against whom preventive powers can be used; to justify the use of such measures; or to serve all these purposes.

---

[14] E Symeonidou-Kastanidou, 'Defining Terrorism' (2004) 12 *European Journal of Crime, Criminal Law and Criminal Justice* 14, 16–17.

[15] C Walker, 'The Legal Definition of "Terrorism" in United Kingdom Law and Beyond' (2007) *Public Law* 331, 335.

[16] Ibid, 335–36.

[17] C Gearty, *The Future of Terrorism* (London, Phoenix, 1997) 56.

[18] D Cole and J Lobel, *Less Safe, Less Free: Why America is Losing the War on Terror* (New York, The New Press, 2007) 103.

[19] Commission (EC), 'Report from the Commission based on Art 11 of the Council Framework Decision of 13 June 2002 on combating terrorism' COM (2007) 681, Brussels, 6 November 2007, p 10.

II. THE DEFINITION OF TERRORISM IN EU LAW

The Framework Decision on Combating Terrorism was adopted by the European Council on 13 June 2002. The use of the framework decision meant that the measure fell outside of the strong rule of law that was established in the internal market.[20] As a result, its operation is heavily reliant on its correct transposition into national law by Member States. In the urgent atmosphere of the early days of the 'war on terror', the Council set an ambitious deadline of December 2002 for transposition into national law. As only six of the then fifteen Member States had existing counter-terrorism legislation, it should have been obvious that the deadline was unlikely to be met. While initially disappointed, by the adoption of the revised Council Action Plan in March 2007, 22 out of 27 Member States had completed implementation.[21] Although the legislation has now been transposed into Member State law its operation remains problematic. Two evaluation reports have been published by the European Commission that demonstrate the failure of Member States to correctly implement the law.[22]

A. EU Definition of Terrorism

The EU definition of terrorism is contained in Article 1(1) FDCT. That article requires Member States to take 'necessary measures' to ensure that certain acts, as defined under national law, and which 'given their nature or context, may seriously damage a country or an international organisation', are deemed 'terrorist offences', where those offences are committed with a particular aim. It is useful to analyse the EU definition of terrorism in relation to the three key aspects of the phenomenon identified by Schmid: the action, motivation and actor. The Commission evaluation reports focus their analysis on the former two elements, respectively referred to as the objective and subjective aspects of the offence. However, it is in examining the actors targeted that some of the more difficult questions of defining terrorism are addressed.

---

[20] The Framework Decision's legal basis was Arts 29, 31(e) and 34(2)(b) EU(N).

[21] European Council, Action Plan on Combating Terrorism, Brussels, 9 March 2007.

[22] Commission (EC), 'Report from the Commission based on Art 11 of the Council Framework Decision of 13 June 2002 on combating terrorism' COM (2004) 409, Brussels, 8 June 2004 (hereafter, First Evaluation Report); Commission (EC), 'Report from the Commission based on Article 11 of the Council Framework Decision of 13 June 2002 on combating terrorism' COM (2007) 681, Brussels, 6 November 2007 (hereafter, Second Evaluation Report). For a comparative study of implementation in six Member States see EJ Husabø, *Fighting Terrorism through Multilevel Criminal Legislation: Security Council Resolution 1373, the EU Framework Decision on Combating Terrorism and Their Implementation in Nordic, Dutch and German Criminal Law* (Leiden, Martinus Nijhoff Publishers, 2009). For a critical discussion of the process of implementation in one Member State see D Walsh, 'Parliamentary Scrutiny of EU Criminal Law in Ireland' (2006) 31 *European Law Review* 48.

i. Prohibited Action

For an act to be classified as a 'terrorist offence' under Article 1(1) FDCT it must be one of those listed in Article 1(1)(a)–(i). The acts listed are attacks on a person's life or physical integrity;[23] kidnapping or hostage taking;[24] causing extensive destruction to government, public or private property or infrastructure;[25] seizing means of transport;[26] possession of weapons;[27] release of dangerous substances, or causing fire, flood or other such event which endanger human life;[28] interfering with water supply or supply of other fundamental resources;[29] or threatening to do any of the above.[30] The definition draws together the crucial elements of the UN conventions against terrorism. Each of the acts corresponds to, and in many cases duplicates the language of, the comparable international treaty.[31] However, the framework decision has a wider scope than some of the previous treaties—Articles 1(1)(d)–(f) are wider than their equivalents in the UN Conventions.[32] Article 1(1) (h), which protects natural resource supplies, is entirely new, as is Article 1(1)(i) in respect of threatening the other actions.[33] These clauses were introduced by the European Commission in the proposal for a framework decision.[34]

As the two Commission evaluation reports make abundantly clear, seeking to approximate national criminal law has proven problematic, even in respect of the objective element of the definition of terrorism which sets out the prohibited action. The Second Evaluation Report noted that most Member States did not adopt transposing provisions, but rather referenced existing offences in domestic law.[35] Furthermore, while some Member States included all of the objective element (eg Czech Republic, Hungary, Malta, Netherlands), other Member States omitted certain aspects of the objective element (eg Greece, Latvia, Lithuania), and some failed to transpose the objective element entirely (eg Poland, Germany).[36] Although the text of the framework decision does refer to the acts 'as defined under national law', if some of those acts are not criminalised at all, or the existing crime is not linked to terrorism, then the Member State cannot be said to have

---

[23]   Art 1(1)(a)–(b) FDCT.
[24]   Art 1(1)(c) FDCT.
[25]   Art 1(1)(d) FDCT.
[26]   Art 1(1)(e) FDCT.
[27]   Art 1(1)(f) FDCT.
[28]   Art 1(1)(g) FDCT.
[29]   Art 1(1)(h) FDCT.
[30]   Art 1(1)(i) FDCT.
[31]   E Dumitriu, 'The EU's Definition of Terrorism: The Council Framework Decision on Combating Terrorism' (2004) 5 *German Law Journal* 585, 593.
[32]   Ibid, 595.
[33]   Ibid.
[34]   Commission (EC), 'Proposal for a Council Framework Decision on combating terrorism' COM (2001) 521 final, 19 September 2001.
[35]   Commission (EC), 'Commission Staff Working Document Annex to the Report from the Commission based on Article 11 of the Council Framework Decision of 13 June 2002 on combating terrorism' SEC (2007) 1463, Brussels, 6 November 2007 (hereafter, Second Evaluation Report Annex) 5.
[36]   Commission (EC), Second Evaluation Report Annex 9–12.

correctly transposed the law. The Commission's reports raise concerns in relation to the lack of uniformity in transposition. The second report noted that piecemeal transposition 'may disrupt the systematic and political aim of the framework decision and clarity of implementation, and can hinder the full implementation of related provisions'.[37] This raises the question of just how much can be expected of a law that 'approximates' rather than 'harmonises' national law.

The Commission reports also note that in respect of the objective element, some Member States (eg Luxembourg) have gone further than the requirements of the FDCT. The reports declare that 'nothing prevents Member States from going beyond the minimum standards set up by this instrument, provided that the requirements regarding fundamental rights are respected'.[38] This may give rise to concern about the principle of legality. If that which is considered 'terrorism' in Luxembourg is not so classified in Germany, the individual cannot know what is and is not permitted within the EU as a jurisdiction, thus also affecting the accessibility and foreseeability of the law—key aspects of legal certainty.

ii. Terrorist Motivation

The EU definition of terrorism set out in the framework decision is noteworthy as it focuses on the overall aim of those perpetrating the criminal acts.[39] It is not the actions themselves which prompt the label 'terrorist' but the motivation behind them. A terrorist offence is committed when one of the actions is carried out with the aim of

— seriously intimidating a population, or
— unduly compelling a Government or international organisation to perform or abstain from performing any act, or
— seriously destabilising or destroying the fundamental political, constitutional, economic or social structures of a country or an international organisation.[40]

This brings into play a subjective element absent from most of the UN conventions on terrorism. The principal precedent for a subjective element is found in the 1999 International Convention on the Suppression of the Financing of Terrorism (Terrorist Financing Convention). The Convention prohibits the collection of, or provision of funds for any act

---

[37] Ibid, 9.
[38] Ibid, 12.
[39] The Shanghai Co-operation Organization, founded on 15 June 2001, immediately adopted the Shanghai Convention on Combating Terrorism, Separatism and Extremism (2001). This Convention also deploys a subjective definition, with some aspects in common with the FDCT. See: Saul, *Defining Terrorism*, n 7 above, 160–62.
[40] Art 1(1) FDCT.

intended to cause death or injury to a civilian, or to any other person not taking an active part in the hostilities in a situation of armed conflict, when the purpose of such act, by its nature or context, is to intimidate a population, or to compel a government or international organisation to do or abstain from doing any act.[41]

The language of the Terrorist Financing Convention is similar but not identical to that in the framework decision. The EU law entails a higher standard, through the requirements of serious intimidation or undue compulsion (perhaps suggesting that the EU can envisage an acceptable level of intimidation or compulsion). Furthermore, the EU law applies this test to all of the prohibited acts and not just the financing of terrorism. In addition, the Terrorist Financing Convention clause is limited to acts that are 'intended to cause death or injury to a civilian', whereas the framework decision contains no such limitation. The framework decision is thus a broader measure in this regard, also covering actions that intend to cause damage to property or to non-civilian targets. Subjective definitions such as these target the core of terrorism: the use of political violence to send a message, by reducing the immediate targets of the act to a means. It is by turning its immediate victims into mere instruments of communication that political violence violates core human rights and the rule of law.[42] However, in attempting to define and condemn such action, counter-terrorism inevitably runs into difficulties as many groups that have used violent tactics have—either at the time, or afterwards—been seen as legitimate political actors.

One element of the motivation test is entirely new. The third part of the test relates to fundamental structures of the state. Chalmers argues that the institutions protected by this part—the 'fundamental political, constitutional, economic or social structures'—demonstrate the EU's ongoing focus on market society. He claims that 'the central actions taken in the war on terror ... have been to protect the European Union market society'.[43] There is some evidence for this claim. At the time of adoption of the framework decision, Italy was hopeful that the definition would be sufficiently broad to cover the anti-globalisation protestors that targeted a G8 summit in Genoa.[44] If this is indeed the case, the definition plays a role in preserving the ideological status quo in the EU. However, any law aimed at preserving particular political principles would likely be contestable. The European Parliament proposed an amendment to replace these words with 'the fundamental freedoms, democracy, respect for human rights, civil liberties and rule of law on which our societies are based'.[45] The concepts cited in the European Parliament's

---

[41]   Art 2(1)(b) Terrorist Financing Convention.

[42]   For a broad discussion see: C Gearty, 'Terrorism and Human Rights' (2007) 42 *Government and Opposition* 340.

[43]   D Chalmers, 'Political Rights and Political Reason in the European Union in Times of Stress' in W Sadurski (ed), *Political Rights under Stress in 21st Century Europe* (Oxford, Oxford University Press, 2006) 70–71.

[44]   Saul, *Defining Terrorism*, n 7 above, p 165.

[45]   European Parliament, Recommendation on the role of the European Union in combating terrorism (2001) OJ C 72 E/135, Preamble recital G.

list are just as contested as those contained in the framework decision itself. Perhaps this third part should be omitted entirely as the first two encapsulate the core of what is popularly considered 'terrorism': political violence aimed at communicating a message to peoples or states. The first part protects the public, and the second part protects the government. The third part is superfluous and may unnecessarily limit legitimate political action. In this respect it is noteworthy that while the draft comprehensive UN Convention on International Terrorism includes a subjective definition of terrorism, the idea of terrorism undermining fundamental 'political, constitutional, economic or social structures' is not included.[46]

The reference in Article 1(1) FDCT to the 'nature or context' of the act, which means that the act 'may seriously damage a country or international organisation' has given rise to some confusion. For some commentators, it is a separate consideration for criminal justice authorities when examining a case.[47] Saul argues that 'a likelihood or even a possibility of damage is sufficient'.[48] However, it seems more likely that the reference to serious damage caused by the nature or context of the act is a descriptive statement of the acts listed, rather than a separate criterion to be fulfilled for the act to be deemed terrorist. Saul also claims that the phrase 'which given their nature or context' is an enabling one that might render the motivation requirement redundant.[49] However, there is no basis for this claim in the text, where the phrase in question is part of Article 1(1) and does not appear to be an alternate requirement to the three parts of the motivation test in Article 1(2).

These nuanced points may, nevertheless, be irrelevant. As the two evaluation reports clearly demonstrate, transposition of the subjective element of the terrorism definition is even more varied than transposition of the objective element. The Commission noted that several Member States implemented the subjective element almost verbatim, with 'nearly literal transposition' in one state and implementation 'almost word by word' in another.[50] However, other Member States did not transpose the subjective element at all and some implemented the subjective aspect but did not link it to the objective elements.[51] When deficient implementation of both the objective and subjective parts of the definition is taken into account, the European Commission identifies Germany, Italy, Lithuania, Luxembourg, Poland, Slovenia and the UK as having failed to correctly transpose

---

[46] Although the draft Convention does include a somewhat similar provision in relation to the action, if not the aim. Art 2(3) refers to 'serious damage to a State or government facility, a public transportation system, communication system or infrastructure facility with the intent to cause extensive destruction of such a place, facility or system, or where such destruction results or is likely to result in major economic loss.'
See: Draft Comprehensive Treaty Against International Terrorism.

[47] Saul, *Defining Terrorism*, n 7 above, p 164; Dumitriu, n 31 above, p 592.

[48] Saul, *Defining Terrorism*, n 7 above, p 164.

[49] Ibid.

[50] Commission (EC), Second Evaluation Report Annex 7. The two Member States in question were Malta and Poland.

[51] Ibid.

the definition. Based on population, this effectively means that merely half of EU residents are subject to a criminal law that defines terrorism in accordance with the framework decision.

iii. Culpable Actors

Much of the debate about definitions of terrorism focuses on who can be a terrorist. The EU definition of terrorism is ambiguous on this point and in particular on whether it includes state actors. Terrorism challenges the state's claim to a monopoly of legitimate coercive force within its territory. To determine who can be culpable under EU law it is first necessary to consider if violence by the state can be classified as terrorism; and second, to examine whether it is possible for non-state actors to use political violence without attracting the label of terrorism.

a. State Terrorism

While the French Revolution's *terreur* is the origin of the term 'terrorism' and states have been responsible for some of the worst political violence in history the idea of state terrorism remains highly controversial.[52] Academic opinion is divided on whether or not state terrorism is included in the EU definition and the point may be moot.[53] One cannot imagine Spain, for example, being prosecuted in English courts for terrorist offences—such a suit would be highly undiplomatic.[54] Furthermore, such a safeguard may not be necessary within the EU. Articles 2 and 7 EU provide a check on Member States' actions.[55] Any systemic breaches of human rights amounting to state terrorism could be dealt with through this mechanism. Furthermore, the oversight of the Council of Europe is designed to protect citizens from human rights abuses. There is arguably no need for a further check on European states in this respect. A similar conclusion was arrived at by the UN High Level Panel when it excluded 'state terrorism' from its definition.[56] The Panel argued that 'the legal and normative framework against State violations [of human rights] is far stronger than in the case of non-State actors' and as such it was not necessary to includes states within the definition of terrorism. However, while it may be unlikely that an EU Member State would be found guilty of terrorism, it is not unthinkable that other states could carry out acts of political violence in the EU, and therefore be subject

---

[52] Chomsky, n 5 above.

[53] O Bures, 'EU Counterterrorism Policy: A Paper Tiger?' (2006) 18 *Terrorism and Political Violence* 57; Dumitriu, n 31 above; S Peers, 'EU Responses to Terrorism' (2003) *International and Comparative Law Quarterly* 227.

[54] Though note *Ireland v UK* (1978) 2 EHRR 25, where five interrogation tactics used by British state agents in the context of counter-terrorism were held to breach Art 3 ECHR.

[55] Art 2 TEU sets out the values upon which the EU is founded, while Art 7 TEU provides a means for action by the European Council with the consent of the European Parliament to take action where there is a 'clear risk of a serious breach by a Member State' of those values.

[56] UN High Level Panel, n 3 above, pp 51–52.

to EU law.[57] It is therefore worth exploring whether the definition can be said to cover state terrorism.

The relevant part of the framework decision is Article 7 on the liability of legal persons. Article 7 is peculiar in that, unlike similar EU measures, states or international organisations are not excluded from the definition of a legal person.[58] The Preamble does exclude armed forces from the law.[59] However, the exclusion is limited to forces in armed conflicts governed by international law.[60] Other instances of state liability—outside of armed conflict—could arise.[61] Furthermore, the Preamble is not legally binding, though it would likely guide interpretation of the operative clauses should ambiguity arise. Dumitriu argues that the FDCT excludes state liability.[62] She bases her case on the text of Article 7(1) which declares that an individual committing terrorism must hold a 'leading position' within the legal person for the latter to be liable. Furthermore, the offence must be for the benefit of the legal person. This would seem to limit potential liability to heads of state or government, or in extremis, members of government. To trigger state liability for terrorist offences, the head of state or government would need to be directly involved in the terrorist offences. This certainly seems unlikely, particularly in terms of EU governments. However, in relation to offences linked to terrorism government involvement is not inconceivable. A head of state might fund an act of terrorism against a strategic enemy for the state's benefit. Such action might incriminate the state. Of further interest is Article 7(2), which requires liability where 'the lack of supervision or control' by a person in a leading position has enabled the commission of an offence for the benefit of the legal person. Here, it is possible that an insufficiently accountable state body—a security service, for instance—might carry out an action for the benefit of the state. Again, the possibility of liability cannot be ruled out.

However, Dumitriu argues that the EU cannot seek to criminalise state actions through an essentially domestic legal measure. Generally, incrimination of subjects of international law can only be achieved through a treaty provision, not through national criminal law. This is a stronger argument than those based on the text of the framework decision. Furthermore, state immunity may apply to certain actions by heads of state (though not, surely, to those committed by security services).[63] Therefore, despite the arguments to the contrary, it would be misleading to conclude that the law provides for incrimination. Rather, while the

---

[57] Art 9 FDCT.

[58] Peers, n 53 above, p 234.

[59] The relevant recital to the Preamble provides that 'Actions by armed forces during periods of armed conflict, which are governed by international humanitarian law within the meaning of these terms under that law, and, inasmuch as they are governed by other rules of international law, actions by the armed forces of a State in the exercise of their official duties are not governed by this Framework Decision'.

[60] Peers, n 53 above, pp 234–35.

[61] Ibid.

[62] Dumitriu, n 31 above, pp 600–02.

[63] Dumitriu, n 31 above, pp 600–02; Peers, n 53 above, p 235.

EU does not exclude 'state terrorism' from its definition of the phenomenon, nor does it envisage the prosecution of state officials for such offences.

b. Non-State Terrorism

If the framework decision is not aimed at controlling terrorism by states then it is reasonable to conclude that it is principally targeted at non-state terrorism and non-state terrorist groups. In addition to the clauses on the culpability of legal persons, the legislation also provides a definition of a 'terrorist group'. Article 2(1) describes such a group as

> a structured group of more than two persons, established over a period of time and acting in concert to commit terrorist offences … a group that is not randomly formed for the immediate commission of an offence and that does not need to have formally defined roles for its members, continuity of its membership, or a developed structure.

On the basis of this definition, a terrorist group has to be more than a mere ad hoc collective formed for a single act, but nevertheless it may still be a rather loose 'structured group'—without hierarchy, division of labour or even formal membership. The definition therefore takes note of the ample literature on violent organisations, highlighting the existence of multiple types of such groups, in particular the 'network' form of organisation of which Al-Qaeda is considered the prime example.[64] Such loosely structured groups were also envisaged by the European Parliament's recommendation, which makes reference to 'the activities of networks operating at international level', and the Preamble to the amending legislation of 2008.[65]

Article 2(2) FDCT requires Member States to adopt measures to ensure criminalisation of directing and participating in the activities of such a group. Directing a group is not defined by the framework decision, which might be taken to mean that all directions, including directions to cease operations, are included in the definition.[66] Furthermore, unlike when 'participating' in the group, the offence of directing the group does not require the offender to have knowledge of the group's illegal activities.[67] This gives rise to the peculiar situation whereby a greater level of culpability is required for participation than direction. Participation is defined as including

---

[64] See, eg, M Sagemann, *Understanding Terror Networks* (Philadelphia, University of Pennsylvania Press, 2004).

[65] European Parliament, Recommendation on the role of the European Union in combating terrorism (2001) OJ C 72 E/135, Preamble recital G; Council Framework Decision 2008/919/JHA of 28 November 2008 amending Framework Decision 2002/475/JHA on combating terrorism (amending Framework Decision), Preamble Recital 3.

[66] Saul, *Defining Terrorism*, n 7 above, p 168.

[67] Ibid.

supplying information or material resources, or by funding its activities in any way, with knowledge of the fact that such participation will contribute to the criminal activities of the terrorist group.[68]

Two distinct points may be made about the definition of participation. First, there is a wide range of activities that are sufficient to criminalise a 'participant'— including the supply of information, resources, or funding. Those caught by this wide definition are then subject to heightened criminal penalties. Member States are required to establish maximum sentences of not less than fifteen years for directing a terrorist group, and not less than eight years for participation in one.[69] Notably, the legislation also provides that these sentences may be reduced if those convicted renounce terrorism and provide the authorities with information that enables the prevention of other offences or assists in the pursuit of other offenders.[70] These provisions—for heightening punishment and incentivising co-operation with authorities—offer a means by which terrorist groups can be targeted, and if infiltrated, broken up. This approach is pre-emptive as it seeks to disrupt or incapacitate such groups before they can pose a threat. However, it may also undermine political discourse as extremist but not necessarily violent groups may be targeted.

Second, the emphasis on the group's 'criminal' rather than 'terrorist' activities is important. Under this definition, it is possible to be guilty of participation in terrorism if one aids a group that engages in terrorist activities, even if one is only aware that the group engages in non-terrorist criminal activities. Take, for example, a person who knowingly supports an animal rights group that graffiti the windows of a fast food restaurant (a criminal offence). Unbeknownst to the supporter, the group also plans and carries out the successful disruption of the water supply to a major European city (a terrorist offence). The framework decision holds the person who consciously supports the first activity equally culpable for the second, whether or not they had knowledge of it.[71] Involvement in political activism, therefore, entails much greater risk for the individual under terrorism law than under ordinary criminal law.

A related concern in this respect is the law's protection of all governments and international organisations. This approach treats a group which engages in direct action against a totalitarian state the same as one that targets a democratic state. The European Parliament's opinion on the draft law included a safeguard for those engaged in political protest. The Parliament's amendment noted that '[t]errorist groups as defined in this Framework Decision are distinct from groups in the European Union who resist totalitarian regimes and repression in third countries

---

[68] Art 2(2)(b) FDCT.
[69] Art 5(3) FDCT.
[70] Art 6 FDCT.
[71] Art 2(2)(b) FDCT.

or who support such resistance'.[72] However this amendment was not adopted by the Council. If the Council intended to exempt those acting to restore or establish democracy then that intention is not reflected in the substantive text. When the definition of terrorism is being considered, exemptions are often called for for two groups in particular: first, domestic protesters exercising their political rights to freedom of expression and freedom of association; and second, those groups that are fighting to overthrow oppressive governments overseas. There are no explicit exemptions for such groups under the operative clauses of the EU law.

There are some potential safeguards for such protesters and opposition groups. Recital 10 to the Preamble and Article 1(2) FDCT may offer some protection to domestic political protesters. The recital refers to political rights, and declares that the framework decision 'respects' them. Article 1(2) FDCT specifies that the framework decision does not alter the obligation to respect fundamental rights and the rule of law in Article 6 TEU. In a strictly legal sense such statements are superfluous as fundamental principles are higher order norms. The inclusion of the caveat suggests the Council or at least some of its members sought to highlight the importance of Article 6 TEU. Douglas-Scott notes that the 'clarification' was included to address concerns that legitimate protest would be caught by the definition.[73] Welcome though the clause may be, a declaratory statement does not remedy the ambiguities of the broad definition of terrorism.

Recital 11 of the Preamble may provide some protection for those fighting oppression overseas. This clause aims to exclude 'actions by armed forces during periods of armed conflict, which are governed ... by international law' from the remit of the FDCT. Bures relies on this clause and cites the first and second Protocols to the Geneva Conventions, which recognise as legitimate armed forces those who are 'fighting against colonial domination and alien occupation and against racist regimes ... and dissent armed forces or other organised armed groups'.[74] The effect of the Geneva Conventions, he claims, is that those groups that the European Parliament sought to protect are safeguarded by international humanitarian law.[75] This is less than satisfactory. First, the Preamble does not enjoy the binding force of law. Second, if one of the justifications for defining terrorism is to invoke the symbolism of the criminal law to denounce illegitimate political violence, that denouncement should be explicit in its exemption of legitimate political violence. The approach of the framework decision is to condemn all and hope the criminal justice process is used judiciously to prevent abusive prosecutions. This tendency to afford broad discretion to national criminal justice

---

[72] European Parliament, Legislative resolution on the Commission proposal for a Council framework decision on combating terrorism OJ C153 E/275 (27 June 2002).

[73] S Douglas-Scott, 'The Rule of Law in the European Union: Putting the Security in the "Area of Freedom, Security and Justice"' (2004) 29 *European Law Review* 219, 231.

[74] Bures, n 53 above, p 67.

[75] Ibid.

systems is a recurring feature of EU counter-terrorism action and counter-terrorism after September 11 in general.

iv. Jurisdiction

The legislation contains detailed rules on jurisdiction aimed at ensuring that offences do not go unpunished by falling between two criminal justice systems. Indeed, the converse is more likely to occur. The broad jurisdiction afforded to Member States makes it quite likely that more than one Member State could have jurisdiction over an offence. Member States are required to establish jurisdiction over offences committed 'in whole or in part' in their territory.[76] However, they may extend jurisdiction if the offence is committed in the territory of any Member State. This latter rule establishes what has been referred to as a 'regional universal jurisdiction' insofar as all Member States can exercise jurisdiction over an offence anywhere in the EU.[77] They must also establish jurisdiction over offences committed against EU institutions, or where the offender is a national or institutions, or where the offender is a national or resident, or where the offence is committed for the benefit of a legal person established in its territory. Imagine if an Irish national committed an offence for the benefit of a violent group established as a political part in Germany on a British-registered ship in Zeebrugge, Belgium. Ireland, the UK, Germany and Belgium all should have jurisdiction while every other Member State may have jurisdiction. The legislation does offer guidance on how to resolve the competing claims. The Member States are to co-operate with the aim of holding a single proceeding. 'Sequential account' should be taken of the state in which the act was committed, the state of nationality or of residence of the perpetrator, the state of origin of victims and the state in which the perpetrator is caught. A final provision of the legislation may well trump all others. The framework decision's rules of jurisdiction 'shall not exclude the exercise of jurisdiction in criminal matters as laid down by a Member State in accordance with its national law'. This provision would appear to ensure that any Member State that wishes to exercise jurisdiction may do so as long as there is a basis for it in national law. Taken as a whole the rules on jurisdiction are permissive and empowering. The evaluation reports indicate that there remains the possibility of 'positive conflicts' with more than one Member State being in a position to claim jurisdiction.[78] However, the reports do not offer any indication as to whether this problem has arisen in practice to date.

---

[76] Art 9(1)(a) FDCT.

[77] F Naert and J Wouters, 'Of Arrest Warrants, Terrorist Offences and Extradition Deals: an Appraisal of the EU'S Main Criminal Law Measures Against Terrorism after "11 September"' (2004) 41 *Common Market Law Review* 909.

[78] Commission (EC), First Evaluation Report Annex, p 34; Commission (EC), Second Evaluation Report, pp 6–7.

v. The Dangers of the EU Definition

It is clear that there are several difficulties with the EU definition of terrorism. The law is clear about the objective aspect of the definition of terrorism: the reference to the nine categories of 'terrorist action' in Article 1(1) is precise and succinct. However, transposition of these nine categories in national law has given rise to discrepancies across the jurisdiction that undermine the idea that there is a common definition of terrorism in EU law. The subjective aspect of the definition has three parts, each of which provides an alternative 'terrorist motive'. The first two—in relation to the public, a government or international organisation—include a requirement of seriousness. This is commendable as it ensures a certain degree of protection for political action. The third part protects particular political principles which increase the political nature of the definition. Transposition of the terrorist motives into national law has also produced divergence across the EU as some Member States have transposed the test literally while others have done so partially or not at all. The problems caused by the vague EU law and divergent national implementation combine to cast a wide net over political action.

While the framework decision effectively excludes state actors from liability it exposes a wide range of non-state actors to liability for terrorist offences. Those caught by the definition are subject to heightened penalties and this may have a chilling effect on political action in the EU. Even if group offences are not applicable to an individual, the legislation requires that terrorist offences and related inchoate offences carry heavier custodial sentences than would be available under ordinary criminal law. The danger of broadly construed definitions of terrorism is clear from examples across the EU, such as the eviction and subsequent detention of a senior citizen at the UK Labour Party Annual Conference in 2005 for heckling a member of government,[79] or the attempts by the Italian government to target anti-globalisation protesters.[80] The definition of terrorism in EU law takes a broad approach that may weaken the condemnatory effect of the definition while curtailing legitimate political action.

B. Inchoate and Related Offences

In addition to criminalising 'terrorist offences' and 'terrorist groups', the legislation, as amended, also provides for three other categories of offences. These are offences 'linked to terrorist activities'; inchoate offences of incitement, aiding and abetting, and attempting terrorist and related offences; and further offences of provocation, recruitment and training, as provided for by the amending legislation.

---

[79] 'Heckler, 82, wins apology from Labour' *Guardian* (29 September 2005).
[80] Saul, *Defining Terrorism*, n 7 above, p 165.

i. Offences 'Linked to Terrorist Activities'

The framework decision as originally enacted included three offences 'linked to terrorist activities'.[81] These actions are 'aggravated theft' or 'extortion' for the purpose of a terrorist offence, and 'drawing up false administrative documents' for the purpose of a terrorist offence or for the purpose of participating in a terrorist group. These offences do not have to be classified as 'terrorism', but simply as 'terrorism-linked'. The First Evaluation Report by the European Commission notes that

> these acts could not be directly committed with the defined terrorist intent … therefore they should be considered as a different type of crimes [sic], carried out with a view to committing terrorist acts, but not terrorist acts themselves. The Framework Decision thus merely requires that they are included as 'terrorist-linked' offences. There is not an explicit obligation to incriminate these offences separately as long as the results sought by introducing this category of offences are sufficiently covered.[82]

The three offences were added to by the amending legislation.[83] A further clause, Article 3(2), was also introduced by the amending measure. The law now provides that for an 'offence linked to terrorist activities' to be punishable, 'it shall not be necessary that a terrorist offence be actually committed'. Thus, the link between any actual harm caused by an act of terrorism and the linked offences is tenuous and may even be non-existent. Both European Commission evaluation reports noted that transposition of these provisions has been unsatisfactory. By the time of publication of the second report only nine Member States were deemed to have adequately implemented the measure.[84] That report noted that other Member States might be able to achieve 'partial compliance' by considering the terrorist-linked offences as 'acts of collaboration with a terrorist group or as participation in specific terrorist offences'.[85] However, the lack of uniformity is clear when one compares the position of Germany and the UK with that of the Netherlands. The two large Member States were judged by the first report not to have transposed the provisions, but their respective governments did not comment on the evaluation before the publication of the second report.[86] In contrast the Netherlands 'has perfectly transposed' the clause.[87] Transposition of these offences linked to terrorism in such a divergent way across these Member States exacerbates the

---

[81] Art 3 FDCT.

[82] Commission (EC), Commission Staff Working Paper. Annex to the Report from the Commission based on Article 11 of the Council Framework Decision of 13 June 2002 on combating terrorism SEC(2004) 688 8 June 2004 (hereafter, First Evaluation Report Annex) 15.

[83] The offences were originally set out by Art 3(a)–(c) FDCT and following amendment are now Art 3(d)–(f).

[84] Commission (EC), Second Evaluation Report 5.

[85] Denmark, Finland, France, Greece, Ireland, Malta, Netherlands, Portugal, Spain. See: Commission (EC), Second Evaluation Report 5, 7.

[86] Commission (EC), Second Evaluation Report Annex 58.

[87] Ibid, 20.

differences in national law already caused by divergent implementation of the principal offences.

ii. Inchoate Offences

The framework decision contained a number of inchoate offences even prior to its amendment in 2008. While the text of these provisions has been altered by the amending legislation, the substance has not. Article 4 sets out the offences of inciting, aiding or abetting, or attempting terrorist offences. Following amendment, Article 4(1) FDCT provides that it shall be an offence to aid or abet a terrorist offence, an offence related to a terrorist group, or an offence linked to terrorism. The list of predicate offences includes the recently-added public provocation, recruitment and training offences. In contrast, the incitement offence under Article 4(2) does not include these new offences amongst the list of crimes whose incitement is to be made punishable. Article 4(3), as amended, requires Member States to make punishable attempting to commit a terrorist offence, or any of the three original offences linked to terrorism.[88] Finally, a new Article 4(4) states that Member States may punish any attempt to commit the recruitment or training offences. The optional nature of this provision appears to be a result of diverging opinions within the institutions as to whether criminalising attempted recruitment or training is desirable (or even possible).[89] Permitting, but not requiring Member States to make such behaviour criminal embeds divergence in the EU law itself and undermines the uniformity of EU law in this field.

The Commission has noted that while some Member States adopted specific measures for these offences, most referred to existing criminal law provisions that ensured compliance. The First Evaluation Report identifies a number of difficulties with the aiding and abetting offences as originally enacted. The report noted that effective transposition is dependent on accurate implementation of Articles 1–3 (which has proven problematic).[90] Two specific concerns were raised with regard to the implementation of the attempt and incitement offences. First, transposition of the 'attempt' offence was hampered in France and Belgium by the distinction in those jurisdictions between attempting a 'crime' and attempting a 'délit'.[91] Portugese implementation was also singled out as suffering from 'loopholes'.[92] Second, the European Commission raised the 'lack of a legal definition of "incitement" in the Framework Decision as well as the lack of a convergent

---

[88] Attempting to commit a terrorist offence under Art 1(1)(f) FDCT (possession of certain weapons) or Art 1(1)(i) FDCT (threatening to commit a terrorist offence) is specifically excluded from the definition of attempt.

[89] See, eg: European Parliament, Report on the proposal for a Council Framework Decision amending Framework Decision 2002/475/JHA on combating terrorism (Committee on Civil Liberties, Justice and Home Affairs) 23 July 2008 (hereafter, Parliament Committee Report).

[90] Commission (EC), Second Evaluation Report 10.

[91] Commission (EC), First Evaluation Report Annex 19.

[92] Commission (EC), Second Evaluation Report Annex 60.

concept of incitement in national legislation'.[93] The problem was raised in the First Evaluation Report, and 'confirmed and stressed' in the second.[94] However, the subsequent amendment of the legislation did not improve the situation but instead further complicated matters by providing for the offence of provocation.

iii. Further Offences: Provocation, Recruitment, Training

Despite the existence of inchoate offences in the original legislation, on 28 November 2008 the Council adopted the Framework Decision amending the 2002 FDCT.[95] The Preamble makes reference to UN Security Council resolution 1624 and the Council of Europe Convention on the Prevention of Terrorism as providing the impetus for the amendments. The amendments introduced three new offences related to terrorism: 'public provocation to commit a terrorist offence'; 'recruitment for terrorism'; and 'training for terrorism'.

a. Provocation of Terrorism

The idea that individuals can be 'radicalised' into committing acts of terrorism has underpinned much post-September 11 counter-terrorism.[96] The UK government in particular has pursued the idea of counter-radicalisation as a policy goal.[97] It has sponsored proposals to create offences of incitement or provocation of terrorism at European and international level.[98] The result at global level was UN Security Council resolution 1624 which 'calls upon' states to 'prohibit by law incitement to commit a terrorist act or acts'.[99] In the framework decision provocation is defined as:

> the distribution, or otherwise making available, of a message to the public, with the intent to incite the commission of one of the offences listed in Article 1(1)(a) to (h), where such conduct, whether or not directly advocating terrorist offences, causes a danger that one or more such offences may be committed…[100]

The inclusion of a detailed offence of provocation was a reaction to the problematic offence of incitement in the original framework decision. The Commission proposal drew attention to the pre-existing measure but noted that 'these provisions

---

[93] Commission (EC), First Evaluation Report Annex 19.

[94] Commission (EC), Second Evaluation Report Annex 24.

[95] Council Framework Decision of 28 November 2008 amending Framework Decision 2002/475/JHA on combating terrorism.

[96] Commission (EC), 'Communication from the Commission to the European Parliament and the Council concerning terrorist recruitment: addressing the factors contributing to violent radicalisation' COM (2005) 313 final, Brussels, 21 September 2005.

[97] For a critique of the policy see A Kundnani, *Spooked! How Not to Prevent Violent Extremism* (London, Institute of Race Relations, 2010).

[98] 'UK Seeks UN Crackdown on Incitement to Terrorism', *Guardian* (24 August 2005).

[99] UNSC Res 1624 (14 September 2005).

[100] Art 3(1)(a) FDCT, as amended.

do not explicitly cover the dissemination of terrorist propaganda and terrorist expertise, in particular through the Internet'.[101] While this may be correct, the new offence does nothing to resolve the lack of particularity. Furthermore, if the purpose of the amendment was to remedy the problems with the original incitement offence, it has been unsuccessful. If anything, the new offence broadens the incitement crime rather than making it more specific.

When asked about the need for these provisions by the House of Commons European Scrutiny Committee the then UK Minister of State, Tony McNulty, agreed with the European Commission. The Commission stated that notwithstanding the existence of the Council of European Convention the framework decision had certain advantages: a more integrated legal framework with common interpretation by the ECJ; rules on penalties and jurisdiction; and the triggering of co-operation mechanisms. However, as the Committee concluded, this reasoning is 'open to question'.[102] The central problem with the European Commission's argument is that it exaggerates the extent to which the legislation actually creates a common legal framework—the flaws of the framework decision prevent that goal from being realised.

The drafting of the offence is less than ideal. The requirement that provocation must be intentional is to be welcomed.[103] However, the remainder of the definition is problematic. By stipulating that an offence can be committed whether or not the conduct directly advocates terrorism suggests that one may intentionally indirectly incite terrorism. This rather dramatically extends the nexus between the conduct caught by the definition and the potential social harm. The requirement that the action must 'cause a danger' that an offence 'may be committed' is both too vague and too low a standard to act as an adequate safeguard. If one distributes a message that does not directly advocate terrorism, but causes a danger that an offence will be committed, guilt and innocence rests on proving intention. On the one hand, proving intention in such a case would be quite difficult, but on the other, lowering the burden of proof risks catching legitimate political speech. The alternative definition offered by the European Parliament would have significantly improved the law:

> the distribution, or otherwise making available, of a message to the public clearly and intentionally advocating the commission of one of the offences listed in Article 1(1)(a) to (h), where such conduct manifestly causes a danger that one or more such offences may be committed.

---

[101] Commission (EC), 'Proposal for a Council Framework Decision amending Framework Decision 2002/475/JHA on combating terrorism' SEC(2007) 1424, Brussels, 6 November 2007, 4.

[102] House of Commons European Scrutiny Committee, 'Seventh Report of Session 2007–08' 9 January 2008.

[103] Sottiaux argues that in this regard the framework decision is more protective of extreme speech than the case-law of the European Court of Human Rights. S Sottiaux, '*Leroy v France*: Apology of Terrorism and the Malaise of the European Court of Human Rights' Free Speech Jurisprudence' (2009) *European Human Rights Law Review* 415, 422.

Requiring clear and intentional advocacy of terrorism presents a more straight-forward test to be applied in prosecutions. While those who prefer the European Commission's test may argue that the Parliament's formulation might not catch certain indirect advocacy, it is not clear that such speech could be successfully prosecuted in any event: the mental element of the offence may be impossible to establish to a criminal standard of proof. The European Parliament's definition would also have improved on the causation safeguard by requiring that the con-duct 'manifestly causes a danger'.[104] Nonetheless, the present offence is directed at speech in the 'virtual training camp' of the Internet, where the causation test is not likely to easily be met.[105] Despite this caveat, it is not only the prohibition on expression that is of concern here, but also the imprecise nature of the prohibi-tion's drafting.

The 'provocation' offence is arguably the most dangerous of all the terrorism-related and inchoate offences, setting boundaries on acceptable speech in Europe and raising the possibility of genuine political debate being outlawed as 'terrorist'. The space available for political debate is constrained by the exclusion of radical or extremist political opinion. As with other EU counter-terrorism measures, the European Parliament's recommendations would have done much to improve the legislation. The Parliament preferred 'incitement' rather than 'provocation' as the former term has an existing legal meaning that can be drawn upon in defining the new offence. 'Incitement' was the term used in recent legislation on combating racism and xenophobia.[106] Indeed, after the European Commission had lamented the absence of a common understanding of 'incitement' in its evaluation reports it is inexplicable that the word was included in the definition of provocation. A related problem is the existence of overlapping offences—the incitement offence remains in the amended framework decision. While this duplication is unlikely to have any practical effect it is undesirable nonetheless.[107]

The offence of incitement or provocation of terrorism is challenging for lib-eral democracies as the line between extreme but nonetheless protected speech

---

[104] The latter part of the definition could be further improved by reference to US law. The clas-sic incitement test in *Brandenburg v Ohio* requires an intention to cause 'imminent lawless action', and examines the likelihood that such action would be produced. In the leading US Supreme Court authority, the majority opinion held that 'the constitutional guarantees of free speech and free press do not permit a State to forbid or proscribe advocacy of the use of force or of law violation except *where such advocacy is directed to inciting or producing imminent lawless action and is likely to incite or produce such action*'. *Brandenburg v Ohio* 395 US 444 (1969) (emphasis added). See S Sottiaux, *Terrorism and the Limitation of Rights: The ECHR and the US Constitution* (Oxford, Hart Publishing, 2008), p 67.

[105] Recital 4 to the Preamble of the amending Framework Decision.

[106] European Parliament, Parliament Committee Report, n 89 above, p 17. Art 1(1)(a) of the meas-ure requires Member States to criminalise 'publicly inciting to violence or hatred directed against a group of persons or a member of such a group defined by reference to race, colour, religion, descent or national or ethnic origin'. Council Framework Decision 2008/913/JHA of 28 November 2008 on combating certain forms and expressions of racism and xenophobia by means of criminal law.

[107] As the framework decisions requires national transposing measures to be adopted, it seems reasonable to assume that Member States will adapt their law to cover both Art 4(1) and Art 3(2)(a) offences.

and unlawful incitement must carefully drawn if legitimate speech is not to be criminalised. European human rights law has struggled with this problem for some time.[108] In the post-September 11 world the ECtHR has had to consider a variety of national laws about incitement to, glorification of, or apology for terrorism.[109] In *Leroy* the applicant had been prosecuted for a cartoon in the Basque weekly newspaper, *Ekaitza*, which referred to the 11 September 2001 attack.[110] The prosecution was brought under a French law that dates from 1881. The ECtHR held that the prosecution did not violate the right to freedom of expression. In *Herri Batasuna* the Court considered a decision by Spain to dissolve Herri Batasuna and Batasuna for activities incompatible with democracy. The reason for dissolution was the parties' support for ETA—a violent Basque separatist group. The Court cited the EU offence as an example of international co-operation in this field and found no violation of the right to freedom of assembly.[111] The Commission has claimed the framework decision would not make it 'an offence to hold certain political or other views'.[112] However, these cases, and the permissive approach of the ECtHR to legislation on incitement, demonstrate that European jurisprudence is willing to curtail political rights in the name of securing the polity.

b. Recruitment and Training for Terrorism

The amending legislation also introduced offences of recruitment and training for terrorism. Article 3(2)(b) FDCT forests out the offence of 'recruitment for terrorism'—which is also vague. It is defined as 'soliciting another person to commit one of the offences listed in Article 1(1)(a) to (h), or in Article 2(2)'. This offence is broader than the provocation offence, in that it includes participation in a terrorist group in the list of offences for which recruitment might take place. While not entailing as imprecise a definition as provocation, the exact meaning of 'solicit' is not obvious. This offence received comparatively little attention during the drafting process. The Parliament limited its recommendations to requiring the solicitation to be intentional and excluding the threatening of terrorist offences from the list of measures for which one might recruit, as it is 'very difficult to

---

[108] Sottiaux, *Terrorism and the Limitation of Rights*, n 104 above, pp 88–92. See also VF Comella, 'Freedom of Expression in Political Contexts: Some Reflections on the Case-Law of the European Court of Human Rights' in W Sadurski (ed), *Political Rights Under Stress in 21st Century Europe* (Oxford, Oxford University Press, 2006).

[109] Sottiaux, '*Leroy v France*', n 103 above.

[110] *Leroy v France* (36109/03) Judgment of the European Court of Human Rights of 2 October 2008.

[111] *Herri Batasuna and Batasuna v Spain* (25803/04 and 25817/04) Judgment of the European Court of Human Rights of 30 June 2009. For a summary of the case in English see *European Human Rights Law Review* (2009) 817–20.

[112] Written Question E-3112/01 by Erik Meijer (GUE/NGL) to the Commission (13 November 2001).

conceive' such an offence.[113] The latter recommendation was adopted by the Council, the recommendation that solicitation be intentional was not. The third new offence is 'training for terrorism'. This involves

> providing instruction in the making or use of explosives, firearms or other weapons or noxious or hazardous substances, or in other specific methods or techniques, for the purpose of committing one of the offences listed in Article 1(1)(a) to (h), knowing that the skills provided are intended to be used for this purpose.[114]

This offence is more precisely formulated. To be found guilty of the offence, an individual must provide the training for the purpose of committing a terrorist offence, knowing that the skills are intended to be so used.[115] This appears to require a double intention—on behalf of both the instructor and the instructed. However, the question of proof presents challenges. Does a university teacher, instructing students in the use of 'noxious or hazardous substances', need to make clear that she does not condone their use for terrorism? Must she also be cognisant of potentially violent students and refuse tuition to those she believes to be prospective terrorists? A similar UK law was the subject of criticism when it was introduced in 2006 with the Act described as putting third-level education staff 'in the impossible role of moral gatekeepers'.[116] While these questions may appear to be scaremongering, the possibility of police action cannot be ruled out. In 2008 a student and administrator at Nottingham University were arrested and held for six days for downloading 'an al-Qaeda training manual' for research for a PhD proposal.[117] While neither were charged, their detention for six days demonstrates the broad basis that inchoate offences offer police for interfering with rights. Innocent parties have to rely more on judicious prosecutions than formal safeguards to protect them. The effect of these offences is, in part, to require private actors to police their own behaviour and that of others as part of the EU's effort to counter terrorism. The co-option of private actors as part of the state's counter-terrorism efforts is a recurring theme of post-September 11 counter-terrorism and will also be seen in relation to financial institutions and telecommunications and travel service providers.

iv. Safeguards in the amending Framework Decision

As with original framework decision, the amending legislation contains a number of safeguards. Recitals 13 to 15 of the Preamble contain both general and

---

[113] European Parliament, Parliament Committee Report, n 89 above, p 12.

[114] Art 3(1) as amended.

[115] As with the definition of recruitment, training excludes the threatening offence in Art 1(1) (i) FDCT This exclusion was once more at the recommendation of the Parliament. See: European Parliament, Parliament Committee Report, n 89 above, p 12.

[116] 'Law-Breakers in the Library', *Guardian* (8 November 2005).

[117] 'Researchers Have No "Right" to Study Terrorist Materials', *Times Higher Education* (17 July 2008).

particular statements regarding the protection of human rights. Recital 13 refers to Article 6(2) TEU and the EU Charter of Fundamental Rights. Recital 14 notes that the new offences should not adversely affect 'the dissemination of information for scientific, academic or reporting purposes', and states that the expression of 'radical, polemic or controversial views in the public debate' falls outside the scope of the law. A European Parliament amendment would also have protected artistic expression, but this recommendation was not adopted by the Council.[118] Finally, Recital 15, added at the behest of the Parliament, calls for implementation to be proportional and not arbitrary or discriminatory. While these recitals are to be welcomed, it is significant that once again the safeguards are placed in the non-binding Preamble rather than the substantive text of the legislation. The operation of these safeguards is therefore left to national authorities, and in particular, agents of national criminal justice systems. However, Article 2 of the amending legislation, entitled 'Fundamental Principles relating to Freedom of Expression', goes some way towards remedying this flaw. The article declares that the amending law shall not contradict 'fundamental principles relating to freedom of expression, in particular freedom of the press'. As the amending Framework Decision entirely recasts both the offences linked to terrorism and the inchoate offences, Article 2 should apply to the new and existing offences. It reaffirms the importance of respecting fundamental rights in an otherwise problematic law.

The European Commission has not yet produced an evaluation report on the amending Framework Decision. However, the dangers posed by the broad definition of terrorist offences and offences related to terrorist groups are compounded by the inchoate and related offences. The law is broadly and imprecisely drafted, and neither transposition into national law, nor the opportunity to amend the legislation, has resolved the resulting uncertainty. Instead the legislation criminalises a broad range of political action and provides weak safeguards for legitimate political action.

III. CRIMINALISING TERRORISM AND THE RULE OF LAW

The framework decisions appear at first glance to be ordinary criminal law, albeit criminal law adopted at EU level. The offences seek to approximate Member State law in the field of terrorism to provide a legislative basis for EU counter-terrorism action. The Preamble of the amending Framework Decision confirms this, stating that the legislation 'is the basis of the counter-terrorist policy of the European Union':

> The achievement of a legal framework common to all Member States, and in particular of a harmonised definition of terrorist offences, has allowed the counter-terrorism policy

---

[118] European Parliament, Parliament Committee Report, n 89 above, p 10.

of the European Union to develop and expand, subject to the respect of fundamental rights and the rule of law.[119]

However, in reality the framework decision may be the paradigmatic example of the failure to adopt a European criminal law. The offences are broad and vague—a problem exacerbated by transposition—and they undermine fundamental legal principles. In terms of the rule of law's constitutive role there is little doubt that the framework decisions were correctly based in a power conferred on the EU by the Member States. However, the lack of an infringement procedure for the European Commission has limited that institution's role to producing reports on transposition into national law. Member States can be said to have the power to 'resist' the EU law on two levels—first, in relation to the drafting of the instrument and second, when implementing it into national law.[120] While there are ample examples in the two evaluation reports of problems with transposition the Commission concluded in 2008 that 'implementation of the main provisions can be considered satisfactory, although some deficiencies remain'.[121] The ultimate arbiter on the interpretation of the law, the ECJ, has not had the opportunity to offer definitive interpretations of the more vague clauses. As a result of the lack of oversight there remain problems with the framework decision as a common criminal law.

A. The Framework Decisions as Criminal Law

The first concern relates to the lack of uniformity in the transposition of the definition across the EU. The example of the FDCT suggests that framework decisions did not lead to a uniform criminal law across the EU. It gives cause for much scepticism about the degree to which 'approximation' can lead to a common criminal code. Without the ECJ ensuring that the rule of law can play its constitutive role it is likely that the Member States' criminal law will be inspired by, rather than an implementation of, the framework decision. This might be welcomed by those who are sceptical about the EU's role in criminal law. However, from the point of view of individuals subject to the law haphazard implementation of criminal law is worrying.

The rule of law's safeguarding role requires that the principle of legality is respected. This relates not just to the action having a lawful basis (which it does) but also requires that individuals subject to it can plan their behaviour in accordance with the law. However, the various offences raise serious doubts in this regard as

---

[119] Recital 2 to the Preamble to the amending Framework Decision (emphasis added).

[120] K Nuotio, 'Terrorism as a Catalyst for the Emergence, Harmonisation and Reform of Criminal Law' (2006) 4 *Journal of International Criminal Justice* 998, 1012–13.

[121] Commission (EC), 'Communication from the Commission to the Council and the European Parliament, Report on Implementation of the Hague Programme for 2007' COM (2008) 373 final, Brussels, 2 July 2008.

they are broadly drafted and quite vague. This might be defensible on three separate grounds: if the ambiguities in the law were remedied through transposition; if the ambiguities were addressed through judicial clarification; or if the broad drafting was tolerable based on the particular characteristics of the offences in question. None of these three considerations save the framework decision offences. First, it is clear from the two evaluation reports that transposition has not remedied the vagueness in the offences. When only half of the EU's citizens are governed by laws based on an ostensibly common definition, the law cannot truly be said to be harmonised or even approximated. Second, the preliminary ruling procedure, a key mechanism for clarifying the law and ensuring harmonious interpretation across the EU, is currently only available in a minority of Member States. If a case is referred to the ECJ by a national court, then the interpretation will, of course, be binding across the EU.[122] However, the Court cannot enforce such rulings and the varying availability of the procedure across the EU simply serves to highlight the disparity in this area. Transposition and interpretation problems are inherent in the framework decision as a legislative measure, but are aggravated by the particularly poor drafting of this law. The third potential justification for the breadth of the provisions relates to the nature of the offences. The European Court of Human Rights has tolerated broadly drafted criminal law where such breadth is necessary due to the subject matter of the law.[123] It has held that the 'need to avoid excessive rigidity and to keep pace with changing circumstances means that many laws are inevitably couched in terms which, to a greater or lesser extent, are vague'.[124] However, as terrorism is viewed as a particular reprehensible crime and because it carries heavier sentences than crimes without the terrorist motive, it is reasonable to demand a high level of legal certainty. The broad drafting of the FDCT cannot be saved by implementation or interpretation, or by reference to the character of the offence. As a result, it may well offend the requirements of accessibility and foreseeability that are cornerstones of the principle of legality in criminal law.

The third principal concern with the legislation as criminal law lies in its attribution of culpability for terrorism. This is most clearly demonstrated by the offences of directing and participating in a terrorist group, and recruiting for terrorism. In relation to the former offences, an individual can be culpable for the terrorist activities of a group in which they participate even if they only have knowledge of the group's criminal activities. An individual who directs a group—regardless of the nature of the direction—can be held culpable for any terrorist activities of the group. An individual who recruits another to participate in such a group is also tainted with culpability for any terrorist activities of the group, again notwithstanding their knowledge (or lack thereof) of the terrorist activities of the group. The fact that the group need not actually carry out any offence for the recruiter to be culpable further aggravates the problem of transferred guilt.

---

[122] C-105/03 *Criminal Proceedings against Maria Pupino* [2005] ECR I-5285.
[123] Dumitriu, n 31 above, p 602.
[124] *Müller v Switzerland* (1988) 13 EHRR 212.

The definition of the terrorist motive provided by the framework decision is itself quite broad. The resulting transfer of culpability is a form of guilt by association, but it is guilt by association to an idea: that violent change of the legal, political and socio-economic status quo within or outside the EU may be legitimate. Given the relatively idiosyncratic facts of breaches of the presumption of innocence before the European Court of Human Rights, it is impossible to speculate in the abstract on whether or not the framework decision breaches the principle.[125] Any challenge to national legislation implementing the framework decision is likely to turn on the facts of the particular case. However, even if the legal validity of such a development cannot be conclusively determined, the broader implications for criminal justice are undeniably worrying.

B. A Basis for Co-operation?

The FDCT is a poor example of ordinary criminal law. It is broadly drafted, lacks effectiveness and uniformity, and erodes the presumption of innocence. However, a definition of terrorism can serve another purpose: to identify those against whom heightened powers of investigation and surveillance may be used, and therefore to justify and limit the use of those powers in a jurisdiction. The definition of terrorism in the FDCT has been described as the basis for EU co-operation by academic commentators, and there have also been statements to this effect by the institutions themselves.[126] In proposing the amending Framework Decision, the Commission declared that 'the Framework Decision is a key instrument in the EU policy against terrorism... [it] triggers the European Union co-operation mechanisms referring to the Framework Decision'.[127]

More than one commentator has claimed that the EU definition provides the basis for the application of co-operation mechanisms such as the European Arrest Warrant (EAW) and targeted asset-freezing sanctions.[128] However, on both counts the analysis is erroneous. The framework decision establishing the EAW simplifies the extradition process between Member States in relation to 32 different offences, only one of which is terrorism. Furthermore, it operates on the basis of definitions in national criminal law, not EU law. As implementation of the FDCT has not successfully harmonised national definitions of terrorism, the EAW still operates on the basis of national criminal law which employs different definitions of terrorism. As a result, the link between the two framework decisions is tenuous at best. Furthermore,

---

[125] S Trechsel, *Human Rights in Criminal Proceedings* (Oxford, Oxford University Press, 2005) 163–64. For a recent discussion of the presumption of innocence that includes an analysis of counter-terrorism see A Ashworth, 'Four Threats to the Presumption of Innocence' (2006) 10 *International Journal of Evidence and Proof* 241.

[126] Saul, *Defining Terrorism*, n 7 above, pp 162–63.

[127] Commission (EC), 'Proposal for a Council Framework Decision amending Framework Decision 2002/475/JHA on combating terrorism' COM (2007) 650, 2.

[128] Saul, *Defining Terrorism*, n 7 above, pp 162–63. See also Cassese, n 6 above, p 934.

neither the UN nor the EU sanctions regime requires a group or individual to be guilty of, or even suspected of, an offence under the FDCT. This divergence between the definition of terrorism in EU law and its application in national law and other EU law measures is yet another example of a failure of the rule of law's constitutive role: the law as promulgated is not being effectively enforced. The result offends the principle of legal certainty at the heart of the rule of law.

There are, nonetheless, some measures that do refer to the framework decision explicitly. These include legislation relating to the Visa Information System and Schengen Agreement,[129] cross-border co-operation on combating crime and terrorism,[130] crisis co-operation,[131] anti-money laundering,[132] information exchange,[133] and confiscation of criminal proceeds.[134] However, even a cursory perusal of the EU's *Official Journal* makes clear that while the measures refer to the framework decision, many of them have a much greater impact than the strict confines of counter-terrorism. Terrorism may have given renewed impetus to co-operation, but the laws adopted since 11 September 2001 pursue broader criminal justice objectives. As a result, it would be inaccurate to conclude that the FDCT has clearly delineated legal culpability for terrorism as the basis of greater co-operation and preventive powers. Some of the most revolutionary EU counter-terrorism measures (eg European Arrest Warrant and targeted sanctions) do not rely on the framework decision, or its definition, at all. Those that do make reference to it go far beyond counter-terrorism into broader areas of security and law enforcement.

C. The Framework Decisions and Pre-emption

The fact that the framework decision fails to harmonise national definitions of terrorism and is not used for prevention and co-operation might be welcomed given its many flaws. However, these deficiencies do not prevent the measure playing

---

[129] Council Decision 2008/622/JHA of 23 June 2008 concerning access for consultation of the Visa Information System (VIS) by designated authorities of Member States and by Europol for the purposes of the prevention, detection and investigation of terrorist offences and of other serious criminal offences; Council Decision 2003/725/JHA of 2 October 2003 amending the provisions of Art 40(1) and (7) of the Convention implementing the Schengen Agreement of 14 June 1985 on the gradual abolition of checks at common borders.

[130] Council Decision 2008/615/JHA of 23 June 2008 on the stepping up of cross-border co-operation, particularly in combating terrorism and cross-border crime.

[131] Council Decision 2008/617/JHA of 23 June 2009 on the improvement of co-operation between the special intervention units of the Member States of the European Union in crisis situations.

[132] Directive 2005/60/EC of the European Parliament and of the Council of 26 October 2005 on the prevention of the use of the financial system for the purpose of money laundering and terrorist financing.

[133] Council Decision 2005/671/JHA of 20 September 2005 on the exchange of information and co-operation concerning terrorist offences.

[134] Council Framework Decision 2005/212/JHA of 24 February 2005 on Confiscation of crime-related proceeds, instrumentalities and property.

a role in EU counter-terrorism. First, the framework decision is an example of executive legislation, which empowers law enforcement officials while providing for limited political accountability or legal safeguards. Second, it deploys the morally damaging label of 'terrorism' broadly, permitting action to be taken against those who *might* be dangerous, rather than those who *are* or definitely *will be*. Third, it particularly affects vulnerable minorities—such as those seeking asylum—and restricts their ability to be effective political actors.

A key trait of counter-terrorism is the dominance of executive and administrative actors.[135] The drafting of the framework decision and the instruments which refer to it has been dominated by the Member State governments acting as the Council. Indeed, it is remarkable that of the various measures outlined above that make explicit reference to the framework decision, only the Anti-Money-Laundering Directive was adopted through the co-decision procedure which allowed the European Parliament to play an equal role. The other measures were all adopted based on the consultation procedure, which only requires the Parliament to offer an opinion. In its opinions on both the framework decision and the amending framework decision, the European Parliament demonstrated a far greater desire than the Council to ensure that counter-terrorism action was compliant with the key standards of the ECHR and the EU Charter of Fundamental Rights. In its report on the amending framework decision, the European Parliament's Committee on Legal Affairs noted that any dichotomy between human rights compliance and counter-terrorism action is 'artificial, legally flawed and politically dangerous'.[136] While various European Parliament amendments would have introduced safeguards into the operative text of the legislation, the Council limited those safeguards to the non-binding Preamble, with two notable exceptions. Article 1(2) FDCT and Article 2 of the amending framework decision respectively refer to the general requirement to respect fundamental rights in Article 6 TEU and the specific protections for freedom of expression. However, these safeguards will not have the desired effect if they are left unimplemented.

The European Commission's record on the importance of upholding human rights when implementing the framework decision is mixed. While the two evaluation reports assess the transposition of the criminal offences in line-by-line detail, the safeguards are disposed of in a few short paragraphs. Although one might reasonably argue that it is not for the EU's executive branch to assess its own compliance with human rights standards (and certainly, the European Commission should not be the final arbiter in this matter), the lack of attention given to the transposition of safeguards is nonetheless worrying. Thus, the European Commission used its power to ensure the enforcement of the law but not the safeguards for individuals—in contrast to its answers to questions from the

---

[135] D Curtin, *Executive Power of the European Union: Law, Practices and the Living Constitution* (Oxford, Oxford University Press, 2009) p 51.

[136] European Parliament, Parliament Committee Report, n 89 above, p 21.

European Parliament that it favoured being 'extremely cautious when proposing to incriminate acts on terrorist grounds, as a very extensive conception, contrary to the de minimus principle, could put fundamental rights at stake'.[137] Despite the somewhat mixed signals from the European Commission the framework decision facilitates pre-emptive counter-terrorism.

The lack of adequate safeguards in the operative part of the text gives rise to a Catch-22 situation for Member States.[138] If Member States try to transpose the safeguards from the Preamble into the operative part of the text and improve the law to ensure that there are adequate protections for human rights, then they risk creating further differences in the law across the EU. If Member States do not clarify the offences and improve safeguards, discretion is passed on to law enforcement officials. This may in turn lead to arbitrary prosecutions or abuses of power. For example, in the absence of clear legal rules on who can be subject to prosecution for terrorist related offences, there is scope for law enforcement authorities to exercise their discretion. Obviously, the Member State legal systems themselves contain safeguards against arbitrary state action. Nonetheless, as the source of the potential infringement of rights, it should be EU law and not that of the Member States that ensures that the rule of law is respected.

The pre-emptive approach allows for as many individuals and organisations possible to be targeted by the counter-terrorism action. They are then tarred by the pejorative 'terrorism' label. The symbolic effect of the terrorism label has been referred to as a key reason for specifically and explicitly criminalising political violence. As the framework decision was agreed by Member State governments acting as the Council the lesson from international relations is salient: states tend to believe that political violence can be legitimate except when directed against the state itself. If the purpose of the EU definition of terrorism is symbolic then any objective assessment of that symbolism must consider it diluted on two accounts. First, the symbolic value may be weakened by the lack of uniformity in the definition as implemented by the Member States. Second, and most significantly, the symbolism is eroded by the failure to exempt those whose actions, while violent, may be justifiable. The EU definition may catch domestic political protesters and resistance groups fighting oppression in overseas jurisdictions. The protection for both groups is in the non-binding part of the legislation and as such the dominant theme in the binding text is the preservation of state power.

While the focus on pre-emption and control is dangerous for all individuals, it has the greatest effect on vulnerable groups at the margins of the

---

[137] Written Question E-3107/02 by Cristina Muscardini (UEN) to the Commission (29 October 2002). In the post-Lisbon Treaty EU the European Commission appears to be interested in taking a more active role in ensuring that fundamental rights are upheld in accordance with the EU Charter. See Commission (EC), 'Communication from the Commission: Strategy for the effective implementation of the Charter of Fundamental Rights by the European Union' COM (2010) 573 final, Brussels, 19 October 2010.

[138] For a discussion of how Finland addressed these difficulties see Nuoti, n 119 above, pp 1013–15.

political community. Consider, for example, the interaction between the definition of terrorism and asylum law. A Commission Working Document published in December 2001 was based on two premises: 'that bona fide refugees and asylum seekers should not become victims of recent events' and 'that there should be no avenue for those supporting or committing terrorist acts to secure access' to the EU.[139] Later that month the Council took action that places those ideas in direct conflict. Council Common Position on Combating Terrorism places those fleeing oppressive regimes in a difficult position.[140] Article 16 of the Council Common Position requires the Member States to ensure 'that the asylum seeker has not planned, facilitated or participated in the commission of terrorist acts'. Furthermore, Article 17 states that Member States must 'ensure that refugee status is not abused by the perpetrators, organisers or facilitators of terrorist acts'. On the one hand, those seeking political asylum must prove they have a well-founded fear of persecution for opposition to a political oppressor to secure refugee status. On the other hand divulging the full extent of their involvement in opposition might result in their criminalisation as a terrorist and the loss of refugee status. This places vulnerable persons in a difficult position when trying to vindicate their rights as asylum seekers under international law. Pre-emptive counter-terrorism has therefore contributed to a broader process of legal and political exclusion.

IV. CONCLUSION: THE POWER OF DEFINITION

Discussing the definition of terrorism, Derrida argues that the dominant power is that which 'manages to impose and, thus, to legitimate, indeed to legalize ... the terminology and thus the interpretation that best suits it in a given situation'.[141] The framework decision allows European governments to legalise the terminology of counter-terrorism with a view to justifying state power and reducing the space for political conflict. This was tacitly acknowledged by the European Commission in response to a question from Frank Vanhecke MEP in October 2001. The Commission drew attention to 'the political declarations, recommendations and decisions regarding terrorism' and declared that it had 'given legal form to those political purposes, consolidating them within a legal text'.[142] If action that challenges state power is terrorism then counter-terrorism can claim to be a legitimate attempt to prevent or even pre-empt a threat. Thus the law offers a means of control over those who associate in any way with a 'terrorist group', who commit any acts that can be 'linked to a terrorist offence', or who make any statements

---

[139] Commission (EC), 'Commission Working Document: The relationship between safeguarding internal security and complying with international protection obligations and instruments' COM (2001) 743 final, Brussels, 5 December 2001.

[140] Council Common Position of 27 December 2001 on combating terrorism (2001/930/CFSP).

[141] Jacques Derrida in G Borradori (ed), *Philosophy in a Time of Terror: Dialogues with Jürgen Habermas and Jacques Derrida* (Chicago, University of Chicago Press, 2003) p 105.

[142] Written Question E-2653/01 by Frank Vanhecke (TDI) to the Commission (1 October 2001).

that may 'provoke' terrorism. Because the safeguards are not binding the law requires individuals to rely on the discretion of law enforcement authorities to respect human rights and not to use their powers beyond what is strictly necessary. The framework decision claims to approximate Member States' criminal law and provide the basis for co-operation and prevention. In reality it serves a less distinct and less distinguished purpose. It provides a legal mechanism by which to stigmatise a wide range of groups and individuals. Once labelled as 'terrorist', they become the subject of coercive powers. But these powers are fragmented and vary across the EU. Nonetheless, the EU definition and associated measures offers much more than mere legal utility. It seeks to legitimate state power by drawing the boundaries of acceptable political action in Europe.[143] It is the central plank of the EU's pre-emptive counter-terrorism: influencing and interacting with other measures to the detriment of vulnerable groups and without limiting the effects to the purported 'worst of the worst'.[144]

---

[143] This process has been described as the development of a 'militant democracy' in Europe. See the various contributions in W Sadurski (ed), *Political Rights Under Stress in 21st Century Europe* (Oxford, Oxford University Press, 2006).

[144] As the detainees at Guantanamo were referred to by former White House Press Secretary Ari Fleischer. See: K Greenberg, *The Least Worst Place: How Guantanamo Became the World's Most Notorious Prison* (Oxford, Oxford University Press, 2009) 79.

4

Anti-Money-Laundering and Counter-Terrorist Finance

I F THE 'WAR on terror' has seen the criminalisation of behaviour prior to the commission of an offence then in no field is this more true than in counter-terrorist finance.[1] Governments across the globe consider preventing money laundering and countering the financing of terrorism to be key aspects of global counter-terrorism. A Staff Report to the National Commission on Terrorist Attacks upon the United States claimed that 'the fight against al Qaeda financing [is] as critical as the fight against al Qaeda itself' and concluded that 'if we choke off the terrorists' money, we limit their ability to conduct mass casualty attacks'.[2] Despite the vivid imagery, US and EU authorities agree that preventing money flowing to those engaged in political violence is almost, if not entirely, impossible.[3] A Europol report puts it bluntly, noting that 'given the small amount of money required, the prevention of terrorist financing appears to some extent unrealistic'. As a result, 'priority is given to financial investigations into the money trail left by terrorists'.[4] Nevertheless, concerted efforts are made at national, regional and international level to do just that. EU action may be divided into two categories—first, efforts to track and/or prevent the flow of funding to suspected terrorists (anti-money-laundering and counter-terrorist finance); and second, action to freeze the assets of those suspected of providing such funding (targeted asset-freezing sanctions).[5] This chapter addresses anti-money-laundering and counter-terrorist finance in general, while the next chapter considers targeted asset-freezing sanctions. It examines the manner in which governments and non-governmental organisations have developed an increasingly intrusive regime of financial surveillance in

---

[1] For a succinct and critical overview of both the policy field and the literature on it see M Levi, 'Combating the Financing of Terrorism: A History and Assessment of the Control of "Threat Finance"' (2010) 50 *British Journal of Criminology* 650.

[2] National Commission on Terrorist Attacks upon the United States, *Monograph on Terrorist Financing: Staff Report to the Commission* 2, available: http://govinfo.library.unt.edu/911/staff_ statements/ 911_TerrFin_Monograph.pdf, last accessed 13 September 2011.

[3] Ibid. See also: Europol, *EU Terrorism Situation and Trend Report* (The Hague, Europol, 2007) 21.

[4] Europol, n 3 above, p 21.

[5] Admittedly, these categories are more ones of convenience rather than policy coherence. Targeted asset-freezing sanctions are the most invasive and most contested measures in the broad anti-money-laundering and counter-terrorist finance policy sphere. As such, they merit particular attention in this book, and are the subject of chapter five.

an effort to pre-empt any attempts to fund political violence. It concludes that the anti-money-laundering and counter-terrorist finance regime fits with the pre-emptive approach and poses strong challenges to both aspects of the EU rule of law. The implications for both individuals and entities can be profound.

1. ANTI-MONEY-LAUNDERING AND COUNTER-TERRORIST FINANCE IN CONTEXT

Anti-Money-Laundering and counter-terrorist finance is co-ordinated by over-lapping regulatory frameworks with both states and non-state actors operating at multiple levels of governance.[6] The three most pertinent non-EU sites of regulation are the UN, Council of Europe and Financial Action Task Force.[7] The EU's relationship with these bodies has accurately been described as 'symbiotic', with EU initiatives aiming at times to meet, and at others to surpass, the other organisations' standards.[8] Perhaps less symbiotic, but no less important, is the role of the US. Action by the US on counter-terrorist finance has required the EU to enter into a bilateral agreement on the transfer of financial data to facilitate the US Terrorist Finance Tracking Programme. The common themes running through the EU's interaction with each of these bodies are divergence, regulatory overlap and 'policy laundering'.

A. United Nations

The UN was the first global body to act against money laundering when it adopted its 1988 Convention against Illicit Traffic in Narcotic Drugs and Psychotropic Substances (UN Drugs Convention).[9] One of the aims of the Convention was to 'to deprive persons engaged in illicit traffic of the proceeds of their criminal activities and thereby eliminate their main incentive for so doing'.[10] It set out a number of offences concerned with the laundering of the proceeds of

---

[6] See generally: WC Gilmore, *Dirty Money: The Evolution of International Measures to Counter Money Laundering and the Financing of Terrorism*, 3rd edn (Strasbourg, Council of Europe Publishing, 2004).

[7] A number of other bodies have involved themselves in counter-terrorist finance, including the World Bank, International Monetary Fund, Basel Committee on Banking Supervision, Wolfsberg Group, Egmont Group and Interpol. However, as the focus here is on EU law, only one non-legal body is considered—Financial Action Task Force—as it is the one which most shapes global policy. For a discussion of the others, see CJ Shaw, 'Worldwide War on Terrorist Finance' (2007) *Journal of International Banking Law and Regulation* 469; WH Muller, CH Kälin and JG Goldsworth (eds), *Anti-Money Laundering: International Law and Practice* (West Sussex, John Wiley & Sons Ltd, 2007).

[8] V Mitsilegas and B Gilmore, 'The EU Legislative Framework against Money Laundering and Terrorist Finance: A Critical Analysis in the Light of Evolving Global Standards' (2007) 56 *International and Comparative Law Quarterly* 119.

[9] UN Convention against Illicit Traffic in Narcotic Drugs and Psychotropic Substances 1988.

[10] Ibid, Preamble.

narcotics trafficking and related offences. As a result of this early involvement in anti-money-laundering, several UN agencies have a role in its regulation. Chief amongst these is the Global Programme against Money Laundering, which is based at the UN Office for Drugs and Crime and under the broad authority of the General Assembly.[11]

However, since 11 September 2001, the UN Security Council and institutions acting under its authority have dominated UN counter-terrorism. The two key institutions for counter-terrorist finance are the Counter-Terrorism Committee and the '1267 Committee'. The 1267 Committee (a sub-committee of the UN Security Council) was established to administer the UN targeted asset-freezing sanctions regime and so it is examined in Chapter Five. The Counter-Terrorism Committee monitors implementation of the 1999 International Convention for the Suppression of the Financing of Terrorism (Terrorist Financing Convention). Former UN Secretary General, Kofi Annan, describes it as the 'center of global efforts to fight terrorism'.[12] In addition to monitoring compliance with UN Security Council resolution 1373, the Counter-Terrorism Committee also acts as a conduit for technical assistance from donor states to those struggling to implement the Convention.[13]

The Terrorist Financing Convention makes reference to prior General Assembly resolutions calling for counter-terrorism action and prescribes specific counter-terrorist finance measures.[14] Article 2 defines financing terrorism as providing or collecting funds for an offence under the existing UN counter-terrorism conventions,[15] or for any other act that fulfils a specified definition of terrorism.[16] The Terrorist Financing Convention definition takes a similar form to the EU definition of terrorism in the Framework Decision on Combating Terrorism

---

[11] For a brief overview see: E Rosand, 'The UN-led Multilateral Institutional Response to Jihadist Terrorism: is a Global Counterterrorism Body Needed?' (2006) *Journal of Conflict & Security Law* 399.

[12] K Annan, Statement At Ministerial Level Meeting of the UN Security Council, cited in Rosand, n 11 above, at fn 18.

[13] See Counter-Terrorism Committee website: www.un.org/sc/ctc/aboutus.html, last accessed 13 September 2011.

[14] General Assembly resolution 49/60 of 9 December 1994; General Assembly resolution 51/210 of December 1996 para 3(f); General Assembly resolution 52/165 of 15 December 1997; General Assembly resolution 53/108 of 8 December 1998.

[15] Convention for the Suppression of Unlawful Seizure of Aircraft 1970; Convention for the Suppression of Unlawful Acts against the Safety of Civil Aviation 1971; Convention on the Prevention and Punishment of Crimes against Internationally Protected Persons, including Diplomatic Agents 1973; International Convention against the Taking of Hostages 1979; Convention on the Physical Protection of Nuclear Material 1980; Protocol for the Suppression of Unlawful Acts of Violence at Airports Serving International Civil Aviation 1988; Convention for the Suppression of Unlawful Acts against the Safety of Maritime Navigation 1988; Protocol for the Suppression of Unlawful Acts against the Safety of Fixed Platforms located on the Continental Shelf 1988; International Convention for the Suppression of Terrorist Bombings 1997. Note that Art 23 Terrorist Financing Convention allows the Annex containing this list to be amended to include future counter-terrorism treaties, subject to certain conditions.

[16] Shaw, n 7 above, p 471.

(FDCT), but they are overlapping rather than identical.[17] Clearly then, Terrorist Financing Convention obligations are based on a different definition of terrorism to that which operates in EU law. As the Member States are subject to two sets of obligations the law in this field lacks clarity. The Terrorist Financing Convention definition of terrorism is also quite broad. No actual act of terrorism is needed to trigger the terrorist financing offence. In addition to directly financing terrorism, attempting, organising or directing others, or acting as an accomplice to the financing of terrorism is also an offence.[18] The Convention also calls for international co-operation and requires that states put in place the necessary domestic measures to ensure prevention and criminalisation.[19] Prior to the September 11 attacks, the Terrorist Financing Convention had only been ratified by four states. There are now 167 parties and the Convention came into force in April 2002. Ramage has described the Convention as having 'preventive potential aimed at punishing financial preparations before they mature into terrorist violence'.[20] This is clear from the wide range of preparatory offences, the customer identification and monitoring requirements, and the frequent references to 'prevention', 'repression', 'elimination' and 'suppression' of terrorism. In addition to the Terrorist Financing Convention, a number of UN Security Council resolutions are relevant to anti-money-laundering and counter-terrorist finance.[21] In particular, UN Security Council resolution 1373, adopted on 28 September 2001, requires states to criminalise a wide range of terrorism-related activity.[22] Article 1 'decides that all states shall prevent and suppress the financing of terrorist acts'. It requires the criminalisation of terrorist financing and the freezing of assets. Article 3 focuses on international co-operation, and calls upon states to accede to the Terrorist Financing Convention and to fully implement previous resolutions.[23] The UN Security Council thereby used a Chapter VII resolution to reinforce existing international law in this area. The Terrorist Financing Convention was adopted two years prior to the declaration of the 'war on terror' and so its broad preventive regime is evidence of an existing political will for such an approach. On the other hand the low number of ratifications prior to the Al-Qaeda attacks may suggest that governments were willing to commit to regulatory regimes at international level that they were unable or unwilling to transpose into their national legal systems. This may explain the extensive use of 'soft law' in anti-money-laundering and counter-terrorist finance.

---

[17] See ch 3 above for further discussion on definitions of terrorism.
[18] Art 5(2) Terrorist Financing Convention.
[19] Art 18 Terrorist Financing Convention.
[20] S Ramage, '2008 Amendments of the Proceeds of Crime Act 2002 and Other Legislation that Combats Terrorist Financing' (2008) *Criminal Lawyer* 1, 2.
[21] See particularly: UNSC Res 1267 (15 October 1999) and Res 1390 (28 January 2002).
[22] UNSC Res 1373 (28 September 2001).
[23] UNSC Res 1269 (19 October 1999) and UNSC Res 1368 (12 September 2001).

B. Council of Europe

Like the UN, the Council of Europe has had a longer involvement in anti-money-laundering and counter-terrorist finance than the EU. A 1980 Recommendation of its Council of Ministers made reference to 'hold-ups and kidnappings which are becoming more and more frequent in many European countries' and noted that international money laundering can give 'rise to serious problems, encourage the perpetration of further criminal acts and thus cause the phenomenon to spread nationally and internationally'.[24] The Recommendation foreshadowed the agreements that were to come, calling for greater customer checks in the banking industry and closer international co-operation in anti-money-laundering.

The Council of Europe adopted its Convention on Laundering, Search, Seizure and Confiscation of the Proceeds from Crime in 1990. It required states to establish money laundering offences, to investigate such offences, to confiscate the proceeds of crime and to co-operate in international efforts to combat money laundering.[25] As the Explanatory Report to the Convention makes clear, it was principally concerned with money laundering as it related to organised crime and in particular drug trafficking (explicit mention was made of the UN Drugs Convention). However, the Report did make passing reference to possible links between money laundering and terrorism.[26]

The Council of Europe Convention entered into force in 1993. Prior to 11 September 2001, 36 states had ratified the Convention, rising to 48 by the end of 2004. In 2005, despite (or perhaps because of) the widespread ratification of the 1990 Convention, the Council of Europe adopted a new anti-money-laundering Convention.[27] The Explanatory Report to the 2005 Convention cites three principal impetus for the new Convention: first, the need to provide for preventive measures; second, new anti-money-laundering developments, in particular in terms of counter-terrorist finance; and third, the desire to make the Council of Europe rules fit with internationally accepted standards.[28] Of the new developments, both the Convention and Explanatory Report explicitly mention developments in EU law, the growing influence of the Financial Action Task Force and the establishment of Financial Intelligence Units in European and overseas states.[29] The Preamble to the Convention also invokes the Terrorist Financing Convention and UN Security Council resolution 1373. The operative text has

---

[24] Recommendation No R(80) 10 of the Committee of Ministers to Member States on Measures Against the Transfer and the Safekeeping of Funds of Criminal Origin (27 June 1980).

[25] Council of Europe, Convention on Laundering, Search, Seizure and Confiscation of the Proceeds from Crime 1990.

[26] Council of Europe, Explanatory Report to the Convention on Laundering, Search, Seizure and Confiscation of the Proceeds from Crime 1990, paras 1, 8, 27.

[27] Council of Europe, Convention on the Laundering, Search, Seizure and Confiscation of the Proceeds from Crime and on the Financing of Terrorism 2005.

[28] Council of Europe, Explanatory Report to the Convention on the Laundering, Search, Seizure and Confiscation of the Proceeds from Crime and on the Financing of Terrorism 2005, para 15.

[29] Ibid, para 21.

clearly been influenced by the broad scope of the UN and EU measures, as it turns the relatively modest approach of the 1990 Convention into a broad anti-money-laundering and counter-terrorist finance regulatory regime, requiring the adoption of national measures as well as international co-operation. It came into effect in January 2008, and has been ratified by fourteen states to date.[30]

Just as the 2005 Council of Europe Convention makes reference to EU law, so too does EU law refer to the Council of Europe Conventions. Some EU measures have specifically focused on improving implementation of Convention obligations. A 1998 Joint Action and 2001 Framework Decision sought to improve implementation of the 1990 Convention.[31] However, the Council of Europe and EU do not impose identical requirements. The Council of Europe Convention defines the 'financing of terrorism' by reference to the Terrorist Financing Convention.[32] This is in contrast to EU anti-money-laundering and counter-terrorist finance, which uses the substantially different EU definition of terrorism. Therefore, within Europe, there are two overlapping anti-money-laundering and counter-terrorist finance regimes which operate based on different definitions of terrorism. This demonstrates the key theme of global anti-money-laundering and counter-terrorist finance: divergent but mutually reinforcing regulatory regimes.

C. Financial Action Task Force

Unlike the above institutions, the Financial Action Task Force has no basis in international law. The Task Force was formed following a G7 summit in 1987, as 'an inter-governmental policy making body ... that has a *ministerial mandate* to establish international standards'.[33] It has been described as the 'premier international body' in this field.[34] Not all EU Member States are members of the Task Force (and many members of the Task Force are not EU Member States), but the European Commission is an active participant.[35] The Task Force produced 40 anti-money-laundering recommendations in 1990, which were subsequently

---

[30] The list of ratifying states is available at the Council of Europe website: http://conventions.coe. int/, last accessed 18 April 2011.

[31] Joint Action of 3 December 1998 adopted by the Council on the basis of Article K.3 of the Treaty on European Union, on money laundering, the identification, tracing, freezing, seizing and confiscation of instrumentalities and the proceeds from crime (98/699/JHA); Council Framework Decision of 26 June 2001 on money laundering, the identification, tracing, freezing, seizing and confiscation of instrumentalities and the proceeds of crime (2001/500/JHA).

[32] Art 1(h) Council of Europe Convention; Art 2 Terrorist Financing Convention.

[33] Financial Action Task Force, 'Policy Brief: Building Effective Systems to Fight Money Laundering and Terrorist Financing,' 2 (emphasis added), available at www.fatf-gafi.org, last accessed 13 August 2011.

[34] Y-K Heng and K McDonagh, *Risk, Global Governance and Security: The Other War on Terror* (London, Routledge, 2009) 52.

[35] The following EU Member States are not members of Financial Action Task Force: Bulgaria, Cyprus, Czech Republic, Estonia, Hungary, Latvia, Lithuania, Malta, Poland, Romania, Slovakia, Slovenia.

amended in 1996.[36] Its mandate was also expanded that year to cover the proceeds of certain crimes including terrorism. However, the Task Force's focus shifted decisively following the September 11 attacks, and in October 2001 it published eight Special Recommendations on countering the financing of terrorism. In October 2004 the '40 Recommendations' were amended once more and a ninth Special Recommendation was added to the existing eight. A detailed analysis of the substance of the recommendations is beyond the scope of the present work. It suffices to note that the recommendations, elaborated upon in their interpretive notes, represent the core rules and technical standards governing global anti-money-laundering and counter-terrorist finance.[37]

The Financial Action Task Force uses recommendations as 'soft law' to achieve its aims. 'Soft law' is itself a difficult and contentious concept. It can be described as the use of 'rules which do not have legally binding force ... to regulate the exercise of official discretion'.[38] There is a long history of the use of soft law in international law and as part of European legal integration.[39] However, its nature and legal force varies from institution to institution.[40] The boundaries between hard law and soft law are blurred—particularly in the context of international finance.[41] The most pertinent standards in the present context are the Financial Action Task Force recommendations. The recommendations have been described as 'the general and primary reference for international and domestic legislation'.[42] Thus, the international community can reach agreement faster (as states are not legally bound and so are more open to co-operation) and governments can avoid the need for national ratification.[43] Furthermore, Alexander et al note that the reinforcement of Financial Action Task Force recommendations by UN Security Council resolutions can be viewed as 'international law through the back door'.[44] The Financial Action Task Force recommendations certainly have a mutually reinforcing relationship with international law. The recommendations often build on existing treaty obligations, fleshing out the details of broad legal provisions.[45] Special Recommendation 1 requires ratification of all relevant UN instruments of

---

[36] Financial Action Task Force, 'The 40 Recommendations', available at www.fatf-gafi.org, last accessed 14 September 2011.

[37] K Alexander, R Dhumale and J Eatwell, *Global Governance of Financial Systems: The International Regulation of Systemic Risk* (New York, Oxford University Press, 2006) 150.

[38] M Woodley (ed), *Osborn's Concise Law Dictionary*, 10th edn (London, Sweet & Maxwell, 2005).

[39] DM Trubek, P Cottrell and M Nance, '"Soft Law", "Hard Law," and European Integration: Toward a Theory of Hybridity', Jean Monnet Working Paper 02/05 (New York, NYU School of Law, 2005).

[40] C Chinkin, 'The Challenge of Soft Law: Development and Change in International Law' (1989) 38 *International and Comparative Law Quarterly* 850.

[41] Alexander et al, n 37 above, p 141.

[42] A Gardella, 'The Fight against the Financing of Terrorism between Judicial and Regulatory Co-operation' in A Bianchi (ed), *Enforcing International Law Norms Against Terrorism* (Oxford, Hart Publishing, 2004) 418.

[43] J Koh, *Suppressing Terrorist Financing and Money Laundering* (New York, Springer, 2006) 122–24.

[44] Alexander et al, n 37 above, p 152.

[45] Ibid.

law. Special Recommendation 2 calls for the criminalisation of terrorist financing and money laundering and Special Recommendation 3 requires terrorist assets to be frozen. The Terrorist Financing Convention is used to define terrorism for these purposes.[46] Special Recommendation 5 calls for international co-operation.[47] The UN, for its part, has endorsed the Task Force's work: UN Security Council resolution 1617 'strongly urges' states to implement the Financial Action Task Force recommendations.[48]

The Task Force exercises significant power over all states operating in international finance.[49] It has been described as '"socially constructing" into existence a shared consensus about the risk, where none might have existed before'.[50] Over 170 states have now joined the organisation itself or a 'Financial Action Task Force Style Regional Body'.[51] The Task Force's enforcement mechanisms have proven particularly effective, using blacklists of 'Non Cooperative Countries and Territories' and Mutual Evaluation Reports of members to ensure compliance. Of twenty-three countries and territories that were originally listed as non-co-operative, twenty-two have altered their financial policies to achieve de-listing, and only Burma remains on the list.[52] The Task Force is therefore a serious force in global counter-terrorism, albeit one which lacks both transparency and accountability in its activities.[53] It has been criticised as an attempt by the US (and the Bush administration in particular) to ensure dominance over counter-terrorist finance. The extent to which the EU is an autonomous actor and is not merely subservient to American hegemony remains contested.[54]

D. Bilateral Agreements: The United States

It is clear that the US has been at the vanguard of counter-terrorist finance since the September 11 attacks. The US has exerted much influence through the use of soft power in international networks. However, one particular action has required a formal bilateral co-operation between the EU and US. In the aftermath of September 11 2001, the US government began acquiring data on financial

---

[46] Financial Action Task Force, 'Interpretative Note to Special Recommendation II: Criminalising the financing of terrorism and associated money laundering; Interpretative Note to Special Recommendation III: Freezing and Confiscating Terrorist Assets', available: www.fatf-gafi.org, last accessed 13 September 2011.

[47] Financial Action Task Force, '9 Special Recommendations (SR) on Terrorist Financing (TF)', available at www.fatf-gafi.org, last accessed 13 September 2011.

[48] UNSC Res 1617 (29 July 2005).

[49] Koh, n 43 above, 124–43.

[50] Heng and McDonagh, n 34 above, p 65.

[51] Financial Action Task Force, 'Policy Brief: Building Effective Systems to Fight Money Laundering and Terrorist Financing', 2, available at www.fatf-gafi.org, last accessed 13 September 2011.

[52] Financial Action Task Force, 'Annual Review of Non-Cooperative Countries and Territories 2006–2007: Eighth NCCT Review', available: www.fatf-gafi.org, last accessed 13 September 2011.

[53] V Mitsilegas, *EU Criminal Law* (Oxford, Hart Publishing, 2009) 312–14.

[54] Heng and McDonagh, n 34 above, p 67.

transactions from the largest financial communication network in the world, the Society for Worldwide Interbank Financial Telecommunication (SWIFT), as reported in the *New York Times*.[55] SWIFT provides secure messaging services to the global banking sector. With no regulatory oversight, SWIFT had been transferring information to the US for use by the Central Intelligence Agency, the Federal Bureau of Investigation and other law enforcement agencies. The *New York Times* article prompted outrage on both sides of the Atlantic, with the European Parliament expressing 'serious concern ... that a climate of deteriorating respect for privacy and data protection' was being created.[56] As an example of a data surveillance instrument, the resulting bilateral agreement, the Terrorist Finance Tracking Programme Agreement, is considered in detail in Chapter Six.

E. Divergence, Regulatory Overlap and 'Policy Laundering'

Three points are made to conclude this critical overview of the global anti-money-laundering and counter-terrorist finance infrastructure. First, action by the UN, Council of Europe, and Financial Action Task Force in anti-money-laundering predates the September 11, 2001 attacks. The Task Force and the UN had already begun to address terrorism, most notably through the adoption of the Terrorist Financing Convention. However, the September 11, 2001 attacks resulted in heightened activity in all three international fora and a hurried effort to react to unilateral US action in counter-terrorist finance. This is most clear in terms of ratification of the Terrorist Financing Convention, which became an international priority in 2001. Thus, as with other counter-terrorism policies, the attacks appear to have accelerated pre-existing policy processes.

Second, the merging of anti-money-laundering and counter-terrorist finance narratives appears to be a direct result of the attacks. It is worth noting that this merging, though superficially logical, is not necessarily appropriate. McCulloch and Carlton point to salient differences. Anti-money-laundering, originating in efforts against organised crime, targets large sums of money garnered from crime and kept as profit. Counter-terrorist finance on the other hand, is concerned with small amounts of money used for crime and driven by political goals, rather than profit.[57] Levi disputes the importance of this difference and argues that it is 'mistaken to dismiss the value of [anti-money-laundering] measures to countering terrorist financing' simply because some violent acts can be carried out on a low budget.[58] The paucity of

---

[55] E Lichtblau and J Risen, 'Bank Data Sifted in Secret by US to Block Terror' *New York Times* (23 June 2006).

[56] European Parliament, 'Resolution on the interception of bank transfer data from the SWIFT system by the US secret services' P6_TA(2006)0317,7 July 2006. See further the discussion in ch 6 below.

[57] J McCulloch and B Carlton, 'Preempting Justice: Suppression of Financing of Terrorism and the "War on Terror"' (2005–2006) 17 *Current Issues in Criminal Justice* 397, 403.

[58] Levi, n 1 above, p 662.

empirical data on the funding of attacks makes it difficult to come to an authoritative conclusion. Regardless of the coherence of anti-money-laundering and counter-terrorist violence it appears unlikely that they will be decoupled in the foreseeable future. Indeed, they may be subsumed by a larger and even more amorphous policy field known as 'threat finance'. This broader field can cover not just the financing of terrorism and organised crime, but the financing of weapons of mass destruction and drug and human trafficking.[59] The change entails a shift in the type of preventive logic used by regulators: 'countering the financing of terrorism presupposes a different risk perception concept than that of classic anti-money-laundering'.[60] Based on the new logic, all financial transactions are potentially suspect, as terrorism may just as easily be supported by licit funds as by illicit ones. This shift marks the difference between prevention and pre-emption: the former operates on the basis of targeted evidence while the latter relies on generalised suspicion.

The third point pertains to the relationship between the different agencies and their rules. For example, legal privilege rules have been eroded by obligations placed upon lawyers to report on their clients: an FATF obligation that has been enshrined in EU law. Steinhardt has warned of 'policy-laundering': 'the cycling of policies that lack political legitimacy through outside institutions in order to bring them into circulation despite their lack of acceptance'.[61] While all areas of EU counter-terrorism are susceptible to policy-laundering, this is perhaps most true of counter-terrorist finance. Mitsilegas and Gilmore have noted that EU actions are 'always in parallel with international developments in the field, in particular initiatives by the Financial Action Task Force'.[62] When the EU took action to control cash entering or leaving the jurisdiction the relevant legislation referred to FATF Special Recommendation IX.[63] It is clear that each of the international organisations and bilateral co-operation with the US contributes to EU anti-money-laundering and counter-terrorist finance. The relationship between Financial Action Task Force soft law and international and European hard law and the lack of accountability of those who devise the technical standards are matters of concern when identifying the origins of relevant EU law.

II. EU ANTI-MONEY-LAUNDERING AND COUNTER-TERRORIST FINANCE

Although the EU has in some respects had to react to US initiatives on counter-terrorist finance, it has a significant history of action in anti-money-laundering. It adopted its first act in this area in 1991 after earlier action by other international

---

[59]   Levi, n 1 above, p 661.

[60]   M Pieth, 'Criminalizing the Financing of Terrorism' (2006) *Journal of International Criminal Justice* 1074, 1083.

[61]   B Steinhardt, 'Problem of Policy Laundering', American Civil Liberties Union, 13 August 2004.

[62]   Mitsilegas and Gilmore, n 8 above, 120.

[63]   Regulation No 1889/2005 of the European Parliament and of the Council of 26 October 2005 on controls of cash entering or leaving the Community OJ L309/9 (25 November 2005).

organisations. The EU has taken action against money laundering using a wide range of legislative instruments—resulting in a somewhat busy legal landscape. While the EU had taken action prior to the September 11 attacks, those events did result in a transformation of this policy field.

A. EU Anti-Money-Laundering before September 11 2001

The EU had taken action against money laundering before the al-Qaeda attacks. Three anti-money-laundering directives have been promulgated, and it is only the latest that treats terrorist financing as a central (and titular) concern. In addition, a number of third pillar measures have been adopted to strengthen the broad anti-money-laundering regime.

i. First Anti-Money-Laundering (AML) Directive (1991)

The first Anti-Money-Laundering Directive was adopted in 1991 following the earlier UN and Council of Europe Conventions.[64] The first directive focused on drug trafficking and organised crime. In the operative part of the text, the directive reads like a criminal statute. Article 2 sets out the central action: 'Member States shall ensure that money laundering as defined in this directive is prohibited'. The directive required customer identification, the maintenance of identification records in banking, examination of transactions that are 'particularly likely' to be related to money laundering, and notification of relevant national authorities.[65] It provided that financial institutions should refrain from carrying out suspect transactions and refrain from disclosing their suspicions or reports to customers.[66] It left the matter of penalties to the discretion of the Member States.[67] Therefore, the First AML Directive was a more traditional and concise form of criminal law than the sprawling international and domestic measures that have followed. Nonetheless, it did foreshadow the risk-orientated thinking to come. The fifth recital to the Preamble noted that a penal approach should 'not be the only way to combat money laundering'. The ninth recital cited the use of money laundering in relation to terrorism and stipulated that Member States should define money laundering 'to include the proceeds of such activities, to the extent that they are likely to result in laundering operations justifying sanctions'. Furthermore, the seventeenth recital declared that Member States may provide that information gathered for anti-money-laundering purposes may be used

---

[64] Council Directive of 10 June 1991 on prevention of the use of the financial system for the purpose of money laundering (91/308/EEC) (hereafter, First AML Directive).

[65] Art 5 First AML Directive.

[66] Arts 7–8 First AML Directive.

[67] Art 14 First AML Directive.

for other purposes, thus previewing the broad scope of financial surveillance to come.

ii. Third Pillar Measures (1998–2001)

In addition to taking action through the European Community the Member States also chose to act through the then third pillar. In 1998, a Council Joint Action on Money Laundering was adopted. It aimed to improve compliance with the Council of Europe Convention and improve co-operation between national anti-money-laundering authorities. The joint action referred to the UN and Council of Europe Conventions but, for the first time in an EU legislative measure, also referred to the Financial Action Task Force and its 40 Recommendations.[68] The joint action also demonstrated an increased emphasis on prevention. The Preamble made reference to the 'potential for disrupting criminal activity'.[69] Furthermore, Article 5(1) calls on Member States to 'take all necessary steps to minimise the risk of assets being dissipated', if necessary by freezing or seizing assets to prevent their future confiscation from being frustrated. Disruption and preventive measures are central tenets of a risk-oriented approach. Despite a tendency towards prevention, joint actions did not legally oblige Member States to act and therefore the joint action was of limited legal significance in developing EU anti-money-laundering.

In light of the legal instrument's questionable effect, the joint action was replaced in June 2001 with a Framework Decision on Money Laundering.[70] Like its predecessor, the framework decision focused on ensuring compliance with the 1990 Council of Europe Convention by instructing Member States not to make or uphold reservations to its key articles.[71] However, while more effective than a joint action, a framework decision is still dependent on Member State transposition. The Commission has produced two evaluation reports to date. The first concludes that 'not all Member States have timely transmitted to the Commission all relevant texts of their implementing provisions'.[72] Compliance with the framework decision was judged to be variable. Article 1, which called for Member States not to make or uphold reservations in respect of certain aspects of the 1990 Council of Europe Convention, was complied with by 'a large majority [12] of Member States'. In comparison, compliance with Article 4, which called

---

[68] Joint Action of 3 December 1988 adopted by the Council on the basis of Article K.3 of the Treaty on European Union, on money laundering, the identification, tracing, freezing, seizing and confiscation of instrumentalities and the proceeds of crime OJ L333/1 (9 December 1998).

[69] Ibid, Preamble.

[70] Council Framework Decision of 26 June 2001 on money laundering, the identification, tracing, freezing, seizing and confiscation of instrumentalities and the proceeds of crime (2001/500/JHA).

[71] Mitsilegas and Gilmore, n 8 above, p 121.

[72] Commission (EC), 'Report from the Commission based on Article 6 of the Council Framework Decision of 26 June 2001 on money laundering, the identification, tracing, freezing, seizing and confiscation of instrumentalities and the proceeds of crime' COM (2004) 230 final, Brussels, 5 April 2004 (hereafter, First Evaluation Report) 20–21.

for mutual assistance in anti-money-laundering, was undetermined for want of evidence.[73] The second Commission report offered a slightly improved survey of implementation, although some Member States' information (notably, Germany) remained inadequate.[74] Of course, the Framework Decision is not the primary measure criminalising money laundering in the EU. As such, its transposition is not vital to implementation of EU anti-money-laundering by the Member States. Nonetheless, varying transposition across the EU does undermine the uniformity of the legal order. Following the adoption of the framework decision, the European legal landscape was cluttered. The Member States were already parties to the 1990 Council of Europe Convention and subject to the Anti-Money-Laundering Directive. The Framework Decision blurred the line between EU and Council of Europe action, and undermined the clarity of the law both within the EU legal order itself and for those subject to the broad anti-money-laundering regulatory regime.

In addition to improving compliance with the Council of Europe Convention, the EU was also concerned with the confusion relating to the different national authorities empowered by different Member States' implementing law. The First AML Directive required credit and financial institutions to report to national authorities, without specifying who these national authorities were to be. This discrepancy led to three types of national authority developing: independent/administrative, police/intelligence and judicial.[75] David Thomas, Director of the UK authority based at the Serious Organised Crime Agency, stated that these 'Financial Intelligence Units' (FIUs) are

> split between what is described as administrative, which may be based within a central bank, for example, or within law enforcement, or within a prosecutor's office, a judicial FIU, or be a hybrid of all of those things. Within the EU it is reasonably well split between administrative and law enforcement based. I think there are 11 administrative, 11 law enforcement, one judicial and two hybrids.[76]

The diversity of models across EU states gave rise to problems for co-operation as a judicial body in one Member State may not be able to co-operate with an administrative body in another.[77] It left those subject to the directive in a different legal situation in each Member State: because the type of institutions varied so too did relevant procedures. Thorny's 1996 survey identified a number of different reporting procedures in different EU Member States—which made matters unnecessarily complicated for financial service providers operating across

---

[73] Ibid.

[74] Commission (EC), 'Second Commission Report based on Article 6 of the Council Framework Decision of 26 June 2001 on money laundering, the identification, tracing, freezing, seizing and confiscation of instrumentalities and the proceeds of crime' COM (2006) 72 final, Brussels, 21 February 2006 (hereafter, Second Evaluation Report) 2.

[75] Mitsilegas and Gilmore, n 8 above, p 122.

[76] House of Lords European Union Committee *Money laundering and the financing of terrorism* (London, The Stationary Office, 2009) 22.

[77] Mitsilegas and Gilmore, n 8 above, p 122.

the EU.[78] In 2000, the Council sought to address these problems by adopting a Decision on Financial Intelligence Units. The Decision defined a financial intelligence unit as

> a central, national unit which, in order to combat money laundering, is responsible for receiving (and to the extent permitted, requesting), analysing and disseminating to the competent authorities, disclosures of financial information which concern suspected proceeds of crime or are required by national legislation or regulation.[79]

The definition stems from an agreement of the Egmont Group, an informal forum for co-operation between different FIUs.[80] It is a clear example of soft law becoming EU hard law. Article 3 of the decision sought to address the difference between different national authorities by stating that the performance of duties by FIUs 'shall not be affected by their internal status'. The decision further provided for the exchange of information between FIUs, subject to the principles of proportionality and data protection. The decision is still in force today, despite the fact that some of its provisions are duplicated by the third Anti-Money-Laundering Directive: another example of overlapping legal measures.

iii. Second Anti-Money-Laundering (AML) Directive

While these various measures were being adopted, the Commission had been pursuing a second directive. The Financial Action Task Force amended its 40 Recommendations in 1996 and in the Commission's view the amendments required transposition into EU law. The 1996 amendments broadened and strengthened the Financial Action Task Force anti-money-laundering regime. It was broadened by widening the range of anti-money-laundering predicate offences beyond narcotics trafficking to include (amongst others) terrorism. It was also broadened by bringing non-financial institutions and persons within the remit of the Recommendations. The regime was strengthened by amending the requirements in relation to customer identification, reporting of suspicious transactions and asset seizure and confiscation.[81] In light of these amendments, the Commission proposed a new Directive in 1999. However, some of the proposals proved contentious, with the European Parliament particularly concerned about the extension of the reporting requirements to lawyers in relation to their clients. At the time of the

---

[78] J-F Thorny, 'Processing Financial Information in Money Laundering Matters: The Financial Intelligence Units' (1996) *European Journal of Crime, Criminal Law and Criminal Justice* 257, 261–62.

[79] This definition is almost identical to that provided for by the 2005 Council of Europe Convention, with the exception that the latter (post-September 11) agreement also makes reference to 'potential financing of terrorism'. This discrepancy is remedied by Art 21(2) of the third Anti-Money Laundering Directive.

[80] Mitsilegas and Gilmore, n 8 above, p 122.

[81] See generally: WC Gilmore, *Dirty Money: The Evolution of International Measures to Counter Money Laundering and the Financing of Terrorism*, 3rd edn (Strasbourg, Council of Europe Publishing, 2004) 100–02.

September 11 attacks the Second AML Directive was at conciliation stage between the Council and Parliament and at risk of lapsing.[82]

Even prior to the onset of the 'war on terror', the EU had already positioned itself as a world leader in anti-money-laundering efforts. Actions by the Commission and Council evidence a strong desire to pursue a preventive regime, with criminalisation complemented by the more preventive measures of customer identification, suspicious transaction reporting, and asset freezing. However, despite the extension of anti-money-laundering predicate offences, the focus remained on proceeds of crime. As such, the anti-money-laundering regime was centred on identifying such proceeds, rather than a broader surveillance regime scrutinising all financial transactions. Furthermore, the ongoing opposition of the European Parliament appeared likely to prevent adoption of the second Directive, thus protecting legal privilege and (more broadly) the right to a fair trial. However, the events of 11 September 2001 provided the impetus to break the political deadlock.

B. EU Action since September 11

The EU responded quickly to the political pressure to adapt anti-money-laundering regulation for counter-terrorist purposes after the 11 September 2001 attacks. Section 3.5 of the Council Action Plan on Combating Terrorism is devoted to the issue. It requires the EU to continually appraise its implementation of the Financial Action Task Force recommendations and explicitly mentions four of the nine Special Recommendations, specifically those relating to codes of conduct for non-profit organisations, payer information accompanying transfer of funds, regulating alternative remittance systems and the regulation of cash couriers.[83] In addition to the Action Plan, a series of Strategy Terrorist Financing plans have been produced.[84] The strategy's objectives include transposing the nine Special Recommendations, and strengthening co-ordination with the Financial Action Task Force, International Monetary Fund, World Bank and UN Office on Drugs and Crime. However, the first legislative effect of the 11 September 2001 attacks was the adoption of the second Anti-Money-Laundering Directive.

i. Second Anti-Money-Laundering Directive (2001)

The second Anti-Money-Laundering Directive was adopted in December 2001.[85] It did not explicitly refer to terrorism, but amended the existing directive to

---

[82] Mitsilegas and Gilmore, n 8 above, p 123.

[83] European Council, 'Action Plan on Combating Terrorism', Brussels, 9 March 2007.

[84] European Council, Strategy Terrorist Financing (16089/04) and its updates (11325/05 and 14349/05).

[85] Directive 2001/97/EC of the European Parliament and of the Council of 4 December 2001 amending Council Directive 91/308/EEC on prevention of the use of the financial system for the purpose of money laundering hereafter, Second AML Directive).

take account of developments in money laundering practices. As with other developments in this regard, Financial Action Task Force standards played a significant part in the directive. The Second AML Directive broadened the scope of the regime, by extending the list of predicate offences, heightening the degree of scrutiny required when identifying customers, and requiring a wider range of actors to comply with the terms of the directive.[86] Following the September 11 attacks, the European Parliament and the Council quickly reached agreement on the extension of the regime to cover legal professionals. The political compromise reached resulted in the Member States being given the choice as to the extent to which reporting obligations would apply to lawyers. The developments precipitated by the 1996 Financial Action Task Force amendments and implemented by the Second AML Directive resulted in more intensive regulation of individuals' finances and a step towards greater preventive regulation of financial transactions. The most troubling development—the erosion of legal privilege—undermines the uniformity of the law as Member States were permitted but not obliged to provide for exemptions for the legal profession.

Perhaps unsurprisingly, the relevant provisions of the directive were the subject of litigation, first before the Belgian Arbitragehof, and then on preliminary reference before the ECJ. The case concerned the compatibility of the reporting obligations with the principles of legal privilege and the right to a fair trial. It turned on the question of whether legal privilege was based on Article 6 ECHR (fair trial) or Article 8 ECHR (privacy). In his Opinion, Advocate General Maduro found that the privilege rule was most accurately based on both Article 6 and Article 8 and that it derives its rational basis from the need for trust between the client and the legal professional.[87] He found that the national implementing law did not violate these articles as long as they took account of recital 17 of the Preamble to the directive.[88] Thus, the Advocate General harnessed the due process protections in the Preamble to ameliorate the potentially severe encroachment into legal privilege that the operative part of the text might allow.

The Court's judgment took a narrower approach. Based on the limited question referred from the national court, the ECJ held that it was not required to consider

---

[86]   Mitsilegas and Gilmore, n 8 above, p 124.

[87]   Opinion of Advocate General Maduro in C-305/05 *Ordre de barreaux francophones et germano-phone, Ordre francais des avocats du barreau de Bruxelles, Ordre dex barreaux flamands, Ordre néerlandais des avocats du barreau de Bruxelles v Conseil des Ministres* [2007] ECR I-5305, para 61.

[88]   Recital 17 provides:
However, where independent members of professions providing legal advice which are legally recognised and controlled, such as lawyers, are ascertaining the legal position of a client or representing a client in legal proceedings, it would not be appropriate under the Directive to put these legal professionals in respect of these activities under an obligation to report suspicions of money laundering. There must be exemptions from any obligation to report information obtained either before, during or after judicial proceedings, or in the course of ascertaining the legal position for a client. Thus, legal advice remains subject to the obligation of professional secrecy unless the legal counsellor is taking part in money laundering activities, the legal advice is provided for money laundering purposes, or the lawyer knows that the client is seeking legal advice for money laundering purposes.

Article 8 ECHR in relation to the directive. Furthermore, it held that the reporting obligation, insofar as it applied to what might be referred to as 'non contentious business', did not engage the right to a fair trial as protected by Article 6 ECHR. As such, there was no breach of the provision.[89] The Court's limited approach is logically unsustainable. If trust between client and counsel is the basis of the privilege, then it is unreasonable to expect lawyers to be under an obligation to monitor their clients until a contentious matter begins. Such a practice would entirely destroy trust in the professional relationship.

ii. Third Anti-Money-Laundering Directive (2005)

Action in anti-money-laundering and counter-terrorist finance continues to be driven by political pressure to react to acts of terrorism. In the wake of the 2004 bombings in Madrid, a joint EU–US Declaration on Combating Terrorism was agreed and adopted at Dromoland Castle. The declaration made explicit and detailed reference to counter-terrorist finance, highlighting both UN and Financial Action Task Force obligations. The EU and US committed to 'actively support the work of the Financial Action Task Force on all issues regarding the financing of terrorism'.[90] They would ensure that their domestic legal systems are 'fully adapted' to both the special recommendations and the interpretive notes. The declaration also noted the need to prevent the misuse of alternative remittance systems, wire transfers, cash couriers, and the non-profit sector. Later in 2004, and following the updating of the Financial Action Task Force Recommendations, the European Commission tabled a proposal for a new directive. The Third Anti-Money-Laundering (AML) Directive was adopted on 26 October 2005.[91] The Third AML Directive repealed the previous two and so recast all first pillar anti-money-laundering law. The directive evidences its intentions in the sensationalist first recital to the Preamble:

> Massive flows of dirty money can damage the stability and reputation of the financial sector and threaten the single market, and terrorism shakes the very foundations of our society. In addition to the criminal law approach, a preventive effort via the financial system can produce results.

The recital is noteworthy in its assertion of the effectiveness of anti-money-laundering and counter-terrorist finance (despite evidence to the contrary).[92] The directive is the lengthiest of the anti-money-laundering measures, and the focus

---

[89] C-305/05 *Ordre de barreaux francophones et germanophone, Ordre francais des avocats du barreau de Bruxelles, Ordre dex barreaux flamands, Ordre néerlandais des avocats du barreau de Bruxelles v Conseil des Ministres* [2007] ECR I-5305, para 33.

[90] EU-US Declaration on Combating Terrorism, Dromoland Castle, June 26 2004.

[91] Directive 2005/60/EC of the European Parliament and of the Council of 26 October 2005 on the prevention of the use of the financial system for the purpose of money laundering and terrorist financing (hereafter, Third AML Directive).

[92] J McCulloch and B Carlton, 'Preempting Justice: Suppression of Financing of Terrorism and the "War on Terror"' (2005–2006) 17 *Current Issues in Criminal Justice* 397, 405.

here is on the four chapters that most clearly demonstrate the post-September 11 shift: Chapter I (Scope of the Directive); Chapter II (Customer Due Diligence); Chapter III (Reporting Obligations); and Chapter V (Enforcement).

a. Scope of the Directive

Chapter I sets out the scope of the directive and includes some key definitions. Article 1(1) declares that 'Member States shall ensure that money laundering and terrorist financing are prohibited'. The Article 1(2) definition of money laundering is almost identical to the 2005 Council of Europe Convention. Money laundering is the intentional and knowing conversion, transfer, concealment, disguise, acquisition, possession or use of property where it is derived from criminal activity. Such activity is 'any kind of criminal involvement in the commission of a serious crime'. 'Serious crime' is in turn defined very broadly, including any crime punishable by a custodial sentence with a maximum of more than one year. A number of inchoate offences are also included within the definition, including participation in and association with, attempting, aiding, abetting, facilitating and counselling the principal offences. The definition of money laundering is broad and consistent with developments in global anti-money-laundering. On the other hand, the definition of 'terrorist financing' is, as discussed above, unique. It is the provision or collection of funds (both defined broadly) with the intention or in the knowledge that they are to be used to carry out an offence under Articles 1–4 FDCT. In this regard, there is a distinction between the definition of terrorist financing under Council of Europe and UN law (both based on the Terrorist Financing Convention) and under EU law (based on the Framework Decision on Combating Terrorism). EU Member States have to criminalise all activity covered by both definitions to fully comply with their obligations. Adding to the confusion, Article 5 of the directive permits Member States to adopt or retain national provisions that are stricter than the directive requires. This provision appears to be contrary to the purpose of the directive: to harmonise the regulation of anti-money-laundering and counter-terrorist finance in the EU. On the other hand, some Member States have even been slow to adopt the provisions of the directive: the Commission has taken action against six Member States for failure to transpose the measure.[93] The result is a regulatory regime that is broad but far from uniform.

b. Customer Due Diligence

One of the key traits of post-September 11 anti-money-laundering and counter-terrorist finance is financial surveillance. In keeping with previous anti-money-laundering measures, Chapter II requires Member States to ensure that those

---

[93] House of Lords European Union Committee, n 76 above, p 16. The six Member States are Belgium, France, Ireland, Poland, Spain and Sweden.

institutions subject to the directive adopt appropriate customer due diligence processes. Such processes are to be followed, inter alia, 'when establishing a business relationship' or 'when there is a suspicion of money laundering or terrorist financing'.[94] Due diligence entails identifying the customer and verifying their identity; identifying the beneficial owner of the property; obtaining information regarding the purpose of the business relationship; and

> ongoing monitoring of the business relationship including scrutiny of transactions undertaken throughout the course of that relationship to ensure that the transactions being conducted are consistent with the institution's or person's knowledge of the customer, the business and risk profile, including, where necessary, the source of funds and ensuring that the documents, data or information held are kept up-to-date.[95]

Customer due diligence requires systematic surveillance of the financial transactions of anyone that interacts with those subject to the directive. The onerous burden this imposes and the invasiveness for customers is to be ameliorated by three mitigating factors. First, a number of directive provisions make reference to a 'risk-sensitive' approach.[96] As a result, low-risk individuals may be subject to more relaxed due diligence. Second, the directive explicitly provides for 'simplified due diligence' in certain cases.[97] Third, the directive provides for derogation from the due diligence requirements in certain limited circumstances.[98] However, in reality, these mitigating factors do little to ease the regulatory burden or relax the surveillance regime. As with a number of technical areas of the directive, the details of simplified due diligence and what constitutes low-risk is left to the Commission's determination.[99] The Commission, for its part, has determined that simplified due diligence 'should be restricted to a limited number of cases'.[100] Furthermore, the directive also provides for 'enhanced due diligence' for 'politically exposed persons', shell banks, correspondent banking, and other specified scenarios. Enhanced due diligence may result in more stringent identity checks and verifications and restrictions on financial transactions.[101] Where an institution cannot comply with the due diligence requirements, it must 'consider' reporting the customer to the relevant FIU.[102] No further guidance is given as to what factors should influence the 'consideration'. While due diligence requirements

---

[94] Art 7 Third AML Directive.
[95] Art 8 Third AML Directive.
[96] Art 8(2) Third AML Directive.
[97] Arts 11–12 Third AML Directive.
[98] Arts 6, 9, 23 Third AML Directive.
[99] Art 40 Third AML Directive.
[100] Recital 6 to the Preamble of Commission Directive 2006/70/EC of 1 August 2006 laying down implementing measures for Directive 2005/60/EC of the European Parliament and of the Council as regards the definition of 'politically exposed person' and the technical criteria for simplified customer due diligence procedures and for exemption on grounds of a financial activity conducted on an occasional or very limited basis.
[101] Art 13 Third AML Directive.
[102] In this respect, Member States are 'not obliged' to apply the reporting requirement to legal and other professionals acting to ascertain the legal position of their client.

may sometimes be carried out by third parties, responsibility remains with the institution subject to the directive.[103] The EU's legislative approach has therefore been to strictly limit the use of low-risk and simplified due diligence. Ordinary due diligence is established as the standard used in the vast majority of cases, with enhanced due diligence in certain situations. Such an approach appears blatantly disproportionate, as the majority of the general public are innocent of anti-money-laundering and counter-terrorist finance offences but are subject to monitoring in the hope of catching suspect transactions by a few individuals. However, the regime is indicative of a pre-emptive approach: using suspicion to capture a wide range of targets and then relying on discretion exercised by private financial institutions, FIUs and law enforcement authorities to discern between the guilty and the innocent.

c. Reporting Obligations

Customer due diligence is one half of the financial surveillance regime. The reporting obligations in Chapter III of the directive are the other. Article 21 obliges the Member States to establish FIUs. Such a body is defined as 'a central national unit', which is the focal point for information concerning 'potential money laundering [or] potential terrorist financing'. This definition is identical to that in the 2000 decision on FIUs, with the exception that the directive extends the remit of the FIUs to cover counter-terrorist finance.[104] The institutions are to have access to the 'financial, administrative and law enforcement information' necessary to perform their role. Article 20 sets out a sweeping reporting obligation on those covered by the directive. They must

> pay special attention to any activity which they regard as particularly likely, by its nature, to be related to money laundering or terrorist financing and in particular complex or unusually large transactions and *all unusual patterns of transactions which have no apparent economic or visible lawful purpose* (emphasis added).

This broad monitoring obligation is bizarrely drafted. It would appear, at the very least, to require financial institutions to pay particular attention to ascertain if any 'unusual' transactions have an 'apparent economic or visible lawful purpose'. It is not clear what such a test entails. It is difficult to define 'economic purpose' in any way other than as a tautology and requiring a 'visible lawful purpose' is tantamount to a presumption of guilt. Institutions must inform the relevant FIU when they 'know, suspect or [have] reasonable grounds to suspect' that money laundering or terrorist financing is or has been committed or attempted.[105] They must also refrain from carrying out suspicious transactions, unless to do so would frustrate the anti-money-laundering and counter-terrorist finance goals of the

---

[103] Art 14 Third AML Directive.
[104] Art 21 Third AML Directive.
[105] Art 20 Third AML Directive.

directive.[106] Institutions must not inform the customer that they are the subject of suspicion or of an investigation.[107] On the other hand, individuals in such institutions are to be protected from liability for their report to the FIU, and from being exposed to 'threats or hostile action'.[108] Thus this chapter of the Third AML Directive requires action based on suspicion. As one witness told the UK House of Lords EU Committee: 'You smell a rat and you report it'.[109] Transactions must be clearly lawful or they will be reported to a regulator who will determine whether further action should be taken. The result is the empowering of administrators and the undermining of legal certainty for individuals, whose finances must not just be lawful but also appear to be lawful.

d. Enforcement Measures

Chapter V is the final section of particular interest and relates to enforcement measures. The manner in which the directive requires anti-money-laundering rules to be enforced impacts upon the actual enforcement of EU law in this field. Article 34(1) imposes yet another broad obligation on those covered by the directive to adopt 'adequate and appropriate policies' to 'forestall and prevent operations related to money laundering or terrorist financing'. This essentially imposes an obligation on private actors to pre-emptively police financial transactions. Member States must ensure there is appropriate supervision of such institutions.[110] They must also ensure that infringements are subject to criminal penalties and/or administrative sanctions, both of which should be 'effective, proportionate and dissuasive'.[111] The European Commission is to facilitate information exchange between FIUs.[112] While private actors regulate financial transactions, Member States must use their legal systems to ensure that those actors do not shirk their duties. Thus, the directive places strong emphasis on the enforcement of the EU regulatory regime.

Mitsilegas and Gilmore describe the Third AML Directive as taking a two-pronged approach: criminalisation and prevention.[113] Broadening criminal offences and increasing use of regulatory intervention combine to blur the distinction between what is lawful and what is treated as unlawful. Furthermore, the use of suspicion and the monitoring of licit as well as illicit funding (required once anti-money-laundering was merged with counter-terrorist finance) marks the evolution from a preventive approach to a pre-emptive one.

---

[106] Art 24 Third AML Directive.
[107] Art 28 Third AML Directive.
[108] Arts 26–27 Third AML Directive.
[109] House of Lords European Union Committee, n 76 above, p 32.
[110] Arts 36–37 Third AML Directive.
[111] Art 39 Third AML Directive.
[112] Art 38 Third AML Directive.
[113] Mitsilegas and Gilmore, n 8 above, p 119.

III. FINANCIAL REGULATION, PRE-EMPTION AND THE RULE OF LAW

The increased use of financial regulation for the purpose of crime prevention
and counter-terrorism has had a significant impact on the EU rule of law. It is
possible to understand EU anti-money-laundering and counter-terrorist finance
as contributing to EU criminal law, to co-operation in criminal justice and crime
prevention, and to pre-emptive counter-terrorism.

A. Financial Regulation and Criminal Law

The anti-money-laundering and counter-terrorist finance legislation and the
directives in particular, are effectively, if not always explicitly criminal law. As such
there is likely to be little difficulty in triggering the higher standard of protection
that applies in criminal justice. However, viewing the anti-money-laundering
and counter-terrorist finance legislation as ordinary criminal law gives rise to a
number of related concerns. First, in terms of the constitutive aspect of the rule
of law, the adoption of the legislation on dubious legal bases ignores the principle
of conferred competences central to EU law. Second, in relation to safeguarding
aspect of the rule of law, the breadth of certain measures gives rise to potential
violations of the principle of legality. Third, certain provisions offend the presumption of innocence by transferring culpability for terrorist offences from
those who commit offences to those who finance (or who may finance) offences.
Fourth, recent developments erode the protection of legal privilege enshrined in
the right to a fair trial.

In 1991, the Council was concerned that the (then) European Economic
Communities did not possess the legal competence to adopt the First AML
Directive. The directive's legal basis showed these concerns were well-founded.
The first directive relied on Articles 57(2) and 100a EEC.[114] This basis is clearly
dubious: the articles provide for the harmonisation of laws pertaining to the internal market and do not appear to anticipate their use for criminal law. To side-step
the problem, the Council used a legislative formula requiring that money laundering 'shall be prohibited'. The use of 'shall be prohibited' instead of 'shall be an
offence' had little effect on Member State implementation as criminal sanctions
have invariably followed.[115] Today, the directives can be viewed as exercising the
criminal law competence established by the *Environmental Crimes* and *Ship Source
Pollution* cases and now enshrined in Article 83(2) TFEU.[116] First, it could be
argued that the laws pursue the common market policies of Article 3(b) and (h) EC.

---

[114] These articles subsequently became Arts 47(2) and 95 EC (Treaty Establishing the European
Community) and are now Art 53 and 114 TFEU.
[115] Mitsilegas and Gilmore, n 8 above, p 136.
[116] C-176/03 *Commission v Council* [2005] ECR I-7879 (*Environmental Crimes*); C-440/05
Commission v Council [2007] ECR I-9097 (*Ship Source Pollution*).

Second, as a directive requiring implementation, Member States are afforded scope to tailor the penalties to suit national legal orders. Thus, while it did not do so in that case, if the ECJ follows the approach of Advocate General Mazak in *Ship Source Pollution*, there is likely to be little difficulty in finding the directive correctly based. Nonetheless, even if there is now a competence that may justify the adoption of the directives, it does not explain their use to facilitate co-operation between national authorities, a matter which would properly be left to the former third pillar. Implementation of the most recent directive has not been without its problems. The European Commission obtained judgments from the ECJ following the failure of several Member States—such as France, Belgium, Ireland, Spain and Sweden—to implement the directive.[117] Of course this procedure, which affords the ECJ the opportunity to uphold the constitutive aspect of the rule of law, was not available for framework decisions.

The second rule of law problem concerns the principle of legality and the lack of legal certainty in this field. Taking the Third AML Directive as the principal measure in the anti-money-laundering and counter-terrorist finance apparatus, three distinct points may be made, each potentially violating the principle of legality. First, the definition of terrorist financing makes reference to Articles 1–4 FDCT. While such cross-referencing should increase the coherence of EU counter-terrorism law, it taints the financing offences with the vagueness of the Framework Decision on Combating Terrorism. If the terrorist offences are broader than permitted by the principle of legality, then the financing offences are also in breach of that provision. Second, the restriction on legal privilege is likely to affect the accessibility of the law as experienced by the individual. It is a staple of ECHR case law that a legislative provision will not be found in violation of the qualitative requirements simply because the individual is required to consult a lawyer to determine their precise meaning.[118] However, if the individual is deterred from consulting a lawyer for fear of having their personal finances reported to the relevant authority, the law may not be accessible to them for the purposes of the principle of legality. As such, the erosion of legal privilege has a consequential effect on the accessibility of the law. Third, while not a problem directly attributable to EU law itself, the surfeit of regulatory measures—in international, EU and domestic law, as well as soft law standards—makes the applicable legal rules almost impossible to ascertain. Though the EU measures may not

---

[117] Case C-170/09 *European Commission v French Republic* Judgment of the Court (Fifth Chamber) of 25 February 2010; Case C-6/09 *Commission of the European Communities v Kingdom of Belgium* Judgment of the Court (Fifth Chamber) of 6 October 2009; C-504/08 *Commission of the European Communities v Kingdom of Spain* Judgment of the Court (Fifth Chamber) of 24 September 2009; Case C-549/08 *Commission of the European Communities v Ireland* Judgment of the Court (Sixth Chamber) of 1 October 2009; Case C-546/08 *Commission of the European Communities v Kingdom of Sweden* Judgment of the Court (Seventh Chamber) of 11 June 2009; Case C-532/08 *Commission of the European Communities v Ireland* Judgment of the Court (Sixth Chamber) of 19 May 2009.

[118] *Sunday Times v UK* (1979–80) 2 EHRR 245, para 49.

be in breach of the principle of legality on this point, the law as experienced by the citizen undoubtedly operates contrary to the spirit of those rules.

The third rule of law problem relates to the right to a fair trial. Specifically, it concerns Article 6(2) ECHR on the presumption of innocence. Insofar as it relates to the financing of terrorism, the anti-money-laundering and counter-terrorist finance legislation provides for inchoate offences. Anti-money-laundering began as a means of retrieving the proceeds of crimes actually committed. However, anti-money-laundering and counter-terrorist finance seeks to deprive (prospective) criminals of the finances necessary to carry out potential future crimes. The extent to which these offences are removed from the actual act of terrorism should not be underestimated. The transfer of culpability within a 'terrorist group' (or from someone committing a 'terrorist offence' to those who are responsible for inchoate acts) challenges the presumption of innocence. The further transference of culpability from such persons to individuals who financially support them makes the link between the terrorist act and the culpability of the suspected financier for that act very tenuous indeed. In the US, this has resulted in the criminalisation of citizens who donate to bona fide charities that may 'free up' assets for organisations designated as 'terrorist'.[119] In *Holder v Humanitarian Law Project* the US Supreme Court had to consider a pre-enforcement challenge to the Antiterrorism and Effective Death Penalty Act 1996 and sought a declaration that the legislation was unconstitutionally vague and a violation of their First Amendment rights. The case was brought by several individuals and organisations that sought to provide training and support to the Kurdish Worker's Party and the Liberation Tigers of Tamil Eelam to assist those groups to pursue their political goals through peaceful means. However, both groups had been designated as 'terrorist' by the US Secretary of State. As such, the applicants feared that any assistance they might provide would constitute material support to terrorism under US law. The Supreme Court employed a wide definition of 'material support' and denied the petition. The judgment has been harshly criticised for its effect on political freedom in the US.[120] It is difficult to envisage a similar decision being upheld in the ECtHR.

Finally, and perhaps most controversially, there is the subjection of legal professionals to identification and notification requirements since the adoption of the Second AML Directive. As discussed above, these requirements potentially infringe legal privilege principles that are protected by European law. The Convention system protects legal privilege in the context of two ECHR provisions: the right to a fair trial (Article 6) and the right to respect for private life (Article 8).[121] In EU law, 'professional secrecy' is protected by Article 41 of the EU Charter of Fundamental

---

[119] See D Cole and J Lobel, *Less Safe, Less Free: Why America is Losing the War on Terror* (New York, The New Press, 2007) 49–50.

[120] 'What Counts As Abetting Terrorists', *New York Times* (21 June 2010).

[121] See, eg, *Niemietz v Germany* Judgment 16 December 1992 (Art 6 ECHR); *Foxley v United Kingdom* Judgment 20 June 2000 (Art 8 ECHR).

Rights.[122] In *AM & S*, the ECJ noted that 'any person must be able, without constraint, to consult a lawyer whose profession entails the giving of independent legal advice to all those in need of it'.[123] It is difficult to read the ECJ judgment in the Belgian legal privilege case as anything other than a repudiation of that statement. Advocate General Maduro's approach was to harness the Preamble to ensure that the operative text did not undermine legal privilege. A contrary, and worrying, example is provided by the Opinion of Advocate General Kokott in *Akzo Nobel*. In that case the ECJ had to consider whether privilege was extended to in-house legal counsel. The Advocate General noted that while the Preamble of the Third AML Directive suggested that privilege should be extended such an extension would be contrary to FATF recommendations which 'are to be relied on for the purposes of interpreting that directive'. She concluded that the directive 'cannot be construed as providing a clear signal in favour' of extending privilege to in-house counsel. The interpretative power afforded to the FATF recommendations by the Advocate General evidences the corrosive effect that this soft law can have in the EU legal order.[124] While the ECJ's opinion in the earlier case stricto sensu protects privilege in 'non-contentious' business, it effectively leaves individuals in a situation where they cannot assume that legal services will be provided confidentially. The ECJ's decision therefore appears to run contrary to the spirit of the principle of legal privilege. As any erosion of legal privilege has some impact on the certainty of the law and also on the right to a fair trial, it is to be hoped that future litigation provides the ECJ with the opportunity to clarify its position.

In conclusion, the anti-money-laundering and counter-terrorist finance legislation can only be viewed as ordinary criminal law if it is permitted to seriously erode the rule of law values that underpin the EU legal system. Its very adoption challenged the principle of conferred competences and opened the Pandora's Box of first pillar criminal law. However, it must be acknowledged that these problems with the constitutive role of the rule of law predate the 11 September 2001 attacks. Perhaps more significantly, the regime breaches the principles protected by the rule of law's safeguarding aspect, breaches that can clearly be attributed to post-September 11 developments.

B. Prevention and Co-operation

In addition to setting out certain criminal offences, the anti-money-laundering and counter-terrorist finance legislation also acts as the basis for preventive

---

[122] Art 41 of the EU Charter on Fundamental Rights refers to 'the legitimate interests of confidentiality and of professional and business secrecy'.

[123] *AM & S* (1982) ECR 1575 [19].

[124] Case C-550/07 P *Akzo Nobel Chemicals Ltd and Akcros Chemicals Ltd v European Commission* Opinion of Advocate General Kokott delivered on 29 April 2010, para 112. The Court of Justice did not did not refer to the directive in its judgment but followed the Advocate General's Opinion on the outcome of the case. Judgment of the Court (Grand Chamber) of 14 September 2010.

interventions against suspicious financial transactions and to facilitate co-operation between FIUs and other institutions subject to the legislation. Preventive interventions are considered first before co-operation is analysed.

Three distinct interventions are required by the anti-money-laundering and counter-terrorist finance regime: first, the broad due diligence and monitoring requirements that have developed in the successive directives; second, the obligation on a wide range of persons and institutions to report suspicious transactions; third, the requirement that persons and institutions refrain from carrying out such transactions. The first of these interventions is clearly pre-emptive, as it operates based on generalised suspicion of all financial transactions, both illicit and licit. It is this change that marks the transition from a focus on ordinary crime prevention to one that is pre-emptive. The obligations to report suspicious transactions, and to refrain from carrying out such transactions, may raise problems for the EU rule of law. The idea that an individual's financial transactions would be reported to a regulatory body and frozen based on the suspicion of a private actor is problematic. The anti-money-laundering and counter-terrorist finance legislation is vague on what constitutes an acceptable basis for that suspicion. The extent to which being reported to an FIU, or having one's transaction frozen for being suspicious has a punitive effect is likely to depend on the legal consequences of a report within the various Member States. Furthermore, the anti-money-laundering and counter-terrorist finance regime offers little accountability if the suspicion is proven false. It is impossible to assess the number of reports that prove unfounded. Even if individuals knew they had been reported, it is highly unlikely that they would be able to access the report due to law enforcement and national security exemptions from data protection principles.[125] The absence of any role for the reported person denies them the opportunity to interact with the system to ensure that any intervention complies with accepted due process.

The national authorities to whom these reports are made are FIUs. These bodies may be administrative, police or judicial in nature. The various measures on FIUs present two challenges to the rule of law's constitutive aspect. First, the provision for co-operation between FIUs in the Third AML Directive is legislation for the co-operation of criminal justice agencies and therefore would be most appropriately based in the third pillar.[126] Second, while the third directive makes provision for FIUs, the existing third pillar law remains on the statute books. The persistence of multiple legal instruments ostensibly regulating the same authorities benefits neither the authorities (who cannot know the source and so the extent of their power) nor those regulated (who will find it difficult to discern their duties and the powers of the authority over them). Furthermore, the differing legal status

---

[125] House of Lords European Union Committee, n 76 above, pp 48–50.

[126] Of course, a third pillar basis, though more appropriate for the community of law, may contribute to the undermining of principles of protection due to the limitations on the ECJ's jurisdiction outside of the first pillar. This rule of law conundrum is returned to in ch 6 below in relation to the data surveillance legislation.

of the FIUs in each Member State continues to make co-operation difficult. As a result of these flaws, it is possible to conclude that the anti-money-laundering and counter-terrorist finance legislation is as poor a basis for preventive intervention and co-operation as it is for ordinary criminal law. It once again demonstrates a disregard for the principles that are the foundation of the legal order and the principles of protection that aim to safeguard the individual against the excesses of the state.

Since the adoption of the First AML Directive in 1991, the emphasis of the EU's action in this field has changed from denying criminals the enjoyment of the proceeds of crime, to monitoring all financial transactions based on generalised suspicion.[127] Pre-emptive counter-terrorism has resulted in three related developments: the dominance of executives, bureaucrats and private administrators over the system of regulation; the change from targeted action after crime to generalised surveillance based on suspicion and a process of 'Othering' through financial exclusion.

Executive actors tend to dominate pre-emptive counter-terrorism action. Both international and European anti-money-laundering and counter-terrorist finance action has borne witness to the use of executive instruments to bolster the effectiveness of other norms. Following the September 11 attacks, a UN Security Council Chapter VII resolution (the strongest legal measure the UN can adopt) was used to 'call upon' all states to sign and ratify the Terrorist Financing Convention. In Europe, the Framework Decision on Money Laundering required Member States not to enter reservations in the 1990 Council of Europe Convention. Notably, whereas the former attempt at executive-driven action followed the September 11 attacks, the latter attempt predates those attacks. However, both demonstrate the same tendency: coercing compliance notwithstanding states' sovereign right to decide whether or not to ratify the relevant treaties.

The focus on ensuring the effectiveness of the global anti-money-laundering and counter-terrorist finance regime goes further, as evidenced by the 'hardening' of soft law into binding legal norms. Such processes have occurred at both international and EU level. EU soft law was used when the Joint Action on Money Laundering was adopted in 1998.[128] It was 'hardened' into the Framework Decision on Money Laundering the Amsterdam Treaty (and of course, the 'hardened' framework decision required compliance with the Council of Europe Conventions). While soft law is subject to the acquiescence of the EU legislature before it becomes binding 'hard law', such is the strength of the Financial Action Task Force that the hardening of its recommendations appears inevitable. The treatment of the legal privilege exemption demonstrates the point. Having provided an exemption that allowed legal professionals to warn clients about the reporting of suspicion transactions, the Commission's proposal for the third

---

[127] P Shaughnessy, 'The New EU Money-Laundering Directive: Lawyers as Gate-Keepers and Whistle-Blowers' (2002–2003) 34 *Law and Policy in International Business* 25, 26.

[128] Joint actions are described as 'soft law' in E Baker and C Harding, 'From Past Imperfect to Future Perfect? A Longitudinal Study of the Third Pillar' (2009) 34 *European Law Review* 25, 43.

Anti-Money-Laundering Directive sought to repeal of this exemption. The reason offered was the incompatibility of the exemption with the revised Financial Action Task Force recommendations.[129] Therefore, an EU law which had been drafted to respect individual rights was amended to comply with Task Force soft law.

The Framework Decision on Combating Terrorism was described as 'executive legislation' because the instrument was adopted using the third pillar criminal law competence. As the exercise of that competence largely sidelines the European Parliament, the measures may have better preserved the rule of law if the Parliament was involved through co-decision rather than consultation. In the present context, it is noteworthy that it was the European Parliament that opposed the infringement of legal privilege (until September 11 2001 provided the political pressure to force agreement). The ongoing role of the European Commission in updating certain definitions, and determining what constitutes high and low risk for the purpose of due diligence is a further example of the empowerment of executives. Since 2008, the procedure for adopting such standards has been subject to the scrutiny of the European Parliament.[130] It remains to be seen how the Parliament will use its powers, and whether it will act as a check on the Commission's uncritical implementation of Financial Action Task Force standards. Anti-money-laundering and counter-terrorist finance also falls within the competence of both Europol and Eurojust—two bodies whose own legal authority has been the subject of critique.[131]

A further aspect of anti-money-laundering and counter-terrorist finance is the use of private actors to enforce both hard and soft law. In pursuing its anti-money-laundering and counter-terrorist finance goals, the EU requires 'a broad group of professional service providers to act as de facto deputies'.[132] As a result 'many of the control functions have been de facto outsourced to the private sector without proper guidance and accountability'.[133] The need to co-ordinate across the public and private sectors has itself posed problems for the efficacy of EU action in this field.[134] There is also a lack of accountability of private actors who are subject to the anti-money-laundering and counter-terrorist finance provisions. A private

---

[129]   Commission (EC), 'Proposal for a Directive of the European Parliament and of the Council on the prevention of the use of the financial system for the purpose of money laundering, including terrorist financing' COM (2004) 448 final, Brussels, 30 June 2004, p 6.

[130]   Directive 2008/20/EC of the European Parliament and of the Council of 11 March 2008 amending Directive 2005/60/EC on the prevention of the use of the financial system for the purpose of money laundering and terrorist financing, as regards the implementing powers conferred on the Commission.

[131]   Council Decision of 6 April 2009 establishing the European Police Office (Europol) (2009/371/ JHA); Council Decision 2009/426/JHA of 16 December 2008 on the strengthening of Eurojust and amending Decision 2002/187/JHA setting up Eurojust with a view to reinforcing the fight against serious crime.

[132]   Shaughnessy, n 127 above, p 26.

[133]   N Passas, 'Setting Global CFT Standards: A Critique and Suggestions' (2006) 9 *Journal of Money Laundering Control* 281.

[134]   O Bures, 'EU's Fight against Terrorist Finances: Internal Shortcomings and Unsuitable External Models' (2010) 22 *Terrorism and Political Violence* 418, 425.

actor who has 'reasonable grounds for suspecting' that a financial transaction is related to money laundering or terrorist financing must refrain from carrying out the transaction and report the matter to the relevant authority. To ensure that private actors operate unencumbered by concerns of personal or corporate liability for any loss incurred by the target of their actions, anti-money-laundering and counter-terrorist finance rules protect 'whistle blowers' from liability for disclosure. This liability shield is quite broadly drafted. While protecting bona fide employees, the shield would also appear to prevent accountability for decisions which can have a profound effect on the lives of those reported. The European Data Protection Supervisor has described the imposition of criminal justice functions on private actors as 'one of the most important tendencies of the recent years' and has highlighted both the TFTP Agreement and the Third AML Directive as examples. They are described as 'derogations from the purpose limitation principle' and are 'often very privacy-intrusive'. Such requirements should only be imposed where there is 'very strong evidence' of their necessity and individual rights should be 'fully safeguarded'.[135] Despite the mandatory language used it is clear that financial dataveillance is not limited to action 'based on suspicions on specific persons' but rather is a system of generalised surveillance.

C. Suspicion, Surveillance and Financial Exclusion

The merging of anti-money-laundering and counter-terrorist finance has also resulted in a proliferation of the logic of suspicion. Indeed, insofar as it requires action to be taken against 'suspicious' transactions, the EU anti-money-laundering regime operates on the basis of a presumption of guilt. As counter-terrorist finance is concerned with the use of illicit and licit money to fund crime, due diligence and monitoring of financial transactions can no longer be limited to identifying and tracing funds that are the proceeds of crime. Rather, it must carry out surveillance of all financial transactions to determine if they might be used for terrorist purposes. Thus, the evolution of anti-money-laundering into anti-money-laundering and counter-terrorist finance has resulted in broader surveillance powers for public and private financial regulators alike. This fits a trend identified as 'dataveillance', 'the proactive surveillance of what effectively become suspect populations, using new technologies to identify "risky groups"'.[136] This trend will be returned to in Chapter Six, which addresses the Passenger Name Record Agreements and the Data Retention Directive. In the present context dataveillance is relevant in terms of the widespread surveillance of financial transactions of ordinary customers

---

[135] Opinion of the European Data Protection Supervisor on the Communication from the Commission to the European Parliament and the Council on an area of freedom, security and justice serving the citizen C 276/8 (17 November 2009), paras 63–65.

[136] M Levi and D Wall, 'Technologies, Security and Privacy in the post 9/11 European Information Society' (2004) 31 *Journal of Law and Society* 194, 200.

and economic undertakings. The approach taken by EU anti-money-laundering and counter-terrorist finance is remarkably similar to the approach taken by the Framework Decision on Combating Terrorism to extreme political action. The framework decision uses a broad definition of terrorism and terrorist offences to potentially criminalise a wide range of action and relies on prosecutorial discretion to prevent fundamental rights from being infringed. The EU anti-money-laundering and counter-terrorist finance directives require due diligence and ongoing monitoring of customers' financial transactions and rely on a collection of private and public authorities to prevent action from being taken against those that are 'innocent'.

Anti-money-laundering and counter-terrorist finance can have a particularly detrimental effect on those who rely on informal or alternative remittance systems such as *hawala*.[137] These systems allow for the secure transfer of funds around the world and cater in particular for diaspora communities sending monies to Asia, Africa and the Middle East. Such systems suffer from difficulties in complying with customer due diligence and suspicious transaction reporting requirements. Furthermore, some—such as Al-Barakaat—have been specifically targeted by the UN sanctions system aimed at freezing the funds of the Taleban, Al-Qaeda and Osama bin Laden and those associated with them.[138] These actions have disproportionate effects on those communities on political margins. The targeting of such systems is notwithstanding the National Commission on Terrorist Attacks Upon the United States' conclusions that the funds that supported the September 11 attacks were not transferred using the *hawala* system. Indeed, there is little evidence that *hawala* is used more than ordinary wire transfer systems to fund political violence.[139] Thus, actions since 11 September 2001 to target such systems amount to unjustifiable financial exclusion of already vulnerable groups.

IV. CONCLUSION: CONTROL THROUGH A POLICY MILIEU

EU counter-terrorism action empowers executive, administrative and private actors to operate in an invasive manner while evading or eroding the rule of law principles that would ordinarily protect individuals. Perhaps most worrying is the apparent consensus that the infringement of rights has not necessarily resulted in any increase in security.[140] Prior to the September 11 attacks, the US government

---

[137] McCulloch and Carlton, n 92 above, p 403.

[138] This is despite the fact that US law enforcement agencies have not proven any link between al-Qaeda and al-Barakaat. National Commission on Terrorist Attacks Upon the United States, n 1 above, p 10.

[139] J McCulloch and S Pickering 'Suppressing the Financing of Terrorism: Proliferating State Crime, Eroding Censure and Extending Neo-Colonialism' (2005) 45 *British Journal of Criminology* 470, 479.

[140] McCulloch and Carlton, n 92 above, p 404.

was itself questioning the cost effectiveness of anti-money-laundering efforts.[141] It is accepted that the measures adopted by the various governmental and non-governmental institutions since 11 September 2001 would probably not have caught the funds used to finance the World Trade Center and Pentagon attacks.[142] Surveillance of international finance, no matter how rigorous, will not catch funds that are raised locally and used for acts of violence—such as those used in Madrid in 2004 and London in 2005.[143] Furthermore, these measures have caused legitimate fears within the financial industry regarding liability for offences and an onerous regulatory burden—fears that are exacerbated in the case of individuals and non-profit organisations.[144] McCulloch and Carlton put it bluntly: 'the available evidence suggests that there is little or nothing to distinguish terrorist financing that originates from legitimate sources from other finances'.[145]

The 9/11 Commission Report concluded that 'trying to starve the terrorists of money is like trying to catch one kind of fish by draining the ocean'.[146] Nevertheless, development of this policy field continues apace as anti-money-laundering and counter-terrorist finance remains a priority. In addition to the regulation on cash flows, a recent directive aims to ensure the 'prudential supervision' of electronic money.[147] The Lisbon Treaty has provided a clear and explicit basis for the adoption of criminal law in the fields of terrorism and anti-money-laundering.[148] The EU Internal Security Strategy calls for EU legislation in this field to 'to enhance the transparency of legal persons and legal arrangements'.[149] The Stockholm Programme calls for the further development of information exchange between FIUs, legislation confiscating the proceeds of crime in line with the 1990 Council of Europe Convention, and further dialogue with Latin-American and Caribbean countries on transnational crime including money-laundering. Reference is also made to the 'framework of the FATF'. Counter-terrorist finance initiatives must be 'adapted to the new potential vulnerabilities' and 'new payment methods used by terrorists'. Charitable organisations are to have increased 'transparency

---

[141] Passas, n 133 above, p 281.

[142] Ibid, p 287.

[143] Heng and McDonagh, n 34 above, p 73.

[144] Passas, n 133 above, 283.

[145] McCulloch and Carlton, n 92 above, p 404.

[146] National Commission on Terrorist Attacks Upon the United States, *The 9/11 Commission Report: Final Report of the National Commission on Terrorist Attacks Upon the United States* (New York, WH Norton & Co, 2004) 382.

[147] Regulation No 1889/2005 of the European Parliament and of the Council of 26 October 2005 on controls of cash entering or leaving the Community OJ L309/9 (25 November 2005); Directive 2009/110/EC of the European Parliament and of the Council of 16 September 2009 on the taking up, pursuit and prudential supervision of the business of electronic money institutions amending Directives 2005/60/EC and 2006/48/EC and repealing Directive 2000/46/EC OJ L267/7 (10 October 2009).

[148] Art 83(1) TFEU.

[149] Commission (EC), 'Communication from the Commission to the European Parliament and the Council: The EU Internal Security Strategy in Action: Five Steps Towards a More Secure Europe' COM (2010) 673 final, Brussels, 22 November 2010.

and responsibility' in line with FATF SR VIII. There is also a call for improved feedback to financial institutions on 'the outcome of their cooperation' with counter-terrorist finance. Furthermore the Commission is to 'examine the possibilities to track terrorist financing within the Union'. The Stockholm Programme Action Plan requires the Commission to produce a communication on the feasibility of such a programme during 2011. This brief summary of the Stockholm Programme's contents on anti-money-laundering and counter-terrorist finance suggests that the direction of travel is unlikely to change over the next half decade. The next chapter addresses the most troubling area of counter-terrorist finance, targeted asset-freezing sanctions, which raise similar rule of law concerns, while having an even more detrimental impact on affected individuals.

5

Targeted Asset-Freezing Sanctions

JUST AS EU action in anti-money-laundering predates the 11 September attacks so too did asset-freezing sanctions exist before the 'war on terror'. However, sanctions systems have become far more intensive since the attacks. An individual, group or entity can now be subject through the UN sanctions list to the freezing of their assets based on their 'association' with Al-Qaeda, Osama bin Laden or the Taleban. In addition, an individual, group or entity may be targeted based on a suspicion that they support terrorism in general. These sanctions entail the worst effects of pre-emptive action on the individual: subjecting them to a system that seriously infringes their rights but in a way that appears to be immune to swift correction by the legal process. They strain both the constitutive and safeguarding aspects of the rule of law. They were adopted (at least at first) on dubious legal basis, the system is not based on clearly defined rules and they deprive those targeted of even the most basic due process. The UN sanctions list has been the subject of almost a decade's worth of litigation and one of the most discussed judgments of the ECJ in history. In *Kadi I*, the Court held that in the absence of due process the designation of Mr Kadi as a person 'associated with' the Taleban, Osama bin Laden and Al-Qaeda was unlawful.[1] The judgment has been the subject of much debate as it raises several questions of international and EU law. However, despite the decision in his favour, Mr Kadi remains subject to the sanctions system at global and European level.[2]

I. SANCTIONS AT INTERNATIONAL LEVEL

The use of economic sanctions as a tool to preserve international peace and security has a long history, much of which is not relevant to the present study as it does

---

[1] Joined Cases C-402/05 P & C-415/05 P, *Yassin Abdullah Kadi, Al Barakaat International Foundation v Council of the European Union* [2008] ECR I-6351. For a useful discussion of the issues arising see *Symposium on Kadi* in Eeckhout and Tridimas (eds), *Yearbook of European Law* (Oxford, Oxford University Press, 2009).

[2] The General Court handed down its decision in Case T-85/09 *Kadi v Commission* on 30 September 2010 (*Kadi II*). The Court held that the listing of Mr Kadi was unlawful due to breaches of his due process rights and ordered that he be delisted. An appeal is pending before the European Court of Justice. See Joined Cases C-584/10 P, C-593/10 P and C-595/10 P OJ C 72 (5 March 2011).

not pertain to post-September 11 counter-terrorism.[3] Here, the consideration begins with the change to 'smart sanctions': sanctions that target individuals within belligerent governments or systems rather than entire states. The previous model of sanctions, used perhaps most notably against Iraq, was strongly criticised in the 1990s as hurting innocent populations of targeted states rather than the often brutal governments that oppressed those populations.[4] In response to these criticisms, the UN Security Council developed the practice of adopting 'smart' or 'targeted' sanctions. Although these resolutions are binding under international law, the idea that the resolutions would target particular individuals is revolutionary.[5] In the context of counter-terrorism, and the 'war on terror' in particular, two strands of targeted sanctions operate at European and international level. The primary sources of the sanctions are UN Security Council resolution 1267 (and further amending resolutions) and resolution 1373.[6] The first strand of sanctions, established by resolution 1267, targets individuals and entities because of their 'association' with Osama bin Laden and Al-Qaeda. The second strand of sanctions, based on resolution 1373, is a general list devised by the EU itself to implement the Member States' international law obligations.

A. Resolution 1267: UN sanctions list

The first strand of asset-freezing sanctions is founded on resolution 1267. Prior to its adoption, the Security Council had placed an arms embargo on Afghanistan due to concerns for regional security arising from internal strife in the country.[7] However in 1999, following the bombing of two US embassies in Nairobi and Dar es Salaam, the more specific resolution 1267 was adopted. It called on the Taleban to immediately cease providing safe haven for terrorists and to turn over Osama bin Laden to a state where he would be 'effectively brought to justice'.[8] The Taleban's failure to comply with these demands resulted in broad diplomatic and economic sanctions against the system. In 2000, the sanctions system was directed against Osama bin Laden himself, as well as the al-Qaeda organisation and those 'associated with' it.[9] As with the previous resolutions, compliance by the Taleban would have resulted in the sanctions on Afghanistan being lifted. In any event they were operational for one year only, at which point they were to be reviewed.[10]

---

[3] C Eckes, *EU Counter-Terrorist Policies and Fundamental Rights: The Case of Individual Sanctions* (Oxford, Oxford University Press, 2009).

[4] GL Simons, *The Scourging of Iraq: Sanctions Law and Natural Justice* (London, Macmillan, 1996).

[5] Ibid.

[6] UN Security Council resolution 1267 (15 October 1999) (hereafter, UNSC Res 1267; resolution 1267); UN Security Council resolution 1373 (28 September 2001) (hereafter, UNSC Res 1373; resolution 1373).

[7] UN Security Council resolution 1076 (22 October 1996).

[8] Art 2 UNSC Res 1267.

[9] UN Security Council resolution 1333 (19 December 2000).

[10] Ibid.

As is the usual practice, the Council delegated responsibility for devising the list of individuals and entities to a Sanctions Committee (the 1267 Committee). This is a subcommittee of the Security Council whose membership mirrors that of the Security Council itself. The 1267 Committee has responsibility for maintaining the lists of individuals who are to be targeted due to their 'association' with the Taleban, Osama bin Laden and al-Qaeda. It is worth pointing out that though the turn towards 'targeted' sanctions occurred before the 2001 attacks on the US, at that time there was still a clear link to a belligerent system with territorial control (ie the Taleban in Afghanistan).

Following the events of 11 September 2001, a new resolution was adopted strengthening the resolution 1267 sanctions system. In addition to requiring sanctions freezing assets, movement, and diplomatic relations, the Security Council urged all states to adopt any necessary domestic legislation to give effect to these obligations.[11] Notably, no provision was made for lifting these sanctions in the event that the Taleban complied with the Security Council's demands. This marks a clear shift from a sanctions system aimed at achieving a particular end (bringing bin Laden to face prosecution) to one that has the broader purpose of incapacitating him and the organisation and system that supported him and anyone associated with them. Furthermore, the link to a defined territory and a belligerent system was severed once the US invaded Afghanistan in the autumn of 2001. The sanctions system that remained was one which targeted individuals 'associated' with the amorphous entities of the Taleban, Al-Qaeda and Osama bin Laden.

The basic post-September 11 sanctions system has been amended several times to clarify and intensify the restrictions to be imposed, to provide for certain limited exemptions and to alter the listing and delisting procedures. In 2002, a resolution made allowance for exemptions from asset-freezing for basic living expenses such as food, accommodation and legal costs.[12] Amendments in 2003 and 2004 focused on improving the provision of information to the 1267 Committee when a state is requesting a listing.[13] The 2004 resolution also required that the individual or entity concerned be informed that action was being taken against them.[14] A 2005 resolution clarified the concept of individuals 'associated with' those targeted.[15] It provided further guidelines on information required to list an individual, and requested that the 1267 Committee develop de-listing procedures.[16] In 2006, a more detailed procedure for listing[17] and delisting was adopted.[18] In 2008, a resolution clarifying certain aspects of the sanctions system also set in motion a review of the entire list of targeted individuals and groups which was completed

---

[11]   Art 8 UN Security Council resolution 1390 (28 January 2002).
[12]   UN Security Council resolution 1452 (20 December 2002).
[13]   UN Security Council resolution 1455 (17 January 2003).
[14]   Arts 17–18 UN Security Council resolution 1526 (30 January 2004).
[15]   Arts 2–3 UN Security Council resolution 1617 (29 July 2005).
[16]   Ibid, Arts 4–6, 18.
[17]   Arts 5–12 UN Security Council resolution 1735 (22 December 2006).
[18]   Ibid, Arts 13–14.

in July 2010.[19] The 2008–10 review was heavily dependent on states, in particular designating states, to co-operate. At its conclusion the UN announced that following the review of over 500 listed individuals and entities, 45 individuals were being delisted. While this was a welcome announcement for the 45 individuals concerned, it was slow justice and undoubtedly dismayed the 90 per cent of listed persons whose listing was upheld.[20]

The listing and delisting procedures are central to both the sanctions systems and the controversy they cause. The procedure for listing individuals has evolved since its inception and the most recent description of it is in UN Security Council resolution 1989 and the updated Committee Guidelines.[21] The procedure operates based on submissions for listing from states which are then considered by the 1267 Committee. The Committee Guidelines set out that states requesting a listing shall submit as much information as possible to support the request for listing.[22] However, it is clearly stated that a 'criminal charge or conviction is not necessary' for an individual to be listed due to the 'preventive nature' of the sanctions.[23] There is no real deliberation process—rather listing is an administrative task carried out by the Committee. Until the adoption of resolution 1989 in 2011 the 1267 Committee took all decisions by consensus and consensus is still the standard form of decision-making for the Committee.[24] Once a listing request is received it is to be considered by the Committee by written procedure within ten days. Alternatively a state may request that a listing request be placed on the Committee's agenda for more detailed discussion. As such, it is possible for an individual or group to be listed based on the suspicion of one UN member state so long as the members of the 1267 Committee acquiesce with the request. After a listing is confirmed, it is communicated through diplomatic channels, including by issuing an Interpol–United Nations Security Council Special Notice.

The delisting procedure is also unsatisfactory in terms of due process. Originally, an individual was entirely dependent on the government of his state of nationality or residence to bring his petition before the 1267 Committee.[25] The Committee's delisting procedures focused on consensus and obtaining the consent of the government that requested the listing in the first place. Subsequent amendments to Security Council resolutions and the Committee Guidelines have attempted

[19] UN Security Council resolution 1822 (30 June 2008) (hereafter, resolution 1822; UNSC Res 1822).

[20] UN News Centre, 'UN panel removed 45 names from Taliban sanctions list after reviewing nearly 500' (2 August 2010), available at www.un.org.

[21] Ibid Art 9–18; 1267 Committee, Guidelines of the Committee for the Conduct of its Work (Adopted on 7 November 2002, as amended on 10 April 2003, 21 December 2005, 29 November 2006, 12 February 2007, 9 December 2008, 22 July 2010, 26 January 2011 and 30 November 2011) (hereafter, 1267 Committee Guidelines), available: www.un.org/sc/committees/1267/pdf/1267 _guidelines.pdf>, last accessed 25 January 2012.

[22] S 6(g) 1267 Committee Guidelines.

[23] S 6(d) 1267 Committee Guidelines.

[24] S 4(a) 1267 Committee Guidelines.

[25] S 7(e) 1267 Committee Guidelines.

to address the inadequate due process provided by these procedures. Between 2006 and the end of 2009 it was possible for a listed person to apply directly to the UN for delisting through a 'Focal Point'. However, the Focal Point was a mere administrative office which gathered information relating to the request and facilitated discussion amongst governments and the 1267 Committee.[26] The delisting decision-making process was not delegated to an independent assessor as some states wished.[27] In 2009 an Office of Ombudsperson was established to replace the Focal Point. The Ombudsperson is certainly an improvement on its predecessor. The office was established by UN Security Council resolution 1904, which declares that

> the Committee shall be assisted by an Office of the Ombudsperson, to be established for an initial period of 18 months from the date of adoption of this resolution, ... and further *decides* that the Ombudsperson shall perform these tasks in an independent and impartial manner and shall neither seek nor receive instructions from any government.[28]

The Ombudsperson for the Committee, Kimberly Prost, previously served as a judge at the International Criminal Tribunal for the former Yugoslavia. However, any hope that the Ombudsperson might offer full due process for those seeking delisting has not yet been borne out. At first the Ombudsperson's role was rather restricted. Her powers were greatly enhanced by UN Security Council resolution 1989.[29] The resolution separated sanctions relating to the Taleban from those relating to Al-Qaeda. The latter sanctions remain subject to the 1267 system—though the delisting process has been significantly altered. The Ombudsperson may now recommend that an individual or entity be removed from the Al-Qaeda list. Her recommendation will take effect unless the 1267 Committee decides by consensus to maintain the listing. However, a single member of the 1267 Committee may refer the matter to the Security Council itself. Once a recommendation is referred to the Security Council the vetoes of the permanent members enable any one of them to prevent delisting. As such, the diplomatic nature of the delisting procedure persists.

Despite the establishment and development of an independent office, the fundamental flaw of the system—the diplomatic means by which it operates— remains. An individual or entity may be listed without playing any part in the decision-making process. While the listed individual or entity can now ensure their case for delisting is at least raised at UN level and the Ombudsperson can recommend delisting it is still possible for a single permanent member of the Security Council to ensure that an individual or entity remains listed. This is an

---

[26] UN Security Council resolution 1730 (19 December 2006).
[27] UN Security Council, Minutes of the 5599th meeting (16 December 2006) UN Doc S/PV.5599.
[28] UN Security Council resolution 1904 (17 December 2009).
[29] UN Security Council resolution 1989 adopted by the Security Council on 17 June 2011 (hereafter resolution 1989).

absurd situation given the poor information used for listings in the first place.[30] The difficulties in achieving delisting are borne out by the statistics. In 2008 ten requests for delisting were received. Three individuals were delisted (including one deceased person), while the remaining seven requests were refused.[31] Despite the comprehensive review of the list in 2010, which recommended the delisting of 45 individuals, only 40 names were removed from the list in that year.[32] At international level, despite the reforms, the system continues to operate based on diplomacy and not due process.

B. Resolution 1373: EU sanctions list

The second strand of the sanctions system is based on Security Council resolution 1373, adopted on 28 September 2001 in the immediate aftermath of the New York and Washington attacks.[33] The meeting at which the resolution was adopted lasted three minutes.[34] Despite the rather brief meeting, the resolution has been referred to as 'hegemonic' insofar as it requires sweeping changes to states' laws to criminalise terrorism and related action. Paragraph 1 of the resolution requires states to suppress and criminalise all forms of terrorist financing, as well as to freeze the assets of 'persons who commit, or attempt to commit, terrorist acts or participate in or facilitate the commission of terrorist acts ... and associated persons and entities'.[35] Resolution 1373 does not specify what constitute 'terrorist acts' in this regard. Furthermore, unlike the 1267 sanctions list, the resolution 1373 sanctions leave it to the states themselves to draw up and implement the list. Therefore, in this case, the 1267 Committee is not involved at all. Within the EU, the Member States opted to implement their resolution 1373 obligations through the EU though some also have national systems of designation.

In 2004, a subsequent Security Council resolution established a working group of its members to draw up proposals for action to be taken against 'individuals, groups or entities involved in or associated with terrorist activities, other than those designated by the [1267] Committee'.[36] The action to be considered included:

> more effective procedures considered to be appropriate for bringing them to justice through prosecution or extradition, freezing of their financial assets, preventing their

---

[30] *Kadi II*, n 2 above, para 78.

[31] UN Security Council, 'Report of the Security Council Committee established pursuant to resolution 1267 (1999) concerning Al-Qaida and the Taliban and associated individuals and entities' (31 December 2008) [6].

[32] UN Al-Qaida/Taliban Sanctions Committee, 'Annual Statement of Information for the Year 2010 on Updates to the Consolidated List', New York (December 2010).

[33] See further the discussion in ch 1 above.

[34] UNSC, 'Security Council Unanimously Adopts Wide-Ranging Anti-Terrorism Resolution' (New York, 28 September 2001) Press Release SC/7158.

[35] Art 1(c) UNSC Res 1373.

[36] Art 9 UN Security Council resolution 1566 (8 October 2004) (hereafter, resoution 1566).

movement through the territories of Member States, preventing supply to them of all types of arms and related material.[37]

However, while the working group paid due regard to the efforts of the Financial Action Task Force, the 1267 Committee, and other official bodies, it did not recommend the establishment of an expanded list, '[o]wing to various reasons including the lack of consensus'.[38] One commentator has attributed the lack of consensus to 'differing priorities on the part of Council members, as well as the inherent difficulties in determining the nature of the criteria to be used in such identification, and the source and strength of the information required to make such a determination'.[39] The failure to reach consensus is to be welcomed. If the UN devised a general list of individuals, groups and entities whose assets were to be frozen then it would be duplicating the action it required states to take in resolution 1373. However, the potential problems with a general UN system of sanctions are themselves a critique of the system put in place by resolution 1373.

C. Assessing the UN Action

It is reasonable to expect, given the profound implications for designated individuals, groups and entities, that the sanctions system would be carefully constructed to ensure its proportionality as well as its effectiveness. However, the construction of the UN sanctions system was marked by rushed ad hoc drafting. The piecemeal development of the UN sanctions list and in particular the 1267 Committee procedures is indicative of an 'act first, plan later' approach. Furthermore, the adoption of a measure as far-reaching as resolution 1373 in a meeting that lasted a mere three minutes is profoundly worrying in terms of the lack of scrutiny possible with so short a public deliberation. Although diplomatic agreements are often deliberated upon before being ratified in a formal meeting, the same process cannot be justified for resolutions that amount to global legislation targeted at individuals.

The UN Security Council, or at the very least some of its members, have reacted to the September 11 attacks by pursing an aggressive counter-terrorist agenda. There has been a shift from the use of UN General Assembly resolutions and international conventions to combat terrorism to a reliance on UN Security Council resolutions. Whereas each UN member has a representative in the General Assembly, only fifteen states are represented on the Security Council: five permanent members and ten further members selected on a rotating basis. Therefore the shift from the

---

[37] Ibid.

[38] UN Security Council, Report of the working group established pursuant to resolution 1566 (2004) (NY 31 December 2007).

[39] J Boulden 'The Security Council and Terrorism' in V Lowe, A Roberts, J Welsh and D Zaum (eds), *The United Nations Security Council and War: The Evolution of Thought and Practice since 1945* (Oxford, Oxford University Press, 2008) 617–18.

General Assembly to the Security Council causes concerns regarding the legitimacy of UN counter-terrorism action. The sanctions system has not gone unnoticed by the General Assembly, which has called on the Security Council 'to ensure that fair and clear procedures exist for placing individuals and entities on sanctions lists and for removing them'.[40] Targeted sanctions leave individuals subject to overlapping coercive systems legislated for by diplomatic compromise and executed by a largely unaccountable administration. It is far easier to be listed than delisted. Furthermore, there are no clear standards used in deciding whether or not to list an individual or entity: an entirely unacceptable situation given the consequences for those concerned. Resolutions 1267 and 1373 are a key source of EU counter-terrorism policy. They demonstrate a worrying tendency towards the pre-emptive exercise of power: the empowerment of executives, the lack of clear rules and the absence of due process.

II. EU ACTION ON TARGETED ASSET-FREEZING SANCTIONS

The Member States acted quickly through the EU to implement the UN sanctions systems. Though the various Security Council resolutions do not directly bind the EU, the Member States chose to fulfil their UN obligations through the Common Foreign and Security Policy. They adopted common positions to implement the Member States' obligations under both UN Security Council resolution 1267 and resolution 1373. Regulations were then used to give full legal effect to the sanctions within the EU legal order.

A. EU Legislation on Targeted Sanctions

At the time of the September 11 attacks, the EU Treaty provided the Council with the power to adopt common positions to 'define the approach of the Union to a particular matter of a geographical or thematic nature'.[41] A common position could be implemented in the internal market by a binding regulation. This was the approach taken with regard to the sanctions. The earliest common position in this field concerned Afghanistan itself, making no reference to freezing the funds of private parties.[42] Subsequent common positions froze the assets of the

---

[40] UN General Assembly, Resolution Adopted by the General Assembly A/RES/60/1 24 October 2005, para 109.

[41] Art 15 EU(N). The provision has now been replaced by Art 29 EU which provides for the Council to adopt 'decisions'. For a discussion of the nature of a 'decision' see P Eeckhout, *EU External Relations Law* 2nd edn (Oxford, Oxford University Press, 2011) 183–84.

[42] Council Common Position of 17 December 1996 (96/746/CFSP). Art 1 declares 'An embargo on the export of arms, munitions and military equipment shall be imposed on Afghanistan'.

Taleban and then bin Laden.[43] The common positions make direct reference to the UN sanctions list and provide that the EU shall take action under its first pillar to implement the sanctions.[44] The EU adopted Regulation 881/2002 based on Articles 60, 301 and 308 EC to do so. The regulation freezes the assets of all persons and entities listed in an Annex to the regulation and empowers the Commission to amend the Annex following listing decisions of the 1267 Committee.[45] Attempting to circumvent the sanctions 'shall be prohibited' and Member States' penalties in this respect must be 'effective, proportionate and dissuasive'.[46] In 2003, following amendments to the relevant Security Council resolutions, a new common position and regulation provided for certain exemptions for essential living costs, subject to the approval of the 1267 Committee.[47] The Annex to the regulation, which contains the EU's duplication of the UN sanctions list, has since been amended by the Commission over one hundred times. The Commission has faithfully followed the 1267 Committee in listing and delisting targeted individuals and entities. If it did not do so, the Member States would have to either implement the UN sanctions list themselves or risk being in breach of their international law obligations.

Regulation 881/2002 has been subject to several amendments in recent years.[48] The two principal reasons for the amendments were the ECJ decision in the *Kadi I* case and the adoption of UN Security Council resolution 1882. Regulation 1286/2009 inserts an Article 7(a) in the principal law. Article 7(a) requires the Commission to 'take a decision' to include any person, entity, body or group listed by the 1267 Committee once a statement of reasons has been released. The Commission must communicate the decision to the listed person and provide him with an opportunity to express his views. Following the receipt of any observations, the Commission must forward the observations to the Sanctions Committee and review its decision. The results of the review must then be communicated to both the listed person and the Sanctions Committee. A further

---

[43] Council Common Position of 15 November 1999 concerning restrictive measures against the Taliban (1999/727/CFSP); Council Common Position of 26 February 2001 concerning additional restrictive measures against the Taliban and amending Common Position 96/746/CFSP (2001/154/CFSP); Council Common Position of 5 November 2001 concerning restrictive measures against the Taliban and amending Common Positions 1996/746/CFSP, 2001/56/CFSP and 2001/154/CFSP (2001/771/CFSP).

[44] Arts 1–3 Council Common Position of 27 May 2002 concerning restrictive measures against Usama bin Laden (2002/402/CFSP).

[45] Arts 1–3, 7 Council Regulation (EC) No 881/2002 of 27 May 2002.

[46] Arts 4, 10 Council Regulation (EC) No 881/2002 of 27 May 2002.

[47] Council Common Position 2003/140/CFSP concerning exceptions to the restrictive measures imposed by Common Position 2002/402/CFSP; Council Regulation (EC) No 561/2003.

[48] Council Regulation (EU) No 1286/2009 of 22 December 2009 amending Regulation (EC) No 881/2002 imposing certain specific restrictive measures directed against certain persons and entities associated with Usama bin Laden, the Al-Qaida network and the Taliban OJ L 346/42 (23 December 2009); Council Regulation (EU) No 754/2011 of 1 August 2011 amending Regulation (EC) No 881/2002 imposing certain specific restrictive measures directed against certain persons and entities associated with Usama bin Laden, the Al-Qaida network and the Taliban OJ L 199/23 (2 August 2011).

review can only be carried out following the presentation of 'substantial new evidence'. Article 7(c) provides for the same means of review to be made available to those who have already been listed by the UN and EU. Further amendments were implemented in 2011 to give effect to the separation of the Al-Qaeda and Taleban sanctions lists by UN Security Council resolutions 1988 and 1989.[49] To date, it would appear that the new procedure for listing has had no substantive effect on the situation in which targeted individuals find themselves. Every individual or entity listed by the UN Security Council since the adoption of Regulation 1286/2009 has been followed by a listing decision of the Commission.[50] However, the new regulation does appear to require the Commission to take an independent decision on listing. Such a decision presents scope for further judicial review at EU level. Thus, if nothing else, the new regulation may hasten the day when the ECJ decides whether or not to engage in substantive review of the sanctions (to date its decisions have been limited to procedural review).[51] Such a judgment would provide a better understanding of the Court's views on the relationship between fundamental rights and national security than has been available to date.

When it came to fulfilling their obligations under UN Security Council resolution 1373, the Member States took a similar approach to their implementation of the UN sanctions list, acting through the EU. However, resolution 1373 was implemented by a common position based on the EU's powers in Common Foreign and Security Policy and in Police and Judicial Co-Operation in Criminal Matters.[52] The use of the CFSP recognises the international origin of the measure and PJCCM acknowledges the role of the Member States' criminal justice system. The legislation to implement the system was circulated to the Member States the day after Christmas in 2001 and adopted a day later through a written procedure.[53]

The common position draws on both the language of the UN resolutions and the Framework Decision on Combating Terrorism (FDCT).[54] It repeats exactly the definitions of 'terrorist offence' and 'terrorist groups' used in the FDCT.[55] It requires that the EU sanctions list is drawn up on the basis of decisions by a 'competent authority', defining such an authority as a 'judicial authority ... or an

---

[49] Ibid.

[50] This conclusion can be reached by comparing the notices on the 1267 Committee website with the Commission Regulations amending the Annex to Regulation 881/2002. All individuals and entities listed by the Security Council up until 5 September 2010 were also listed by the Commission, with the maximum delay between decisions being 13 days.

[51] In *Yusef*, the applicant is challenging the sanctions by claiming that the European Commission has failed to take an independent decision on listing. See: Case T-306/10 *Yusef v Commission* OJ C260 (25 September 2010).

[52] Council, Common Position of 27 December 2001 on the application of specific measures to combat terrorism (2001/931/CFSP) based on Articles 15 and 34 EU (N).

[53] G Sullivan and B Hayes, *Blacklisted: Targeted Sanctions, Preemptive Security and Fundamental Rights* (Berlin, European Centre for Constitutional and Human Rights, 2011).

[54] Council Framework Decision of 13 June 2002 on combating terrorism (2002/475/JHA).

[55] Art 1 Council Common Position 2001/931/CFSP; Arts 1–4 Council Framework Decision of 13 June 2002 on combating terrorism (2002/475/JHA).

equivalent competent authority'.[56] The list must contain sufficient details to avoid identification errors and be reviewed at least every six months.[57] As with the common position implementing the UN sanctions list, the common position establishing the EU sanctions list was implemented by a regulation based on Articles 60, 301 and 308 EC.[58] The regulation provides for the freezing of assets of persons listed under the common position and prohibits the provision of financial services to such persons.[59] The Council, acting unanimously, may designate natural or legal persons committing, attempting, facilitating or participating in terrorist acts; natural persons acting under the direction of or for the benefit of such a person; or legal entities owned by such a person.[60] Member States may allow frozen funds to be used for 'essential human needs', subject to certain conditions.[61] Finally, mirroring the UN sanctions list regulation, any attempt to circumvent the sanctions 'shall be prohibited' and subject to penalties that are 'effective, proportionate and dissuasive'.[62] The EU sanctions list clearly and explicitly provides an example of the blurring of internal and external security matters that terrorism is oft-cited as causing.[63] The sanctions system presents overlapping tools by which economic coercion can be deployed against those suspected of terrorism.

B. EU Case Law

Litigation relating to the sanctions system has kept the European Courts quite busy in the decade since 11 September 2001. While the common positions could not be reviewed by the ECJ, the regulations implementing those common positions could and have been challenged. The litigation has spawned libraries' worth of literature as both General Court and the ECJ have handed down several judgments on both the UN and EU sanctions lists. The analysis focuses on four points which relate to the constitutive and safeguarding aspects of the EU rule of law: the question of competence; the interaction between the EU and national legal orders; the availability of judicial review; and the protection of human rights.

i. Competence

The matter of the EU's competence to adopt the sanctions systems is perhaps the most troubling of developments from the point of view of EU constitutional law.

---

[56] Art 1(4) Council Common Position 2001/931/CFSP.

[57] Art 1(5)–(6) Council Common Position 2001/931/CFSP.

[58] Council Regulation 2580/2001 of 27 December 2001 on specific restrictive measures directed against certain persons and entities with a view to combating terrorism (21 December 2001).

[59] Art 2 Regulation 2580/2001.

[60] Art 2(3) Regulation 2580/2001.

[61] Arts 5–6 Regulation 2580/2001.

[62] Arts 3, 9 Regulation 2580/2001.

[63] P Bobbit, *The Shield of Achilles: War, Peace and the Course of History* (London, Penguin, 2003).

Several competing theories as to the correct legal basis for the sanctions have been offered. However, following the *Kadi I* judgment from the ECJ, it is clear that all organs of government at EU level view the EU competent to adopt the sanctions on the basis of Articles 60, 301 and 308 EC. Both the UN sanctions list and the EU sanctions list have been implemented on this basis.

Originally, the sanctions against the Taleban as the rulers of Afghanistan were implemented using Articles 301 and 60 EC, which were designed for exactly this purpose: putting in place a 'bridge' between the Common Foreign and Security Policy and the internal market.[64] However, Articles 301 and 60 EC only covered the implementation of sanctions targeted at third countries. The question which arose following the fall of the Taleban was whether these provisions could form the basis for targeting individuals without a link to a sanctioned 'third country'. To address this issue, the Council extended the legal basis to include Article 308 EC.[65] Article 308 permitted the Council to act to attain one of the objectives of the (then) European Community where the EC Treaty did not provide necessary powers. In its *Kadi I* decision, the Court of First Instance (CFI) declared that none of the articles could themselves provide sufficient legal basis.[66] A plain reading of Article 308 would indicate that it can only be used to pursue an internal market objective. To side-step this problem, the Court held that the 'bridge' established by Articles 60 and 301 EC was 'widened' by Article 308 EC allowing the internal market to be used to pursue a foreign policy objective. The CFI judgment did not elaborate on which objectives might travel across the bridge to be pursued using internal market mechanisms. The CFI's reasons for allowing this widening relate to the need for the EU to be consistent in its external affairs and are entirely unconvincing. Indeed, it is difficult, if not impossible to justify the Court's decision solely on the basis of the text. Rather, the real reason for allowing this widening of the 'bridge' is that '[s]tates can no longer be regarded as the only source of threat to international peace and security'.[67] Commentators who disagree on the validity of this point nevertheless agree that it is the true motivation for the decision.[68] On appeal, the ECJ ruled that Council practice cannot derogate from Treaty rules, and that Article 308 cannot be used to effectively amend the Treaty.[69] It may well be desirable that the Member States be able to take action against suspected terrorists through a binding regulation. However, there is a difference between desirability and legality. The constitutive aspect of the rule of law requires that when action

---

[64] Council Regulation 337/2000; Council Regulation 467/2001.
[65] Council Regulation 881/2002.
[66] T-315/01 *Kadi* [2005] ECR II-3649, para 121.
[67] Ibid, para 133.
[68] C Tomuschat, 'Case T-306/01, *Ahmed Ali Yusuf and Al Barakaat International Foundation v Council and Commission*; Case T-315/01, *Yassin Abdullah Kadi v Council and Commission*' (2006) 43 *Common Market Law Review* 537; P Eeckhout, 'Community Terrorism Listings, Fundamental Rights, and UN Security Council Resolutions. In Search of the Right Fit' (2007) *European Constitutional Law Review* 183.
[69] Eeckhout, n 68 above, p 197.

is taken it is not just desirable but that it is in accordance with the principle of conferred powers. The means by which new competences are to be provided is by amending the Treaty (as has now been done). The CFI judgment is therefore most unconvincing on this point.

The CFI itself had provided a logically convincing basis for using Articles 60 and 301 EC in its decision in the analogous *Minin* case.[70] That case involved sanctions concerning Liberia and its former ruler Charles Taylor. The sanctions were grounded in Articles 60 and 301 EC. Noting that Taylor no longer controlled the country, the CFI held that the sanctions were still validly grounded as Taylor continued to pose a threat to that country, which constituted a sufficient link for the purposes of the Treaty basis.[71] One does not have to engage in mental gymnastics to reason that the same argument could be made in respect of al-Qaeda and Afghanistan. Had the CFI followed this logic in *Kadi I*, many of the problems of that judgment would have been avoided.

A somewhat similar approach was adopted by Advocate General Maduro in *Kadi I*.[72] Having noted that governments do not 'function as gatekeepers for the economic relations and activities of each specific entity within their borders', he held that 'by affecting economic relations with entities within a given country, the sanctions necessarily affect the overall state of economic relations between the Community and that country'.[73] He noted that Article 301 EC should be construed in this fashion to give it its full effect. By way of contrast, the Advocate General held that Article 308 EC had no cross-pillar function.[74] As a result, he found that the sanctions were appropriately based on Articles 60 and 301 EC. This decision represents the best basis for the sanctions in EU law, as it avoids the problems of the CFI judgment without engaging in the ECJ's convoluted reasoning in *Kadi I*. The latter Court's somewhat laborious musings on the matter concluded that the correct legal basis was indeed Articles 60, 301 and 308 EC. Nonetheless, it offered different reasoning to that of the CFI. While Articles 60 and 301 could only be used to target states, Article 308 EC could be used to extend the ambit of the sanctions *ratione materiae*. Articles 60 and 301 EC were held to contain the Community objective to be pursued: that of 'making it possible to adopt such measures through the efficient use of a Community instrument'.[75] As this and the other criteria for the use of Article 308 EC were met, that provision could be used to extend the scope of the sanctions system.[76] Tridimas notes that this reasoning 'confuses means with objectives and is self-contradictory'.[77] As Articles 60 and 301

---

[70] T-362/04 *Minin* [2007] ECR II-2003 [72].

[71] Id [70–75].

[72] C-402/05 *Kadi* Opinion of Advocate General Maduro 16 January 2008.

[73] Ibid, para 13.

[74] Ibid, paras 14–15.

[75] C-402/05 *Kadi* ECJ Judgment 3 September 2008, para 226.

[76] Ibid, para 236.

[77] T Tridimas, 'Terrorism and the ECJ: Empowerment and Democracy in the EC Legal Order', *Queen Mary School of Law Legal Studies Research Paper*, No 12/2009, p 7.

EC only envisage the use of sanctions against states, it is illogical to claim they have the objective of imposing sanctions against individuals.

The reasoning is perhaps best understood as the ECJ struggling to find the sanctions correctly based on Articles 60, 301 and 308 EC while attempting to avoid the pitfalls of the CFI's decision. Advocate General Maduro was correct in identifying the salient issue as whether or not the EU possesses the power to adopt economic sanctions in an era where the international community has begun to use them against individuals as well as states. Just as scholars of international law have questioned the use of binding resolutions to target individuals, so too do questions of appropriateness arise in relation to the constitutive aspect of the EU rule of law. Sanctions against states and sanctions against individuals are qualitatively different and the legal powers used for the former should not necessarily be used for the latter.[78] These problems are all replicated in respect of the EU sanctions list regulation as it rests on the same legal basis. Indeed, arguably the above criticisms with regard to links to third countries are all the sharper with respect to the EU sanctions list, as it targets 'domestic' as well as 'international' terrorists. However, when considering the question of legal basis, the CFI merely cited its *Yusuf* and *Kadi I* judgments which, it claimed, 'provided exhaustive answers'.[79]

The Lisbon Treaty provides a clear and unequivocal legal basis for sanctions in Article 75 TFEU and one could be forgiven for thinking that the question of competence is now merely a historic curiosity.[80] However, the Treaty on the Functioning of the European Union offers not just one, but two potential legal bases. Article 75 TFEU allows the EU, when it is necessary to achieve an area of freedom, security and justice, to 'define a framework' for administrative measures against terrorism, such as the freezing of assets. Article 75 TFEU is thus the obvious solution to the tortured debate on the legal basis. From the point of view of the legitimacy of the system Article 75 TFEU has the benefit of providing that action should be taken through the ordinary legislative procedure which affords equal power to the Council and the European Parliament.

However, Article 75 TFEU is not the only potential legal basis of targeted asset-freezing sanctions. Article 215 TFEU provides for the adoption of 'restrictive measures'. It begins by providing a procedure for the adoption of restrictive measures against states but also declares that restrictive measures can also be adopted against 'natural or legal persons and groups or non-State entities'. Such action should 'include necessary provisions on legal safeguards'. The procedure through which this action is taken requires the Council to act on a joint proposal from the High Representative of the Union for Foreign Affairs and Security Policy and

---

[78]   C Eckes, 'Judicial Review of European Anti-Terrorism Measures: The *Yusuf* and *Kadi* Judgments of the Court of First Instance' (2008) 14 *European Law Journal* 74, 78.

[79]   T-47/03 *Sison* CFI Judgment 11 July 2007 para 100.

[80]   As the present author did: CC Murphy, 'Fundamental Rights and Security: The Difficult Position of the European Judiciary' (2010) 16 *European Public Law* 289, 304. The new litigation on the legal basis is Case C-130/10 *European Parliament v Council of the European Union* OJ 2010 C134.

the European Commission. The European Parliament is merely to be informed. When the Member States decided to amend the legislation that implements the Al-Qaeda and Taleban sanctions in EU law they chose to act through Article 215 TFEU rather than through Article 75 TFEU.[81] As a result the European Parliament launched the litigation now before the European Court of Justice.

The debate about legal bases may seem academic. However, the choice of basis determines what procedure is used and therefore what role the European Parliament is given. This has a direct impact on the democratic legitimacy of the legislation. The constitutive aspect of the rule of law includes the principle of conferred powers which requires that the EU acts on the correct legal basis. If that legal basis affords the European Parliament a greater role it may strengthen the safeguarding aspect of the rule of law if the Parliament insists on a more human rights compliant sanctions system.

It is unclear which basis is more appropriate. Article 215 TFEU might appear the obvious successor to Articles 60 and 301 EC which, along with Article 308 EC, provided the legal basis for the sanctions before the Lisbon Treaty came into force. Nonetheless, an examination of the Table of Equivalences published in the *Official Journal* offers a more complicated answer. Article 60 EC is described as 'moved' to Article 75 TFEU while Article 301 EC is described as 'replaced' by Article 215 TFEU. The Table is therefore of little help (and indeed given the differences between Article 60 EC and Article 75 TFEU proves itself to be positively unhelpful). On balance, the best view may be to consider Article 75 TFEU as *lex specialis* because it refers explicitly to terrorism. Thus, Article 215 TFEU should be used for restrictive measures against states and individuals in general, with Article 75 TFEU used in the particular context of counter-terrorism. The latter article has the added advantage of affording the European Parliament co-decision powers which improves the legitimacy of the system. Indeed the ECJ has noted that participation of the European Parliament 'reflects a fundamental democratic principle that the peoples should take part in the exercise of power through the intermediary of a representative assembly'.[82] It is also more appropriate as sanctions against states may be temporary and related to a particular conflict (eg Libya) and thus merit swift action by the EU.[83] Sanctions in the field of counter-terrorism appear to be a permanent fixture of EU law which affects a wide range of individuals and so it is appropriate that they be enacted by the full EU legislature acting through the ordinary legislative procedure. The use of this procedure might not have any effect on the substance of the sanctions system. However, a legislative process

---

[81] Council Regulation 1286/2009 of 22 December 2009.

[82] C-300/89 *Commission v Council* [1991] ECR I-2867, para 20. The case concerned an environmental directive that could have been adopted on one of two possible legal bases. The Court accepted a *lex specialis* argument in determining that the (then) Art 130s EEC was not the correct legal basis for the law.

[83] See, eg, Council Regulation No 204/2011 of 2 March 2011 concerning restrictive measures in view of the situation in Libya.

that involved the European Parliament might improve the transparency of the legislative process and thus the legitimacy of the system as a whole.

ii. Availability of Judicial Review

The key debate on the applications for annulment of sanctions listings concerns the availability of judicial review. The attitude of the EU courts has evolved from a deferential one in early cases before the CFI to a robust reassertion of the right to judicial review in judgments following the ECJ's *Kadi I* decision. Looked at as a system, the EU courts might be said to have moved from a more deferential approach to one which is robust in its defence of the rule of law.[84] However, the reality is that the Court of First Instance took a bold, but erroneous, decision in *Kadi I* which was reversed by the ECJ. Since then the *Kadi I* decision of the ECJ has dominated the legal landscape in this field and has been followed by the General Court. The appeal of *Kadi II* from the General Court to the ECJ is pending at the time of writing—it remains to be seen if the ECJ will revise the position it established in *Kadi I*.[85]

Prior to the decision of the ECJ in *Kadi I*, the CFI held different positions with regard to the UN sanctions list and the EU sanctions list. In relation to the UN sanctions list, the Court's decision on judicial review was a consequence of its determination that the EU was under an obligation to adopt the contested measures. It found, by virtue of EU law itself, that the Community was bound to comply with international law and give effect to UN Security Council resolutions. The CFI then reaffirmed that the European legal order is based on the rule of law, a vital component of which is judicial review.[86] However, it found its jurisdiction limited in accordance with its obligation to give effect to international law. It would not review the contested regulation against European human rights standards, as to do so would be tantamount to indirectly reviewing the UN Security Council resolution against those standards.[87] The CFI was willing to hold the UN list to account against *ius cogens* standards—peremptory norms of international law that are binding on the UN itself.[88] It caused much concern within the academy as the level of review required was quite low. In addition, the UK cross-appealed this point in *Kadi I*. However, *ius cogens* was not discussed by the ECJ.[89] The idea of *ius cogens* review offered little assistance to the applicants and it might damage the international legal order if a regional court were considered competent to interpret and apply universal rules. However, as long as the ECJ decision

---

[84] F Fabbrini, 'The Role of the Judiciary in Times of Emergency: Judicial Review of Counterterrorism Measures in the United States Supreme Court and the European Court of Justice' in Eeckhout and Tridimas (eds), *Yearbook of European Law* (Oxford, Oxford University Press, 2009).

[85] See *Kadi II*, n 2 above.

[86] *Kadi I*, n 1 above, para 209.

[87] *Kadi I*, n 1 above, para 215.

[88] *Kadi I*, n 1 above, para 226.

[89] Eeckhout, n 68 above, pp 194–97.

in *Kadi I*, discussed in full below, remains valid law the *ius cogens* point is moot as EU constitutional review surpasses the level of protection offered by *ius cogens*. A cleavage emerged in the CFI case law when it annulled the EU sanctions list regulation insofar as it related to the *Organisation des Modjahedines du peuple d'Iran (OMPI*: 'People's Mujahidin of Iran'). In that case the CFI found itself competent to review the legality of that listing, and ordered the delisting of the organisation in question.[90] The CFI distinguished the *Kadi I* line of cases on the basis that in those cases designation was by the UN directly, whereas in relation to the EU sanctions list, the UN had left states the discretion to decide who to designate.[91] Though this distinction should not be understated, the result—individuals within the EU may seek judicial review depending on what institution suspects them of illegal activity—was hardly satisfactory.

The Opinion of Advocate General Maduro in *Kadi I* reasserted the importance of the constitutional role of the EU courts in reviewing EU legislation, regardless of its origins. For Advocate General Maduro, the test for whether the courts may exercise review is to be answered by reference to the EU treaties, not the UN Charter.[92] Thus, he notes that in *Bosphorus*, the ECJ had no qualms about reviewing European law that sought to implement UN sanctions.[93] The absence of effective judicial review of the decision to list Mr Kadi (and later, Al Barakaat) was a breach of the applicant's due process rights, and therefore he recommended the annulment of the regulation insofar as it referred to the applicant.[94] The decision of the ECJ in *Kadi I* was equally assertive. Just as the CFI's decision on judicial review stemmed from its opinion on the interaction between the EU and international law, so too did that of the ECJ. However, in beginning its consideration of the relationship, the ECJ noted that the EU 'is based on the rule of law'.[95] The Court went on to note the need to respect international law, in particular when Chapter VII resolution of the UN Security Council were concerned.[96] However, the Court stressed the 'free choice' of Member States when implementing such resolutions, the 'autonomy' of the European legal order, and the fundamental importance of Article 6(1) EU and the rule of law.[97] It found no basis in either the UN Charter or the EC Treaty to oust the Court's power to review,[98] and held that generalised immunity from review was not justified due to the lack of judicial protection at UN level.[99] Invoking *Les Verts*, it reasserted the autonomy of the European legal system and the role of the ECJ in reviewing acts of the institutions

---

[90] T-228/02 *Organisation des Modjahedines du peuple d'Iran* [2006] ECR II-4665 (hereafter, *OMPI I*).
[91] Ibid, para 100.
[92] Opinion Advocate General Maduro in *Kadi I*, para 24.
[93] Opinion Advocate General Maduro in *Kadi I*, n 1 above, paras 26–28.
[94] Opinion Advocate General Maduro in *Kadi I*, n 1 above, para 55.
[95] *Kadi I*, n 1 above, para 81.
[96] *Kadi I*, n 1 above, paras 291–94.
[97] *Kadi I*, n 1 above, paras 301–16.
[98] *Kadi I*, n 1 above, paras 299–300.
[99] *Kadi I*, n 1 above, para 322.

and the Member States against the Treaty.[100] The Court reiterated the importance of fundamental rights in the European legal order, and that 'respect for human rights is a condition of the lawfulness' of European law.[101] This reasoning was not revolutionary—but merely an application of existing jurisprudence.[102] What was remarkable was that the ECJ chose to adopt a 'business as usual' approach in the field of international peace and security where questions of jurisdiction and competence might have mitigated in favour of a more deferential approach. In doing so it found itself at the forefront of the defence of the rule of law in the 'war on terror'.

Despite its robust approach, the Court was careful to point out that it was reviewing the lawfulness of the European law and not the UN Security Council resolution.[103] Furthermore, the Court rejected any notion that it had jurisdiction to review the resolution, even against *ius cogens* norms.[104] That particular can of worms, unhelpfully opened by the CFI, can now be considered closed. In short the ECJ overturned the CFI decision on the major points of principle, and asserted that the EU is a legal order with the same relationship as one might expect to find in a sovereign state taking a dualist approach to international law. Once it had established the autonomy of the EU legal order the Court quickly concluded that the absence of due process for Mr Kadi rendered his designation unlawful. It therefore annulled the listing but delayed the effect of its judgment for three months.

The ECJ decision in *Kadi I* now dominates the jurisprudence of the EU courts in this area and may be seen as merging the two strands of case law.[105] In *Othman*, the Council requested that in the event of a judgment annulling Othman's listing, the CFI delay the effect of that judgment for a short period, as the ECJ had done in *Kadi I*.[106] The CFI refused the request. The Court noted that over three months had elapsed since the ECJ judgment in *Kadi I* (in fact, over nine months had elapsed) and within that time the Council should have taken steps to remedy the procedural breaches.[107] After the *Kadi I* litigation, Mr Kadi was sent a copy of the UN narrative summary of the reasons for his listing. No evidence was provided before he was once more listed by the EU. In *Kadi II*, the General Court noted that the ECJ decision required 'in principle full review'. It noted that the European Commission did not possess the evidence used as the basis for Mr Kadi's designation—rather this is held by the members of the UN Security Council. The

---

[100]   *Kadi I*, n 1 above, paras 280–81.

[101]   *Kadi I*, n 1 above, para 284.

[102]   P Eeckhout, 'Kadi and Al Barakaat: Luxembourg is not Texas—or Washington DC' *EJIL:Talk!* (25 February 2009).

[103]   *Kadi I*, n 1 above, para 286.

[104]   *Kadi I*, n 1 above, para 287.

[105]   This is clear from its recent citation with approval in Case C-27/09 P *French Republic v PMOI*, Judgment of the Court of Justice (Grand Chamber) of 21 December 2011.

[106]   T-318/01 *Othman v Council & Commission* CFI Judgment 11 June 2009.

[107]   Ibid, para 99.

General Court was dismissive of the role played by the Ombudsperson—referring to the review offered at international level as a 'simulacrum'. As a result it annulled the listing of Mr Kadi.

iii. Interaction between EU and National Law

Although the relationship between international and EU law has been much-examined, far less attention has been paid to the interaction between EU law and national law in the context of the sanctions systems. However, this relationship is important insofar as it determines how the law is actually applied within the EU. The regulations establishing both the UN and EU sanctions systems in EU law offer conflicting directions on the need for transposition: one regulation raises it, the other ignores the problem. This was considered in *M & Others*. The UK High Court judge noted that the state had adopted 'fairly detailed measures' to give effect to the UN Security Council resolution.[108] The judge supposed that this course of action was taken 'from an abundance of caution' to ensure that the UK would have implemented the resolution regardless of the validity of the EU Regulation.[109] He identified three differences between the Order and the Regulation.[110] Thus, the key point in deciding *M & Others*, whether social security payments to the spouses of listed persons fell within the sanctions system, was subject to different rules under EU and UK law.[111] This discrepancy has not yet received appropriate judicial attention. In the UK litigation the further up the UK judicial system the case progressed, the lesser the attention paid to the potential for conflict between the domestic statutory instrument and the directly applicable EU regulation. Though the potential conflict was simply ignored by the highest court in the UK, it might become relevant if, for example, the regulation were found invalid or a UK authority decided to comply with the domestic instrument rather than EU law. In either circumstance, the UK might continue to freeze the assets of the listed person despite the finding in EU law. In a recent case before the UK Supreme Court, their Lordships noted that in addition to being subject to the directly effective EU regulations implementing the UN Security Council sanctions system, several Member States also gave effect to that system by means of national law.[112]

In a speech in 2010 former Court of Justice Judge Timmermans stated that any implementation in national legislation as well as EU legislation would 'raise

---

[108] [2006] EWHC 2328 (Admin) para 41. The Al-Qa'ida and Taliban (United Nations Measures) Order 2002.

[109] Ibid.

[110] The Al-Qaida and Taliban (United Nations Measures) Order 2006.

[111] The earlier regulations have since been replaced by the Al-Qaida (Asset-Freezing) Regulations 2011.

[112] *HM Treasury v Ahmed & Others* [2010] UKSC 2, para 22. For a discussion of the UK law that considers it in light of EU law see T Tridimas, 'Economic Sanctions, Procedural Rights and Judicial Scrutiny: Post-Kadi Developments' (2010) *Cambridge Yearbook of European Legal Studies* 455.

questions under EU law'. Judge Timmermans did not elaborate in his speech on what those implications might be.[113] National implementation of a sanctions system that is already provided for by an EU regulation is likely to be unlawful under EU law. Regulations are directly applicable and EU law is supreme over national law. In *Amsterdam Bulb*, the Court of Justice held that a Member State could not adopt national law to implement a regulation if doing so would 'conceal the Community nature and effects of any legal provision from the person to whom it applies'.[114] Some implementing measures may be allowed or even required. In *Azienda Agricola*, the ECJ noted in relation to regulations that 'some of their provisions may none the less necessitate, for their implementation, the adoption of measures of application by the Member States'.[115] For example, if the regulation does not provide for penalties for breaches of European law then national law may so provide.[116] On this basis national implementing measures may be permissible to implement Article 10 of Regulation 881/2002 or Article 9 of Regulation 2580/2001 through national law. These provisions call for penalties to be imposed on those who attempt to undermine the sanctions system but do not specify what penalties should be imposed. However, in relation to the system itself, a simple application of *Amsterdam Bulb* would suggest that national measures duplicating the regulations are impermissible. Member States might seek to distinguish the case by arguing that the sanctions' true origin is in UN law, not EU law and therefore *Amsterdam Bulb* should not apply; or that the national measures do not conceal the European nature of the system (if an explicit reference was made to the regulation). If either argument were accepted then national measures duplicating the sanctions system might be permissible.

The adoption of national measures as insurance against the potential invalidity of a listing under EU regulations is problematic for the constitutive aspect of the rule of law (which requires obedience to the law) and for its safeguarding aspect (which requires legal certainty). However, the key legal conceit which prevents the *Kadi I* judgment from undermining the international legal order is that finding a listing unlawful under EU law does not violate the Member States' obligations under international law, it simply prevents them from fulfilling those obligations through the EU.[117] If the ECJ ordered the delisting of an individual and the Member States were bound by that decision as a matter of EU law, the Member States would be in violation of a Chapter VII resolution. At that point

---

[113] C Timmermans, 'The European Court of Justice as a Human Rights Court?' Annual Lecture, Centre of European Law, King's College London, 6 May 2010.

[114] Case 50/76 *Amsterdam Bulb* [1977] ECR 137, para 7.

[115] C-403/98 *Azienda Agricola Monte Arcosu v Regione Autonoma della Sardegna* [2001] ECR I-103, para 26.

[116] Para 32.

[117] This too is contentious. For a discussion of Member States' compliance with their UN obligations following the most recent litigation, see M Tzanou and S El-Droubi 'Case T-318/01, *Omar Mohommad Othman v Council of the European Union and Commission of the European Communities*, Judgment of the Court of First Instance of 11 June 2009 (Seventh Chamber), not yet reported' (2010) 47 *Common Market Law Review* 1233.

the EU legal order would be in open revolt against the international legal order and would be even more susceptible to the scorn of those who were critical of *Kadi I*.[118] However, despite becoming more willing to examine how the system operates, the Court of Justice has not yet satisfactorily resolved the relationship between international, EU and national law in this context.

iv. Substantive Human Rights Infringements

In the course of the many cases contesting the sanctions system, individuals have claimed violations of a wide range of human rights in addition to their due process rights. Most prominent amongst these are the rights to property, to respect for private and family life, and to be free from inhuman and degrading treatment.[119] However, it remains impossible to accurately assess the level of protection of human rights that the European Courts are likely to offer once the problems with due process are remedied. In one respect the system may be heading towards a crisis. If the courts ever deem themselves satisfied with the listing process, they will be forced to either undertake a substantive review on the facts, or to defer to the judgment of the EU executive organs leaving the applicants with no effective review of their listing. Substantive human rights infringements, and the extent to which they are remedied by the courts, are indicative of how well the safeguarding aspect of the rule of law is upheld.

The sanctions systems have a profound effect on the human rights of those targeted but also on those who have relationships (personal or financial) with listed individuals and organisations. Further litigation has considered the effect on such related individuals. In *Möllendorf*, the ECJ examined whether the registration of a transfer of ownership of a property was included within the sanctions system. It was held that such registration was covered by the sanctions system, although the ECJ left resolution of the case itself to the national court. In *M & Others*, the Court addressed whether social security payments to spouses of listed persons fall within the scope of the system. In that case, despite the existence of arguments to the contrary, the Court found that the payments fell outside the scope of the system. Thus the ECJ signalled a willingness to engage more actively with the operation of the sanctions system in national law. This willingness was reinforced by the judgment in *Criminal Proceedings against E & F*.[120] The Court examined the prosecution of two individuals in Germany for fundraising for a group listed on the EU's domestic sanctions list. It intervened on the basis that it was EU law which effectively determined the scope of criminal liability under national law.

---

[118] See, in particular, G De Búrca, 'The EU, the European Court of Justice and the International Legal Order after *Kadi*' (2010) 51 *Harvard International Law Journal* 1.

[119] See eg: *Othman*, n 103 above, para 59.

[120] Case C-550/09 *Criminal Proceedings against E & F*, Judgment of the European Court of Justice (Grand Chamber) of 29 June 2010, nyr, paras 60–62.

The robust defence of due process and human rights in the operation of the sanctions system since *Kadi I* has had its limits. *Fahas v Council* concerned the EU sanctions list.[121] Mr Sofiane Fahas, an Algerian resident in Germany, has been listed since 12 December 2002 on suspicion of involvement with the 'Al Takfir and Al-Hira' group, a dissident group in Algeria. A warrant for his arrest was issued in Italy in 9 October 2000—this warrant was the reason for his initial listing. In 2008 he was charged with four offences before Italian courts, three of which related to terrorism. Mr Fahas sought a declaration from the General Court directing the Council not to relist him unless a 'final judicial decision' proved his involvement in terrorist activities and financial compensation for the harm caused to him and his wife. Based on rather deferential reasoning, the General Court rejected the applicant's claim that the Council has failed to state reasons, that he has not been given effective judicial protection and that the presumption of innocence has been violated. While the General Court's decision might be too deferential, its examination of the applicant's claims of an error of assessment or a misuse of power by the Council is more thorough. Indeed, given the text of Regulation 2580/2001, it is difficult to argue with the judgment on this ground. The Council's decision was based on that of Italian investigating judge which constitutes a competent national authority for the purpose of the sanctions regime. Thus on this point, and the related claim for damages, the judgment is difficult to fault on doctrinal grounds. However, if this action is indeed lawful then it further demonstrates the potentially great interference with rights based on ostensibly temporary measures.

One could argue that a system of temporary sanctions aimed at freezing the assets of those suspected of terrorism pending criminal trial is the most human rights compliant system that could be devised. However, *Fahas* demonstrates the potentially fatal flaw in such a system: the slow justice delivered by Member States' criminal justice systems. A temporary system of sanctions would need to be precisely that—temporary. It took eight years for Mr Fahas to be charged following the issuing of an arrest warrant and the charges against him are still pending. Under these circumstances the sanctions are better described as indefinite rather than temporary and the interference with his rights is consequentially much greater. There has been some debate in the academy on whether replacing the system of global lists of suspected terrorists with national ones would improve human rights compliance. *Fahas* demonstrates that it is not merely the level of governance at which listing takes place that poses the problem, but also the extent and duration of the interference with rights.

III. SANCTIONS, PRE-EMPTION AND THE RULE OF LAW

A doctrinal legal analysis of the sanctions system makes clear the challenge posed to both the constitutive and safeguarding aspects of the rule of law. However, it

---

[121] Case T-47/09 *Fahas v Council* Judgment of the General Court of 7 December 2010.

is when taking a broader view of the law in action that the full consequences of the system become apparent. The system is the tip of the sword of EU counter-terrorism and yet their true nature is not clear. The classification of the measures as temporary or indefinite, precautionary or punitive may have a significant effect on the degree of rights protection that is appropriate. There have been suggestions in the literature that the sanctions are a form of criminal punishment.[122] While the sanctions systems' interference with human rights might be tantamount to such punishment an examination of European human rights law suggests that the tests for 'criminal charge' and 'criminal sanction' are not met. However, the sanctions are not an ordinary form of preventive action—they go beyond what would ordinarily be considered acceptable prevention. Rather, they exhibit all of the tendencies of pre-emptive counter-terrorism action and the related corrosion of the rule of law.

A. Sanctions as Criminal Punishment?

Faced with the severe effects of the targeted sanctions systems, individuals might well wonder if they are being subjected to criminal sanctions. In its judgment in *Kadi II*, the General Court noted that the description of the Al-Qaeda sanctions as 'temporary' may need to be revised. It cited with approval a UN report which noted that 'the question of the classification of the measures in question as preventative or punitive, protective or confiscatory, civil or criminal seems now to be an open one'. However, in *Fahas*, the General Court returned once more to the refrain that the sanctions are 'precautionary' and 'do not imply any accusation of a criminal nature'. While the two cases dealt with different regimes the sanctions' substantive effect is the same. If the different statements on the nature of the regimes reflect differences in attitude between the General Court's Fourth Section (*Kadi II*) and Second Section (*Fahas*) then clarification is needed. This point has been emphasised by the UN itself. The Preamble to UN Security Council resolution 1822 reiterates that the sanctions 'are preventative in nature and are not reliant upon criminal standards set out under national law'.

The approach taken by European human rights law to the criminal and civil divide is rather formalistic. Though arguably just as punitive as a criminal sanction, the formalistic definitions of 'criminal charge' and 'criminal sanction' adopted by the European Courts is likely to render the targeted sanctions as non-criminal within the EU legal order. The judgments of the ECtHR in *Welch* and *Jamil* are not very clearly reasoned but appear to require conviction for a criminal offence as a prerequisite for a sanction to be considered a 'criminal penalty' under the terms of Article 7 ECHR.[123] Conviction or charge for a criminal offence is

---

[122] See I Cameron, 'UN Targeted Sanctions, Legal Safeguards and the European Convention on Human Rights' (2003) 72 *Nordic Journal of International Law* 159.

[123] *Welch v UK* (1995) 20 EHRR 247; *Jamil v France* (1995) 21 EHRR 65. On Art 7 ECHR and the definition of 'criminal penalty' see CC Murphy, 'The Principle of Legality in Criminal Law under the ECHR' (2010) *European Human Rights Law Review* 192.

not required for inclusion on the UN sanctions list. While the EU sanctions list requires a decision of a competent national authority, there is no requirement that such a decision be in the context of the criminal justice system. Thus, OMPI (for example) has been listed at various times based on the decision of the UK Home Secretary and a French prosecutor.[124] As such the test under Article 7 ECHR is unlikely to be met. To determine if the proceedings relate to a 'criminal charge' under Article 6 ECHR the ECtHR looks to national characterisation of the proceedings; the nature of the offence; and the sanction that may be imposed following the outcome of the proceedings.[125] The first and third considerations do not point towards a 'criminal' classification of the sanctions system as it is characterised as preventive and the action as temporary. One might argue that the nature of the alleged 'offence'—involvement in or association with 'terrorism'—could be sufficient to classify the sanctions as 'criminal', but this seems unlikely given the ostensibly preventive and temporary nature of the action. As a result, it is unlikely that the higher-level protections available in criminal cases under Articles 6 and 7 ECHR would be triggered. The result is lowered standards in terms of the requirements of accessibility and foreseeability and fair trial rights.

While the targeted sanctions themselves may not meet the test for 'criminal penalties', the EU law is also ambiguous in relation to the enforcement clauses. The regulations establishing both the UN and EU sanctions lists in EU law use the phrase 'shall be prohibited' in relation to attempts to circumvent the sanctions system. Both note that the determination of the penalties is a matter for the Member States, but call for them to be 'effective, proportionate and dissuasive'.[126] Whether or not criminal penalties are envisaged in the present case, the use of the language is troublesome as it suggests that Member States may have to take action to implement the ostensibly directly effective regulations into national law. Indeed, while the EU sanctions list regulation is silent on the matter, Article 10(2) of the UN sanctions list regulation states that national legislation may be necessary.[127]

There are clear implications here for the constitutive role of the rule of law. It is a fundamental aspect of the EU legal order that the EU may only act if the power to do so has been conferred upon it. The legal basis for the sanctions in the EU was dubious before the adoption of the Lisbon Treaty and remains contested. The system therefore places considerable strain on the constitutive aspect of the

---

[124] Case T-284/08 *People's Mojahedin Organization of Iran v Council of the European Union* CFI Judgment 4 December 2008.

[125] *Engel v Netherlands* (1979–80) 1 EHRR 647.

[126] The language of 'effective, proportionate and dissuasive' can be traced to the ECJ's judgment in C-68/88 *Commission v Greece* [1989] ECR 2965.

[127] Pending the adoption of such legislation, the regulation provides that the penalties shall be those determined in accordance with regulation 467/2001, Art 13. This is of no real use, as it in turn points to regulation 337/2000, Art 10: a clause identical to Art 10(1) of regulation 881/2002. The result of the journey down the rabbit hole is that Art 10(1) and Art 10(2) of regulation 881/2002 appear to be identical in their legal effect—requiring 'effective, proportionate and dissuasive' penalties.

rule of law. In terms of the safeguarding aspect of the rule of law the problem is more one of evasion. By avoiding being characterised as 'criminal penalties', the sanctions escape higher requirements of legality and due process. Nonetheless, it is clear that the system as it exists at present violates the principle of legality and breaches even civil due process standards.

B. Co-operation and Prevention

The sanctions may not amount to criminal penalties, notwithstanding the effect on individuals. However, as seen throughout this book, counter-terrorism laws may also provide the basis for law enforcement co-operation and extraordinary preventive powers for use solely against those suspected of terrorism. A system aimed at preventing the financing of crime would logically fulfil two general conditions: first, the freezing of assets would be linked to a criminal investigation and second, the investigation would be for clearly defined crimes relating to terrorism. It is conceivable that prior to the bringing of criminal proceedings against an individual, the state may wish to freeze their assets to prevent their dispersal or use for criminal activities. In the alternative, the state may confiscate a convict's assets following their successful conviction for criminal offences. Neither scenario can be said to accurately describe the sanctions system in place in the EU. Rather, the EU has frozen the assets of individuals and entities based on the suspicion that they can be linked to criminal activity (terrorism).

If a temporary system of sanctions were to be devised then it could only be appropriate to target any individuals groups or entities based on their 'linking' to a clearly defined crime. This would be a first step towards compliance with the principle of legality. In the EU, it might reasonably be expected that the definition of the crime (terrorism) against which such individuals' actions would be judged would be those provided in the relevant criminal law (Framework Decision on Combating Terrorism). The definitions of 'terrorist act' and 'terrorist group' in the framework decision are law across the EU. In considering whether or not this is indeed the basis for the targeting of particular individuals and entities, it is necessary to consider the UN and EU sanctions lists separately. In terms of the former, although the common position implementing the UN sanctions list contains the EU definition of terrorism, there is no causal link between an individual's activities, the definition, and their listing under the sanctions system. Indeed, the Commission's list simply mirrors that of the 1267 Committee, which in turn operates based on information supplied by national authorities. This situation might be sustainable if the 1267 Committee itself operated on the basis of a clear definition of terrorism. UN Security Council resolution 1822 makes clear that an individual can be targeted if they are suspected of participating in, financing, planning, facilitating, preparing or perpetrating acts by, under the name of, on behalf of, or in support of; supplying, selling or transferring arms to; recruiting for; or 'otherwise supporting acts or activities of' 'Al-Qaeda, Osama bin

Laden or the Taleban, or any cell, affiliate, splinter group or derivative thereof'.[128] Given the breadth of this definition, it would be worrying enough if the 1267 Committee were operating on this basis. However, the 1267 Committee lists individuals based on requests from states. In the case of Mr Kadi, the request for the listing came from the US Treasury Department.[129] It is not clear if Mr Kadi is suspected of supporting terrorism based on a definition in US law, based on US Treasury Department administrative rules, or based on the definition contained in UN Security Council resolution 1822. However, it is clear that at no point were his actions judged against the definition of terrorism operating in EU law. The request of the US Treasury Department was simply carried out by the 1267 Committee and subsequently the European Commission.

One might reasonably expect the situation to be better with regard to the EU sanctions list. Resolution 1373 requires states to adopt appropriate measures to freeze the assets of those linked to terrorist acts.[130] No definition of terrorism is provided by the resolution. Thus, it is reasonable to assume that it calls for the freezing of assets of individuals and entities involved in terrorism as defined under national law. This is itself problematic, given the academically contested and politically controversial nature of any such definition. The UN resolution essentially offers broad scope for repressive (and indeed ostensibly liberal) systems to identify and target certain political actors as 'terrorists' and take intrusive coercive action against them. Within the EU the test should be that provided for by the Framework Decision on Combating Terrorism. At a legislative level, this is indeed the case, with the relevant measures including the definitions in the framework decision.[131] However, practically the EU sanctions list operates based on decisions of national authorities. Any notion that such authorities are using the EU definition of terrorism can be dispelled by examining the failure to transpose the definition into national law.

The obvious conclusion is that even if the sanctions system is viewed as an extraordinary preventive counter-terrorism measure, it still breaches key rule of law principles. First, the absence of any clear rules on why any particular individuals or entities are targeted by either the UN or EU sanctions list is a breach of the principle of legality. The presence of multiple definitions of terrorism, and the apparent application of none of them, is a clear breach of this cornerstone of the constitutive aspect of the rule of law. Problems with the constitutive aspect of the rule of law have consequential effects for the rule of law's safeguarding aspect. If the relevant rules are vague and are not applied then the individual cannot know what rules they are subject to. Furthermore, the procedures by which individuals are listed lack transparency and are not open to participation by those subject to them.

---

[128] Art 2 UNSC Res 1822.
[129] *Newsweek* 'Terror Watch: Antiterror Victory?' (22 June 2005).
[130] Art 1 UNSC Res 1373.
[131] Art 1 Council Common Position 2001/931/CFSP; Arts 1–4 Council Framework Decision of 13 June 2002 on combating terrorism (2002/475/JHA).

C. Understanding the Sanctions as Pre-emption

The sanctions system does not amount to criminal law but nor is it appropriately characterised as preventive—certainly not if basic rule of law principles are to be observed. Rather, the system is best characterised as one that is pre-emptive. It uses executive and administrative power to deploy coercive power against the individual with little accountability for those affected. It undermines the principle of individual culpability and uses 'guilt by association' to identify those targeted. The system imposes sanctions that evidence an emphasis on incapacitation rather than on prosecution and punishment. It is by understanding the sanctions system as pre-emptive that the problems for the rule of law come clearly into focus. The trend towards pre-emption is evidenced by the empowering of executives and administrators, the shift away from a focus on individual culpability and the use of the financial system for control.

i. Executive and Administrative Power

A recurring feature of EU counter-terrorism action is the empowerment of executive and administrative actors with little provision for accountability mechanisms. Nowhere is this more accurate a criticism than in the case of the sanctions system. Individuals subject to the UN sanctions list are added at the request of national governments: the executive organ of the state acting on information from police intelligence agencies. Prior to the adoption of UN Security Council resolution 1989 a request for delisting required the support of a member state government to succeed. Within the EU, national authorities' reactions to delisting requests have been mixed. For example, the Swedish government engaged in much diplomacy on behalf of Mr Yusuf and his fellow litigants.[132] Other governments were less helpful. For example, in the *Hassan* case, the applicant had little hope of assistance, as the British government intervened against him in the litigation.[133] Without the support of a national government, an individual could not be removed from the UN sanctions list. The improvements in the delisting process have removed the need for government support for delisting—but retained the need for the UN Security Council to acquiesce in delisting. The process remains diplomatic rather than judicial. The ECJ's efforts in *Kadi I* have formally asserted the rights of those listed, to judicial review but at UN level that review does not come with an effective remedy.

Executive and administrative power is also prominent in the operation of the EU sanctions list. Those targeted are added based on the decision of a 'competent national authority'. Ideally this should be a judicial authority, but the *OMPI* case makes clear that the authority may be an executive actor at ministerial or

---

[132] CC Murphy, 'Questioning *Yusef*: quis custodiet ipsos custodes?' (2006) *University College Dublin Law Review* 109; CC Murphy, '*Ayadi v Council*: Competence and Justice in the 'War on Terrorism' (2007) 29 *Dublin University Law Journal* 426.

[133] T-49/04 *Hassan v Council and Commission* [2006] ECR II-52.

prosecutorial level.[134] Indeed, the experience of OMPI demonstrates a clear divergence between the law as set out in the relevant regulation and its operation in practice. In the later OMPI cases the Council was unable to convince the Court that it could reasonably base the listing on the decision of a competent national.[135] The authority was said to be the UK Home Secretary until his decision was overturned by a judicial authority in that jurisdiction. Thereafter, OMPI was relisted based on a decision of a French prosecutor. As the CFI has noted, the basis for that decision is itself dubious: OMPI has been implicated largely on the basis of arrests of certain persons who may or may not be members of the organisation.[136] Reading the OMPI cases, it is difficult not to come to the conclusion that the Council, acting at the instigation of the UK government, decided to list OMPI regardless of the decisions of 'competent national authorities'. The eventual delisting of OMPI in January 2009 came after not just several court judgments, but a concerted political effort that included a petition signed by parliamentarians from across the EU.[137]

A final relevant point relates to the multi-layered nature of the sanctions. In the EU, there are global (UN), regional (EU) and several national asset-freezing sanctions systems in place.[138] If the purpose of the system is to identify and proscribe financial activity by those suspected of terrorism, then the logical approach would be to harmonise—or at the very least co-ordinate—the systems. The seeming impossibility of unravelling the administrative procedures that lead to listing, and to hold the appropriate authorities to account presents clear problems in a jurisdiction whose legal system is based on the rule of law. However, it fits as part of a system of control that harnesses all forms of power to achieve a particular end. In this case that end is the continued listing of Mr Kadi and other targeted individuals and entities—regardless of the pronouncements of courts or the requirements of legal principles such as the rule of law.

ii. Individual Culpability and Presumption of Innocence

The presumption of innocence is a key principle of European human rights law.[139] However, the sanctions system offends the principle by transferring culpability from persons convicted of, or suspected of, terrorist acts to those merely 'associated' with them. As Cole points out in relation to the equivalent US laws, this is

---

[134] T-284/08 *People's Mojahedin Organization of Iran v Council of the European Union* CFI Judgment 3 December 2008.

[135] Case T-256/07 *People's Mojahedin Organization of Iran v Council of the European Union* CFI Judgment 23 October 2008, para 185; T-284/08 *People's Mojahedin Organization of Iran v Council of the European Union* CFI Judgment 3 December 2008, paras 64–65.

[136] Ibid, para 56.

[137] Reuters UK, 'EU Takes Iran Opposition Group Off Terror List' (26 January 2009).

[138] Eg, the UK operates a national scheme under the Terrorism Acts. See S Marques da Silva and CC Murphy, 'Proscription of Organisations in UK Counter-Terrorism Law' in Cameron (ed), *Legal Aspects of EU Sanctions* (Mortsel, Intersentia, forthcoming 2012).

[139] Art 6(2) ECHR; Art 48 EU Charter.

very much modern 'guilt by association'.[140] Even if the lists were devised based on the legal rules setting out terrorist offences within the EU, those rules have been shown in previous chapters to be broad, vaguely drafted, and inconsistently transposed into national law, even within the EU. It is difficult, if not impossible, to defend a system that does not require an individual to be convicted of, or even charged with, a criminal offence when the available offences cast so wide a net. Furthermore, at least one of the two lists (the UN sanctions list) operates based on a factual presumption of guilt. Any person seeking delisting is required to submit evidence to demonstrate that they 'no longer [meet] the criteria' for listing.[141] The presumption is therefore that, at the very least, they once did meet those criteria.

A further breach of the presumption of innocence is to be found in the new policy of publishing narrative statements relating to each listing. The ECtHR found a breach of the presumption of innocence in the somewhat similar case of *Allenet de Ribemont*. In that case, members of the French government and prosecuting authorities announced on television that the perpetrator of a high profile murder had been apprehended, naming the applicant. The Court held that the presumption of innocence was breached even though no charges were ever brought.[142] It is difficult therefore not to find fault with a UN Security Council statement of case that includes the following excerpt:

> According to investigations by the Federal Public Prosecutor, there is good reason to believe that HARRACH [the listed individual] has been a member of the foreign terrorist organization Al Qaeda since March 2007. The threats he has distributed via the Al Qaeda media office demonstrate his willingness as a member of Al Qaeda to participate in its terrorist activity all the way to suicide attacks.[143]

Making such a public statement certainly breaches the spirit of the ruling in *Allenet de Ribemont*. While the EU itself is not responsible for the actions of the UN Security Council, by implementing the sanctions within its jurisdiction it can hardly be said to uphold the principle of presumption of innocence. Furthermore, it is not clear what is to be achieved by publishing these narrative statements. The 1267 Committee could easily transmit the statement of reasons to the relevant state authorities for the purpose of informing the individuals and entities concerned as to the reasons for their listing. The release of the information into the public domain is entirely unnecessary for the effective operation of the sanctions system. Rather, it may be an attempt to garner public support for the system by publishing unverifiable and highly pejorative statements about individuals as proven fact. The 1267 Committee website is host to numerous other examples of such

---

[140] D Cole 'Terror Financing, Guilt by Association and the Paradigm of Prevention in the 'War on Terror' in A Bianchi and A Keller (eds), *Counterterrorism: Democracy's Challenge* (Oxford, Hart Publishing, 2008).

[141] s 7(d) 1267 Committee Guidelines.

[142] *Allenet de Ribemont v France* [1995] 20 EHRR 557.

[143] UN Security Council Department of Public Information, News and Media Division, 'Statement of Case against Bekkay Harrach', SC/9667 (New York, 28 May 2009).

narrative statements.[144] Insofar as this operates to reinforce counter-terrorism action it fits with a pre-emptive approach by perpetrating a particular discourse to attempt to justify the action taken. It strips the individual of protections that are key to the safeguarding aspect of the rule of law.

iii. Financial Sanctions as Control

The final element to be considered from the point of view of pre-emption is the practical effect of the sanctions. Control through incapacitation is a central tenet of pre-emption. The targeted asset-freezing sanctions represent the very real incapacitation of those targeted. While the anti-money-laundering legislation aims to convict criminals, the sanctions systems do not. An example serves to illustrate the point. Mr Ayadi was refused permission to obtain a taxi license by the Irish authorities as to issue such a license (and to allow him to work as a taxi driver) would allow him access to economic resources in breach of the sanctions system. When considering this refusal, the CFI noted that nothing prevented Mr Ayadi from working, the authorities would simply freeze his salary and he and his family would subsist on state support.[145] The effect on organisations is arguably even more severe. For a political organisation, freezing of assets and related sanctions effectively sounds the death-knell for its activities. However, such lists are unlikely to have much impact on groups truly committed to political violence. For example, there is little evidence that the proscription by the British and Irish Governments had any effect on the activities of the Provisional IRA in Northern Ireland in the 1980s.[146] Thus, by listing political organisations, the EU effectively shrinks the space for political debate in Europe without necessarily reaping any security dividend. The targeted sanctions thus have an even more detrimental effect on the public sphere than the political or financial exclusion discussed in previous chapters—potentially ending the political activities of those targeted.

That the sanctions are coercive is clear. Though they are not, strictly speaking, 'criminal penalties', they are clearly punitive and cannot realistically be called temporary. Therefore, though the measures do not result in a criminal conviction, the result so infringes human rights that it can only be described as punitive. The UN system was aptly described as 'financial Guantánamo' by David Anderson QC in 2006.[147] This is not mere hyperbole. Faced with such coercive control, it is entirely understandable that the applicant in *Othman* claimed that the system 'interferes extremely seriously with [his] dignity' and 'makes it impossible for

---

[144] See: www.un.org/sc/committees/1267/, last accessed 16 May 2011.

[145] T-253/02 *Ayadi v Council* [2006] ECR II-2139. In 2011 Mr Ayadi became one of the first individuals to be delisted following a recommendation of the Ombudsperson under the UN Security Council resolution 1989 procedures. See UN Security Council Press Release SC/10413 of 17 October 2011.

[146] Marques da Silva and Murphy, n 138 above.

[147] D Anderson, Centre of European Law Annual Conference, King's College London, 10 March 2006.

[him] to have the means of enjoying the normal aspects of civilised existence'.[148] Individuals targeted are unable to carry out an ordinary life while subject to the sanctions, some of which have been in place for almost a decade. This is longer than the minimum maximum sentences provided for by the Framework Decision on Combating Terrorism for the offence of participating in a terrorist group. It is impossible to equate different state interventions and it is not suggested that the targeted sanctions are equivalent to incarceration. However, the comparison is nonetheless striking.

The move to potentially permanent incapacitation may be traced to the pre-emptive shift since 11 September 2001. Prior to the attacks on that day, it was clear to those listed by the 1267 Committee what action would prompt delisting. However, all revisions of the Security Council resolutions since that day have removed the possibility that the individuals would be delisted if they altered their behaviour. The EU sanctions list operates in a similar vein. While OMPI was listed, the relevant authorities noted explicitly that the question to be considered was not whether OMPI were linked to terrorist activities in the past or at present, but whether they were *likely to do so* in the future.[149] This language is patently that of pre-emption, with the basis for government action being the prediction of future activity and not an assessment of guilt for previous acts.

IV. CONCLUSION: THE LIMITS OF THE RULE OF LAW?

Mr Kadi's experience demonstrates the limits of the rule of law—that is the limited ability of the legal process to correct state action where that action subverts the principles of the legal order itself. The European judiciary have responded to Advocate General Maduro's call to arms and delivered a judgment which, if considered by the academic reaction alone, offered almost everything a plaintiff could hope for. However, that has to date changed little of the applicant's practical situation: all of his assets in the EU remain frozen while the legal process reasserts the rule of law inch by inch. The targeted sanctions demonstrate the danger of trying to deviate from a rule of law approach to counter-terrorism action. Once the basic tenets of the principles of legality and due process are undermined through the political process, the legal system can seriously struggle to rectify the situation to the detriment of those subject to the law. Judicial review of European implementation of the Al-Qaeda and Taleban list remains the 'right fit' to secure the rule of law in the absence of due process at international level.[150]

---

[148] *Othman*, n 103 above, paras 63–64.

[149] T-256/07 *People's Mojahedin Organization of Iran v Council of the European Union* CFI Judgment 23 October 2008 [110].

[150] Eeckhout, n 68 above. For support from a UN point of view see: M Scheinin, 'Is the ECJ Ruling in *Kadi* Incompatible with International Law?' in P Eeckhout and T Tridimas (eds), *Yearbook of European Law* (Oxford, Oxford University Press, 2009) 637.

In conducting that review, the ECJ must necessarily address several difficult questions including the relationship between different legal orders, the appropriate level of judicial review in times of emergency and the extent to which human rights may be interfered with in the absence of criminal prosecution. The abject failure of the UN sanctions system to provide any due process allowed the ECJ to annul the measure without having to address in detail what level of review it would consider appropriate. The Court was also able to fashion a distinction between review of the EU law and review of the UN resolution it sought to implement—thus dodging the problem of regional review of international law. It is unlikely to be able to avoid the problem for long. The Stockholm Programme notes that the Union 'must ensure that its policies are in full compliance with international law, in particular, human rights law'. Nonetheless, it commits the EU to continuing to work towards 'enhancing the design, implementation and effectiveness of sanctions by the UN Security Council with a view to safeguarding fundamental rights and freedoms and ensuring fair and clear procedures'.[151]

In his report to Parliament on 28 February 2011 the Financial Secretary to the Treasury noted that there was £140,000 of assets frozen in the UK under the general EU/UK sanctions regime and just under £140,000 of assets across 112 accounts frozen in the UK under the Al-Qaeda and Taleban sanctions regime.[152] These are not large sums of money—but political violence does not necessarily require large sums of money to make an impact. Targeted sanctions are a rather cumbersome tool of counter-terrorist finance which presents problems for constitutional governance while having a questionable effect on counter-terrorism. The 9/11 Commission Report notes that shifts in how violence is funded might render existing counter-terrorist finance tools outdated.[153] However they will persist as long as they are considered a useful tool of 'diplomacy'[154] to designate individuals, groups and entities and to restrict their political actions. If the EU is to continue to support this system then it must be drastically overhauled. It exhibits characteristics of 'counter-law'—law that operates in a manner that is contrary to the very principles upon which legal systems are based.[155] The result is the subversion of the legal system for political aims to the detriment of both the system itself and the individuals whose lives it regulates.

---

[151] OJ C115/25 (4 May 2010).

[152] M Hoban, Hansard HC col 3WS (28 February 2011).

[153] National Commission on Terrorist Attacks Upon the United States, *The 9/11 Commission Report: Final Report of the National Commission on Terrorist Attacks Upon the United States* (New York, WH Norton & Co, 2004) 383.

[154] As they are intriguingly described in the *9/11 Commission Report*:
Public designation of terrorist financiers and organizations is still part of the fight, but it is not the primary weapon. Designations are instead a form of diplomacy, as governments join together to identify named individuals and groups as terrorists. They also prevent open fundraising. (ibid, p 382)

[155] R Ericson, *Crime in an Insecure World* (Cambridge, Polity Press, 2007) 24.

6

Data Surveillance

S URVEILLANCE IS THE broadest of the EU's actions to counter terrorism. The terrorist offences, targeted sanctions and other counter-terrorist finance measures already considered are primarily, though not entirely, limited in their effects to those suspected of involvement in terrorism. In contrast surveillance systems can impact upon the whole population. Even before counter-terrorism became the dominant paradigm for government the use of surveillance for crime control was growing at pace.[1] The EU, which had not yet asserted its role in relation to criminal justice, used databases extensively in immigration and border controls. Today surveillance systems target not just immigrants, asylum seekers and suspected criminals but also the whole population. The breadth of the data surveillance systems as well as the manner in which they have been put in place has implications for the rule of law. In terms of the constitutive aspect of the rule of law, state action is increasingly based on technological rationales empowered by law that confers broad discretion (and obligations) on executive, administrative and private actors. If discretion is conferred its use should be subject to review so as to comply with the rule of law. However, many data surveillance systems fail this basic rule of law requirement. Mass surveillance removes the link between unlawful behaviour and interference with human rights. Thus the safeguarding role of the rule of law is affected as the entire population is held to account for what a minority might do. Surveillance in the EU since the events of 11 September 2001 has exhibited both trends—it is in relation to financial, telecommunications and travel data. Though the different schemes interfere with privacy in different ways and to a different extent the overall trend is towards 'digital panopticism'—the total surveillance of the population as a whole.

I. DATA SURVEILLANCE AND DATA PROTECTION IN THE 'WAR ON TERROR'

The EU had already used data surveillance systems even prior to 11 September 2011. A communication from the Commission to the European Parliament and

---

[1] B Bowling, A Marks and CC Murphy, 'Crime Control Technologies: Towards an Analytical Framework and Research Agenda' in R Brownsword and K Yeung (eds), *Regulating Technologies* (Oxford, Hart Publishing, 2008) 61–63.

the Council in 2010 opened with an observation that 'neither the Schengen area nor the EU internal market could function today without cross-border data exchange'.[2] Early EU databases thus include the Schengen Information System and Customs Information System which became operational in 1995. The Commission communication notes the impact of the attacks in New York, Madrid and London on the development of policy in this area. It sets out in rigorous detail, over 28 pages, the wide range of data collection, storage and exchange instruments in EU law. The majority of these are aimed at surveillance and control of asylum, migration and crime. The Commission concludes that the EU should 'enhance the coherence and effectiveness of current and future instruments in a manner that fully respects citizens' fundamental rights'.[3]

While asylum and migration was the initial focus of EU data surveillence the growth in EU criminal justice has seen the focus broaden to security in general. Following 11 September 2011, the Council Action Plan on Combating Terrorism made several references to such systems.[4] Under 'Border Control', it referred to implementation of a Council Decision and Regulations on the next generation of Schengen; a Council Regulation on the Visa Information System; and the introduction of biometrics in EU passports. Most notably, under 'Information Gathering, Analysis and Exchange', the Action Plan referred to the drafting of framework decisions to simplify information exchange between law enforcement authorities and on the principle of availability; referred once again to the Visa Information System and the new Schengen system; called for the implementation of the Data Retention Directive; and sought better information exchange between national authorities and Europol and Eurojust. The latter two bodies also operate their own databases, the Europol Information System and the Eurojust Information System.

It is therefore clear that the 'war on terror' has seen an increased focus in the EU on the use of data surveillance as a tool of counter-terrorism action.[5] This is, nonetheless, part of a wider change in the use of surveillance. In the field of border control, for example, Mitsilegas notes five transformational trends in recent years. These are the linking of immigration with security and counter-terrorism, increasing use of biometrics, a shift towards prevention, widening access to data

---

[2] Commission (EC), 'Communication from the Commission to the European Parliament and the Council: Overview of Information Management in the Area of Freedom, Security and Justice' COM (2010) 385 final, Brussels, 20 July 2010.

[3] Ibid.

[4] European Council, EU Action Plan on combating terrorism (Brussels, 9 March 2007).

[5] For a historical view see T Mathiesen, 'The Globalisation of Control: Towards an Integrated Surveillance System in Europe' in P Green and A Rutherford (eds), *Criminal Policy in Transition* (Oxford, Hart Publishing, 2000). For an overview of the databases currently operational under EU law, see: V Mitsilegas, *EU Criminal Law* (Oxford, Hart Publishing, 2009) ch V: Databases. For an overview of US surveillance since September 11, 2001 see LK Donohue, *The Cost of Counterterrorism: Power, Politics, and Liberty* (Cambridge, Cambridge University Press, 2008) 218–66.

by police and security agencies and the use of risk assessments.[6] These trends are present not just in border controls but in surveillance in general. The growth in use of surveillance has been in accordance with a 'utilitarian' logic: 'information must be seen as a tool for collective benefits like fighting terrorism … everything must be done to ensure that information is available when needed'.[7] This idea of 'availability' runs counter to the traditional data protection principle of limiting the use of data to purposes specified in advance of data collection.[8] The reversal is most evident in relation to the Data Retention Directive which explicitly amended the earlier e-Privacy Directive which had required deletion rather than retention of data once it was no longer needed for billing purposes.[9]

In addition to collecting, storing and exchanging a greater volume of data within jurisdictions there has also been an increased emphasis on exchange of data between jurisdictions. Since 11 September 2001 the EU and US have increasingly sought to co-operate through the sharing of data related to internal security. EU–US co-operation is made problematic by the different constitutional frameworks and cultures of privacy in the two jurisdictions.[10] In legal terms the protection of privacy in general and data privacy in particular is less clear-cut in the US whereas in Europe it is based on eight key principles.[11] In terms of culture the difference has been described as a US focus on liberty in contrast to a European focus on dignity.[12] Whether legal, cultural, or both, it is clear that the difference exists and that it has impacted upon EU–US co-operation since 11 September 2011.

Within the EU, insofar as the safeguarding role of the rule of law requires the protection of fundamental rights, it requires a system of protection of data privacy. In particular, any data surveillance within the EU must comply with both

---

[6] V Mitsilegas, 'The Transformation of Border Controls in an Era of Security: UK and EU Systems Converging?', (2010) 24 *Journal of Immigration Asylum and Nationality Law* 233.

[7] H Hijmans and A Scirocco, 'Shortcomings in EU Data Protection in the Third and The Second Pillars. Can the Lisbon Treaty be Expected to Help?' (2009) 46 *Common Market Law Review* 1485, 1490.

[8] The principle of availability is defined in the Hague Programme as entailing that 'throughout the Union, a law enforcement officer in one Member State who needs information in order to perform his duties can obtain this from another Membeer State and that the law enforcement agency in the other Member State which holds this information will make it available for the stated purpose, taking into account the requirement of ongoing investigations in that state.'
Commission (EC), 'The Hague Programme: Ten Priorities for the Next Five Years' COM (2005) 184 final.

[9] See text following n 113 below.

[10] S Sottiaux, *Terrorism and the Limitation of Rights: The ECHR and the US Constitution* (Oxford, Hart Publishing, 2008) 265–322. See further JQ Whitman, 'The Two Western Cultures of Privacy: Dignity Versus Liberty' (2004) 113 *Yale Law Journal* 1151–221. In the US, while there is no explicit protection for a general right to privacy in the Bill of Rights, most legal theorists infer one from the specific rights in the First, Fourth, Fifth and Nineth Amendments. The classic case is presented by SD Warren and LD Brandeis 'The Right to Privacy' (1890) 4 *Harvard Law Review* 193. However, as Sottiaux notes, the patchwork nature of this protection and the largely legislative basis for it has left privacy rights in the US vulnerable to executive and legislative interference in the post-September 11 environment.

[11] Sottiaux, *Terrorism and the Limitation of Rights*, n 10 above, pp 266–68.

[12] Whitman, n 10 above, p 1219.

constitutional and legislative standards on data protection.[13] The right to data protection is enshrined at a constitutional level through the general privacy right in Article 8 of the European Convention on Human Rights as well as the more specific right to protection of personal data in Article 8 of the EU Charter of Fundamental Rights.[14] At a legislative level the EU has adopted two directives: the Data Protection Directive in 1995 and the e-Privacy Directive in 2002.[15] In 2008 a framework decision was adopted to provide similar protection in relation to police and judicial co-operation in criminal matters (as this field of activity is explicitly excluded from the Data Protection Directive).[16] However these instruments do not comprehensively cover all data processing and their operation in practice may be problematic. Although the Lisbon Treaty offers the potential for improvement in this area the system of protection to date remains incomplete.[17]

There is not the space here to discuss the legislative framework governing data protection in the EU in detail. The central principles can be found in Article 8 of the Charter. The article states that individuals have the right to protection of personal data. Article 8(2) elaborates on the right stating that

> such data must be processed fairly for specified purposes and on the basis of the consent of the person concerned or some other legitimate basis laid down by law. Everyone has the right of access to data which has been collected concerning him or her, and the right to have it rectified.

Finally the Charter requires that compliance 'shall be subject to control by an independent authority'. The rights afforded by the Charter require implementation in any EU surveillance instruments if they are to be effective. However, many

---

[13] For a useful overview of data protection as a legal concept see H Hijmans and A Scirocco, 'Shortcomings in EU Data Protection in the Third and The Second Pillars. Can the Lisbon Treaty be Expected to Help?' (2009) 46 *Common Market Law Review* 1485, 1487–89.

[14] In *Marper* the Court noted that the concept of private life is 'a broad term not susceptible to exhaustive definition'. The right to privacy under the ECHR protects 'a right to personal development, and the right to establish and develop relationships with other human beings and the outside world'. In addition, 'mere storing of data relating to the private life of an individual amounts to an interference within the meaning of Article 8'. The Court also noted that

> in determining whether the personal information retained by the authorities involves any of the private-life aspects mentioned above, the Court will have due regard to the specific context in which the information at issue has been recorded and retained, the nature of the records, the way in which these records are used and processed and the results that may be obtained. (*S. and Marper v UK* [2008] ECHR 1581 paras 66–67)

Art 8 of the EU Charter of Fundamental Rights is also reflected in the jurisprudence of the European Court of Justice. See Case C-275/06 *Promusicae* [2008] ECR I-271, Joined Cases C-465/00, C-138/01, C-139/01 *Osterreichischer Rundfunk and Others* [2003] ECR I-4989.

[15] Directive 95/46/EC of the European Parliament and of the European Council of 24 October 1995 on the protection of individuals with regard to the processing of personal data and on the free movement of such data; Directive 2002/58/EC of the European Parliament and of the Council of 12 July 2002 concerning the processing of personal data and the protection of privacy in the electronic communications sector.

[16] Council Framework Decision 2008/977/JHA of 27 November 2008 on the protection of personal data processed in the framework of police and judicial co-operation in criminal matters.

[17] Hijmans and Scirocco, n 13 above, p 1496.

of the instruments that establish counter-terrorism data surveillance systems have failed to adequately provide oversight mechanisms. In light of the shift in emphasis after September 11, 2001 data protection has played a secondary role as governments focus on data collection and data mining. The analysis of EU instruments that follows makes it clear that 'creating a stable and unequivocal system of data protection was not a priority'.[18]

II. DATA SURVEILLENCE IN EU COUNTER-TERRORISM

The EU legislative landscape is cluttered with various measures that can be and are used for data surveillance and counter-terrorism action. An examination of three EU policy initiatives in this field—the Terrorist Finance Tracking Programme (TFTP), the Passenger Name Record (PNR) systems and telecommunications data retention—provides evidence of trends contrary to the rule of law. The Agreements and legislation afford greater power to executive and administrative agencies on dubious legal bases with little accountability. In doing so they open up a space in which security services that lack legitimacy can act while subject to limited legal and political safeguards and thus present challenges to both the constitutive and the safeguarding roles of the rule of law.

A. Terrorist Finance Tracking Programme

Counter-terrorist finance has been a key policy area for both the EU and US over the past decade. The US Terrorist Finance Tracking Programme is a system and overlaps the counter-terrorist finance and data surveillance policy areas which has its origin in US counter-terrorism in the aftermath of the September 11 attacks. Based in Belgium and the US, the Society for Worldwide Interbank Financial Telecommunication (SWIFT) provides secure messaging services to the global banking sector. The SWIFT database in the US not only stored information relating to financial transactions in that country—it also held a copy of all financial transaction messages processed by SWIFT's European base in Belgium.[19] The increased focus on the financing of terrorism prompted US law enforcement agencies to issue sub poenas to SWIFT to access all data held on its servers relating to financial transactions. Thus, with no regulatory oversight, SWIFT had been transferring EU financial transaction information for use by the Central Intelligence Agency, the Federal Bureau of Investigation and other law enforcement agencies. The practice came to light following the publication of a *New York Times* article which provoked outrage on both sides of the Atlantic. The European

---

[18] Hijmans and Scirocco, n 13 above, p 1496.
[19] E Lichtblau and J Risen, 'Bank Data Sifted in Secret by US to Block Terror', *New York Times* (23 June 2006).

Parliament expressed 'serious concern ... that a climate of deteriorating respect for privacy and data protection' was being created.[20] Furthermore, the Article 29 Working Group, a data protection working group set up by the EU Data Protection Directive, issued a highly critical opinion.[21] In response, the operation of the TFTP system was altered to comply with the 'Safe Harbour' principles which allow US companies to self-regulate in accordance with EU data protection rules.[22]

In the face of criticism of the system SWIFT established a new data repository in Switzerland to house European financial messaging information where it would not be subject to sub poena by US authorities. To allay the fears of both EU and US governments losing access to TFTP data negotiations began for an agreement on data transfer. In September 2009 the European Parliament adopted a resolution expressing concern that any EU–US co-operation in this field be strictly limited to what is necessary and proportionate and that it respect human rights and the rule of law.[23] On 30 November 2009 the Council adopted a decision concluding an agreement with the US (TFTP-I). However, in February 2010 the Parliament withheld its consent from TFTP-I.[24] The Council and Commission then altered their negotiating stance on the issue—a move that was welcomed by the Parliament as a 'new spirit of cooperation'.[25] There remained deficiencies in the Agreement's protection of individual privacy.[26] In July 2010, notwithstanding the Agreement's flaws, the European Parliament consented to the conclusion of a second agreement (TFTP-II).[27]

---

[20] European Parliament, 'Resolution on the interception of bank transfer data from the SWIFT system by the US secret services' P6_TA(2006)0317, 7 July 2006.

[21] Art 29 Data Protection Working Group, 'Opinion 10/2006 on the processing of personal data by the Society for Worldwide Interbank Financial Telecommunication (SWIFT)', Brussels, 22 November 2006.

[22] MR VanWasshnova, 'Data Protection Conflicts Between the United States and the European Union in the War on Terror: Lessons Learned from the Existing System of Financial Information Exchange' (2006–2008) 29 *Case Western Reserve Journal of International Law* 827. See the letters exchanged between the US and the EU on June 28 2007 and published in OJ C166/17 (20 July 2007).

[23] European Parliament, Resolution of 17 September 2009 on the envisaged international agreement to make available to the United States Treasury Department financial payment messaging data to prevent and combat terrorism and terrorist financing OJ C224 E/8 (19 August 2010).

[24] European Parliament, Legislative resolution of 11 February 2010 on the proposal for a Council decision on the conclusion of the Agreement between the European Union and the United States of America on the processing and transfer of Financinal Messaging Data from the European Union to the United States for purposes of the Terrorist Finance Tracking Program 2010/C 341 E/25 OJ C341 E/100 (16 December 2010).

[25] European Parliament, Resolution of 5 May 2010 on the Recommendation from the Commission to the Council to authorise the opening of negotiations for an agreement between the European Union and the United States of America to make available to the United States Treasury Department financial messaging data to prevent and combat terrorism and terrorist financing OJ C81 E/66 (15 March 2011).

[26] Opinion of the European Data Protection Supervisor on the proposal for a Council Decision on the conclusion of the Agreement between the European Union and the United States of America on the processing and transfer of Financial Messaging Data from the European Union to the United States for purposes of the Terrorist Finance Tracking Program (TFTP-II) OJ C355/10 (29 December 2010).

[27] For a descriptive overview of the TFTP-II Agreement see V Pfisterer, 'The Second SWIFT Agreement Between the European Union and the United States of America: An Overview' (2010) 11 *German Law Journal* 1173.

The first Commission report following a joint review of the operation of the system sheds light on implementation of TFTP-II.[28] The operation of the programme is supervised on the European side by Europol though that supervision has been criticised by the European Parliament.[29] The US authorities request a bulk data transfer from SWIFT (referred to as the 'designated provider' in the Agreement) on a monthly basis. That request is verified by Europol who may, and do, ask for further justification for the request before approving it. Once the data has been transferred to the US it may be searched by those who operate the TFTP. Searches must be individualised (ie not based on arbitrary signifiers such as race, ethnicity or religious belief) and a 'terrorism nexus' must be established *before* the search is carried out. The operation of the Agreement is overseen by supervisors who have the authority to refuse to permit a search to go ahead. US authorities carried out 27,006 searches in the period between August 2010 and February 2011. Leads resulting from these searches were transmitted to US law enforcement agencies, to the EU and to several third countries. The Commission report notes that it is difficult to assess the necessity or effectiveness of the system as those in receipt of intelligence derived from TFTP are not aware of the source of the information. Despite an overall satisfactory assessment from the Commission there remain problems with the programme which have led to heated disputes within and between European institutions.[30]

i. Legal Basis

In the United States the initial collection, storage and processing of financial messaging information by SWIFT was based on mandates in statutes and Executive Orders. However the system did not have a basis in EU law. The action was possible by virtue of European data being 'mirrored' on SWIFT's US server and thus subject to US law. Though the US legislative framework is not the subject of the present analysis it is noteworthy that the situation is far from clear on that side of the Atlantic. While SWIFT did its utmost to comply with the US sub poenas it could have refused to do so. In that case their enforceability before US courts could have been challenged on the ground that they breach foreign (ie EU) law. Though a moot point today, the existence of the question casts doubt on the legality of the whole Terrorist Finance Tracking Programme.[31] The 'Safe Harbour'

---

[28] This report follows two reports by the 'eminent European person', Judge Jean-Louis Bruguière, who was appointed to oversee the system prior to the implementation of the TFTP-II Agreement. See: Judge Jean-Louis Bruguière, 'Second Report on the Processing of EU-Originating Personal Data by the United States Treasury Department for Counter Terrorism Purposes: Terrorist Finance Tracking Programme', January 2010.

[29] EDRI.org, 'SWIFT agreement implementation not respecting data protection safeguards', 9 March 2011.

[30] EDRI.org, 'EU Commissioner criticises US for the data protection negotiations', 12 January 2011.

[31] PM Connorton, 'Tracking Terrorist Financing Through SWIFT: When U.S. Subpoenas and Foreign Privacy Law Collide' (2007) 76 *Fordham Law Review* 101.

compliance with EU data protection principles was not a legal agreement but a diplomatic one based on an exchange of letters between the EU and the US. There was therefore no EU oversight of the system and so no legal basis for it in EU law. It was not until SWIFT took action to cease mirroring European bank data onto its US server that a formal agreement—and therefore a formal legal basis—was required.

The Council Decision of 30 November 2009 which provided for the conclusion of the TFTP-I Agreement was based on Articles 24 and 38 EU(N). The legal basis used simply requires the Council to adopt the Agreement with no requirement that the European Parliament be involved. The Lisbon Treaty amended this procedure so that the Parliament's consent is now required to conclude such agreements.[32] The decision by the Council to adopt the decision on the eve of the coming into force of the Lisbon Treaty and the new procedure exposes it to criticism and allegations that it was trying to sideline the Parliament. Four Member States—Austria, Germany, Greece and Hungary—abstained in the Council vote while Ireland and Denmark opted not to be part of the instrument. The legal basis has also been the subject of dispute by some Members of the European Parliament. A Belgian MEP, Sophie in 't Veld, sought full access to the Council Legal Service's opinion on the legal basis of the recommendation to opening negotiations on the TFTP-I Agreement. While a redacted version was provided Ms in 't Veld contended that the redaction prevented her from gaining knowledge of the substance of the analysis on the legal basis. A challenge has been brought before the General Court seeking an annulment of the Council's decision to refuse full access.[33]

The coming into force of the Lisbon Treaty empowered the European Parliament in relation to the conclusion of international agreements. Thus, the Council submitted the proposal for a Council Decision to conclude the Agreement to the European Parliament for the latter's consent. Due to delays in translation the Parliament only received the Agreement on 25 January, mere days before its provisional entry into force on 1 February. The resolution refusing consent was adopted on 11 February by 378 votes to 196. Monar argues that the acclaim the European Parliament received following its rejection of the TFTP-I may embolden it in relation to future agreements and thus give it a stronger voice in political wrangling during negotiations.[34] The Council Decision to sign the second Agreement, known as TFTP-II, was based on Articles 87(2)(a) and 88(2) TFEU in conjunction with Article 218(5) TFEU.[35] This legal basis required the consent of the European Parliament. The Second Agreement did not adhere to all of the principles set out in the Parliament's 2009 Resolution. However, the Parliament

---

[32]   See Art 218(6) TFEU.

[33]   Case T-529/09 *In 't Veld v Council* OJ C 80/32 27 March 2010.

[34]   J Monar, 'Editorial Comment: The Rejection of the EU–US SWIFT Interim Agreement by the European Parliament: A Historic Vote and Its Implications' (2010) 15 *European Foreign Affairs Review* 143.

[35]   For a critical discussion of the operation of Art 218 TFEU see P Eeckhout, *EU External Relations Law* (Oxford, Oxford University Press, 2011) 193–211.

nonetheless offered its consent to the the TFTP-II Agreement. The granting of consent notwithstanding the flaws with the TFTP-II Agreement is further evidence that the Parliament may become a more pragmatic political actor when it has actual power to exercise.

While the PNR and data retention instruments have been challenged before the ECJ on grounds of legal basis the same is not true of the TFTP Agreements. Nonetheless the political wrangling over the Agreements demonstrates that legal basis is often a proxy battle over institutional power. This might sometimes be beneficial for the rule of law (if the successful institution uses its power to promote rule of law principles). But—as both the PNR and Data Retention Directive sagas will show—institutional power struggles can also act to undermine the rule of law.

ii. Breadth and Operation of the System

It is clear from the Commission's report on the first Joint Review that the system operates based on a monthly bulk transfer of data from the EU branch of SWIFT to the US.[36] While US authorities could originally obtain the data using administrative sub poenas the migration of SWIFT's European data to Switzerland ended this access to EU financial messaging data. Article 4 TFTP-II requires the US to identify 'as clearly as possible' the data that is requested, 'clearly substantiate the necessity of the data' and ensure that the request is 'tailored as narrowly as possible in order to minimise the amount of data requested'. The request is then subject to verification by Europol.[37] Once verified, the request has 'binding legal effect as provided under U.S. law, within the European Union as well as the United States'.[38] The Commission's report on the first Joint Review suggests that while bulk data is transferred it may be limited by geographic scope, time period or message category.[39] The report does not offer an indication of the volume of data that has been transferred between August 2010 and February 2011. The volume of data transferred is pertinent to the proportionality of the system as a whole. The more data that is transferred the greater the potential infringement of rights and the greater the need for justification through a demonstration of the necessity of the transfer.

Following the transfer of data it can be searched by operators of the TFTP system. The data was searched by the US authorities 27,006 times in the first

---

[36] Commission (EC), 'Commission report on the joint review of the implementation of the Agreement between the European Union and the United States of America on the processing and transfer of Financial Messaging data from the European Union to the United States for the purposes of the Terrorist Finance Tracking Program 17–18 February 2011', Brussels, 16 March 2011 (hereafter, Commission Joint Review Report).

[37] Europol's role is itself a matter of some interest. See the explanatory note from the Commission to the Justice and Home Affairs Council on Europol's role (2010/0177) Brussels, 18 June 2010.

[38] Art 4(5) TFTP-II.

[39] Commission (EC), n 36 above, p 8.

6 months of the operation of TFTP-II. The Agreement specifically excludes data mining 'or any other type of algorithmic or automated profiling or computer filtering'.[40] Searches of the data must be based on 'pre-existing information or evidence which demonstrates a reason to believe that the subject of the search has a nexus to terrorism or its financing'.[41] The concept of a 'nexus to terrorism' is not defined in the Agreement. However, Article 2, which sets out the scope of application, includes a de facto definition of terrorism that is similar, but not identical to, the definition in the Framework Decision on Combating Terrorism. If an EU authority (or an authority of an EU Member State) wishes to request a search of the TFTP data then it must be satisfied that there is 'reason to believe that a person or entity has a nexus to terrorism' as defined by the Framework Decision on Combating Terrorism. This suggests that searches initiated by the US do not have to adhere to the EU definition of terrorism but searches at the request of the EU do. The EU requested 15 such searches in the first 6 months of operation of TFTP-II and received a lead from the US in each case.[42] These searches represent a minute fraction of the overall number of searches and so it appears that the TFTP is a tool used principally by US law enforcement authorities.

Searches of the TFTP data must be narrowly tailored and must be logged. Oversight of searches is provided by 'independent overseers' as provided for in the Agreement.[43] The overseers may 'review in real time and retrospectively all searches made', they may query the searches, request additional justification for the 'terrorism nexus' and may block searches that are in breach of the safeguarding rules.[44] However, it is questionable whether the overseer can provide effective scrutiny of the searches given the sheer volume of queries conducted. In that period the overseers queried 304 searches (many on a routine auditing basis) and was satisfied with over 90 per cent of the searches as formulated. However, this leaves a not insignificant percentage of cases where the overseers were not satisfied—and this is based on the querying of just over 1 per cent of all searches. The Commission Joint Review Report states that data from a TFTP search is neither the start of an investigation (as a nexus to terrorism is needed) nor the end of one.[45] This sets the system apart from those which are based on automated data mining processes. However, the searches are so numerous that it is difficult to gauge—without access to the necessary evidence—just how targeted the system actually is.

Once data has been extracted and 'leads' produced those leads can be transferred to law enforcement authorities within the US, to the EU or its Member States, and to certain third countries. In the first 6 months of TFTP-II 84 reports on investigation subjects were supplied to EU Member States or to Europol.

---

[40] Art 5(3) TFTP-II.
[41] Art 5(5) TFTP-II.
[42] Commission (EC), n 36 above, p 19.
[43] Art 12 TFTP-II. The overseers include 'a person appointed by the European Commission, with the agreement of and subject to appropriate security clearances by the United States'.
[44] Art 12 TFTP-II.
[45] Commission (EC), n 36 above, p 5.

Seventy of these reports were provided 'spontaneously'—that is, without their having been requested by the European authorities.[46] This may well be the most worrying aspect of the whole TFTP system. No matter how strict the system of searching is, and no matter how rigorous the oversight, once data has been transferred to other agencies the TFTP operatives have no control over it. Thus, data security, retention periods and deletion requirements are impossible to enforce.[47] The loss of control facilitates the evasion of rule of law standards. The principles of the rule of law may or may not be upheld by authorities to whom data is transferred—but it is impossible to determine whether they are or not.

iii. Human Rights Infringements

The TFTP's principal interference with human rights is caused by the bulk transfer of personal data from the EU to the US. Mass surveillance, in contrast to many of the rights infringements by EU counter-terrorism, amounts to a widespread interference with rights. This makes it difficult to carry out an assessment of the proportionality of the system. Its necessity is asserted for reasons of national security and the infringement with any one individual's rights is seemingly minor. The typical balancing act conducted by courts to determine proportionality is impossible to convincingly carry out.

The TFTP Agreement provides for a variety of rights, including the right of access, right to rectification, erasure, or blocking and right to redress.[48] While individuals are provided with the means to ascertain if their data has been accessed it is not clear that the system operates satisfactorily in practice. An individual may only access their data if a search has been performed for it. Thus, there is no means for an individual to ascertain if their data has been transferred to the US if that data has not been the subject of a search. However, if the data has been the subject of a search then there must be, according to the Agreement, a pre-established 'terrorism nexus'. In that case it is worth considering if the US authorities would be willing to inform the individual that the data had been accessed. In the first 6 months of the operation of the Agreement only one inquiry was received and it was not processed due to a failure to supply the US authorities with the necessary information.

iv. The Development of an EU System

In July 2011, the European Commission presented a paper to the Parliament and Council to lay out the background to, and options for, a European Terrorist Finance Tracking System (TFTS). The two goals of such a system are described as

---

[46] Commission (EC), n 36 above, p 19.

[47] See S Marques da Silva, 'The TFTP Agreements: A Legal and Contextual Analysis', King's College London LLM Dissertation 2011 (copy with author).

[48] See Arts 15, 16 and 18 TFTP-II. For a critical discussion see Marques da Silva, n 47 above.

making an 'effective contribution to the fight against terrorism' and contributing to 'limiting the amount of personal data transferred to third countries'. The development of an EU system follows the utilitarian logic behind post-September 11 data collection. Indeed, press reports have suggested that Member State governments were 'by no means pleased' with SWIFT's attempts to comply with EU data protection principles by moving its European operation from the US to Switzerland.[49] In this case it appears that a private actor has been greatly inconvenienced to facilitate a surveillance system in the name of counter-terrorism.

The development of systems to track terrorist finances is in many ways paradigmatic of both EU data surveillance and EU–US co-operation on data surveillance in the 'war on terror'. First, understanding the operation of the system requires a forensic analysis of a labyrinth of documents. Second, the system has come about as a result of the bypassing of constitutional politics and continues to suffer from a lack of political accountability. Third, the TFTP challenges several rule of law principles. It was established on an initially non-existent legal basis, it offers little formal protection to individual rights and even less de facto protection, and is marked by an absence of judicial oversight in the EU. The overview provided of terrorist finance tracking therefore introduces several of the themes that are also found in the remaining systems in this chapter. The operation of the system in practice demonstrates the difficulties of accountability for transnational law enforcement—with relations between the European Parliament and the Commission, Council and Europol strained as the former struggles to exercise effective oversight of the actions of the latter institutions and agency.[50]

B. EU–US Passenger Name Record Agreements

While the TFTP Agreements have attracted attention within legal and political debate the operation of passenger screening has also caught the popular imagination. Following the adoption in the US of the Aviation and Transportation Security Act 2001, airlines in Europe operating in the US were faced with a legal dilemma. In light of the clash between their obligations under US law to disclose PNR data and under EU law not to disclose that data, the airlines faced the difficult decision of determining which of the two legal systems to disobey. Any attempt to comply with the US requirements would breach EU data protection principles while compliance with the EU system of protection would preclude the data transfer required by the US authorities. To solve this problem, the effects of the US legislation were delayed and the Commission embarked on a rushed negotiation process with US authorities.[51] The saga unfolded as follows: The EU

---

[49] F Aldhouse, 'Comment: SWIFT and the new EU–US data transfer agreement' (2010) 7 *Data Protection Law and Policy*.
[50] For a full account see Marques da Silva, n 47 above.
[51] VanWasshnova, n 22 above, p 834.

Data Protection Directive declares that no personal data should be transferred to any third country unless its data protection system has been determined as 'adequate' by the Commission.[52] Prior to the adoption of the EU–US PNR Agreements, no such determination had been made in relation to the relevant US authorities, hence the development of the 'Safe Harbour' scheme. However, this scheme has been criticised as insufficiently clear and precise, and the Commission determined that it was not appropriate for a PNR Agreement with a state department (the Customs and Border Protection agency).[53] In 2004 the Commission adopted an Adequacy Decision in respect of the US.[54] This paved the way for an EU–US PNR Agreement (the First Agreement) adopted on the basis of Article 95 EC in conjunction with Article 300(2) EC. In 2006, the ECJ annulled the Adequacy Decision and the First Agreement as they pertained to criminal justice co-operation and not the regulation of the internal market.[55] The Council subsequently adopted two further Agreements on the basis of competences in police and judicial co-operation in criminal matters. In late 2006, an Interim Agreement was adopted to allow for the continuation of transatlantic flights until a more permanent agreement could be reached.[56] In 2007, the Council and US Department of Homeland Security concluded a new EU–US PNR Agreement (the Second Agreement), which is in effect today.[57]

Since the adoption of the Second Agreement, the EU has concluded similar agreements with Canada and Australia.[58] However, neither the Canadian nor the Australian agreement is as objectionable as the EU–US PNR Agreement. For example, Canada is authorised to retain PNR data for a maximum of 6 years and Australia for a maximum of 5 years and 6 months. In contrast, the US is authorised to retain the data for up to 15 years. These discrepancies suggest that the retention

---

[52] Art 25(6) Data Protection Directive.

[53] VanWasshnova, n 22 above, p 832.

[54] Commission Decision 2004/535/EC of 14 May 2004 on the adequate protection of personal data contained in the Passenger Name Record of air passengers transferred to the United States Bureau of Customs and Border Protection; Council Decision 2004/496/EC of 17 May 2004 on the conclusion of an Agreement between the European Community and the United States of America on the processing and transfer of PNR data by Air Carriers to the United States Department of Homeland Security, Bureau of Customs and Border Protection (hereafter, First Agreement).

[55] Joined Cases C-317/04 and C-318/04 *European Parliament v Council of the European Union and Commission of the European Communities* [2006] ECR I-4721.

[56] Council Decision on the signing, on behalf of the European Union, of an Agreement between the European Union and the United States of America on the processing and transfer of passenger name record (PNR) data by air carriers to the United States Department of Homeland Security, Brussels, 11 October 2006 (hereafter, Interim Agreement).

[57] Council Decision 2007/551/CFSP/JHA on the signing, on behalf of the European Union, of an Agreement between the European Union and the United States of America on the processing and transfer of Passenger Name Record (PNR) data by air carriers to the United States Department of Homeland Security (DHS) (hereafter, Second Agreement).

[58] Agreement between the European Community and the Government of Canada on the processing of Advance Passenger Information and Passenger Name Record data (2006); Agreement between Australia and the European Union on the Processing and Transfer of European Union-Sourced Passenger Name Record (PNR) Data by Air Carriers to the Australian Customs Service (2008).

periods may owe more to political negotiations than they do to any objective assessment of the necessessity of retention.[59] If the retention period was based on a rational case for a particular retention period one would expect greater convergence between retention periods in different Agreements. The variance between the American, Australian or Canadian agreements casts doubt on arguments concerning the necessity and proportionality of the retention periods.

i. Legal Basis

The European Parliament challenged the First EU–US PNR Agreement on grounds of legal basis. Even prior to that litigation the Article 29 Working Group questioned whether the US law regarding PNR data processing actually required the extensive regime put in place by the Bush administration.[60] The First EU–US PNR Agreement involved two EU acts: first, a Commission Adequacy Decision, based on Article 25(6) of the Data Protection Directive and adopted on 14 May 2004; and second, a Council Decision based on Article 95 EC and adopted on 17 May 2004.[61] The choice of Article 95 EC can be attributed in large part to that being the basis of the Data Protection Directive and the adoption of the Commission's Adequacy Decision based on that provision. The European Parliament challenged the Agreement on several grounds, but the ECJ annulled it on the ground of the absence of a legal basis.

Advocate General Léger offered a more detailed analysis of the legal framework than the European Court of Justice.[62] On the matter of legal basis, the Advocate General and the Court proved to be of one mind. The Advocate General noted that the criminal law nature of the data processing meant that the Agreement fell outside of the scope of the Data Protection Directive, and furthermore that Article 95 EC could not be used as the basis for a measure which has public security as its principal aim. The Advocate General then addressed the question raised by the Commission: whether there was any basis in the first pillar upon which the EU could adopt the Agreement. Although the analysis is brief, the conclusion is clear. Due to the nature of the data processing—the provision by one public authority (the EU) to another (US Customs and Border Protection) of data for the prevention of terrorism—the action fell outside the scope of the first pillar. To confirm this point, the Advocate General quoted the CFI judgment in *Kadi*, that 'the fight

---

[59] P de Hert and V Papakonstantinou, 'The EU PNR Framework Decision Proposal: Towards Completion of the PNR Processing Scene in Europe' (2010) 26 *Computer Law and Security Review* 368.

[60] Art 29 Data Protection Working Party, Opinion 6/2002 on Transmission of Passenger Manifest Information and other Data from Airlines to the United States, Brussels, 2002.

[61] See n 56 above.

[62] Opinion of Advocate General Léger in *Parliament v Council and Commission* 22 November 2005.

against international terrorism … cannot be made to refer to one of the objects which Articles 2 EC and 3 EC expressly entrust to the Community'.[63]

Though clear, the Advocate General's logic is not unproblematic. There is a discrepancy between the legal basis used for the First Agreement and that used for an internal EU measure to provide advanced passenger information.[64] A Directive to provide for the latter matter was based on Articles 62(2)(a) and 63(3)(b) EC which pertain to border control and illegal immigration.[65] While the measure may be justifiably based in the first pillar as it pertains to immigration (a first pillar competence), the legislation has also been identified as aiding counter-terrorism and so the difference between the Advance Passenger Information Directive and the PNR Agreement is less clear.[66] In light of the reversal of the decision on appeal, the CFI judgment in *Kadi* is likely no longer good precedent for the proposition that competences linked to the internal market cannot be used for counter-terrorism. Whatever its probity at the time, the merging of police and judicial co-operation in criminal matters by the Lisbon Treaty has rendered this point moot today.

The two EU acts were considered separately by the Court. The annulment of the Commission Adequacy Decision was swiftly explained by the ECJ. The Data Protection Directive excluded processing of personal data for activities relating to (amongst others) 'public security, defence, State security and the activities of the State in areas of criminal law'.[67] The Court quickly concluded that transferring the data to the US authority was for precisely such a purpose. As such, the Commission could not lawfully use the Data Protection Directive to adopt the Adequacy Decision and it was annulled.[68] The Court gave even shorter shrift to the Council Decision. Its reasoning was simple: the Council Decision relates to the processing of data outside the scope of the Data Protection Directive. As the Commission was not competent on that basis to adopt the Adequacy Decision neither was the Council competent to conclude the Agreement. Therefore the Council Decision was also annulled.[69]

The Council's response to the decision was to negotiate the Interim and Second Agreements on the basis of Articles 24 and 38 EU(N) (the same legal basis as the TFTP-I Agreement). The former provision permits the Council to authorise the Presidency of the EU, 'assisted by the Commission', to negotiate international agreements to be concluded by the Council. The latter provision simply notes that such agreements may cover matters that fall under Police and Judicial Co-operation in

---

[63] Ibid, paras 157–62.

[64] Mitsilegas, *EU Criminal Law*, n 5 above, p 303.

[65] Council Directive 2004/82/EC of 29 April 2004 on the obligation of carriers to communicate passenger data.

[66] Mitsilegas, *EU Criminal Law*, n 5 above, p 303.

[67] Art 3(2) Data Protection Directive.

[68] Joined Cases C-317/04 and C-318/04 *European Parliament v Council of the European Union and Commission of the European Communities* [2006] ECR 1-4721, para 61.

[69] Ibid, para 70.

Criminal Matters (PJCCM). It is therefore clear that the conclusion of the Interim and Second Agreements under the authority of PJCCM was more in keeping with the nature of those competences. Nonetheless, it had significant consequences for the regulatory framework within which the Agreements operate. The adoption of the Interim and Second Agreements on the new legal basis affected the role of both European and national parliaments and the ECJ in terms of democratic and judicial oversight. The European Parliament did not have the right to be consulted on the adoption of the Agreements under the third pillar and only thirteen Member States permitted their national parliaments to scrutinise the measure.[70] On the other hand, while the new legal basis placed the burden of negotiating the subsequent Agreements on the Presidency of the Council, the Commission once again played a large part in the dialogue. In addition, the ECJ's jurisdiction in this field was extremely limited. Thus, as Gilmore and Rijpma point out, the judgment in the PNR case is something of a 'poisoned chalice' from the point of view of improving the human rights and data protection compliance of the Agreements.[71] The perverse result is that the constitutive role of the rule of law played a part in undermining the principle's safeguarding role. Although this was a consequence of the incomplete system of judicial protection in the EU it highlights once more the potential negative impact of institutional power struggles on the rule of law.

ii. Breadth of the Agreements

The breadth of the First, Interim and Second Agreements has provided cause for concern on a number of grounds. These include the categories of PNR data to be transmitted to the US authorities; the various agencies that may access the PNR data; the scope of application of the PNR data; the retention period for the data; and the broad qualification clauses that feature in the Agreements.

The First Agreement included 34 fields of PNR data that would be 'pulled' from the airlines' databases by the US authorities.[72] The data fields to be transmitted were not mentioned explicitly in the Interim Agreement, and so it can be assumed that the original 34 fields continued to be used.[73] While the fields of PNR data to be transmitted were rationalised from 34 to 19 by the Second Agreement, most of the original fields were retained but were merged to give the appearance of

---

[70] G Gilmore and J Rijpma, 'Joined Cases C-317/04 and C-318/04, *European Parliament* v. *Council and Commission*, Judgment of the Grand Chamber of 30 May 2006, [2006] ECR I-4721' (2007) 44 *Common Market Law Review* 1081, 1098.

[71] Ibid, p 1099.

[72] Undertakings of the Department of Homeland Security, Bureau of Customs and Border Protection (CBP) (2004), para 4.

[73] Department of Homeland Security, 'Letter to the Council Presidency and the Commission from the Department of Homeland Security (DHS) of the United States of America, Concerning the Interpretation of Certain Provisions of the undertakings Issued by DHS on 11 May 2004 in Connection with the Transfer by Air Carriers of Passenger Name Record (PNR) Data', hereafter (2006 US Letter), available at: www.statewatch.org/news/2006/oct/eu-usa-pnr-letter-13738.pdf, last accessed 10 September 2009.

a reduction.[74] Furthermore, under the Second Agreement, the Department of Homeland Security was permitted to use 'sensitive data' in certain cases where 'the life of a data subject or of others could be imperilled or seriously impaired'.[75] This is a broad test and leaves sensitive data open to widespread use by US law enforcement authorities. Finally, certain data—relating to baggage and frequent flier information—was added to the regime.[76] Thus, in a trend that is repeated in other aspects of the Agreements, the effect of the ECJ judgment was to allow the US to renegotiate broader access to personal data in the Interim and Second Agreements.

The list of agencies permitted to access the PNR data under the terms of the First Agreement was lengthy and included law enforcement agencies such as the Federal Bureau of Investigation, Interpol and the Secret Service. However, it also included certain authorities whose role in combating terrorism is more questionable: the Inland Revenue Service, Department of Alcohol, Tobacco and Firearms, and Animal Plant Health Inspection Service.[77] These bodies are not specifically concerned with counter-terrorism though they clearly have a more general criminal justice role. Notwithstanding this already lengthy list, the Interim Agreement added other agencies, including the Office of the Department of Homeland Security Secretary and 'all entities that directly support it'.[78] The varied nature of the agencies and departments permitted to access the PNR data give lie to the claim that its retention is aimed solely at countering terrorism and serious transnational crime. Rather, it appears that the wide range of PNR data retained is to be made available to US government departments and agencies for the broad purpose of law enforcement. That conclusion is borne out by the expansion of scope of the Agreement following the ECJ judgment. Under the terms of the First Agreement, the PNR data could be used for preventing and combating terrorism and 'related crimes', 'other serious crimes, including organised crime, that are transnational in nature' and to prevent flights from warrant or custody for such crimes.[79] These terms alone offer sufficient scope for broad interpretation, with 'serious crimes … that are transnational in nature' potentially including political violence, organised crime, drug trafficking, human trafficking, and piracy (of intellectual and other property).[80] However, the Interim and Second Agreements

---

[74] V Papakonstantinou and de Hert, 'The PNR Agreement and Transatlantic Anti-Terrorism Co-operation: No Firm Human Rights Framework on Either Side of the Atlantic' (2009) 46 *Common Market Law Review* 885, 914.

[75] Department of Homeland Security,' 'US Letter to the EU', III 'Types of Information Collected' OJ L204/21 (4. August 2007) (hereafter, 2007 US Letter).

[76] Van Wasshnova, n 22 above, p 839.

[77] For a detailed discussion see DR Rasmussen 'Is International Travel *Per Se* Suspicion of Terrorism? The Dispute Between the United States and European Union over Passenger Name Record Data Transfers' (2008) 26 *Wisconsin International Law Journal* 551.

[78] Ibid, p 585.

[79] Undertakings of the Department of Homeland Security, Bureau of Customs and Border Protection (CBP) (2004), paras 2–3.

[80] Department of Homeland Security, 2007 US Letter 'I *Purpose for which PNR is used*'.

provide for even broader scope, by the inclusion of certain clauses which effectively act as qualifiers on the safeguards in the agreement.

The First Agreement set a retention period of 3 years and 6 months for PNR data transferred to the US authorities. However, any information accessed within that period would be stored by Customs and Border Protection for a further 8 years. Thus, the First Agreement set an upper limit of 11 years and 6 months for retention of PNR data.[81] However, the Interim Agreement notes that the destruction of the data would have to be addressed by future negotiations.[82] The Second Agreement extended the data retention period to a total of 15 years. The data would be retained in an 'active analytical database' for 7 years, before being moved to 'dormant non-operational status' for 8 years (during which it would be accessible under slightly more stringent procedures).[83] However, the Second Agreement did not explicitly provide for the deletion of the data at the end of that period, noting that the US authorities 'expect' that the data will be deleted, but that such deletion would be a matter for 'further discussions'.[84] Thus, as with other areas of potential breadth, the presence of limits is significantly undermined.

The final manner in which the Agreements are broad is in the inclusion of certain clauses that appear to almost vitiate all that has preceded them. Thus, the Undertakings provided by the US government as part of the First Agreement provide that none of the preceding provisions 'shall impede the use or disclosure of PNR data to relevant government authorities, where such disclosure is necessary for the protection of the vital interests of the data subject or of other persons'.[85] Furthermore, the Undertakings shall not 'impede the use or disclosure of PNR data in any criminal judicial proceedings or as otherwise required by law'.[86] These statements reduce the preceding safeguards and limitations to little more than political gloss on broad powers of retention and processing of personal data for various US government authorities. Indeed, they were the basis for the subsequent 'interpretation' of the Undertakings by a Letter from the Department of Homeland Security that effectively unilaterally amended the Interim Agreement.[87] The breadth of the Agreements is anathema to the EU data protection regime, which requires clear and precise rules on data collection, retention and processing.[88] Therefore it is unsurprising that the Agreements have given rise to numerous human rights concerns.

---

[81] Undertakings of the Department of Homeland Security, Bureau of Customs and Border Protections (CBP) (2004), para 15.

[82] Department of Homeland Security, 2006 US Letter, n 73 above, p 6.

[83] Department of Homeland Security, 2007 US Letter, n 75 above, 'VII Data retention'.

[84] Ibid.

[85] Undertakings of the Department of Homeland Security, Bureau of Customs and Border Protections (CBP) (2004), para 34.

[86] Ibid, para 35.

[87] Department of Homeland Security, 2006 US Letter.

[88] Directive 95/46/EC of the European Parliament and of the European Council of 24 October 1995 on the protection of individuals with regard to the processing of personal data and on the free movement of such data; Directive 2002/58/EC of the European Parliament and of the Council of

iii. Human Rights Infringements

The PNR system has the same potential for human rights infringements as the TFTP does. Throughout the course of the negotiation of the various Agreements, the European Parliament, Article 29 Working Group, European Data Protection Supervisor, and national parliamentary bodies such as the UK House of Lords EU Committee all expressed serious concerns relating to privacy protections under the regime.[89] The potential for human rights infringements by the PNR system is much the same as that which exists in relation to the TFTP Agreements. Certain data protection principles may be violated by the transfer of personal data from the EU, with its relatively high level of protection, to the US. The Article 29 Working Party opined in 2003 that the categories of data to be transferred were broader than could be considered 'adequate, relevant and not excessive'.[90] The Supervisor argued that purpose of data processing should be strictly limited to terrorism and a specified list of related offences, and the list of agencies with access to the data should be specific and justified.[91] Furthermore, the transfer of 'sensitive data' should be abandoned altogether to ensure compatibility with the Data Protection Directive.[92] The matter of a system of redress, and independent supervision of the scheme was also raised by the Working Party.[93] Despite repeated opinions from the Working Party and the European Data Protection Supervisor and resolutions from the European Parliament, the standard of protection in the Agreements has not improved.[94] While the First Agreement, adopted under the first pillar, was subject to the Data Protection Directive, the same is not true of the Interim and Second Agreements. A consequence of the Court's PNR judgment has been the adoption of those subsequent Agreements under the third pillar, where the Data Protection Directive does not apply. At the time of negotiation of the Agreement there was no EU system of data protection for police and judicial co-operation in criminal matters. As a result the Agreement operated in a vacuum of judicial protection which is difficult to justify in light of the degree of interference with individual rights.

Even in the absence of a specific set of data protection standards, the general right to privacy is still applicable and while the ECJ did not consider this point in its judgment, the Advocate General did.[95] Basing his analysis on the ECHR,

---

12 July 2002 concerning the processing of personal data and the protection of privacy in the electronic communications sector.

[89] For a useful summary of the debate, see Rasmussen, n 77 above, pp 573–87.

[90] Article 29 Data Protection Working Party, 'Opinion 4/2003 on the Level of Protection ensured in the US for the Transfer of Passengers' Data', 13 June 2003, p 7.

[91] Ibid.

[92] Ibid, p 8.

[93] Ibid.

[94] For a useful collection of documents, see: <http://www.statewatch.org/pnrobservatory.htm>, 10 September 2011.

[95] Opinion of Advocate General Léger in Joined Cases C-317/04 and C-318/04 *European Parliament v Council of the European Union and Commission of the European Communities* [2006] ECR 1-4721, para 193.

the Advocate General pronounced himself satisfied that the interference with privacy was 'in accordance with law' and 'pursued a legitimate aim'.[96] As is usual in such determinations, the case turned on the test of whether the Agreement was 'necessary in a democratic society'. The Advocate General applied a wide 'margin of appreciation' based on the national security and 'politically sensitive' context of the Agreement.[97] As such, his review was limited to considering whether the Agreement was 'manifestly inappropriate' to achieve its objectives.[98] Although it is not proposed to conduct a complete review of the applicable standards of review here, it is worth noting that the degree of deference shown stands in stark contrast to the subsequent decision of Advocate General Maduro in *Kadi*.[99] The subsequent erosion of rights is also noteworthy: whereas the Advocate General's reading of the safeguards in the US Undertakings considered that the data would be deleted after the prescribed period, the reality is that the US no longer commits to deleting the data after the (rather long) retention period.[100] In conclusion the interference with rights is broad: undermining the data protection principles as outlined above constitutes a serious infringement of personal privacy as understood by the EU legal system. On the other side of the balancing act, no evidence has been adduced as to the usefulness of PNR data for countering terrorism and other crime. As such, it is difficult to conclude that it is 'necessary in a democratic society'.

Subsequent action by the US may be taken as an indication that the Department of Homeland Security is willing to unilaterally alter the terms of the Agreement. Following the adoption of the Second Agreement, the US took steps in its domestic and its foreign policy to undermine the operation of the Agreement.[101] Domestically, the Department of Homeland Security published an updated record system for PNR data that may undermine the protections provided by the Privacy Act. In foreign policy, the US is negotiating bilateral agreements with EU Member States based on their visa-waiver policies. These agreements have been used to obtain greater access to data on citizens of those Member States when travelling to the US.[102] The recurring theme of the PNR saga is EU acquiescence to a US data processing programme that seriously breaches the fundamental tenets of data protection principles. Thus, the Interim Agreement is 'unusual in that the United States was able to achieve everything its legislation required with no concessions to the national law of EU member nations'.[103] Indeed, the overall trend has been one of less protection, not more, as the Agreements have been renegotiated.[104]

---

[96] Ibid, paras 221, 224.
[97] Ibid, paras 225–62.
[98] Ibid, para 232.
[99] Opinion of Advocate General Maduro in C-402/05 *Kadi* 16 January 2008.
[100] Ibid, para 241.
[101] Papakonstantinou and de Hert, n 74 above, p 917.
[102] Ibid, pp 917–18.
[103] Rasmussen, n 77 above, p 576.
[104] Mitsilegas, n 5 above, p 307.

iv. The Development of An EU PNR System

The European Commission has proposed a framework decision and subsequently a Directive on the use of an EU PNR system for law enforcement.[105] The framework decision would have required the collection and processing of PNR data for all passengers arriving into or leaving the EU by air. If the flaws in the EU–US Agreements were solely the fault of the uncompromising negotiating stance taken by the US, then one might expect an EU system on PNR data to better reflect EU human rights standards.[106] However, the original Commission proposal would have introduced many of the problematic aspects of the EU–US Agreement into EU law and the Council sought to broaden certain aspects of the regime.[107] The proposed amendments would broaden the application of the framework decision beyond air travel to other modes of transport, to broaden the scope beyond terrorism and organised crime to other offences, to process sensitive data and to retain PNR data relating to intra-EU flights. The European Data Protection Supervisor had, unsuprisingly, expressed concern over the proposed measure.[108]

The coming into force of the Lisbon Treaty afforded the European Commission the opportunity to launch a new legislative proposal under the ordinary legislative procedure. The proposal for a Directive on EU PNR was published in February 2011 and has become the subject of controversy once more. Both Ireland and the UK have expressed their intention to opt-in to the legislation.[109] A statement explaining the UK opt-in to the House of Commons emphasised the UK government's intention that an EU PNR system would also cover intra-EU flights but also suggested that the system be targeted at 'routes of high risk'.[110] Nonetheless the extension of the system to internal flights remains the subject of dispute among the Member States. The Commission proposal defines 'terrorist offences' with reference to the Framework Decision on Combating Terrorism and 'serious crime' with reference to the list of offences in the Framework Decision on European Arrest Warrant. A further aspect to be resolved is the establishment of Passenger Information Units which will have responsibility for processing the PNR data for individuals arriving or departing from their respective Member State. The current proposal calls for these units to be set up by each Member

---

[105] Commission (EC), 'Proposal for a Council Framework Decision on the use of Passenger Name Record (PNR) for law enforcement purposes' COM (2007) 654 final, Brussels, 6 November 2007; 'Proposal for a European Parliament and Council Directive on the use of Passenger Name Record data for the prevention, detection, investigation and prosecution of terrorist offences and serious crime' COM (2011) 32 final, Brussels, 2 February 2011.

[106] Ibid.

[107] Mitsilegas, n 5 above, p 271.

[108] European Data Protection Supervisor, Opinion of the European Data Protection Supervisor on the draft Proposal for a Council Framework Decision on the use of Passenger Name Record (PNR) data for law enforcement purposes, Brussels, 20 December 2007.

[109] See Council of the European Union document 9932/11, Brussels, 12 May 2011 (Ireland opt-in) and Council of the European Union document 9941/11, Brussels, 12 May 2011.

[110] Statement to the House of Commons by the Minister for Immigration on Tuesday 10 May 2011.

State (two or more Member States may share a unit)—which is likely to add to the cost of the system. The proposal has been criticised for violating the right to non-discrimination, privacy and data protection, for impinging upon free movement of EU citizens, for its high costs and for its failure to harmonise the law in relation to purpose limitation, data retention, third country transfers, rights and remedies and powers of supervision.[111] These flaws are also present in the final instrument examined in this chapter—the Data Retention Directive—and have led to widespread recognition of the need to radically overhaul that system of data retention. However, while there remains significant differences of opinion on the details of the EU PNR system it seems likely that such a system will be legislated for in the near future.[112]

C. Data Retention Directive

The adoption of the Data Retention Directive is a classic example of acts of political violence providing the impetus for unpalatable legislation. Following the attacks in Madrid on 3 March 2004, four Member States tabled a proposal for a Framework Decision on Data Retention. Faced with strong opposition from the European Parliament (opposed to the choice of legislative measure and concerned with the human rights implications of the legislation) and the European Commission (which sought to bring forward its own legislative proposal), the proposal was eventually dropped.[113] However, in the aftermath of the attacks in London on 7 July 2005, data retention came to prominence once more, and the Data Retention Directive was quickly adopted by qualified majority (with the Parliament co-legislating, and Ireland and Slovakia opposing the measure in the Council).[114] Opposition to the measure from the European Parliament was effectively suppressed by strong pressure from the UK during its Presidency of the EU.[115] The rationale behind the measure was the information that mobile telephones had been used in co-ordinating the attacks in Madrid and London, and (unsubstantiated) claims were made that telecommunications information was vital to police investigations.

---

[111] Meijers Committee, 'CM1108 Directive on the use of PNR data for the prevention, detection, investigation and prosecution of terrorist offences and serious crime' COM (2011) 32, Utrecht, 21 June 2011.

[112] See Council of the European Union, Document 11392/11, Brussels, 14 June 2011.

[113] Draft Framework Decision on the retention of data processed and stored in connection with the provision of publicly available electronic communications services or data on public communications networks for the purpose of prevention, investigation, detection and prosecution of crime and criminal offences including terrorism 2004/0813/CNS.

[114] Directive 2006/24/EC of the European Parliament and of the Council of 15 March 2006 on the retention of data generated or processed in connection with the provision of publicly available electronic communications services or of public communications networks and amending Directive 2002/58/EC.

[115] *Euractiv.com*, 'Data Retention: Parliament caves in to Council pressure', December 14 2005.

The central action of the directive is laid out in the first Article. The directive:

aims to harmonise Member States' provisions concerning the obligations of the providers of publicly available electronic communications services or of public communications networks with respect to the retention of certain data which are generated or processed by them, in order to ensure that the data are available for the purpose of the investigation, detection and prosecution of serious crime, as defined by each Member State in its national law.

The directive was to be implemented by September 2007, but provided for an optional 18 month extension to the transposition period in relation to the retention of data on internet traffic. At the time of adoption of the directive, 16 Member States expressed their intention to avail themselves of this extension, or reserved their right to do so in the future.

i. Legal Basis

The Data Retention Directive was adopted on the basis of Article 95 EC. Following the adoption of the directive, Ireland (supported by Slovakia) brought an application for annulment before the ECJ. The Council and Parliament, as defendants, were supported by Spain, the Netherlands, the Commission and the European Data Protection Supervisor. The plea in the case was that the directive was inappropriately based on Article 95 EC specifically, and within the first pillar generally, as its 'centre of gravity' lay in the third pillar in that it aimed to facilitate access to information by national police and security forces. Much of the discussion focused on the various recitals to the Preamble, which invoked both the public security goals relating to counter-terrorism and the need to avoid distortion of the internal market.

Advocate General Bot and the Court came to broadly similar conclusions: that the measure had as its purpose the harmonisation of the internal market. First, the Court noted that Member State legislation for data retention may give rise to different standards in different Member States. Second, it acknowledged that the directive amended the Privacy and Electronic Communications Directive, which itself was based on Article 95 EC. Third, it noted that the directive does not in itself 'involve intervention by the police or law-enforcement authorities of the Member States'.[116] Fourth, the Court distinguished the PNR judgment on the basis that its reasoning in that case was that although the collection of PNR data by Member States fell within the first pillar, the transfer of PNR data to law enforcement authorities did not. Because the Data Retention Directive aims to harmonise the retention of data by private actors in order to avoid a distortion of competition within the internal market and does not provide the mechanism for transfer the PNR judgment was deemed inapplicable.[117]

---

[116] C-301/06 *Ireland v European Parliament and European Council* [2009] ECR I-593, para 82.
[117] Ibid, paras 60–94.

The rationale is unconvincing. The fundamental reason for adopting the measure was to provide a lawful basis for the retention of traffic and location data and effectively permit derogation from the terms of the data protection principles which would require such information to be deleted once it was no longer necessary for billing purposes. The reason that such derogation was permitted was for law enforcement, specifically to aid in combating terrorism and other serious crimes. While the directive does not specify the details of access for law enforcement authorities, it makes such access possible. The attempt to distinguish it from the PNR Agreements on this ground is not convincing.

ii. Breadth of the Directive

The directive is broad in a number of respects, including the range of crimes for which the data may be used and the authorities to whom access may be granted, the retention period and the provision of compensation to service providers. As the impetus for the directive was the attacks in Madrid and London, early drafts would have limited its application to investigations relating to terrorism and serious organised crime.[118] However, the measure as adopted allows the information to be used for 'serious crime, as defined by each Member State in its national law'.[119] Furthermore, the information is to be made available to 'competent national authorities'.[120] The failure to agree on definitions as to who may access the information and for what purpose has led to different practices in different Member States. The most recent European Commission report on the operation of the directive notes that all Member States which have transposed the directive allow national police forces to access the data, while all non-common law systems also allow prosecutors access. Some Member States allow military services, security and intelligence services, tax and customs authorities, or border authorities access.[121] There is no EU definition of 'serious crime' and practices differ within the Member States on the purpose for which access to retained data is granted. This latter point has been of particular concern and the Council has issued a discussion paper which calls for debate on whether a standard definition of 'serious crime' should be adopted or some other means to be found to limit the purpose for which retained data can be accessed.[122]

The directive also permits divergence in respect of the retention period. Member States must require the retention of data for no less than 6 months and

---

[118] Commission (EC), 'Proposal for a Directive of the European Parliament and of the Council on the retention of data processed in connection with the provision of public electronic communication services and amending Directive 2002/58/EC' COM (2005) 438 final, Brussels, 21 September 2005.

[119] Art 1 Data Retention Directive.

[120] Art 4 Data Retention Directive.

[121] Commission (EC), 'Report from the Commission to the Council and the European Parliament: Evaluation report on the Data Retention Directive (Directive 2006/24/EC)' COM (2011) 225 final Brussels, 18 April 2011, p 9.

[122] Council of the European Union, Document 9439/11, Brussels, 27 April 2011.

no more than 24 months.[123] When the proposed measures were being drafted, the Commission noted that there existed a range of 3 months to 4 years in national law.[124] The Commission argued that a lack of uniformity had to be addressed to prevent distortion of the internal market. Although the adopted measure reduces the potential divergence in Member State laws, a relatively broad range of retention periods—18 months—remains. The potential for diverging national law has been borne out in practice. The retention periods vary widely—though 10 Member States have an apparent consensus of 1 year for all kinds of data retained.[125] Other Member States have different periods for different types of data and these periods include 2 years, 18 months, 1 year and 6 months.[126] Furthermore, a peculiar clause in the directive permits Member States to extend the retention period beyond the 2 year maximum if they face 'particular circumstances'.[127] The extension is subject to the approval of the Commission, who shall review it for compliance with the requirements of the internal market.[128] It is not clear why the extension clause is deemed necessary and it has not been used to date.[129] As a form of generalised surveillance, it is difficult to imagine circumstances whereby, in the aftermath of an act of political violence, the Member State affected would need to retain data for longer. Furthermore, it is not clear why the Commission should review the measure for compliance with the internal market, rather than compliance with data protection principles.[130]

Each of the political compromises that led to the scope for divergence has undermined the instrument's claim to harmonise the internal market in this field. A final failure—to agree to provide compensation to service providers for the cost incurred—is likely to lead to significantly different market conditions across the EU. One author estimates that the requirement to retain data on unanswered calls alone will cost 'millions of euros'.[131] The European Commission has cited a study which estimates that an internet service provider servicing half a million customers could expect to spend $375,240 in the first year and $9,870 in operational costs every month thereafter.[132] Variable compensation across the EU is a reality. Eight Member States provide compensation for the capital or operational costs of the scheme. On the other hand some Member States, such as Germany, have made clear that no such compensation will be provided. Indeed the German Federal

---

[123] Art 6 Data Retention Directive.

[124] Commission (EC), n 118 above, p 1.

[125] Commission (EC), n 121 above, p 13.

[126] Ibid.

[127] Art 12 Data Retention Directive.

[128] Art 12(2) Data Retention Directive.

[129] Commission (EC), n 121 above, p 13.

[130] M Vilasau, 'Traffic Data Retention v Data Protection: The New European Framework' (2007) *Computer and Telecommunications Law Review* 52, 58.

[131] S Blakeney, 'The Data Retention Directive: Combating Terrorism Or Invading Privacy?' (2007) *Computer and Telecommunications Law Review* 153, 155.

[132] Commission (EC), n 121 above, p 26.

Constitutional Court considered the burden on service providers in its judgment on the German implementing legislation, but found it to be constitutional.[133]

The failure to harmonise EU law in this field is a result of political disagreements within the Council and between the Council and the Parliament. The Commission proposal was a much more precise piece of legislation. It would have provided for retention periods of 1 year (telephone data) and 6 months (internet data); a clear provision on compensation for service providers; and limited access to the data for 'the prevention, investigation, detection and prosecution of serious criminal offences, such as terrorism and organised crime'.[134] It is difficult not to read the legislation as adopted as being unfit for purpose: insofar as its aim was to harmonise data retention schemes across Europe it has resolutely failed to do so. Indeed, this is now common ground between those who have criticised the directive and those who seek to salvage a data retention system. It is on the future development of the programme, rather than its failure to date, that much of the debate is focused.

iii. Human Rights Infringements

The human rights concerns in relation to the directive focus, as with the TFTP and PNR systems, on the right to privacy and the principles of data protection. The Data Retention Directive is a direct reversal of the requirements of the e-Privacy Directive 2002, which required the deletion of traffic and location data after it was no longer needed for billing purposes.[135] Unfortunately, while Ireland challenged the Data Retention Directive, it did so solely on grounds of legal basis, and did not raise any pleas on human rights grounds.[136] Therefore, the ECJ is yet to have the opportunity to consider the measure on these grounds. The European Data Protection Supervisor intervened on behalf of the respondents in *Ireland*, arguing that the Article 95 EC legal basis ensured that the directive was subject to the rules of the Data Protection Directive.[137] An action by the Irish civil society group, Digital Rights Ireland, is to be referred to the European Court of Justice. It will provide the court with its first opportunity to consider the human rights implications of the Data Retention Directive and, indeed, of EU surveillance in the name of counter-terrorism.

This is not an easy question to answer. Understood in classic European human rights law terms a data retention system would have to comply with three key principles to be a lawful interference with the right to privacy: whether it is 'in accordance with law', whether it pursues a legitimate aim, and whether it is 'necessary in a democratic

---

[133] Bundesverfassungsgericht, 1 BvR 256/08, 1 BvR 263/08, 1 BvR 586/08, Judgment of 2 March 2010.

[134] Commission (EC), n 118 above, pp 9–15.

[135] Art 6 of the Directive 2002/58/EC of the European Parliament and of the Council of 12 July 2002 concerning the processing of personal data and the protection of privacy in the electronic communications sector.

[136] Prior to the adoption of the directive, Ireland had legislated for a three year retention period for the types of data covered by the directive. As such, it is not surprising that Ireland did not challenge the directive on human rights grounds. See: Criminal Justice (Terrorist Offences) Act, 2005.

[137] C-301/06 *Ireland v European Parliament and European Council* [2009] ECR I-593.

society'. The first and second of these tests are straightforward in comparison with the third. Whether the interference is 'in accordance with law' is certainly doubtful given the breadth of the directive and the vagueness of its terms—which have, as even the Commission has conceded, undermined legal certainty across the EU. However, as Advocate General Léger's Opinion in the PNR case demonstrates, few measures are found to be unlawful on this ground.[138] The second test is easily met—the directive claims to pursue the legitimate aim of national security. The debate on the directive's lawfulness thus effectively turns on whether or not it is 'necessary in a democratic society'. It is impossible to adjudicate on this matter in the abstract. Nonetheless, as with the PNR Agreements, the blanket interference with rights based on little evidence of a pressing national security threat is difficult to justify. In addition to interfering with the rights to privacy and data protection, the Data Retention Directive may also pose a threat to freedom of expression and even the right to property.[139] Furthermore, while not a criticism of the EU law per se, there is also a risk of law enforcement agencies breaching Article 14 ECHR, the right not to be discriminated against, if they engage in profiling that uses race, ethnicity, religious belief or nationality as grounds for data processing. Much will turn on how the directive is subsequently used by law enforcement officials, a matter which in itself is cause for concern given the degree of discretion bestowed upon them. It is for this reason that the directive has been the subject of mass legal and political resistance since it has come into operation.

iv. Legal and Political Resistance

Among the instruments considered in this chapter it is the Data Retention Directive that has been the subject of the greatest legal and political resistance. The Bulgarian Supreme Administrative Court, Romanian Constitutional Court, Czech Constitutional Court and German Federal Constitutional Court have all found some aspects of the national implementing legislation to be in contravention of fundamental legal principles.[140] On the other hand, failure by Ireland, Greece and Sweden to transpose the directive has resulted in enforcement proceedings being brought by the European Commission against those Member States.[141]

---

[138] Opinion of Advocate General Léger in Joined Cases C-317/04 and C-318/04 *European Parliament v Council of the European Union and Commission of the European Communities* [2006] ECR 1-4721.

[139] P Breyer, 'Telecommunications Data Retention and Human Rights: The Compatibility of Blanket Traffic Data Retention with the ECHR' (2005) 11 *European Law Journal* 365, 368–70.

[140] Decision No 13627 of 12 November 2008 of the Supreme Administrative Court of Bulgaria in relation to Ordinance No 40 of 07 January 2008; Romanian Constitutional Court, Decision no 1258 of 8 October 2009 regarding the unconstitutionality exception of the provisions of Law no 298/2008 regarding the retention of the data generated or processed by the public electronic communications service providers or public network providers, as well as for the modification of law 506/2004 regarding the personal data processing and protection of private life in the field of electronic communication area; Czech Constitutional Court Decision Pl. ÚS 24/10 94/2011 Coll. 2011/03/22.

[141] Case C-211/09 *European Commission v Hellenic Republic* ECJ Judgment 26 November 2009; Case C-202/09 *European Commission v Ireland* ECJ Judgment 26 November 2009; Case C-185/09 *European Commission v Kingdom of Sweden* ECJ Judgment 4 February 2010.

The decision of the German Federal Constitutional Court merits particular attention—both because of the weight which judgments of that court have held in the past and the rigour of its reasoning. German jurisprudence has a well-developed system of data protection—and one which is based on a theoretically informed conception of privacy.[142] German data protection is based on the right to informational self-determination. German law requires the protection of three personal spheres: the individual, the private and the intimate.[143] The right to manage one's affairs so as to keep separate these different aspects of one's life is a key facet of German data protection. The German court held that the German implenting legislation went beyond the requirements of the directive itself. In doing so it violated the right to informational self-determination in German law and therefore had to be annulled. The decision marks the most detailed judicial treatment yet of not just the Data Retention Directive, but of counter-terrorism mass surveillance in general.

The directive is currently the subject of political review at EU level. The Commission convened a conference in December 2010 entitled 'Taking on the Data Retention Directive' at which civil society groups, law enforcement operators and members of the European institutions came together to discuss the problems with the directive and potential solutions. After a moment in which it appeared as though the whole system might be abandoned the Commissioner for Home Affairs stated clearly that 'data retention is here to stay'.[144]At the same conference the European Data Protection Supervisor stated that the directive was at its 'moment of truth'. He called for any future system to provide not just for data retention but also for rules on access by law enforcement and associated safeguards.[145]

The future development of telecommunications data retention will indicate the current political consensus in the EU on the level of surveillance citizens can expect to be subjected to in the interests of national security and crime prevention. Whereas PNR data is targeted at borders and thus part of a general system aimed at the exclusion of 'others', and TFTP systems have, to date, been comparatively unknown, the retention of telecommunications data affects those within the EU and therefore represents action against both citizens and 'others'. It is for this reason that the directive has fomented so much opposition amongst the public at law. It is the cornerstone of the EU's surveillance architecture which views both citizens and non-citizens as potential suspects.

---

[142] For an overview see G Hornung and C Schnabel, 'Data Protection in Germany I: The Population Census Decision and the Right to Informational Self-Determination' (2009) 25 *Computer Law and Security Review* 84 and 'Data Protection in Germany II: Recent decisions on Online-Searching of Computers, Automatic Number Plate Recognition and Data Retention' (2009) 25 *Computer Law & Security Review* 115.

[143] C DeSimone, 'Pitting Karlsruhe Against Luxembourg? German Data Protection and the Contested Implementation of the EU Data Retention Directive' (2010) 11 *German Law Journal* 291.

[144] C Malmstrom, 'Taking on the Data Retention Directive' Speech/10/723 Brussels, 3 December 2010.

[145] P Hustinx, 'The Moment of Truth for the Data Retention Directive' Brussels, 3 December 2010.

III. SURVEILLANCE, PRE-EMPTION AND THE RULE OF LAW

Several common themes emerge from an analysis of EU data surveillance. It is note-worthy that both the PNR Agreements and Data Retention Directive have faced criticisms on grounds of not having a legal basis. The EU is clearly in uncharted waters here in terms of its competence to adopt the legislation in question. The respective decisions of the ECJ on the matter leave many questions pertaining to the legal basis provided by the Article 95 EC and the competence of the EU more generally. It is difficult to reconcile the decisions in the two cases. Whereas the PNR decision appears to adopt a strict division of competences between the market and criminal law, the clear lines of that decision are blurred by the ruling on the Data Retention Directive. The latter judgment allowed a particularly broad reading of Article 95 EC in terms of the relationship between market rules and public security. Many aspects of criminal law and procedure may have an effect on the internal market and yet it would be unsustainable to use Article 95 EC as a basis for EU action in every case. The brevity of the ECJ's PNR decision might be lamented. However, it is worth recalling the collegiate nature of the Court, the fact that the judgment was one of the Grand Chamber (thus entailing a panel of 13 judges) and that there are, of course, no dissenting judgments in the EU legal system. Thus, the brief judgment may simply indicate that the Court was agreed on the outcome, but not on the precise rationale for it. Subsequent development of the law in this area is therefore likely to be instructive. It is unfortunate that the ECJ did not take the opportunity to articulate its thoughts on the right to privacy, and the principles of data protection in the litigation on either instrument. While the opportunity may not arise again in relation to the PNR Agreements, it will in respect of the Data Retention Directive when a reference from the Irish High Court, in an action brought by an advocacy group, reaches the Court.[146]

A. Prevention and Co-operation: The Alternatives

The principal purpose of both the EU data surveillance systems and the EU's co-operation with the US in this field is to glean as much information as possible for law enforcement authorities for general crime prevention purposes. Looked at in terms of the rule of law the principal problem then is the use of broad interventions and the granting of wide powers without sufficient safeguards. It is note-worthy that there were alternatives that the EU might have considered but which ultimately were given short shrift by the institutions.

Both the PNR Agreements and the Data Retention Directive could have been drafted to operate as more traditional surveillance measures: targeted at indi-viduals suspected of involvement in criminal activity. It is possible to devise a

---

[146] 'European Court to Rule on Data Storage Law', *Irish Times* (5 May 2010).

system of prior notification of passenger information that would not so offend the rule of law. Under such a system, requiring advanced passenger information and conducting surveillance of electronic communications would be based on pre-existing intelligence that some crime had taken place or was likely to take place. The programme already in existence within the EU for the transfer of Advance Passenger Information, for example, could form the basis for such a system. Informed of the passenger manifest 72 hours prior to departure, national agencies such as Customs and Border Patrol could then check that data against existing criminal justice databases and request further information based on evidence of suspected terrorism or related criminal behaviour. However, the US has vigorously pursued a broader approach to data transfer that goes far beyond a traditional preventive approach.

In relation to the Data Retention Directive, an alternative system of data surveillance was proposed during the passage of the legislation, but seemingly ignored by the Council and Commission.[147] This 'quick freeze' system would allow law enforcement authorities to request that telecommunications companies retain traffic and location data pertaining to certain persons, even though the authorities could not yet produce sufficient evidence to justify the disclosure of that data. Once the authorities had amassed sufficient evidence to obtain a warrant from a judicial officer, the data could be released by the telecommunications companies.[148] This system would not be unproblematic. It is easy to imagine a situation whereby police believe there is an imminent threat to public security which may be allayed by the processing of data that has been retained for a number of months. Faced with a compelling and urgent case from the police in an application where the target was not represented and where the only infringement on human rights related to electronic privacy, courts would no doubt be co-operative with law enforcement agencies. Nonetheless, such a process, regardless of how lenient, would at least require law enforcement officials to develop suspicions before infringing rights.

B. Data Surveillence as Pre-emptive Counter-Terrorism

Of course, any discussion of alternatives ignores what may well be the reality of the situation: broadening the scope of surveillance is the aim—not a collateral effect—of most data surveillance systems. The extent to which EU data surveillance constitutes a form of pre-emptive counter-terrorism can be demonstrated through four separate aspects of the regimes. These are the empowerment of administrators

---

[147] Art 29 Data Protection Working Party, 'Opinion 4/2005 on the Proposal for a Directive of the European Parliament and of the Council on the Retention of Data Processed in Connection with the Provision of Public Electronic Communication Services and Amending Directive 2002/58/EC' COM (2005) 438 final, 21 September 2005, 21 October 2005, p 6.

[148] Ibid.

and private actors; the focus on mass surveillance and generalised suspicion; the resulting self-disciplining effect; and targeting 'suspect communities'.

i. Empowerment of Administrators and Private Actors

As with other areas of counter-terrorism action addressed in previous chapters, data surveillance legislation empowers a wide range of executive and administrative actors while relying on weak safeguards to protect rule of law principles. Those empowered by EU data surveillance legislation include the following: executive actors, in particular the US Department of Homeland Security and other US law enforcement agencies, police and law enforcement authorities in the EU, and private actors, most notably telecommunications providers and airlines. Furthermore, if the Framework Decision on PNR is adopted then a whole new form of executive/administrative body will be established in each Member State: the Passenger Information Unit.

The PNR Agreements empower a wide range of US law enforcement authorities to process data on EU citizens in a manner which many EU law enforcement agencies cannot. Perhaps the most peculiar aspect of the PNR Agreements with the US is the use of 'letters' to both elaborate on the details of the agreements and finally conclude them. Some commentators note that this use of letters may allow for informal amendment of the PNR Agreement, or even unilateral alteration of its terms.[149] If so, then the idea of a community of law is undermined as the polity is governed not by the acts of a legislature, but by executive fiat. Furthermore, the Data Retention Directive offers the potential for broad access to personal data to national law enforcement agencies, without putting in place any safeguards in relation to the processing of that data. Thus, as with other areas, the EU is empowering executive actors without providing adequate safeguards to protect targeted individuals. Anecdotal evidence from one Member State highlights the potential for abuse—in Poland two civil society groups have alleged that police and security services have used their powers to investigate journalists in an effort to uncover their sources.[150]

The co-option of private actors is evidenced in both the PNR Agreements and the Data Retention Directive. Both PNR data and the telecommunications data were already being retained by service providers in the ordinary conduct of their business. The personal data in question—be it financial, travel or communication related—is remarkably banal. The common feature of these regimes is that they relate to 'vast categories of personal data linked with ordinary, everyday and mostly legitimate activity'.[151] By requiring those undertakings to transfer (or make available) pre-existing data to law enforcement authorities, the EU has side-stepped a number of legal and pragmatic difficulties that would be

---

[149] Papakonstantinou and de Hert, n 74 above, p 909.

[150] Hensinka Fundacja Praw Czlowieka and Fundacja Panoptykon, Joint Statement Regarding the Evaluation of Directive 2006/24/EC, 5 November 2010.

[151] Mitsilegas, n 5 above, p 272.

encountered were state authorities themselves to try to collect the data in question. The private actor that has faced the greatest difficulties as a result of data surveillance has been SWIFT. Having gone to great lengths to ensure its operation did not breach EU law by discontinuing its practice of mirroring European data on US servers it found that it was ultimately forced to continue to provide data to US authorities by the EU–US TFTP Agreements. The case of SWIFT demonstrates that private actors are not just tools of EU counter-terrorism but also subjects of it. There remain doubts as to whether the administrative sub poenas issued to SWIFT under US law would be upheld by US courts in light of their violation of foreign law.[152] Nonetheless the private actor expended much by way of financial resources to comply with its obligations under an evolving legal regime.

These problems each contribute to an erosion of the idea that the polity is governed by a system of rules constituted through law. The most insidious aspect of this erosion is the manner in which legal rules pertaining to the way in which norms are devised, the applicable standards of proof, and rational procedures for their application are eroded by increased reliance on technologies of risk. Whereas this poses problems for the individual it also poses problems for the idea of a community governed through law as legal rules recede while technological rationalities are shifted to the fore.[153] Those technological rationalities are themselves the product of power relationships as evidenced by the Comitology Committee's power over the risk assessment process—but the power relationships can be masked by the seemingly scientific methods used. Thus the transparency, accountability and certainty provided by legal rules properly promulgated is lost as a technocratic process is used to make decisions. The more blatant aspect of the erosion is the way the EU–US PNR Agreements have effectively given the force of law to mere 'undertakings' and 'letters' from the US Department of Homeland Security. This is a clear breach of the principle of legality, simply understood, and permits the US authorities to exercise de facto power within the EU. While the fact of that exercise of power is contrary to the constitutive aspect of the rule of law it is clear that the manner in which the power is actually being exercised is also contrary to the safeguarding aspect of the rule of law. The result is the subversion of the EU legal system for US law enforcement purposes.

ii. Mass Surveillance & Generalised Suspicion

The most obvious manner in which EU data surveillance represents a pre-emptive approach is in its generalisation of suspicion. Both the PNR system and the Data Retention Directive affect all individuals, regardless of their prior criminal record, or the presence (or absence) of any reason for suspecting them of criminal behaviour.

---

[152] Connorton, n 31 above, pp 283–322.
[153] Michel Foucault, quoted in L Amoore, 'Risk before Justice: When the Law Contests Its Own Suspension', (2008) 21 *Leiden Journal of International Law* 847, 847.

As one commentator notes, 'the sharp departure after [11 September 2011] was to move from individualised surveillance to mass suspicion'.[154] Thus, data surveillance operates based on one of two assumptions. Either every individual is a potential terrorist, or the interference with the rights of the general population is justifiable to capture the minute percentage of individuals actually guilty of terrorism.

The European Commission proposal is most blatant in this regard. Noting that the EU already requires the transfer of Advance Passenger Information (which includes the type and number of travel document used, nationality, full name and date of birth of passengers, amongst other data) the proposal goes on to declare that such information is sufficient 'only for identifying *known* terrorists and criminals'.[155] PNR data on the other hand 'are a very important tool for carrying out risk assessments of the persons, for obtaining intelligence and for making associations between known and *unknown* persons'.[156] This emphasis on 'unknown persons' echoes Donald Rumsfeld's infamous 'unknown unknowns' and is a typical trait of pre-emptive counter-terrorism.

This generalisation of the regulatory effects of counter-terrorism outside the confines of the criminal justice system can be explained as the dispersal of control from the institutions to wider society. The effect on the rule of law is clear: individual autonomy is infringed without any link between the infringement and the individual's conduct. As the remainder of analysis in this section demonstrates, that infringement is made without sufficient safeguards, in violation of both procedural and substantive human rights.

iii. Effect on General Population

Data surveillance does not entail the use of overt force against suspected individuals. Whereas legislating for criminal offences involves deploying the state's coercive force in the form of the criminal justice system, data surveillance measures may not involve any force at all. However, the use of force cannot be ruled out, since law enforcement or security agencies may use surveillance information as the basis for subsequent action. Yet, for the vast majority of people subject to surveillance, the exercise of power will never become visible. Nonetheless, the surveillance regimes may affect the behaviour of the population subject to them. It is worth considering the potential reactions of two ideal-types: first, the 'guilty', those who knowingly engage in illegal activity and second, the 'innocent', those who do not knowingly engage in illegal activity.

In terms of the first ideal-type, the 'guilty', it seems likely that the data surveillance systems will have little impact. Breyer notes that 'traffic data retention cannot stop more

---

[154] Interview with Marc Rotenberg, Director of the Electronic Privacy Information Center and senior counsel, Washington, DC, 30 October 2007, quoted in Amoore, 'Risk before Justice', n 153 above, p 855.

[155] Commission (EC), n 105 above, p 3.

[156] Ibid.

experienced criminals from preventing the generation of incriminating traffic data'.[157] The use of such databases is not foolproof and various techniques may be used to ano-nymise computer usage and render the databases redundant. If the counter-terrorism action is aimed at the 'worst of the worst', it is reasonable to assume that such individu-als will alter their communication practices to avoid detection.[158] Furthermore, given the finite amount of information available from PNR data, it may be possible to avoid or reduce the likelihood of detection. Levi has highlighted the complicity of Lloyds Bank in London with Iranian banks to avoid tracking through TFTP.

> The UK branches or subsidiaries of Iranian banks would send electronic messages via the SWIFT electronic banking payments system to Lloyds and other banks. Employees at Lloyds would then re-key the data into a new SWIFT message, carefully removing any reference to Iran or its banks. The sophisticated screening software at American banks would have raised red flags if the true source of the funds had been revealed, but coming from respected European financial institutions, they were not questioned.[159]

It is clear therefore that sophisticated operators may evade data surveillance—rendering the security dividend from generalised surveillance is far from certain.[160] While Lloyds was ultimately forced to agree a settlement with the Manhattan District Attorney in exchange for a deferred prosecution for enabling the evasion of surveillance the example is illustrative of the questionable efficacy of terrorist finance tracking against those willing to consciously evade detection.

There is obvious scope for affecting the everyday life of the second ideal-type: the 'innocent'. Individuals who know that their telecommunications traffic and location data is being retained may alter their usage to avoid attracting the atten-tion of the law enforcement authorities. There is clear potential for a 'chilling effect' on the general public as individuals avoid websites discussing subversive political material for fear that their activity is monitored by law enforcement authorities. While those authorities might consider such an outcome a positive benefit, the result is an interference with the rights to privacy and freedom of expression (which includes, under Article 10 ECHR, the right to receive informa-tion) and the shrinking of the space for political debate. The mass surveillance thus complements other, more specific, restrictions on the public sphere.

In some respects, it seems unlikely that the implementation of PNR data reten-tion will affect individuals' travel habits, especially as the use of PNR regimes becomes more widespread (with the US, Canada, Australia and soon the EU operating such schemes). However, there remains scope for altering behaviour.

---

[157] Breyer, n 139 above, p 369.

[158] Ibid.

[159] M Levi, 'Combating the Financing of Terrorism: A History and Assessment of the Control of "Threat Finance"' (2010) 50 *British Journal of Criminology* 650, 665.

[160] Indeed, the gain in security from the generalised surveillance of travel has largely been asserted rather than proven. See, eg: Meijers Committee, 'CM1108 Directive on the use of PNR data for the prevention, detection, investigation and prosecution of terrorist offences and serious crime' COM (2011) 32, Utrecht, 21 June 2011, at p 4 for a refutation of the necessity from a security point of view of PNR data processing.

In the US, frequent flyers are encouraged to submit biometric data to enable them to pass more swiftly through airport security. A similar programme has been instituted at Amsterdam Schiphol, where for an annual fee and the submission of certain biometric information, EU passport holders can enjoy speedier security checks when using the airport and frequent flyer benefits.[161] In the United Kingdom the introduction of a 'Trusted Traveller' programme operates on a similar basis and facilitates faster passage through airport security through an iris scan.[162] These systems encourages users to agree to a greater interference with their privacy in exchange for an improved user experience. While on the one hand this might be seen as placing control in the hands of the user to make their own determination as to how great an interference they are willing to tolerate it also disadvantages those who are not in a position to do so—for example because they cannot afford the annual fee.

iv. Suspect Communities

The final point of note is that though the surveillance is generalised, action taken based on data surveillance tends to target certain 'suspect communities'. The widespread use of data surveillance led to the coining of the term 'dataveillance': 'the proactive surveillance of what effectively become suspect populations, using new technologies to identify "risky groups"'.[163] For example, Amoore describes communications between US and UK authorities regarding the abolition of the US visa waiver for British citizens of Pakistani origin. Following the suspected plot to simultaneously attack eight transatlantic flights in 2006, the Secretary of Homeland Security, Michael Chertoff, is reported to have raised the matter with his British counterpart.[164] If true, this episode demonstrates most clearly the relationship between the pre-emption and measures directed against certain suspect communities. However, in this example, even the supposedly scientific nature of the risk assessment has ben entirely abandoned with a group—British citizens of Pakistani origin—explicitly identified solely on the basis of nationality and ethnicity. In this respect it is clear that at least some risk assessments are little more than the twenty-first century equivalent of demonised 'others'.[165]

The PNR databases and many of the others that exist at EU level relate to travel and migration. The definition of terrorism was drafted in such a way that asylum seekers may have to choose between revealing their opposition to an oppressive regime and being labelled a 'terrorist' or concealing that information and being refused political

---

[161] L Amoore and M de Goede, 'Governance, Risk and Dataveillance in the War on Terror' (2005) 43 *Crime, Law and Social Change* 149, 167.

[162] See V Mitsilegas, 'The Transformation of Border Controls', n 6 above, p 243.

[163] M Levi and D Wall, 'Technologies, security and privacy in the post 9/11 European Information Society' (2004) 31 *Journal of Law and Society* 194, 200.

[164] Amoore, n 153 above, p 847.

[165] For a broader discussion see L Weber and B Bowling, 'Valiant Beggars and Global Vagabonds: Select, Eject, Immobilize' (2008) 12 *Theoretical Criminology* 355.

asylum. The use of surveillance technologies for security purposes can also target vulnerable migrants. The Commission's proposal for a European Border Surveillance System (EUROSUR) is a case in point. The aim of EUROSUR is to reach 'full situational awareness at the ... external border', with the first phase seeking to 'interlink and streamline existing surveillance systems and mechanisms at Member State level'.[166] One of the three key aims of the surveillance system is to counter 'cross-border crime such as terrorism'.[167] The proposition that preventing illegal migration will counter terrorism is an unproven assertion. It is offered notwithstanding the fact that the perpetrators of the September 11 attacks entered the US legally, and those responsible for the 7 July bombings in London were British citizens.

Under the various PNR programmes, those who are confident of their digital footprint will move unhindered to Australia, Canada, the US, and soon, the EU. They may even use programmes such as that at Schiphol airport to speed their passage through airport security. Others will (at best) be singled out for heightened security checks, or (at worst) refused permission to fly. Others still may even opt not to fly to avoid the attention of law enforcement authorities and so fulfil the purpose of a digital 'Panopticon': the exercise of control through surveillance without the use of, or need for, any overt force.[168]

IV. CONCLUSION: THE DIGITAL PANOPTICON?

Since 11 September 2011, the logic of pre-emption has been deployed beyond the strict confines of counter-terrorism, and used as justification for broader surveillance regimes that target vulnerable minorities as well as the population as a whole. Data surveillance shares two characteristics with anti-money-laundering and counter-terrorist finance. Both evidence practices of policy-laundering and both generalise suspicion far beyond those against whom evidence of criminal behaviour can be brought. Data surveillance also shares characteristics with the Framework Decision on Combating Terrorism discussed. As with the Framework Decision, the dataveillance laws may interact with efforts to control (legal and illegal) migration to the detriment of vulnerable minorities. If targeted asset-freezing sanctions are EU counter-terrorism at its most coercive, data surveillance is pre-emption at its broadest. Decoupled from any evidence of criminality or deviance on the part of those targeted, it seeks to control behaviour through self-government and the selective deployment of coercive technologies.

---

[166] Commission (EC), Examining the creation of a European Border Surveillance System (EUROSUR) MEMO/08/86, Brussels, 13 February 2008.

[167] Ibid.

[168] The idea of a 'panopticon' was first developed by Jeremy Bentham as a form of prison where a single warden could view all prisoners from a central point while remaining out of sight. The concept was developed by Michel Foucault in *Discipline and Punish*. Foucault described a society in which individuals exercise 'self-discipline' to comply with societal norms without any overt force having to be exerted against them. See M Foucault, *Discipline and Punish: The Birth of the Prison*, new edn (London, Penguin, 1991).

7

European Warrants

THE EUROPEAN ARREST Warrant (EAW) was announced, along with the Framework Decision on Combating Terrorism (FDCT), as a central plank of EU counter-terrorism.[1] The EAW revolutionises the approach to the transfer of individuals suspected or convicted of crimes within Europe. The arrest warrant has become the most well-known of EU counter-terrorism instruments, with high profile cases such as that of Julian Assange, the founder of Wikileaks, attracting much media attention. However, the legislation's impact goes beyond the high profile cases as there have been 54,689 EAWs issued in the five years between 2005 and 2009.[2] The European Evidence Warrant (EEW) builds on the EAW and several other framework decisions based on the principle of mutual recognition.[3] It aims to facilitate speedier co-operation in the transfer of evidence for criminal proceedings between Member States. Although neither are limited in use to counter-terrorism, both framework decisions are part of the EU Action Plan on Combating Terrorism. As framework decisions, the arrest and evidence warrant instruments are prone to the same problems as the Framework Decision on Combating Terrorism. All framework decisions are heavily dependent on implementation by national legislatures to be effective. Differences in national legislation have given rise to diverging practices—contrary to the rule of law. In addition, civil society groups have raised concerns over the transfer of suspects to Member States with poor rights of defence in their criminal justice system. In many respects the arrest warrant has emerged as a litmus test for the successful operation of an EU criminal justice system—while the evidence warrant demonstrates that the Council learned lessons from the difficulties of the earlier instrument. The evidence warrant is already earmarked for obsolescence with a proposed European Investigation Order due to replace it. The instruments are all based on the principle of mutual recognition which was first established in

---

[1] Council Framework Decision of 13 June 2002 on the European arrest warrant and the surrender procedures between Member States (2002/584/JHA).

[2] Commission (EC), 'Report from the Commission to the European Parliament and the Council: On the implementation since 2007 of the Council Framework Decision of 13 June 2002 on the European arrest warrant and the surrender procedures between Member States' COM (2011) 175 final, Brussels, 11 April 2011 (hereafter, Third Implementation Report) 3.

[3] Council Framework Decision 2008/978/JHA of 18 December 2008 on the European evidence warrant for the purpose of obtaining objects, documents and data for use in proceedings in criminal matters (hereafter, FDEAW).

the internal market before being introduced to criminal justice co-operation by the Tampere Programme. For all of their problems, the European warrants may be examples of the establishment of a new rule of law in EU criminal justice rather than the excesses of pre-emptive counter-terrorism.

I. CRIMINAL JUSTICE CO-OPERATION IN EUROPE

European co-operation in criminal matters predates the existence of the EU, with the Council of Europe taking a leading role in the past.[4] Co-operation focused on six areas: 'extradition, mutual assistance, transfer of prisoners, enforcement of sentences, transfer of proceedings and confiscation of proceeds of crime'.[5] Within the EU, the impetus for greater co-operation in criminal matters was the belief that criminals were benefiting from the free movement ideal that lies at the heart of the internal market. In 1998, the UK Presidency of the EU proposed to make the principle of mutual recognition the cornerstone of increased co-operation in criminal justice in Europe. The principle, as it applies to criminal law, may be defined as the recognition by each Member State of decisions of courts from other Member States 'with a minimum of procedure and formality'.[6] The idea behind the UK proposal was based on an analogy with the internal market where following the *Cassis de Dijon* decision mutual recognition paved the way for the completion of the market.[7] If the same principle could be harnessed in relation to criminal justice, then a European criminal law could be built without facing the difficult task of adopting harmonising instruments.

The logic of mutual recognition, which now pervades much of EU justice and home affairs, has not been uncontroversial. Two principal arguments are offered against transferring the mutual recognition principle from the internal market to criminal justice.[8] First, opponents argue, criminal justice is qualitatively different from rules governing the internal market ('qualitative difference argument'). It entails the protection and limitation of individual rights: a matter which is too close to the role of the state and too dependent on direct democratic legitimacy to be integrated by the blunt instrument of mutual recognition. One way in which there is a clear qualitative difference is the beneficiaries of mutual recognition. In the internal market it was private individuals and undertakings that were permitted to move through the Union without having to consider different regulation in each Member State. Thus it was public power that was limited and private power

---

[4] S Peers, 'Mutual Recognition and Criminal Law in the European Union: Has the Council Got it Wrong?' (2004) 41 *Common Market Law Review* 5, 6.

[5] Ibid.

[6] V Mitsilegas, *EU Criminal Law* (Oxford, Hart Publishing, 2009) 116.

[7] Case 120/78 *Cassis de Dijon* [1979] ECR 649. For a discussion of mutual recognition as a mode of governance see: M Poiares Maduro, 'So Close and Yet So Far: the Paradoxes of Mutual Recognition' (2007) 14 *Journal of European Public Policy* 814.

[8] For a useful summary of the debate see: Mitsilegas, *EU Criminal Law*, n 6 above, pp 101, 117–20.

that benefitted. In criminal justice the converse is true—with state actors able to pursue law enforcement across the EU while private actors find it more difficult to escape a state's criminal justice system.[9] Second, some argue that even if the qualitative difference can be overcome, mutual recognition in the internal market was only successful due to the high level of harmonisation that already existed ('harmonisation argument'). In the absence of similar convergence in Member State criminal law, mutual recognition cannot work. One example of how this convergence could be achieved is through a minimum harmonisation of criminal offences in EU law. Thus, Vermuelen has argued that the EAW should only be available for offences that have been approximated in EU law.[10] These arguments have gained greater acceptance over the past decade but were given little attention by the Council or Commission at the time of the Tampere Council in 1999.

Despite misgivings among the academic community and in civil society groups, the Conclusions of the 1999 Tampere Council noted that in relation to the area of freedom, security and justice, 'the principle of mutual recognition ... should become the cornerstone of judicial co-operation in both civil and criminal matters within the Union'.[11] It set out the rationale behind the European warrants:

35. With respect to criminal matters, the European Council urges Member States to speedily ratify the 1995 and 1996 EU Conventions on extradition. It considers that the formal extradition procedure should be abolished among the Member States as far as persons are concerned who are fleeing from justice after having been finally sentenced, and replaced by a simple transfer of such persons, in compliance with Article 6 TEU. Consideration should also be given to fast track extradition procedures, without prejudice to the principle of fair trial. The European Council invites the Commission to make proposals on this matter in the light of the Schengen Implementing Agreement.

36. The principle of mutual recognition should also apply to pre-trial orders, in particular to those which would enable competent authorities quickly to secure evidence and to seize assets which are easily movable; evidence lawfully gathered by one Member State's authorities should be admissible before the courts of other Member States, taking into account the standards that apply there.[12]

Tampere thus enshrined mutual recognition as the key to EU criminal justice. The Tampere Programme has since been succeeded by the Hague Programme and, most recently, the Stockholm Programme.[13] Throughout the development of these programmes, mutual recognition has been considered the 'motor of European

---

[9] M Möstl, 'Preconditions of Mutual Recognition' (2010) 47 *Common Market Law Review* 405, 409.

[10] See the discussion in F Naert and J Wouters, 'Of Arrest Warrants, Terrorist Offences and Extradition Deals: An Appraisal of the EU's Main Criminal Law Measures Against Terrorism after "11 September"' (2004) 41 *Common Market Law Review* 909, 920.

[11] European Council, 'Tampere European Council 15 and 16 October 1999 Presidency Conclusions 1999', [33].

[12] Ibid.

[13] European Council, 'Presidency Conclusions Annex 1 The Hague Programme: Strengthening Freedom, Security and Justice in the European Union', Brussels, 4–5 November 2004.

integration in criminal matters'.[14] The shift from co-operation to mutual recognition is significant. In the past one state would request co-operation from another. The requested state would then take a decision on assistance subject to the requirements of its own legal system. Following the shift to mutual recognition, the requested state executes a decision taken by the requesting state.[15] Though the requested state retains a certain degree of control, that control is limited by the legal instrument establishing the system. To date, the principle has been the basis for several EU instruments, most notably the framework decisions on the EAW and EEW. It has also been enshrined in the European constitution as Article 82 TFEU provides that judicial co-operation in criminal matters 'shall be based on the principle of mutual recognition of judgments and judicial decisions'.

Moving extradition and evidence transfer from international law conventions to domestic EU legislation was a bold step in itself. The action was rendered even more ambitious by the shift from co-operation to mutual recognition. However, it is clear that the system can only work if Member State authorities have a high level of trust in each others' criminal justice systems. The Commission's efforts to simplify extradition were thwarted prior to 11 September 2001 by a lack of the very trust said to underpin the system. Today, despite ongoing co-operation, the fundamental problem of lack of trust remains. Mutual recognition, notwithstanding its inclusion in the Lisbon Treaty, still appears 'unsettled' in relation to its 'functionality, legitimacy and ... scope'.[16]

II. EU LEGISLATION ON EUROPEAN WARRANTS

The use of framework decisions to introduce both the arrest and evidence warrant left the instruments open to the same problems that plagued implementation of the Framework Decision on Combating Terrorism. Indeed, the very use of a framework decision to regulate a part of criminal justice co-operation previously governed by international conventions was controversial.[17] The warrants have also been subject to scrutiny for appropriation of the concept of 'surrender' from international criminal justice as well as for the partial abolition of the dual criminality requirement. However, the gratest scrutiny, as much be expected, has been on the procedures and safeguards in transferring suspects, convicts and evidence. The Stockholm Programme includes a commitment to replace the evidence warrant with a more comprehensive instrument, the European Investigation Order, which therefore also merits attention.

---

[14] Mitsilegas, n 6 above, p 115.
[15] Ibid.
[16] P Rackow and C Birr, 'Recent Developments in Legal Assistance in Criminal Matters' (2010) 2 *Goettingen Journal of International Law* 1087, 1094.
[17] See the below discussion of C-303/05 *Advocaten voor de Wereld VZW v Leden van de Ministerraad* (hereafter *Advocaten voor de Wereld*) [2007] ECR I-633.

A. European Arrest Warrant

Prior to the adoption of the Framework Decision on the EAW, extradition in the European Union was based on a 1957 Council of Europe Convention and a 1975 Additional Protocol.[18] The European Commission claimed that though these instruments were progressive at the time of their adoption, by 2001 the system of extradition was 'a heavy and obsolete mechanism'.[19] In addition to the Council of Europe Convention, extradition was simplified by two EU Conventions, originally based on provisions of the Schengen Agreement.[20] However, even under these additional instruments, extradition remained 'by definition political and intergovernmental'.[21] Under this system, extradition procedures often involved a two-stage process: an initial judicial decision being reviewed on political grounds by an executive authority.[22] It was therefore a slow and politicised process. The aim of the Commission proposal was to entirely replace these earlier agreements with a new legal apparatus to ensure the swift transfer of suspects and convicts between Member States. Despite the lofty ambitions it took the events of 11 September 2001 to force consensus on a Framework Decision on the EAW. The Commission brought forward a proposal on 25 September 2001. The framework decision was formally adopted on 13 June 2002 and became operational on 1 January 2004. This presented Member States with a relatively short period in which to incorporate the measure, not least because several Member States had to contemplate constitutional amendments to achieve transposition.[23]

The framework decision seeks to abolish the formal extradition procedure between Member States and replace it with a simplified process whereby sought-after suspects and convicts would be 'surrendered' following a brief judicial procedure.[24] It is based on Articles 31(a)–(b) and 34(2)(b) EU(N). The various recitals to the Preamble trace the evolution of extradition within Europe and the EU. The fifth recital sets out that the Framework Decision is part of an effort to ensure the 'free movement of judicial decisions'. It is based on a 'high level of confidence between Member States' and as such, its operation should only be suspended if there is a 'serious and persistent breach' of the founding principles of the EU.[25]

---

[18] European Convention on Extradition 1957; Additional Protocol to the European Convention on Extradition 1975.

[19] Commission (EC), 'Proposal for a Council Framework Decision on the European arrest warrant and the surrender procedures between the Member States' COM (2001) 522 final/2, Brussels, 25 September 2001, p 2.

[20] Schengen Agreement 1985; Convention on the simplified extradition procedure between the Member States of the European Union of 10 March 1995; Convention on the extradition between the Member States of the European Union of 27 September 1996.

[21] Commission (EC), COM (2001) 522 final/2, n 19 above, p 2.

[22] M Plachta, *'European Arrest Warrant: Revolution in Extradition?'* (2003) 11 *European Journal of Crime, Criminal Law and Criminal Justice* 178, 187.

[23] For an overview of implementation by Member States see Naert and Wouters, n 10 above, pp 916–17.

[24] Plachta, n 22 above, p 191.

[25] Preamble, FDEAW.

The Preamble stands out when compared to those of other measures considered in this work: there is but a single reference to terrorism and no reference to prevention or other tropes of EU counter-terrorism.[26]

The framework decision's legal basis was challenged before the ECJ on a reference from the Belgian Arbitragehof. The applicants alleged first, that a framework decision could only be used to approximate the criminal law of the Member States (which, they alleged, the Framework Decision on the EAW did not do) and second, that the Framework Decision could not be used to replace a policy area previously governed by conventions. Advocate General Colomer and the ECJ rejected both claims on similar grounds. In relation to the first claim, the Court pointed out that the Framework Decision did approximate Member State laws, in terms of the rules and procedures relating to extradition.[27] On the second claim, the Court used the principle of effectiveness to uphold the Council's power to choose which legal mechanism was appropriate.[28] The challenge to the legal basis was therefore dismissed. While the Court's decision on competence is entirely rational, it is noteworthy that it invoked the principle of effectiveness in this manner. The decision reinforces the idea that the EU should be able to be an effective actor in criminal justice and signals the ECJ's tacit acceptance of the Union's role in this policy sphere.

The EAW has been the subject of landmark decisions in the Polish, German, Cypriot and Czech constitutional courts and tribunals. It has also been the subject of a reference to the ECJ from the Belgian Arbitragehof. The impact of these cases on the developing law will be considered throughout this chapter. It is not proposed to examine the entire arrest warrant system here as ample efforts have been made to do so elsewhere.[29] The focus is on three key elements: the concept of 'surrender', the partial abolition of the dual criminality requirement and the process by which the warrant is executed and the associated safeguards.

i. The Arrest Warrant as 'Surrender'

Article 1 sets out the basic definition and aims of the legislation. It defines the European Arrest Warrant as:

> a judicial decision issued by a Member State with a view to the arrest and surrender by another Member State of a requested person, for the purposes of conducting a criminal prosecution or executing a custodial sentence or detention order.

The provision goes on to note that the EAW is based on the principle of mutual recognition. Like the FDCT, Article 1 ends with a reaffirmation of the founding

---

[26] Preamble, FDEAW.

[27] *Advocaten voor de Wereld VZW*, Opinion of Advocate General Colomer, para 49; ECJ Judgment, paras 28–30.

[28] Ibid Opinion of Advocate General Colomer, para 65; ECJ Judgment, para 43.

[29] See, eg: S Alegre and M Leaf, *European Arrest Warrant: A Solution Ahead of its Time?* (London, JUSTICE, 2003).

principles of the EU (identical to that in the earlier measure). In keeping with the intentions expressed in the Preamble, the EAW is described as a procedure of 'surrender', and not 'extradition'. Plachta takes issue with the use of 'surrender' to describe the EAW procedure.[30] The idea of 'surrender' originated to allow states that could not 'extradite' nationals to nonetheless hand them over to international criminal tribunals.[31] 'Surrender' is therefore the language of the Rome Statute establishing the International Criminal Court.[32] Its appropriation by EU law as the term to replace 'extradition' within EU law was always likely to be controversial.

The question of 'surrender' is particularly important in relation to Member States' own citizens. Several Member States traditionally refused to extradite their own nationals. One of the goals of the EAW was to remove this impediment to cross-border co-operation. Poland, Germany, Cyprus and the Czech Republic all had to face this problem in the aftermath of transposition. Following a request from the Netherlands for the surrender of a Polish citizen, the Gdansk Regional Court sent a reference to the Constitutional Tribunal regarding the constitutionality of the Penal Procedure Code provisions that implemented the Framework Decision on the EAW. The key question was whether 'surrender' of an individual subject to an EAW amounted to extradition and if so, whether the EAW was in breach of the constitutional prohibition on the extradition of Polish citizens.[33] The Constitutional Tribunal held that the relevant provisions of the Code were not compatible with the Constitution. However, the Tribunal went on to declare that its judgment would not take effect for 18 months, during which time the legislature was expected to address the problem of constitutionality. Following the decision of the Constitutional Tribunal, the Polish Government ensured that the Constitution was amended.[34] The Constitutional Tribunal was afforded a second opportunity to consider the arrest warrant in 2010.[35] The case concerned an individual sentenced to life imprisonment in the UK and then sent to Poland, which typically imposes a much more lenient penalty for the offence, to serve the sentence. The individual claimed a breach of the Polish Constitution and of Article 6 ECHR. However, the Constitutional Tribunal upheld the validity of the contested parts of Polish law implementing the EAW and dismissed the application.

---

[30] Plachta, n 23 above, p 190.

[31] Ibid.

[32] Art 102 Rome Statute of the International Criminal Court 17 July 1998.

[33] Art 55 § 1 of the Polish Constitution plainly stated 'Extradition of a Polish citizen is prohibited.' See: Judgment of Polish Constitutional Tribunal 27 April 2005 Case P 1/05. For a discussion of the Polish litigation on the EAW see: A Lazowski, 'Half Full and Half Empty Glass: The Application of EU Law in Poland (2004–2010)' (2011) 48 *Common Market Law Review* 503.

[34] Commission (EC), 'Report from the Commission on the implementation since 2005 of the Council Framework Decision of 13 June 2002 on the European arrest warrant and the surrender procedures between Member States' COM (2007) 407 final, Brussels, 11 July 2007 (hereafter, Second Evaluation Report) 5.

[35] Judgment of Polish Constitutional Tribunal 5 October 2010 Case SK 26/08.

The German Federal Constitutional Court was not as accommodating. The German case arose from a request by Spanish authorities for a suspect of German and Syrian nationality to be surrendered for prosecution relating to membership of Al Qaeda.[36] The Court held that the German European Arrest Warrant Act was in contravention of the Basic Law, in particular provisions for the non-extradition of German nationals and the availability of recourse to a court. Notably, the Court did not find fault with the framework decision itself, but with the German implementing law.[37] The problem, the Court held, was that the German legislature did not take full advantage of the discretion afforded to it by the parent measure. The Court noted that the framework decision allowed the executing state to refuse surrender where the alleged offences took place in part or in full within the territory of the executing state. This, the Court held, would protect the special affinity the German citizen has for his own legal order. The failure to transpose this into national law made the implementing act offend the proportionality requirement of the Basic Law. As a result of these incompatibilities the Act was declared void. This result represented a distinct lack of 'loyal co-operation' on the part of German Court.[38] In response to the decision, Spain and Hungary suspended the operation of the EAW in respect of Germany, requiring all German requests to be dealt with under the earlier extradition system. The EAW procedure was restored by both countries following the adoption of the new German implementing law in 2006.[39]

The other two Member States to offer constitutional judgments were Cyprus and the Czech Republic. The Cypriot case involved a request from the UK for the surrender of an individual of dual British and Cypriot nationality. The Framework Decision was held by the Cypriot Supreme Court to be incompatible with Article 11(f) of the Cypriot Constitution, which only permitted the extradition of 'aliens'.[40] While the Cypriot Government ensured that the Constitution was amended to facilitate correct implementation, the surrender of Cypriot nationals is limited to crimes committed after Cyprus' accession to the EU.[41] The Czech case focused on similar issues, specifically a provision which prohibited any law forcing a Czech citizen to leave their homeland.[42] However, the Czech Supreme Court offered a different point of view to that of the Cypriot, German and Polish courts. The Court held that if 'Czech citizens enjoy certain advantages, connected with the status of EU citizenship, then naturally in this context that a certain degree of

---

[36] *Europäischer Haftbefehl* 113 BVerfGE 273 (2005). For commentary see: N Nohlen, 'Germany: The European Arrest Warrant Case' (2008) 6 *International Journal of Constitutional Law* 153.

[37] In this regard the approach is similar to that which was subsequently adopted in relation to the German implementation of the Data Retention Directive. See ch 6 above.

[38] Ibid 160.

[39] Commission (EC), Second Evaluation Report, 5.

[40] Judgment of the Supreme Court of Cyprus 7 November 2005 Ap No 294/2005.

[41] Commission (EC), Second Evaluation Report, 5.

[42] Judgment of the Czech Constitutional Court 3 May 2006 Pl Ús 66/04.

responsibility must be accepted along with these advantages'.[43] The arrest warrant was deemed constitutional, exhibiting a far greater degree of trust in the criminal justice systems of other Member States than the other courts discussed above.

The idea of 'surrender' is an innovation in EU criminal justice. The EU has borrowed a concept originally devised to avoid the difficulties of extraditing nationals to international criminal tribunals. However, the use of different nomenclature has not allowed it avoid the difficulties surrounding the surrender of Member States' own nationals. Nonetheless, now that these difficulties have been (largely) dealt with, the term allows a differentiation between extradition from an EU Member State to a non-Member State and extradition within the EU. As such, it is perfectly appropriate. While a change in name alone cannot justify the circumvention of constitutional protections, the change of name in tandem with change in the substantive procedure, and the basis of that change in mutual trust in the EU, signifies an important development in EU criminal law. It represents a key step in establishing a distinct EU criminal justice system by moving beyond the status quo of each criminal law jurisdiction in the EU as an autonomous system. In creating this EU system it may be necessary to rethink certain concepts of criminal justice and co-operation between the Member States. As neither a unitary nor federal system the EU is likely to be innovative in devising instruments that serve public policy goals (such as crime prevention) while upholding constitutional principles such as the rule of law. The idea of 'surrender' replacing extradition is one such innovation. Its successful operation is heavily dependent on mutual trust—which will in turn be built through the provision of appropriate safeguards for those subject to criminal justice co-operation. Before examining those safeguards another innovation, the partial abolition of dual criminality, merits scrutiny.

ii. Partial Abolition of Dual Criminality

One of the most significant substantive changes to extradition brought about by the framework decision is the partial abolition of dual criminality. A Member State may issue an EAW in two different scenarios. First, a warrant may be issued for a person suspected of an offence with a maximum custodial sentence of no less than 12 months, or no less than 4 months if the sentence has been passed. In such instances, the requested state may impose the 'dual criminality' rule that requires the behaviour that has given rise to the warrant to be an offence in both states.[44] Second, a warrant may be issued for a person suspected of one of 32 offences, as defined by the law of the issuing Member State, if the offence carries a maximum custodial sentence of no less than 3 years. In such cases, the dual criminality rule shall not apply.[45] The abolition of the dual criminality rule for 32 offences—including terrorism—is one of the revolutionary aspects of the

---

[43] Ibid.
[44] Art 2(1), 2(4) FDEAW.
[45] Art 2(1), 2(2) FDEAW.

framework decision. In addition to terrorism, the list includes other offences relevant to counter-terrorism such as participation in a criminal organisation, illicit trafficking in weapons and munitions and laundering of the proceeds of crime. Some of the crimes are clearer in their definition than others. While 'rape', 'arson' and 'murder' are all likely to be reasonably well-defined in Member State law, 'swindling', 'racketeering and extortion' and 'sabotage' may not be. The list of offences may be amended by the Council, acting unanimously, following consultation with the European Parliament.[46] The Belgian Arbitragehof asked the ECJ to consider whether the vague drafting of the items on this list offended the principle of legality. However, the Court swiftly dismissed the question, noting that the list does not seek to harmonise national law on the criminal offences themselves, merely with regard to extradition.[47] Furthermore, it is the law of the issuing state that defines the offences and that law should be in compliance with the principle of legality.[48] While this conclusion is logical, this EU practice of 'labelling' rather than defining criminal offences—also evidenced by the Framework Decision on Combating Terrorism—causes persistent difficulties with the clarity of the law.

A further question referred to the ECJ by the Belgian Arbitragehof was whether, in selecting certain crimes to be exempt from the requirement of dual criminality but not others, the Council had operated contrary to the principles of equality and non-discrimination. The response from the ECJ was, unsurprisingly, in the negative. The Court was quick to note that the decision was not arbitrary, but could be justified on objective grounds 'in terms of adversely affecting public order and public safety'.[49] The decision affirms the power of the Council to determine which offences are sufficiently serious to merit the abolition of the dual criminality requirement. It is unlikely that the Court could have arrived at any other decision without restricting the legislature's prerogative to set criminal justice policy. Nonetheless, in this instance the legislature consists of Member State governments. This raises a question about the allocation of institutional power in EU criminal justice. The EU legislature is composed of the Council (ie Member State governments) and the European Parliament. Thus, legislative power is exercised by a hybrid executive/legislative authority. Indeed, when adopting framework

---

[46] Art 2(3) FDEAW.

[47] Notwithstanding the ECJ's argument on this point the list first introduced in the EAW has also been used in the EEW and has been proposed for use as the purpose limitation definition of 'serious crime' for the proposed Directive on a Passenger Name Record System for the EU. As such the vagueness of the list that was first introduced in the aftermath of the 11 September 2001 attacks has migrated into new areas of EU counter-terrorism. See: Commission (EC), 'Proposal for a Council Framework Decision on the use of Passenger Name Record (PNR) for law enforcement purposes' COM (2007) 654 final, Brussels, 6 November 2007; 'Proposal for a European Parliament and Council Directive on the use of Passenger Name Record data for the prevention, detection, investigation and prosecution of terrorist offences and serious crime' COM (2011) 32 final, Brussels, 2 February 2011. See discussion in ch 6 above.

[48] *Advocaten voor de Wereld*, para 52.

[49] Ibid, para 57.

decisions, that authority was vested entirely in the Council.[50] Thus, Member State governments were permitted wide discretion to devise and enforce criminal justice policy—raising obvious concerns for accountability. Though the need to implement framework decisions in national law provided a check on this power it did not necessarily improve compliance with the rule of law due to the divergences in national legislation.

The partial abolition of dual criminality remains problematic. Several Member States did not transpose the relevant provisions of the framework decision correctly. For example, in Poland, the dual criminality rules have become intertwined with the question of surrendering Polish nationals. Following the decision of the Polish Constitutional Tribunal, the new implementing law reintroduced the requirement of dual criminality in the case of Polish citizens, even for the 32 listed offences. Furthermore, Polish citizens would only be surrendered for offences committed after 1 May 2004.[51] Other Member States have also retained the dual criminality requirement in relation to all or some offences. Italy checks the requirement for all of the 32 listed offences, while three other Member States (Belgium, Slovenia and the UK) have retained the requirement in certain circumstances.[52] This deviation from the strict terms of the framework decision undermines the uniformity of the system. In the case of the Polish law the new provision discriminates between Polish citizens and other persons. These measures may potentially be in breach of the principle of non-discrimination. Reluctance to correctly transpose this provision has led to stricter drafting of the Framework Decision on the EEW, discussed below.

iii. Procedures and Safeguards

While the aim of the EAW is for the executing state to recognise the criminal jurisdiction of the issuing state without exercising its own jurisdiction, there are a number of mandatory and optional grounds for refusal to surrender. The mandatory grounds are where there is an amnesty in the executing state; or where the *ne bis in idem* (double jeopardy) principle applies; or where the subject of the warrant is considered a minor under the law of the executing state.[53] In addition, seven optional grounds for refusal exist, including the absence of dual criminality (except in the case of the 32 listed offences) and rules related to territoriality and limitation periods.[54] While these rules are clear and specific, the Commission's 2007 evaluation report identifies eight states that have in some way failed to

---

[50] Although the European Parliament had, mere days before the September 11 attacks, called for greater EU co-operation in counter-terrorism. This included calling on the Council to bring forward a proposal for a European-wide search and arrest warrant. See European Parliament, Resolution of 5 September 2001 on the Role of the European Union in Combating Terrorism, OJ C72/E/135.

[51] Commission (EC), Second Evaluation Report, p 5.

[52] Commission (EC), Second Evaulation Report, p 8.

[53] Art 3 FDEAW.

[54] Art 4 FDEAW.

correctly transpose the grounds for mandatory or optional non-executive of an arrest warrant.[55]

The most recent European Commission report appears to have brought to an end the debate on whether or not the human rights protection referred to in the Preamble and the operative text constitutes a ground for refusal.[56] Although some Member States have used the clauses to create a ground for refusal, the better view, based on a plain reading of the text, is that the relevant provisions are simply broad statements of human rights compliance.[57] First, the clause in question refers to the fact that constitutional rules are not affected by the framework decision. As legislation is subordinate to constitutional rules, the clause is somewhat superfluous. Second, the clause is separate from the grounds for refusal and therefore is clearly not meant to be taken as one of them. As a result, it is unlikely that substantive human rights protection was intended as a ground for refusing a particular EAW request. However, the Commission Report suggests that breach of fundamental rights may be considered a mandatory ground for non-execution in relation to Article 2(1) extraditions (ie those that do not involve the waiving of dual criminality). The Report notes ECHR case law that has found that detention conditions can amount to a breach of Article 3 ECHR. It then states that the Framework Decision on the EAW

> does not mandate surrender where an executing judicial authority is satisfied, taking into account all the circumstances of the case, that such surrender would result in a breach of a requested person's fundamental rights arising from unacceptable detention conditions.[58]

This innovation by the Commission is contrary to the constitutive role of the rule of law in several ways. First, if this is now a ground for refusal then there is a clear difference between the law as promulgated by the EU legislature and the law in action. Second, and even more worrying, the varying implementation of this ground for refusal highlights the potential for EU criminal justice to develop in divergent fashion. Finally, there is the risk that EU criminal justice will be fragmented with power being granted at EU level but subject to safeguards in national law only.[59]

In addition to the grounds for refusal there are certain circumstances under which a judicial authority executing a warrant may require guarantees from the issuing Member State (eg that the suspect, if convicted, be permitted to serve their sentence in the executing state).[60] Furthermore, the framework decision details the rights of the requested person, which include access to legal counsel and an interpreter, the right to be heard before the executing judicial authority, and the

---

[55] Commission (EC), Second Evaluation Report, p 8.
[56] Mitsilegas, n 6 above, p 129.
[57] Commission (EC), Second Evaluation Report, p 8.
[58] Commission (EC), Third Evaluation Report, p 7.
[59] This matter is considered in more detail in Chapter Eight.
[60] Art 5 FDEAW.

right to respect for privileges and immunities.[61] While the rights of the requested person have been fully transposed by all Member States, the Commission's evaluation report notes that some Member States have also included provisions requiring additional guarantees from the issuing Member State.[62] Thus, in attempting to safeguard the rights of requested persons, the Member States have introduced divergence in an ostensibly harmonised system.

The framework decision is quite prescriptive in terms of the content, form, and procedure for issuing and executing a warrant.[63] An EAW may be transmitted through the Schengen Information System, the European Judicial Network, or through Interpol.[64] The extent to which these three networks have actually been used is returned to below. The law requires the surrender decision to be taken swiftly: a requirement that ensures both the efficient operation of justice for the requesting Member State, but also that the subject of the arrest warrant is not kept waiting indefinitely for their case to be decided.[65] Following a final decision, notification must be 'immediate', and surrender effected 'as soon as possible' and in ordinary circumstances no later than ten days after the final decision.[66] The details of transit of the arrested person, the effects of their surrender, and the potential for their future prosecution for other offences in the requesting Member State are also addressed by the framework decision.[67]

iv. Conclusions

The Commission Evaluation Report dubs the EAW a 'success', a verdict that is somewhat justified in terms of its use and effectiveness.[68] It has been credited with reducing the time it takes to transfer an individual from approximately 1 year to between 11 days and 6 weeks.[69] However, concerns persist in relation to differing treatment for domestic nationals and other EU citizens, the vague nature of the list of 32 offences and divergence amongst Member State safeguards. Therefore the flagship measure for mutual recognition in criminal matters has merely started and not ended the debate. In terms of the rule of law the clear conclusion is that the Framework Decision on the EAW has failed to bring about a uniform system for the transfer of suspects and convicts. If anything the instrument has highlighted the need for greater respect for rule of law principles in safeguarding those subject to the arrest warrant. This in turn raises questions about the

---

[61] Arts 11, 14, 19, 20 FDEAW.
[62] Commission (EC), Second Evaluation Report, p 9.
[63] Art 8 FDEAW.
[64] Arts 9–10 FDEAW.
[65] Art 17 FDEAW.
[66] Art 23 FDEAW.
[67] Arts 24–25 FDEAW.
[68] Commission (EC), Second Evaluation Report, p 2.
[69] Commission (EC), 'Communication from the Commission to the European Parliament and the Council: An area of freedom, security and justice serving the citizen' COM (2009) 262 final, Brussels, 10 June 2009, p 3.

appropriate relationship between nascent EU criminal justice and the Member State criminal justice systems it seeks to build upon.

B. European Evidence Warrant

While the Framework Decision on the EAW was adopted relatively quickly following its formal proposal by the Commission, the Framework Decision on the EEW took much longer to agree. The precursor to the evidence warrant is to be found in the Council of Europe 1959 Convention on Mutual Assistance in Criminal Matters and its additional protocols (1978 and 2001).[70] Co-operation within the EU is based on the 1990 Schengen Convention.[71] A comprehensive EU Convention was adopted in 2000 and added to by a protocol in 2001.[72] Neither the Convention nor the protocol had entered into effect when the Commission drafted its proposal for the EEW in 2003. Therefore the legal landscape was cluttered with instruments before the introduction of the EEW.[73] However, as with extradition prior to the arrest warrant, the Commission proposal considered these existing measures to be too slow, complicated, and subject to too many limitations for a jurisdiction such as the EU. The Framework Decision on the EEW was aimed at standardising evidence requests, speeding up the procedures and limiting the grounds for refusal of requests.[74] Unlike the arrest warrant, the evidence warrant legislation did not seek to replace all existing transfer rules and procedures. Rather, it fit within the existing framework of mutual assistance. As such it is a less radical and more complicated piece of legislation.

The evidence warrant had not yet been agreed when the Hague Progreamme was published in 2005. The Programme referred to 'the comprehensive programme of measures to implement the principle of mutual recognition' including a measure on 'the gathering and admissibility of evidence'. It also noted that the Framework Decision on the EEW should have been adopted 'by the end of 2005'. This is the first reference to a deadline for adoption of the instrument.[75] The deadline, however, was missed. The framework decision was not formally adopted

---

[70] Council of Europe 1959 Convention on Mutual Assistance in Criminal Matters; Additional Protocol 1978; Additional Protocol 2001.

[71] Convention of 19 June 1990 implementing the Schengen Agreement of 14 June 1985 on the gradual abolition of checks at the common border.

[72] Convention of 29 May 2000 on Mutual Assistance in Criminal Matters between the Member States of the European Union; Council Act of 16 October 2001 establishing, in accordance with Article 34 of the Treaty on European Union, the Protocol to the Convention on Mutual Assistance in Criminal Matters between the Member States of the European Union.

[73] JR Spencer, 'The Problems of Trans-border Evidence and European Initiatives to Resolve Them' (2007) 9 *Cambridge Yearbook of European Legal Studies* 477.

[74] Commission (EC), 'Proposal for a Council Framework Decision on the European Evidence Warrant for obtaining objects, documents and data for use in proceedings in criminal matters' COM (2003) 688 final, Brussels, 14 November 2003, pp 4–5.

[75] S Peers, The 'Hague Programme' Annotation of final version, approved 5 November 2004, p 33.

by the Council until December 2008 and Member States have until January 2011 to transpose it into national law. The Framework Decision is based on Articles 31 and 34(2)(b) EU(N). As a relatively recent measure, there is no case law to date on its use. Three aspects of the EEW regime are examined in detail here: the general scheme of the legislation, the abolition of dual criminality and judicial control of the evidence transfer process.

i. The General Scheme of the Evidence Warrant

Article 1(1) of the Framework Decision describes the evidence warrant as

> a judicial decision issued by a competent authority of a Member State with a view to obtaining objects, documents and data from another Member State for use in [certain legal proceedings].

Mirroring the Framework Decision on the EAW, Article 1 proceeds to note that the EEW is based on the principle of mutual recognition and also affirms the fundamental principles of the EU legal order. The definition of evidence is that used in the Framework Decision on Orders Freezing Evidence or Property: 'objects, documents and data'.[76] As such, the measure allows for the collection and transfer of a broad range of materials that may assist in criminal proceedings. Despite the apparent breadth of this definition, several types of evidence are explicitly excluded. For example, the execution of a warrant cannot entail the interviewing or taking of statements from suspects, witnesses or victims.[77] The Commission proposal noted that these would require 'special consideration' and are the subject of a separate Green Paper.[78] The taking of DNA evidence or other evidence from a person's body is also excluded, as is any evidence that would require ongoing monitoring or surveillance.[79] Finally, evidence that would require analysis to be carried out by the executing Member State is also excluded.[80] However, excluded material may be requested if it is already in the possession of law enforcement authorities.[81] The exclusion of certain types of evidence demonstrates a key difference between the two european warrants. Whereas the EAW entirely replaced other extradition agreements between the Member States, the evidence warrant legislation is designed to exist alongside existing mutual legal assistance measures.[82] This state of affairs has been described as a 'muddle', but one which is

---

[76] Art 2(e) Council Framework Decision 2003/577/JHA of 22 July 2003 on the execution in the European Union of orders freezing property or evidence (hereafter, FDEEW).

[77] Art 4(2)(a) FDEEW.

[78] Commission (EC), Proposal for a Council Framework Decision on the European Evidence Warrant for obtaining objects, documents and data for use in proceedings in criminal matters COM (2003) 688 final, Brussels, 14 November 2003, pp 7–8.

[79] Art 4(2)(b)–(c) FDEEW.

[80] Art 4(2)(d) FDEEW.

[81] Art 4(4) FDEEW.

[82] Commission (EC), n 78 above, para 10.

tolerable due to its transitory nature.[83] The framework decision also prescribes which proceedings may be the basis for a transfer. These are all criminal proceedings and administrative proceedings that may result in proceedings before a criminal court. In this regard, the framework decision has the same scope as existing mutual legal assistance agreements. Fulfilment of the Hague Programme would have rendered all evidence within Europe subject to transfer based on the principle of mutual recognition.[84] However, this objective was not achieved by the end of 2009 and so has been carried forward to the Stockholm Programme and the proposed EIO Directive.

ii. The Abolition of Dual Criminality

The abolition of dual criminality offers a notable point of comparison between the EAW and EEW legislation. Certain provisions of the Framework Decision on the EEW demonstrate that lessons were learned from the teething problems experienced by the arrest warrant. Reluctance to correctly transpose the arrest warrant legislation has led to stricter drafting of the Framework Decision on the EEW. The Framework Decision on the EAW uses the language 'without verification of the double criminality of the act'.[85] Nonetheless, certain Member States have adopted implementing laws that require verification. The Framework Decision on the EEW uses more stringent language to afford less discretion to national legislatures when implementing the legislation. The dual criminality requirement is almost entirely abolished by the evidence warrant. It is retained for evidence warrants that require search and seizure in their execution.[86] The exception to this rule is that the requirement is not to be applied to certain offences, as defined by the issuing Member State, which carry a minimum maximum sentence of 3 years. The list of relevant offences is the same 32 offence list that features in the Framework Decision on the EAW.[87] The Framework Decision on the EEW legislation is stronger than its predecessor, declaring that evidence warrants requiring search and seizure for such offences 'shall not be subject to verification of double criminality *under any circumstances*'.[88] Whether this difference in drafting is noted in the transposing measures remains to be seen.

One of the key points of contention in the negotiations on the framework decision was the extent to which the issuing Member State would be able to request that the executing Member State carry out coercive measures to obtain the requested evidence and the role of judicial authorities in supervising such requests. The framework decision has significantly limited the scope for such

---

[83] Spencer, n 73 above, p 478.
[84] R Belfiore, 'Movement of Evidence in the EU: The Present Scenario and Possible Future Developments' (2009) 17 *European Journal of Crime, Criminal Law and Criminal Justice* 1, 10.
[85] Art 2(2) FDEAW.
[86] Art 14(1) FDEEW.
[87] Art 14(2) FDEEW.
[88] Art 14(2) FDEEW (emphasis added).

requests. Member States may refuse to carry out search and seizures where the issuing authority is not an actual judicial authority.[89]

iii. Judicial Control of Evidence Transfer

One of the more notable features of the framework decision is its emphasis on judicial control of any evidence transfer. The eighth recital to the Preamble notes the need to maintain trust, and that trust is dependent on appropriate safeguards in each Member State:

> The principle of mutual recognition is based on a high level of confidence between Member States. In order to promote this confidence, this Framework Decision should contain important safeguards to protect fundamental rights. The EEW should therefore be issued only by judges, courts, investigating magistrates, public prosecutors and certain other judicial authorities as defined by Member States in accordance with this Framework Decision.[90]

Within the operative part of the text, the measure describes an 'issuing authority' as 'a judge, a court, an investigating magistrate, a public prosecutor' or 'any other judicial authority as defined by the issuing State'.[91] This distinction between the former type of authority (referred to here as an 'actual judicial authority') and the latter type (referred to here as a 'designated judicial authority') is maintained throughout the measure. The distinction is clearly the result of a legislative compromise as the Commission proposal included references to judges, investigating magistrates and prosecutors only.[92]

Certain provisions emphasise the need for oversight by an actual judicial authority. If the issuing authority is not an actual judicial authority, then the executing authority may refuse to carry out search and seizure to execute the evidence warrant.[93] Furthermore, Member States may require requests from designated judicial authorities to be validated by an actual judicial authority in the issuing state where the measures necessary to execute the warrant would ordinarily require actual judicial authority in the executing state.[94] Actual judicial authorities are also afforded greater power in terms of refusing to recognise or execute an evidence warrant and in postponing the recognition or execution of an evidence warrant. First, one of the grounds for refusing or postponing recognition or execution is that the evidence warrant has been issued by a designated judicial authority and has not been validated by an actual judicial authority.[95] Second, any decision to refuse or postpone must be made by an actual judicial authority unless

---

[89] Art 11(4) FDEEW.
[90] Recital 8 Preamble FDEEW.
[91] Art 2(c) FDEEW.
[92] Commission (EC), n 78 above, para 47.
[93] Art 11(4) FDEEW.
[94] Art 11(5) FDEEW.
[95] Art 13(1)(e) FDEEW (refusal) and Art 16(1)(b) FDEEW (postponement).

the evidence warrant is itself an unvalidated request from a designated judicial authority.[96] The empowering of actual judicial authorities may be attributed to two considerations. First, some Member States have implemented the Framework Decision on the EAW incorrectly by designating central (administrative) authorities as judicial authorities for the purposes of the measure.[97] Second, one of the principal concerns in drafting the measure was the circumvention of ordinary procedural safeguards through the EEW process: the above limitations on designated judicial authorities attempt to prevent such circumvention. Whether those limitations are successful or not will depend in large part on their transposition and operation by the Member States.

The framework decision also provides for more general safeguards. Several grounds exist for refusing to recognise or execute a request, demonstrating considerable overlap with the grounds for refusal to execute an arrest warrant. These include the principle of *ne bis in idem*, the existence of relevant immunities or privileges, or considerations of national security.[98] While the issuing decision can only be challenged in the Member State responsible for it, the framework decision requires Member States to put in place appropriate remedies for 'any interested party, including bona fide third parties' to protect their legitimate interests.[99] The relevant judicial authorities in both the issuing and executing Member States must take steps to facilitate any such action.[100] Furthermore, the executing authority may suspend the transfer of evidence pending the outcome of any such proceedings.[101]

iv. Conclusion

The Framework Decision on the EEW is a more intricate measure than its arrest warrant counterpart. As it must fit within the existing mutual legal assistance framework, rather than replace it entirely, its provisions are more restricted. Furthermore, it attempts to draw fine jurisdictional lines on coercive powers and judicial safeguards. If the experience of the arrest warrant is any guide, much of its success or failure will depend on the implementing legislation adopted by Member States in the coming years. The reception of the arrest warrant by national legislatures and judiciaries and the manner in which the evidence warrant legislation was drafted offers some insights into the operation of mutual recognition in practice. However, even before the transposition period for the Framework Decision on the EEW expired proposals for the instrument's replacement were already being contemplated. In November 2010 a Green Paper called for the replacement of the existing system 'by a single instrument based on the

---

[96] Art 13(2) FDEEW (refusal) and Art 16(3) FDEEW (postponement).
[97] Commission (EC), Second Evaluation Report, p 8.
[98] Art 13 FDEEW.
[99] Art 18 FDEEW.
[100] Art 18(5) FDEEW.
[101] Art 18 (6) FDEEW.

principle of mutual recognition and covering all types of evidence'.[102] The Green Paper noted several difficulties in the current evidence transfer regime. First, the fragmented nature of the regime 'makes the application of the rules burdensome and may cause confusion'. Second, mutual assistance is 'slow and inefficient'. Third, the existing rules 'only cover specific types of evidence and ... provide for a large number of grounds for refusal'. The Commission's solution is to propose a new legal instrument based on mutual recognition covering all types of evidence. The new instrument would include statements from suspects or witnesses, interception of communications, monitoring of financial transactions, analyses of documents, DNA samples and fingerprints.[103] As matters transpired it was a group of Member States rather than the European Commission which brought forward a proposal.

C. The European Investigation Order

The idea for a comprehensive instrument on the exchange of evidence was carried forward into the Stockholm Programme. The Council declared that a new approach should be 'based on the principle of mutual recognition but also taking into account the flexibility of the traditional system of mutual legal assistance'. The Programme suggested that the new instrument could have 'a broader scope' and include 'as many types of evidence as possible'.[104] In April 2010 seven Member States brought forward a proposal for a European Investigation Order (EIO).[105] If adopted, the EIO would replace the EEW for all participating Member States. The UK has decided to opt-in to the instrument. Home Secretary, Theresa May, told the House of Commons that the instrument 'offers practical help for the British police and prosecutors, and we are determined to do everything we can to help them cut crime and deliver justice'. The Home Secretary also pointed out that by opting-in the UK would be able to influence the content of the legislation.[106] While the UK has exercised its option to opt-in at present the EIO would not apply to Denmark, or Ireland, which has yet to exercise its opt-in. Therefore the instrument will not wholly simplify co-operation in this aspect of EU criminal

---

[102] Commission (EC), 'Green Paper on obtaining evidence in criminal matters from one Member State to another and securing its admissibility' COM (2009) 624 final, Brussels, 11 November 2009, p 5.

[103] Ibid.

[104] Council of the European Union, 'The Stockholm programme: An open and secure Europe serving and protecting the citizens', Brussels, 2 December 2009, para 3.1.

[105] OJ C165/22 (24 June 2010). The sponsoring Member States are Austria, Belgium, Bulgaria, Estonia, Slovenia, Spain and Sweden.

[106] House of Commons, *Hansard*, July 27 2010, col 881. For a discussion of the background in the UK see R Lööf, 'Obtaining, Adducing and Contesting Evidence from Abroad: A Defence Perspective on Cross-Border Evidence' (2011) (1) *Criminal Law Review* 40.

justice but will maintain the diversity that has come to mark legislation on freedom, security and justice.[107]

The EIO legislation will be based on Article 82(2)(a) TFEU which relates to mutual recognition in criminal matters. The use of this legal basis means that the directive will be adopted using the ordinary legislative procedure which does not give Member States the opportunity to use the 'emergency brake' that is applicable when other, related legal bases are used.[108] Thus, in contrast to the two framework decisions establishing the European warrants, the legal basis for the new instrument will favour the European Parliament and the majority of the Council at the cost of individual Member States in the Council. The legal basis might be open to query as Article 82 TFEU provides for mutual recognition of judicial decisions, raising the question as to whether an EIO constitutes such a decision.[109]

The proposed instrument will go further than the EEW. Whereas the EEW is limited to evidence that is already in existence, the EIO will not be restricted in this way. It is defined as 'shall be a judicial decision issued or validated by a judicial authority of a Member State ... in order to have one or several specific investigative measure(s) carried out in another Member State ... with a view to obtaining evidence'. Despite being a comprehensive instrument certain activities remain excluded from the definition of an investigative measure.[110] The Order may also be used to obtain evidence already in the possession of law enforcement authorities.[111] An EIO is to be executed on the basis of mutual recognition and in accordance with the directive.[112] An Order may be issued in respect of proceedings which are criminal in nature or which may lead to criminal proceedings.[113] This makes the Order available in a broad range of proceedings making it a potent tool for law enforcement authorities.

The proposed directive contains certain limitations and safeguards that are to be assessed by the issuing authority. Thus, an EIO may only be issued where it is 'necessary and proportionate' to do so and where a similar investigative measure could have been ordered in national law. Furthermore, the principle of validation of requests where they are made by an authority other than an actual judicial

---

[107] The relationship between the EIO and earlier measures such as the EEW for the Member States that do not opt-in to the instrument remains unclear. See S Peers, *Statewatch Analysis: Update: The Proposed European Investigation Order*, available: www.statewatch.org, last accessed 10 September 2011. For a discussion of diversity in freedom, security and justice see: S Coutts, 'The Lisbon Treaty and the Area of Freedom, Security and Justice as an Area of Legal Integration', Presentation to King's College London Centre of European Law, 10 June 2011 (copy with author).

[108] Peers, n 107 above, p 5.

[109] Rackow and Birr, n 16 above, p 1114.

[110] The excluded measures are the establishment of a joint investigation team—a matter already addressed by other EU law instruments. The inclusion of measures involving interception of communications has been controversial. See Art 3 Draft EIO Directive and the annotation of the draft at fn 6 therein.

[111] Art 1(1), Draft Directive of the European Parliament and the Council regarding the European Investigation Order in Criminal Matters, Brussels, 8 June 2011 (hereafter, Draft EIO Directive).

[112] Art 1(2) Draft EIO Directive.

[113] Art 4 Draft EIO Directive.

authority is also incorporated.[114] There are also safeguards under the control of the executing state. These are grounds of non-recognition, non-execution and postponement. Recognition or execution may be refused if there is an 'immunity or privilege' in the law of the executing state, if execution would harm national security interests or if the EIO has been issued in relation to non-criminal proceedings and the investigative measure would not be available under the national law of the executing state.[115] The last ground could potentially be quite wide and may afford much discretion to refuse recognition or execution depending on its implementation in national law.[116] Refusal is also possible if certain rules relating to *ne bis in idem* or territoriality apply.[117] The executing state may postpone recognition or execution if it is necessary to prevent prejudicing an ongoing investigation or prosecution or if the evidence required is being used in ongoing proceedings.[118]

In June 2011 the outstanding issues to be agreed were the grounds for non-execution or non-recognition of an EIO, the legal remedies available and the costs associated with the instrument.[119] The proposed instrument has been the subject of significant criticism. Peers, writing for Statewatch, has referred to it as an 'assault on human rights and national sovereignty'.[120] The European Data Protection Supervisor and the Meijers Committee have both issued opinions criticising the draft proposal. The Data Protection Supervisor recommended a high standard of data protection and some specific safeguards to be incorporated in the EIO legislation.[121] The Meijers Committee has called for the terminology in the draft directive to be defined with greater precision. This is particularly important in relation to the definition of 'judicial authority' given the heightened powers afforded to such authorities by the draft directive. The Committee has also recommended allowing the defence to make use of an EIO, amendments to the grounds for refusal, and the establishment of a common system of remedies.[122]

These proposed developments of the law present significant challenges to EU criminal justice co-operation. First, in calling for all forms of evidence to be exchanged, including evidence not available, the Council and Commission presents the possibility of Polish police intercepting communications at a property in Warsaw at the request of Gendarmerie in Paris. Such integration of Member State criminal justice systems has clear implications for resource allocation within domestic budgets. Second, as the Commission notes, increasing the type of evidence available under the warrant will require detailed rules on the admissibility

---

[114] Art 5a Draft EIO Directive.

[115] Art 10 Draft EIO Directive.

[116] Rackow and Birr, n 16 above, p 1116.

[117] Art 10 Draft EIO Directive.

[118] Art 14 Draft EIO Directive.

[119] See European Council, Draft EIO Directive, n 111 above.

[120] S Peers, *Statewatch Analysis: The Proposed European Investigation Order: Assault on Human Rights and National Sovereignty*, May 2010, available: www.statewatch.org, last accessed 11 September 2011.

[121] European Data Protection Supervisor, Opinion, 2010/C 355/1 29 December 2010.

[122] Meijers Committee, CM1106, Utrecht, June 9 2011.

of such evidence in criminal trials in different Member States. There is little point in the police carrying out the above surveillance if the evidence gathered is not admissible in the French criminal justice system. To solve this problem a third point will have to be addressed: the harmonisation of standards for police conduct in evidence gathering. As envisaged by the Lisbon Treaty, the Commission proposes to adopt common standards for the gathering of evidence to ensure its admissibility.[123]

The EIO may be an example of the maturation of EU criminal justice. It is a far more complex instrument than the simplistic EAW that preceded it by a decade. However, the transfer of evidence and indeed carrying out investigative measures to produce evidence is a far more complex undertaking than the transfer of an individual. Given the existing complexity of the case law on the EAW it is not inconceivable that the EIO would lead to the development of an EU law of criminal procedure.

III. EUROPEAN WARRANTS, PRE-EMPTION & THE RULE OF LAW

The European warrants represent a revolutionary, but somewhat different development of EU criminal law to the counter-terrorism explored in other chapters: rather than subverting Member States' criminal justice systems to allow the greatest possible control to be exercised over those targeted by counter-terrorism actions, the attempt is to integrate the systems to develop more efficient criminal justice within the EU. The many teething problems encountered by the instruments demonstrate that the development of EU law in this field will be far from easy.

A. European Warrants as Criminal Justice Co-operation

As measures which aim to assist in the investigation and prosecution of crime already committed, the European warrants do not have a particular crime prevention purpose (although, by making the European criminal justice system more effective they are presumably intended to increase the deterrent effect of that system). However, it is clear that they aim to improve the system of co-operation in EU criminal justice—once more raising the question as to whether the principle of mutual recognition is a suitable means of doing so.

i. Mutual Recognition and Mutual Trust

The key building block of the new system of EU criminal justice is the principle of mutual recognition. The European warrants aim to promote increased co-operation between the Member States in criminal matters. If this co-operation

---

[123] Commission (EC), Making it easier to obtain evidence in criminal matters from one Member State to another and ensuring its admissibility Memo/09/497, Brussels, 11 November 2009.

is to be successful, Member State governments and judiciaries will need to agree to 'mutually recognise' the validity of each others' criminal justice systems. Much of the criticism of the application of the principle to criminal justice systems overlooks the similarity between the various EU systems. Several domestic courts have addressed the question of mutual trust which must underpin a system of mutual recognition. Most importantly, each Member State's criminal justice system shares the safety net provided by the ECHR, as upheld by the ECtHR. Nonetheless, courts have taken different approach to this safety net. This is apparent from the contrasting dicta of the German Federal Constitutional Court and the Czech Constitutional Court. The German Federal Constitutional Court held that

> the existence of an all-European standard of human rights protection established by the European Convention for the Protection of Human Rights and Fundamental Freedoms do not, however, justify the assumption that the rule-of-law structures are synchronised between the Member States of the European Union as regards substantive law and that a corresponding examination at the national level on a case-by-case basis is therefore superfluous.[124]

The German Federal Constitutional Court has therefore taken a rather cautious view of the safety net provided by the ECHR. On the other hand, the Czech Court takes the opposite view:

> The contemporary standard for the protection of fundamental rights within the European Union does not, in the Constitutional Court's view, give rise to any presumption that this standard for the protection of fundamental rights, through invoking the principles arising therefrom, is of a lesser quality than the level of protection provided in the Czech Republic.[125]

Significantly, neither court explicitly refers to the presence or absence of human rights infringements in other Member States. Rather, while the Czech Constitutional Court is willing to presume that fundamental principles are upheld, the German Federal Constitutional Court is not. Of course, the existence of the ECHR and its Court is no guarantee that human rights will be protected and the rule of law upheld. Figures from 1999–2005 (inclusive) show that the EU Member States were found in violation of the Convention on a total of 2,826 occasions. Both the Czech Republic and Germany were amongst the offenders, with 69 and 47 violations respectively.[126]

---

[124] Europäischer Haftbefehl 113 BVerfGE 273 (2005).

[125] Judgment of the Czech Constitutional Court 3 May 2006 Pl Ús 66/04.

[126] Data taken from S Greer, *The European Convention on Human Rights: Achievements, Problems and Prospects* (Cambridge, Cambridge University Press, 2006) 77–78. Greer's data is in turn compiled from 'Judgments finding at least one violation' from annual 'Violations by Article and by Country' tables, 1999–2005, supplied by the ECtHR's Registry. While not all of these violations will pertain to criminal justice safeguards, Greer notes that there were a total of 3,127 Art 6 ECHR violations in that time (across all Council of Europe members).

However, it should be borne in mind that while increased compliance with human rights standards is of course to be striven for, no legal system is ever likely to have a perfect record in this regard. Therefore, it is likely that there will always be violations of the ECHR. However, so long as those violations are remedied then it can be argued that the system is functional. The key issue here is whether it is acceptable to surrender an individual to another Member State, bearing in mind the possibility of rights violations, as long as it is clear that a system of protection exists. For the German court it is not acceptable. Admittedly, the standard for Member State action to discontinue executing arrest warrants is set quite high by the Preamble to the framework decision. Co-operation should only be suspended in the event of a 'serious and persistent' breach of Article 6 TEU.[127] Nonetheless, the decision in the German case displays a distinct lack of trust in the criminal justice systems of the other Member States.[128] This has been acknowledged by the Commission in its 2011 report on the operation of the arrest warrant system.[129]

Returning then to the arguments in opposition to mutual recognition in criminal matters, it is obvious that Member State judiciaries agree that there is an important qualitative difference between policies in the internal market and those in justice and home affairs. Whereas national courts have accepted mutual recognition in relation to the internal market, they are reluctant to be as accommodating to the EAW. In terms of harmonisation, it is clear from the declaration attached to the Framework Decision on the EEW that the Germans will seek increased convergence of Member State criminal and procedural law before extending mutual recognition.[130] However, as is made clear below in relation to terrorism, harmonisation at EU level, in particular in criminal justice, may not be entirely successful. The qualitative difference argument and harmonisation argument combine to suggest that there is not just a need for convergence in Member State laws but that there is a need for greater procedural safeguards to be put in place as well. These safeguards will be necessary to ensure that trust develops between European judiciaries and other law enforcement authorities and thus to ensure the effective operation of EU criminal justice co-operation.

The Stockholm Programme includes efforts to improve mutual trust. The European Council and the Commission is clearly aware that national police and judiciaries possess the power to determine whether or not that co-operation is successful. As such, the Stockholm Programme recognises the need to improve trust amongst the officials of the criminal justice system. Indeed, it describes

---

[127] Recital 10 Preamble FDEAW.
[128] For a theoretical analysis of the constitutional implications, see: J Komárek, 'European Constitutionalism and the European Arrest Warrant: In Search of the Limits of "Contrapunctual Principles"' (2007) 44 *Common Market Law Review* 9.
[129] Commission (EC), n 2 above, p 6.
[130] Declaration of the Federal Republic of Germany OJ L350/92 (30 December 2008).

the training of 'judges ... prosecutors and other judicial staff' as 'essential to strengthen mutual trust'.[131] It aims to promote such training through, amongst other initiatives, an Erasmus programme for the officials of national criminal justice systems.[132] However, while this may improve judicial trust amongst those officials, wider acceptance of EU criminal justice co-operation may require the sort of convergence on standards of protection that the EU has failed to deliver to date. This is because the qualitative difference between the internal market and the area of freedom, security and justice has implications for how mutual trust is developed.

As it is the rights of citizens that are restricted by the expansion in the power of the state it is European citizens whose trust must be developed.[133] The Stockholm Programme makes reference to the Roadmap for strengthening procedural rights of suspected and accused persons in criminal proceedings drawn up by the Swedish Presidency of the EU.[134] The first of these directives has already been agreed while others are in different stages of the legislative process.[135] In addition the Commission has published a Green Paper on EU criminal justice and detention. The Green Paper acknowledged that transfer to a detention facility where an individual's rights (such as Article 3 ECHR) would be breached is not acceptable.[136] The success of the Roadmap and related initiatives may well be decisive for the Stockholm Programme's broader success and an indicator of the future of mutual recognition in criminal matters. The *de facto* EU law enforcement authorities cannot be assumed to have any particular loyalty to the EU legal order. They are empowered—and held to account—at national level and so it is to the national legal order that their allegiance is. Of course, national law enforcement authorities might be expected to be well-disposed to EU criminal law and criminal justice where it offers institutional benefits. Thus, the enforcement-led co-operation to date has been a welcome addition to law enforcement agencies' arsenal. Of course those authorities that are charged with protecting the rights of suspects - public defenders, members of national judiciaries, and

---

[131] Council of the European Union, 'The Stockholm Programme: An Open and Secure Europe Serving and Protecting the Citizens', Brussels, 2 December 2009, p 25.

[132] Ibid, 9.

[133] Rackow and Birr, n 16 above, p 1113.

[134] Ibid, 17.

[135] Resolution of the Council of 30 November 2009 on a Roadmap for strengthening procedural rights of suspected or accused persons in criminal proceedings OJ C 295/1 (4 December 2009), Directive 2010/64/EU of the European Parliament and of the Council of 20 October 2010 on the right to interpretation and translation in criminal proceedings OJ L 280/1 (26 October 2010), Commission (EC), 'Proposal for a Directive of the European Parliament and of the Council on the right of access to a lawyer in criminal proceedings and on the right to communicate upon arrest' COM (2011) 326 final, Brussels, 8 June 2011. For a discussion see C Rijken, 'Re-balancing Security and Justice: Protection of Fundamental Rights in Police and Judicial Cooperation in Criminal Matters' (2010) 47 *Common Market Law Review* 1455.

[136] Commission (EC), 'Green Paper: Strengthening mutual trust in the European judicial area: A Green Paper on the application of EU criminal justice legislation in the field of detention' COM (2011) 327 final, Brussels, 14 June 2011.

civil society groups—are likely to be sceptical of EU criminal justice. This has proven to be the case to date. One question for the future will arise if a rebalancing of EU criminal justice takes place—will the mutual trust which is said to be the foundation of mutual recognition be improved by increased protection of the rights of suspects? Or will an unlikely coalition form between those groups that advocate on behalf of suspects and those law enforcement authorities that seek to have their powers unfettered by EU rules—to the overall detriment of EU criminal justice. The future development of EU criminal justice will therefore require attention to be paid to both the constitutive and the safeguarding aspects of the rule of law.

ii. Problems of Transposition

A persistent problem with the use of framework decisions is diverging national laws due to a failure to correctly transpose EU legislation into national law. In its second evaluation report on the implementation and operation of the EAW, the Commission noted that twelve Member States still needed to 'make an effort to comply fully' with the framework decision.[137] Amongst this list were large Member States such as Poland and the UK. This failure to correctly transpose the law presents clear problems for the rule of law. By undermining the uniformity of the law, the Member States prevent the EU from developing the rule of law in this sphere of competence. Of course, a principal cause of the lack of uniformity is the constitutional differences between EU powers in different policy areas. The Commission cannot take enforcement proceedings against the Member States and the jurisdiction of the ECJ is limited. The Council has gone to some effort to prevent the same problems from affecting the Framework Decision on the EEW. Whether those efforts will be successful or not remains to be seen following the expiration of the transposition period.

However, the Commission evaluation reports on the arrest warrant legislation makes it clear that Member States have in some cases adopted transposing laws that are so inconsistent with the parent legislation as to be effectively *contra legem*. Thus, the problem is not the precision of the drafting in the parent legislation, but the absence of an effective enforcement mechanism in relation to framework decisions. The problem persists in relation to 12 Member States who were recommended to alter their national legislative framework by the Commission in 2007 but nonetheless failed to do so.[138] Thus, some Member States remain unable or unwilling to correctly implement the framework decision in national law. The persistent problems in this area continue to undermine the establishment of an EU rule of law.

---

[137] Commission (EC), Second Evaluation Report, p 9.
[138] Commission (EC), n 2 above, p 5.

iii. Proportionality

Perhaps the most persuasive criticism of the arrest warrant system in terms of rule of law safeguards is the disproportionality of surrendering an individual in certain circumstances. There are two instances where this might be the case—first, where the offence in question is so trivial as to render surrender under an arrest warrant a disproportionate response to the offence, and second, where the proposed penalty was judged to be too severe. The first scenario recognises that being subject to the criminal justice system can itself be a punitive process—a point which is surely heightened when the individual is transferred across the EU to face charges. In the case of *Zak v Regional Court of Bydgoszcz Poland* the UK High Court was asked to consider whether the use of an arrest warrant for an offence of receipt of a stolen mobile phone was akin to using a sledgehammer to crack a nut.[139] Due to its requirement of compulsory prosecution Poland is foremost amongst the Member States prone to use the arrest warrant for apparantly trivial offences. Although the use of minimum maximum sentences as a threshold in the EAW legislation provides a certain level of protection it is nonetheless a rather low threshold. Davidson, arguing from the point of view of a prosecutor, suggests that reintroducing a triviality rule would allow offenders to evade punishment for offences committed in other EU Member States.[140] The solution she proposes is to ensure the mutual enforcement of non-custodial penalties—a course of action that would reduce dependency on extradition of those suspected or convicted of minor offences.

The second scenario is not concerned with the nature of the offence but with the punishment. It is conceivable that an individual could be subject to a request to face prosecution for an offence that carries a significantly higher penalty in the issuing state than it does in the executing state. One means of addressing this problem would be to introduce a proportionality requirement into the arrest warrant system. The former approach has been advocated by Judge Joachim Vogel of the Higher Regional Court in Stuttgart, Germany.[141] Judge Vogel drew on the German Constitution as well as Article 49(2) of the EU Charter of Fundamental Rights, which provides for the proportionality of criminal offences and penalties, to read a proportionality requirement into the German implementing legislation. In the case at hand the Judge described the penalty sought by a Spanish prosecution for a drug offence as 'very severe' but not in breach of fundamental rights and as such it was not disproportionate to extradite the requested person. The Judge also noted the potential disproportionality of 'extradition arrest' for trivial offences both in terms of the burden placed on the requested person and the executing state. He suggested that a system of 'European summons', which would

---

[139] *Zak v Regional Court of Bydgoszcz Poland* [2008] EWHC 470 (Admin).

[140] R Davidson, 'A Sledgehammer to Crack a Nut? Should There be a Bar of Triviality in European Arrest Warrant Cases?' (2009) *Criminal Law Review* 31.

[141] A translation of the decision has been published, with comment, as J Vogel and JR Spencer, 'Proportionality and the European Arrest Warrant' (2010) *Criminal Law Review* 474.

require individuals to present themselves without the need for arrest, might solve this problem.

The problem of disproportionality has also received attention from the EU institutions. The European Parliament has called on the Member States to respect the principle of proportionality when implementing the EAW system.[142] The Council is also sympathetic to calls for a proportionality requirement. This is not surprising as the execution of arrest warrants in cases where the offence is trivial (rather than ones where the sentence might be considered disproportionate) may be viewed as a waste of resources by the executing state. The Council has addressed this through amending the 'European Handbook on How to Issue an EAW'. The introduction of a proportionality test begs the question as to whether it is for the issuing or the executing judicial authority to adjudicate on proportionality. While Judge Vogel held that it was for the executing authority to do so it is more in keeping with the principle of mutual recognition for the issuing authority to examine the matter. The amendment to the Handbook notes that there is no obligation in the framework decision for the issuing authority to consider proportionality. However, 'considering the severe consequences of the execution of an EAW with regard to restrictions on physical freedom and the free movement of the requested person', the authorities should 'consider proportionality'.[143] The Handbook goes on to set out a non-exhaustive list of factors to be taken into account. These factors include 'seriousness of the offence', 'the possibility of the suspect being detained', 'the likely penalty imposed', 'the effective protection of the public' and the interests of the victims.

This approach is similar to the one taken in the draft EIO Directive which requires the issuing authority to consider if it would be proportionate to request the investigative measures be carried out. Application of the principle of proportionality to arrest warrants would add a rule of law compliant safeguard to the system. The Commission suggests that amending the Handbook is a means to provide consistency of interpretation across the EU. However, the test has been put in place through an amendment to a Handbook for issuing authorities rather than through an amendment to the legislation itself. While national courts will play a role in applying the rules, final interpretative authority should lie with the ECJ rather than Member State courts to ensure uniformity across the EU.[144]

B. European Warrants and Pre-emptive Counter-Terrorism

Though the European warrants are not without their problems they make little contribution to the EU's pre-emptive counter-terrorism action. One clear way in

---

[142] European Parliament recommendation of 7 May 2009 to the Council on development of an EU criminal justice area (2009/2012(INI)) OJ C212 E/116 (5 August 2010).

[143] Council (EC), Document 8436/2/10, Brussels, 28 May 2010, p 3.

[144] See further the discussion of 'autonomous concepts of EU law' at n 157 below.

which the arrest warrant instrument marks a difference in European treatment to political violence is the ending of the political offence exception to extradition. This marks 'the end of an era of sympathy with politically motivated rebellion'.[145] In this respect the arrest warrant fits with the post-September 11 trend of deeming all political violence unacceptable. However, at least within the EU, this is neither hypocritical nor objectionable. It is difficult to imagine justifying political violence within the EU today—any state against which violent rebellion was merited could surely be dealt with through political means.[146] Two aspects of the European warrant systems are relevant to counter-terrorism: the implications for national counter-terrorism offences and the empowerment of administrative actors.

i. National Counter-Terrorism Offences

One manner in which the EAW contributes to counter-terrorism is by ensuring that each Member States' criminal law on terrorism is enforced throughout the EU. Terrorism is listed amongst the thirty-two offences for which the dual criminality requirement is abolished by the EAW. Furthermore, it features in the same list of offences as used in the Framework Decision on the EEW to denote offences for which dual criminality shall not need to be verified under any circumstances. Of course, these definitions only actually apply insofar as the offences are committed within the jurisdiction of the particular Member State. Thus, if an individual is suspected of terrorism within the UK's jurisdiction it may issue an arrest warrant based on its definition of terrorism contained within the Terrorism Act 2000. The EU's success in agreeing on extradition for terrorism represents significant progress on the earlier European agreements which were considered to be undermined by exceptions for political offences.

It is commonplace that mutual recognition works best when the trust upon which it is based is reinforced by measures harmonising or approximating Member State law.[147] The FDCT established an EU definition of terrorism. Thus, one might reasonably expect extradition within the EU for terrorist offences to be based on those offences in Articles 1–4 of the FDCT. However, both the European warrants apply to the offences as defined in national law. Therefore, it is the Member States' definition of terrorist offences, not the EU definition that is relevant. Less than half of EU residents live in a state which the European Commission considers to have correctly transposed the FDCT.[148] Thus, even in this area where there has been harmonisation of criminal law, the European warrants are operating based on vastly differing national definitions of criminal offences.

---

[145] Naert and Wouters, n 10 above, p 922.
[146] Ibid.
[147] Mitsilegas, n 6 above, p 101.
[148] See the discussion in ch 3 above.

In this respect, the adoption by Germany of a declaration in relation to dual criminality and terrorism is noteworthy.[149] Germany has reserved the right in considering an evidence warrant to apply the dual criminality rule for search and seizure in respect of the crime of terrorism, unless the requesting Member State makes a declaration. The requesting Member State would be required to declare that the crime in question was one prohibited by a UN Terrorism Convention, UN Security Council resolution or Articles 1–4 FDCT. The German declaration may have little effect on the operation of the framework decision in practice: Member States simply have to make the declaration for dual criminality to be waived. Furthermore, the offences referred to are sufficiently broad to catch any conceivable request from another Member State. Nonetheless, the declaration indicates a desire on behalf of the German government to limit the operation of this clause. Mitsilegas notes that the reservations expressed by Germany on this point were a result of the internal difficulties it was experiencing with the European Arrest Warrant.[150] However, in tandem with the failure (or refusal) to accurately transpose the Framework Decision on Combating Terrorism, the declaration may be taken at the very least as a sign of unease in Germany regarding the development of EU counter-terrorism.

The European warrants do no more for counter-terrorism co-operation in the EU than they do for any other area of law enforcement. In this respect counter-terrroism is but a small part of the warrants' effect on EU criminal justice. However, the use of an EU measure to increase the reach of the often overly broad national definitions of terrorism is a lamentable side-effect of an approach that focuses on increasing control over those suspected of terrorism.

ii. Empowerment of Judicial Authorities

Most of the instruments of EU counter-terrorism demonstrate a tendency to empower executive and administrative actors, often at the cost of judicial authorities. The same is not necessarily true of the Framework Decision on the EAW. The framework decision puts in place a surrender procedure within the Member States that—on the face of it—removes the executive branch of national governments almost entirely from the process. Nonetheless, the Commission's evaluation reports—that note that certain Member States had designated an executive authority—give cause for concern.[151] Thus, Denmark has designated an executive body as the 'competent judicial authority' for all purposes linked to the framework decision, while five other Member States have done so for some aspects of

---

[149] Declaration of the Federal Republic of Germany OJ L350/92 (30 December 2008).

[150] Mitsilegas, n 6 above, p 127.

[151] Commission (EC), 'Report from the Commission based on Article 34 of the Council Framework Decision of 13 June 2002 on the European arrest warrant and the surrender procedures between Member States' COM (2005) 63 final, Brussels, 23 February 2005 (hereafter, First Evaluation Report); Commission (EC), Second Evaluation Report, p 8.

the process.[152] Despite criticism from the Commission, neither Denmark, nor three of the five other Member States had altered their position by the time of the publication of the 2007 Report. Furthermore, Germany was added to the list of partial offenders.[153] Three Member States gave more discretion to their 'central authorities' than the framework decision permits. Those authorities were to be limited to a facilitating role, whereas Estonia, Ireland and Cyprus have provided them with varying degrees of power.[154] The consequence of this inconsistent implementation has been more stringent drafting in the Framework Decision on the EEW. The distinction struck in that measure between actual judicial authorities and those that are merely designated as such aims to ensure that where judicial control of evidence-gathering is necessary, it is indeed an actual judicial authority that exercises that control. However, these safeguards will be entirely dependent on correct transposition by the Member States. The transposition period expired in January 2011 and a Commission report on implementation of the evidence warrant was due in January 2012. The evolution of the law in this field will continue with the adoption of the EIO Directive.

Administrative bodies play a key role in the transmission of warrants. In 2005, Interpol transmitted 58 per cent of the arrest warrants issued, while the Schengen Information System transmitted 52 per cent of warrants. The remainder of the warrants were transmitted directly between national authorities.[155] Thus, administrative actors are empowered as conduits for the flow of criminal justice documents between Member State authorities. Furthermore, the arrest and evidence warrants effectively empower national police forces, who can obtain the surrender of suspects and evidence more swiftly. The legislation for the EAW and EEW puts in place several safeguards for the protection of the person subject to the arrest warrant and those whose 'legitimate interests' are affected by an evidence warrant. This marks out the European warrants as much more in keeping with a rule of law approach than is found in other counter-terrorism action. Notwithstanding these differences, the warrants rely on national law enforcement authorities to act lawfully and in a manner that respects human rights. Thus the question of mutual trust comes once more to the fore. Civil society groups campaigning against the extradition of individuals subject to the EAW demonstrate that while mutual trust may be presumed by the law, it has yet to be established in practice.[156]

---

[152] Commission (EC), First Evaluation Report, p 3. The Member States were: Estonia, Latvia, Lithuania, Finland and Sweden.

[153] Commission (EC), Second Evaluation Report, p 8. The updated list is: Germany, Estonia, Latvia and Lithuania.

[154] Ibid.

[155] Ibid, 3–4.

[156] See, eg, the campaign by Liberty in the UK, www.extraditionwatch.co.uk, last accessed 13 September 2011.

IV. CONCLUSION: TOWARDS AN EU CRIMINAL JUSTICE SYSTEM?

In many respects, the European warrants represent a counterpoint to the narrative of the pre-emption. While the measures only became politically palatable after the 11 September 2001 attacks, they aim to integrate EU criminal law, rather than to combat terrorism specifically. It is not just the content of the measures which underlines this point, but also the recitals to their Preambles. Apart from one brief reference to extradition under the 1977 European Convention on the Suppression of Terrorism, there is no mention of terrorism or efforts to prevent it in the Preamble to either measure. Rather, the language is the more measured tone of criminal justice co-operation. One manner in which the EAW and EEW has contributed to the approach is by exporting Member States' definitions of terrorism across the EU. While this is true of the definitions of all of the 32 crimes for which the dual criminality requirement has been abolished, it is particularly noteworthy in the case of terrorism where the definition is politically controversial and academically contested.

The developing case law on the EAW may be indicative of the development of an EU law of criminal procedure. In addition to *Advocaten voor de Wereld* a series of cases have considered the operation of the EAW system and its interaction with other EU law, national criminal law and national criminal procedure. Thus, in *Kozlowski*, the ECJ declared that the terms 'resident' and 'staying' in Article 4(6) of the framework decision are 'autonomous concepts of EU law' which must be subject to uniform definition across the EU.[157] Interpretation of Article 4(6) was also at the heart of the judgments in the cases of *Wolzenburg* and *IB v Conseil des Ministres*.[158] The idea of an 'autonomous concept of EU law' was also raised in the case of *Mantello* in relation to the definition of 'same acts' in Article 3(2) of the framework decision.[159] EAW case law has also had implications for EU constitutional law as demonstrated in the cases of *Santesteban Goicoechea* and *Leymann and Pustovarov*, both of which dealt with the use of the Article 35 EU(N) preliminary ruling procedure, amongst other matters.[160]

It seems clear that the EAW and EEW are instruments that owe more to the development of European criminal co-operation than they do to the development of an EU counter-terrorism capacity. The difficulties that the EAW has faced in implementation—lack of trust amongst Member State judiciaries—is more instructive of the difficulty in forging a continent-wide criminal jurisdiction than it is any indication of willingness or reluctance to co-operation

---

[157] Case C-66/08 *Kozlowski* [2008] ECR I-6041.

[158] Case C-123/08 *Wolzenburg* [2009] ECR I-9621; Case C–306/09 *IB v Conseil des Ministres*, judgment of 21 October 2010, nyr. For a discussion of the issues arising in both *Kozlowski* and *Wolzenburg* see E Herlin-Karnell, 'European Arrest Warrant Cases and the Principles of Non-Discrimination and EU Citizenship' (2010) 73 *Modern Law Review* 824.

[159] Case C-261/09 *Mantello*, judgment of 16 November 2010, nyr.

[160] Case C-296/08 PPU *Santesteban Goicoechea* [2008] *ECR* I-6307; Case C-388/08 PPU *Leymann and Pustovarov* [2008] ECR I-8993.

on counter-terrorism. As such, the final instruments examined in this book present an alternative direction that EU criminal justice may pursue in the future. Some evidence for this broader approach may be the omission of the word 'terrorism' from the proposal for the EIO—which suggests that counter-terrorism may be subsumed within more general EU criminal justice policy.

The likelihood that this will lead to a more rule of law compliant approach will be examined in the final chapters.

Part III

The Future of EU
Counter-Terrorism

8

Rule of Law and Pre-Emption Reconsidered

TWO BROAD EFFECTS can be discerned in EU action since 11 September 2001: an acceleration of counter-terrorism and criminal justice co-operation and a shift to a more pre-emptive form of action. The acceleration of EU co-operation has been clearly evident. Certain programmes that were already in place—such as the commitment to mutual recognition in criminal law—were suddenly brought to the top of the legislative agenda. The swift establishment of the European Arrest Warrant was the result. Similarly, the European Parliament's opposition to some of the more controversial elements of the second Anti-Money-Laundering Directive gave way in the face of increased pressure to counter the financing of terrorism. However, it would be incorrect to describe September 11 as a mere catalytic event. It did not just accelerate the development of EU criminal law and counter-terrorism but also altered the course of that development. Following September 11 2001, there has been a shift in focus within the EU that echoes, if not mirrors, the shift observed in the US. The shift is clear in policy documents that frame EU action, such as the Action Plan on Combating Terrorism, in the language used in the Preambles to various legislative acts and in the operative text of those acts. The tenor of the shift is towards pre-emption.

I. SEPTEMBER 11: CATALYSIS AND SHIFT

A pre-emptive approach to counter-terrorism is indicated by two fundamental changes: first, from action based on past harm to that based on future worse-case scenarios; and second, from accepting a certain risk of harm as normal to holding all such risk unacceptable. The result is the adoption of legislation and the pursuit of policies that seek to eradicate the space in which political violence might occur. Despite this change, some measures appear to have emerged relatively unscathed. Though the EAW and to a lesser extent the EEW owe their birth to the September 11 attacks, they show little sign of being substantively influenced by the events of that day. Though they have encountered significant problems the warrants cannot be characterised as pre-emptive in nature. On the other hand, the difference in thinking is clearly evident in relation to anti-money-laundering. This policy area was significantly altered by the September 11 attacks, with 'counter-terrorist finance' added to anti-money-laundering legislation. Extensive changes to the surveillance and intervention regime were brought about by the third Anti-Money-Laundering Directive. In addition, whole new legislative acts, such as the Framework Decision on Combating Terrorism, broadened the scope of EU counter-terrorism. The shift towards a pre-emptive approach can been described as entailing changes to the type of action taken, the target of the action and the actors that are empowered. Table 1 sets out the policy areas examined in this book and sets out their respective actions, targets and actors.

As Table 1 makes clear, EU counter-terrorism actions have wide-ranging, overlapping and yet sometimes diverging effects. Some target particular individuals whereas others affect the entire population. Some result in criminal sanctions, others involve pre-emptive interventions, others broad surveillance. Perhaps

Table 1. EU Counter-Terrorism Action

Action	Type of Action	Target	Actor
FD on Combating Terrorism	Broad criminalisation of 'terrorist motive' and related criminal offences	All individuals and groups with 'terrorist motive'	EurCou, nat. leg., nat. law enf.
Anti-Money Laundering & Counter-Terrorist Finance	Financial surveillance and related criminal penalties	All financial services users, individuals and groups suspected of materially supporting terrorism	EurCou, EurCom, UN SecCou, FATF, nat. law enf., FIU
Targeted Asset-Freezing Sanctions	Freezing of assets and travel bans	Individuals and groups suspected of materially supporting terrorism	UNSC, EurCou, EurCom, nat. law enf.
Data Surveillance	Surveillance of travel and telecommunications	All travellers and telecommunications users	US law enf, EurCou, EurCom, nat. leg., nat. law enf.
European Warrants	Expedited transfer of suspects and convicts	Those suspected and convicted of crimes, including terrorism	EurCou, nat. leg., nat. law enf., nat. jud., Europol.

EurCou: EU Council; EurCom: EU Commission; FATF: Financial Action Task Force; FIU: Financial Intelligence Units; nat. jud.: national judiciaries; nat. leg.: national legislatures; nat. law enf.; national law enforcement; US law enf.: US law enforcement; UNSC: UN Security Council.

one of the most striking aspects of EU counter-terrorism is the range of actors involved. These include EU institutions, Member State governments, legislatures and law enforcement authorities; overseas (in particular US) executive and law enforcement authorities; and private actors that both influence policy (FATF) and execute it (telecommunications service providers). The manner in which these actors have been empowered and the ways in which they have used those powers have had a significant impact on the EU rule of law.

II. THE CONSTITUTIVE ROLE OF THE RULE OF LAW

The first role of the EU rule of law is constitutive—it is concerned with the construction of the EU legal order and the effective enforcement of EU law. The effect of the various EU measures on the constitutive role is discussed under three headings: institutional power; effectiveness and uniformity; and law and coercion.

A. Institutional Power

A key part of the constitutive aspect of the rule of law is conferral of power on the EU and within the EU on different institutions. The shift towards a pre-emptive approach to counter-terrorism has had an impact on this allocation of institutional power. The increased use of framework decisions and common positions has empowered the executive (Member State governments) and the granting of discretion has benefitted law enforcement agencies. This empowering has come at the cost of the European and national parliaments—while the ECJ has been left in a difficult position as it seeks to uphold fundamental principles while adjudicating disputes over institutional power.

i. Empowering Executives and Administrators

A recurring feature of EU counter-terrorism action is its empowering of executive and administrative actors at international, EU and national level. At international level, the greatest beneficiary has been the UN Security Council and its Sanctions Committee.[1] The approach taken by the European Council and Commission to the list of targeted groups and individuals under Resolution 1267 has essentially allowed the Security Council and Sanctions Committee to draft EU law. As the Security Council itself is dominated by its five permanent members (China, France, Russia, UK and US), the EU's 'delegation' of power has particularly benefited two EU Member States and three other states. The US has used this power to target individuals it suspects of terrorism (such as Mr Kadi: listed by

---

[1] JE Alvarez, 'Hegemonic International Law Revisited' (2003) 97 *American Journal of International Law* 873.

the Sanctions Committee at the request of the US Treasury Department). The US has also been empowered by the Passenger Name Record (PNR) and Terrorist Finance Tracking Programme (TFTP) Agreements. Throughout the negotiating process with the EU, the US resisted EU requests for better data protection in the PNR Agreements.[2] The EU acted so swiftly to safeguard the ability of European-based airlines to enter US airspace that it left itself in a weak negotiating position from the outset.[3] The Commission appears not to have considered the effect of a travel ban on US companies and on the US economy. As such, the US negotiators were able to ensure that the PNR Agreements served their purposes almost entirely without compromise. The TFTP Agreements are a further example of apparent EU powerlessness in the face of US demands for co-operation. However, the position in relation to TFTP is perhaps more nuanced than it appears to be at first. While the programme was initially established by the US government it appears that the EU Member States also sought access to leads based on financial messaging data. Thus, the TFTP Agreements may be an example of executive co-operation at the cost of their legislatures. On the other hand, the adoption of the measure amending the UN sanctions list regulation may reassert the autonomy of EU institutions by requiring the Commission to take an independent decision on whether or not to list individuals added to the UN sanctions list by the Sanctions Committee.[4] Though the initial practice appears to simply replicate the UN list in EU law the requirement to take an independent decision has afforded a further ground for review of individual listings.

Other international actors that have benefited from EU pre-emption include organisations such as the Financial Action Task Force that aim to influence policy-making in certain discrete areas. While the Financial Action Task Force was already influential in anti-money-laundering policy-making before 11 September 2001, the expansion of its remit to include counter-terrorism has increased its power. The influence of agencies such as the Task Force may be one of the most worrying developments since the al-Qaeda attacks. As non-governmental institutions, they neither are nor claim to be accountable, despite the power they wield.

At European level, the Council and to a lesser extent Commission have been the strongest actors in EU counter-terrorism. In part, this is due to the use of framework decisions as the legislative instrument of choice in relation to the EU crime of terrorism and co-operative instruments establishing the arrest and evidence warrants. The Interim and Second PNR Agreements were also adopted under legislative procedures that favoured the Council while failure to adequately consult the European Parliament on the negotation of the TFTP-I Agreement resulting in it being rejected. These procedures gave law-making power almost

---

[2] MR VanWasshnova, 'Data Protection Conflicts Between the United States and the European Union in the War on Terror: Lessons Learned from the Existing System of Financial Information Exchange' (2006–08) 29 *Case Western Reserve Journal of International Law* 827, 834.

[3] Ibid.

[4] Council Regulation 1286/2009 of 22 December 2009.

exclusively to the Council, with the European Parliament merely being consulted.[5] Therefore, increased police and judicial co-operation since 11 September 2001 has inevitably led to more EU action being dominated by the Council. Even though the Commission has less power in the field of police and judicial co-operation than it does in the internal market, it has nonetheless engaged vigorously with action in this field insofar as it is competent to do so. Thus, the Commission has written lengthy evaluation reports on the relevant framework decisions and had brought forward a proposal for a Framework Decision on PNR before the coming into force of the Lisbon Treaty. Furthermore, when the Interim and Second PNR Agreements were adopted, the Commission played a significant part in the negotiations, despite the EU Treaty limiting its power.

The final aspect of empowerment is that of national law enforcement authorities, and administrative offices such as the Financial Intelligence Units and the proposed Passenger Information Units. These national authorities and offices benefit from broadly drafted EU law that grants significant powers of surveillance and intervention while providing little by way of safeguards. The same is true of private institutional actors that—in the banking, telecommunications and travel sectors—are required to store information on individuals and liaise with law enforcement authorities to prevent terrorism and other crime. This can impose a significant regulatory burden on such institutions while infringing on human rights of those subject to surveillance.

ii. Undermining Legislatures

A corollary of the empowering of a diverse range of executive, administrative and private actors is the diminution of legislatures. Throughout this book, attention has been drawn to the manner in which the European Parliament has expressed reservations about some of the more troubling aspects of the counter-terrorism measures adopted. However, it was sidelined by the legislative instruments used to pursue much EU counter-terrorism action. The framework decisions that were adopted came into force despite the Parliament's strong reservations about their content.

It is a truism that national parliaments are sidelined by the EU legislative process. While national executives participate through the Council, national parliaments do not. However, it is remarkable that apart from one set of instruments—the regulations establishing the UN and EU sanctions lists—every item of counter-terrorism legislation discussed in this work has required national legislation to be adopted for its transposition. Note though that international agreements such as the PNR and TFTP Agreements did not require transposition. Thus, to claim that national parliaments are powerless would be overstating the point. It is perhaps more accurate to note that when faced with a framework decision or directive to

---

[5] Art 34 EU(N).

be transposed, the scope for action by national legislatures is seriously curtailed. Any action to improve the measures would result in a lack of uniformity in EU law and would be singled out for remedy by the Commission (insofar as it is competent to do so). Furthermore, national legislatures are subject to the particular dynamics of domestic politics: in some cases, such as the UK, the Parliament is effectively controlled by the executive.[6] In others, such as Ireland, the process of implementation was seriously lacking in informed debate and scrutiny.[7] In such cases there is very little scope for effective control of executive action by an independent legislature. While EU law cannot be held to account for national constitutional arrangements, the dominance of executives at both EU and national level allows coercive power to be exercised with little democratic control.

iii. The Difficult Position of Judiciaries

Faced with the difficulties of refereeing institutional conflicts, upholding fundamental principles of the EU legal order and protecting individual rights, the European courts have struggled to articulate clear principles in several leading counter-terrorism cases. For example, it is difficult to reconcile the decision that the EU was not competent to adopt the PNR Agreements under the first pillar, but was competent to adopt the Data Retention Directive on the same legal basis. There is an inherent tension in any litigation on the division of competences between the former first and third pillars. Not only must the judiciary weigh up competing claims for institutional power, they are also subject to a legal dilemma: a decision to find a first pillar competence may overstretch the inherent limits of that pillar, based around the internal market, and increase the coercive means available to the EU at the cost of the Member States. On the other hand, a decision to find a third pillar competence places the Court at a disadvantage due to the lack of judicial oversight and may leave affected individuals and entities without an effective remedy. Thus, in relation to the judgments in the PNR, data retention and *Kadi* cases, the ECJ's willingness to find the legal measures in the latter two cases correctly based in internal market powers may be due to the loss of jurisdiction it suffered as a result of its decision in the PNR case.[8] However, despite its difficult position the ECJ issued a robust defence of the rule of law in *Kadi* and European action in relation to targeted sanctions may be at least in part responsible for the modest improvements in the system at UN level. National judiciaries have also found themselves in difficult territory. As with national legislatures,

---

[6] AW Bradley and KD Ewing, *Constitutional and Administrative Law*, 14th edn (London, Longman, 2008) p 81.

[7] D Walsh, 'Parliamentary Scrutiny of EU Criminal Law in Ireland' (2006) 31 *European Law Review* 48–68.

[8] Joined Cases C-317/04 and C-318/04 *European Parliament v Council of the European Union and Commission of the European Communities* [2006] ECR I-4721; C-301/06 *Ireland v European Parliament and European Council* [2009] ECR I-593; Joined Cases C-402/05 P and C-415/05 P *Yassin Abdullah Kadi, Al Barakaat International Foundation v Council of the European Union* [2008] ECR I-6351.

any attempt by national judiciaries to improve the human rights compliance of EU law may fragment the EU legal order and give rise to accusations of legal nationalism (eg with regard to the EAW). Decisions of the European judiciaries can significantly affect both the effectiveness and uniformity of EU law, to which the analysis now turns.

B. Effectiveness and Uniformity

The constitutive aspect of the rule of law is also concerned with two essential attributes of the EU legal system: the effectiveness and uniformity of the law. While these principles are both important for the functioning of the legal system, increasing pressure to ensure 'effectiveness' has had an adverse effect on the uniformity of the law. The result is a coercive, but fragmented and fragile legal system.

'Effectiveness' in this context can involve the conflation of two different meanings. First, the EU is keen to be an 'effective' actor in the field of counter-terrorism and so it aims to make an effective contribution to efforts to combat terrorism. Second, where the EU takes action through law, that law must be 'effective' and so the law as adopted at EU level must be enforced by the Member States. The adoption of the sanctions lists regulations and the Data Retention Directive on dubious legal basis may be attributed to a concern with the both parts of effectiveness. Similarly, in *Advocaten voor de Wereld*, when the ECJ upheld the legal basis of the Framework Decision on the EAW, it based its decision on the need to ensure the effectiveness of the EU legal order.[9] While the applicant claimed that the measure should have taken the form of a convention, the ECJ held that it was for the Council to decide the legislative form, as it had to be able to ensure the effectiveness of EU law. While the decision in the EAW case was correct on this point, the focus on effectiveness is striking nonetheless: it reinforces the point that the ECJ is preoccupied with enforcing EU law. The decision is one that is best characterised as acknowledging the expediency of upholding the EAW over clear legal principles.

This preoccupation is, to a certain extent, attributable to the nature of the EU legal system. The ECJ has been concerned with the effectiveness of EU law since *Van Gend en Loos*.[10] However, the desire to ensure that the EU can be an effective actor in EU counter-terrorism (in particular) appears to have led to increased divergence in Member States' law. Uniformity is most at risk where the use of framework decisions to harmonise Member State laws has faltered in the absence of the mechanisms for enforcement that make directives so effective. However, divergence is also possible when directives are used. The Data Retention Directive

---

[9] C-303/05 *Advocaten voor de Wereld VZW v Leden van de Ministerraad* [2007] ECR I-633.
[10] Case 26/62 *Van Gend en Loos* [1963] ECR 1.

is the key example. Whereas the Commission proposal would have put in place a strict data retention regime across the EU, the need to achieve agreement amongst the Member State governments in the Council led to divergence on the retention period, the crimes for which and agencies by whom data could be accessed, and the availability of compensation for telecommunications providers. Thus, unlike the divergence in implementing framework decisions, the scope for divergence in this particular measure is provided by the Directive itself. As such, there is little the Commission can do to improve uniformity: the problem is inherent in the instrument. This has been acknowledged by the Commission and by others in the institutions in the subsequent debate on its reform. The Data Retention Directive therefore raises questions concerning how much diversity EU law should permit when attempting to pursue counter-terrorism at EU level.

A further recurring theme is the manner in which the EU provides for the coercive powers for executives and administrators but leaves national legal systems to ensure that safeguards are put in place. As Mitsilegas notes, the trend is towards the transformation of criminal law into 'a field where maximum EU-led enforcement capacity is matched with a shrinking field of applicability of human rights safeguards'.[11] One consequence of this approach is that national legislatures and courts are left with the task of ensuring the rule of law compliance of EU counter-terrorism action. However, leaving protection of the rule of law's safeguarding role to national level can be harmful to both the effectiveness and uniformity of the EU legal order. In addition to affecting the effective operation of the EU legal system, the erosion of uniformity is also of concern to the individual: legal system in which the law is applied uniformly provides greater legal certainty for individuals. If Member States implement EU law with differing national rules, then the individual cannot assume the same set of rules apply across the EU.

C. Law and Coercion

While the EU has evolved into a community of law, it lacks direct coercive force and so it relies on the Member States to ensure that EU law is obeyed. EU counter-terrorism has, to a certain extent, demonstrated the danger of such an approach. While it is impossible to impute causality it is nonetheless striking that as power has increasingly been exercised by the Council, the uniformity of the legal system has suffered as legislation has been adopted that has resulted in diverging rules across the EU. Member State governments, acting through the EU, have adopted vague but coercive laws, focused more on bestowing power than on ensuring uniformity or even coherence. Driven by the desire to act 'effectively' and predisposed to leaving themselves and their law enforcement agencies as much scope for action as possible, legislation has been drafted

---

[11] V Mitsilegas, *EU Criminal Law* (Oxford, Hart Publishing, 2009) 25.

broadly and with insufficient safeguards. Faced with a myriad of legal measures, the ECJ has struggled to articulate a coherent position on the division of competences. Furthermore, the trend towards coercive law being agreed at EU level with safeguards left to Member States runs the risk of national legislatures and judiciaries appearing to reject the supremacy of EU law when they are simply filling in the gaps in protection for individuals. The rule of law's constitutive role has thus been undermined by counter-terrorism action by the EU.

III. THE SAFEGUARDING ROLE OF THE RULE OF LAW

The safeguarding role of the rule of law has been even more clearly threatened by EU action in counter-terrorism since 11 September 2001. The principle's safeguarding role seeks to protect the individual from state excesses. The most significant impact on the rule of law has been on the rights of those individuals, groups and entities suspected of terrorism. However, there have also been implications for broader human rights protections in EU law. The result has been the evasion and erosion of rights in the EU.

A. The Rights of Those Suspected of Terrorism

Most of EU counter-terrorism law is directed, first and foremost, against those suspected of terrorism. Such persons may be prosecuted for a wide range of offences including acts of terrorism, inchoate offences and offences linked to terrorism, money-laundering offences and terrorist-financing offences. Individuals may also have their financial transactions scrutinised, assets frozen and telecommunications and travel data disclosed to law enforcement authorities. If they are selected for attention on the basis of PNR data processing, they may be subject to stricter immigration and security controls, or refused permission to enter the US or any other state operating a PNR screening system. These legislative actions have had implications for the principle of legality, the right to a fair trial and other substantive human rights.

The principle of legality is a cornerstone of the safeguarding aspect of the rule of law. In criminal law it provides that only the law can define a crime and prescribe a penalty. In broader terms, all interferences with substantive rights such as the right to privacy and freedom of religion, expression and association must be prescribed by law. Both criminal and civil law must be sufficiently accessible and foreseeable for it to meet the standard of the principle of legality. EU counter-terrorism legislation may fall foul of this principle in several ways. The terrorist offences, offences related to a terrorist group, inchoate and linked offences in the Framework Decision on Combating Terrorism are all quite broadly drafted. The existing breadth of the law has been exacerbated in some Member States by poor transposition. The other set of measures that result in criminal law are the

Anti-Money-Laundering Directives. As with the framework decision, the offences defined in this measure are broadly drafted. Whether either of these measures violate the requirements of accessibility and foreseeability is impossible to adjudicate in the abstract. However, they have been drafted to catch as many potential suspects as possible, in clear contravention of the spirit of the principle of legality. Finally, the principle of legality is entirely discarded by the targeted sanctions. Those who are listed are selected by national intelligence agencies and listed by either the UN (and subsequently the EU) or the EU. Though the EU has its own definition of terrorism, it is not used when deciding whether or not to list an individual or group. Thus, the principle that the individual's behaviour is judged against a clear standard set down in law is violated by the sanctions system.

The right to a fair trial and broader rights of defence are essential to allow an individual subject to criminal or quasi-criminal proceedings to ensure that their substantive rights are upheld. These rights include access to an independent and impartial adjudicator, the presumption of innocence, the right to a hearing and other related rights. Several potential infringements of the right to a fair trial arise in EU counter-terrorism. First, the requirements on legal professionals to report suspicious transactions by their clients may infringe legal privilege. The decision of the ECJ in its judgment on the second Anti-Money-Laundering Directive did little to allay this fear.[12] According to that judgment, individuals can only rely on professional secrecy once a matter of contentious business has begun. However, that decision erodes the trust that a client may have in the professional relationship and so undermine their ability to receive legal advice. An individual who cannot trust their legal advice cannot ensure that their fair trial rights are upheld. Second, the targeted asset-freezing sanctions are imposed without due process. Both the UN- and EU-level sanctions suffer from an absence of safeguards during both the listing and delisting process. Chapter Five demonstrated the resistance of the European judiciary to these regimes. The ongoing targeted sanctions saga makes clear that judicial review is poor compensation for a decision-making process that is fundamentally unsound, in particular where the executive acts quickly to reverse the decision of the ECJ.[13] Third, much EU counter-terrorism action erodes the presumption of innocence. The sanctions regime most clearly offends the principle: both substantively as assets are frozen without evidence of criminal behaviour, and formally in that individuals are publicly denounced as 'terrorists' without due process. More broadly, all data surveillance action operates on the basis of unproven suspicion, while interventions in counter-terrorism finance can subject those targeted by the authorities to action without any proof of guilt.

---

[12] C-305/05 *Ordre de barreaux francophones et germanophone, Ordre francais des avocats du barreau de Bruxelles, Ordre dex barreaux flamands, Ordre néerlandais des avocats du barreau de Bruxelles v Conseil des Ministres* [2007] ECR I-5305.

[13] Joined Cases C-402/05 P & C-415/05 P, *Yassin Abdullah Kadi, Al Barakaat International Foundation v Council of the European Union*, [2008] ECR I-6351.

In addition to the rights associated with the principles of legality and due process, those suspected of terrorism may also have substantive human rights restricted and even violated. The rights protected in the EU legal system are broad. For those suspected of terrorism, almost the entire gamut of human rights may be infringed. The rights affected include: freedom of expression, including the right to receive information (incitement to terrorism offences and through surveillance of telecommunications), freedom of association (terrorist group offences, targeted asset-freezing sanctions), the right to privacy (surveillance of telecommunications, travel and financial transactions, as well as targeted sanctions), and the right to property (targeted asset-freezing sanctions). In one case, counter-terrorism action has had such an affect on those targeted that the individual has claimed a breach of their right to be free from inhuman or degrading treatment.[14] Though the ECJ has taken a strong line in upholding human rights the result has not provided effective relief for those affected.

B. The Broader Impact on Human Rights

In addition to affecting those suspected of terrorism, EU counter-terrorism also affects the wider public. These wider effects are most notable in relation to freedom of expression and association and the right to privacy. The space for political speech in the EU has been significantly curtailed by a combination of the Framework Decision on Combating Terrorism and the broad financial, telecommunications and travel surveillance programmes. Furthermore, the ongoing development of surveillance systems has significantly restricted the right to privacy for both those suspected of terrorism and the wider public.

Any infringement on these substantive rights must be prescribed by law, be in pursuit of a legitimate aim and be 'necessary in a democratic society'.[15] Of these three tests, it is only the second that is obviously met: with the goal of public safety and national security being entirely legitimate. The first test, which entails the principle of legality, may not be met by the relevant instruments. The Framework Decision on Combating Terrorism is very broadly drafted and its breadth has been exacerbated by Member State transposition. As such, while the infringement of freedom of expression is formally prescribed by law, it is not clear that it is sufficiently accessible and foreseeable to meet the qualitative tests used by the European courts. The various legislative acts on surveillance are also quite broadly drafted—a matter considered by national courts to undermine the lawfulness of the action.

The test of whether the measures are 'necessary in a democratic society' is difficult to discuss in the abstract. The European courts tend to examine such

---

[14] T-318/01 *Othman v Council & Commission* [2009] ECR II-1627.
[15] Arts 8, 10 ECHR.

legislation by examining how it is used rather than the text of the statutes themselves. Furthermore, it is almost impossible to objectively assess this requirement when the necessity of the measures is asserted rather than proven by those who promulgate them. Nonetheless, it is possible to conclude, at the very least, that the human rights of the general public have been restricted by the EU counter-terrorism action. Whether those restrictions amount to violations will be determined on a case-by-case basis.

C. Evasion and Erosion of Rights

As a preliminary point, it is significant problems with the rule of law's constitutive role, in terms of effectiveness and uniformity, translate into problems for the accessibility and foreseeability of the law. Both laws targeted at those suspected of terrorism and laws applicable to the general public are broadly drafted and potentially in violation of these principles. Furthermore, the law affects the rights of both groups in a way that is difficult to hold to account: the denial of due process to those suspected of terrorism (for instance those targeted by asset-freezing sanctions) makes it difficult to prove that the laws which target them are not necessary in a democratic society. Similarly, in the absence of clear evidence as to the necessity of broader restrictions on human rights, whether those infringements are justified or not becomes a matter of political debate rather than legal principle. This may be the greatest threat to the rule of law's safeguarding role: the usurping of legal jurisdiction over the legality of measures and the transfer of that debate into the political sphere where it is subject to ideological abuse.

IV. PERMANENT PRE-EMPTION?

In the United States, counter-terrorism actions since 2001 have been described as 'normalising the exception': putting in place a permanent emergency to allow extraordinary law enforcement and security powers to be extended—potentially indefinitely.[16] Perhaps the greatest distinction between the US and EU approach to counter-terrorism can be caught through this idea of the 'exception'. It has become *de rigueur* to begin any analysis of the Bush administration's response to the 11 September attacks with the citation of Carl Schmitt's statement that 'sovereign is he who decides on the exception'.[17] The attempts by the Bush administration to step 'outside' the legal constraints of the US Constitution, international

---

[16] D Cole and J Lobel, *Less Safe, Less Free: Why America is Losing the War on Terror* (New York, The New Press, 2007).

[17] C Schmitt, *Political Theology: Four Chapters on the Concept of Sovereignty* (Chicago, University of Chicago Press, 2006).

human rights law and laws of war by declaring an 'exception' have been well documented.[18]

However, no such Schmittian declaration has, or could be made, by the EU. The absence of centralised coercive force was identified at the outset of this book. The EU has no such power of its own but relies on that of the Member States. The EU legal system is heavily reliant on the co-operation of domestic and supranational actors to ensure the enforcement of its law. As such, any attempt to 'declare the exception' would be fruitless. It is therefore unsurprising that the language of a 'war on terror' is entirely absent from EU law and policy (though it is sometimes used by Member State governments).[19] However, the absence of coercive powers and reliance on a disaggregated network of actors has left the EU preoccupied with the effectiveness of its law. The requirement—now used by the judicial and legislative branches alike—that breaches of EU law be punished with sanctions that are 'effective, proportionate and dissuasive' has led to criminal law, traditionally the most coercive civilian power available to the state, being deployed to enforce a wide range of policy goals.

Instead of relying on centralised coercion, the EU has co-opted the coercive mechanisms of the Member States to great effect. It is for this reason that EU counter-terrorism is better explained through a more nuanced analysis than through Schmitt's state of exception. However, while less naked in its exercise of power, the coercion that the EU is capable of should not be underestimated. Kennedy described UN Security Council resolution 1373—the basis of the EU sanctions list—as the 'weaponisation of law'.[20] Three broad themes can be discerned: the use of power to develop particular discourses; the dispersal of power amongst a wide range of actors; and an emphasis on control.

A. Power and Discourse

Beginning with the Framework Decision on Combating Terrorism, it is clear that legislative power—law's greatest tool for producing 'truths'—is deployed to shape European and national discourses on 'terrorism'. It is instructive, for instance, that Jackson's discourse analysis of EU counter-terrorism policy documents, speeches and press releases notes that the idea of 'state terrorism' is nowhere to be found.[21] Therefore it is unsurprising that the legal analysis of the definition of terrorism in the FDCT concluded that while terrorism by state actors might be caught by the definition, prosecution for such an offence is not envisaged by that measure. The

---

[18] See: Cole and Lobel, n 16 above.

[19] R Jackson, 'An Analysis of EU Counterterrorism Discourse post-September 11' (2007) 20 *Cambridge Review of International Affairs* 233, 245; 'Britain stops talk of "war on terror"', *Observer* (10 December 2006).

[20] D Kennedy, *Of War and Law* (Princeton, Princeton University Press, 2006) 36–37.

[21] Jackson, n 19 above, p 236.

Italian attempt to draft the measure broadly enough to catch anti-globalisation protesters further evidences the point. The link between the power of the FDCT and the shaping of discourses is sharpest when the offence of provoking terrorism, introduced by the amending framework decision in 2008, are considered. The criminalisation of these actions attempts to shape public discourse on political violence. Less clear in execution, but no less real in effect, is the manner in which anti-money-laundering and counter-terrorist finance measures operate to formulate and perpetuate 'truths'. Both the soft (financial surveillance) and sharp (asset-freezing sanctions) ends of these measures operate on the basis of suspicion. 'Suspicion' in this context is very clearly an expression of power. It is the suspicion of the US Treasury Department that has resulted in the listing of certain individuals by the UN Security Council Sanctions Committee as 'terrorists'. The effect of this suspicion is the promulgation of a 'truth': Mr Kadi is considered to be a financier of terrorism.

An intriguing example can be garnered from a comparison of the Commission's evaluation reports on the implementation of different framework decisions. It was noted that while the Commission evaluation reports spilt much ink discussing the transposition of law enforcement aspects of the Framework Decision on Combating Terrorism, they simply asserted the implementation of the fundamental rights clause.[22] Thus, in terms of the present analysis, the Commission used its power to focus on the construction of a 'law enforcement' truth rather than a rule of law one. This aspect of the counter-terrorism stands in stark contrast to the Commission Evaluation Report on the Framework Decision on the EAW. There, not only did the Commission critique the implementation of the fundamental rights clause, but it also discussed implementation of the related (non-binding) recitals to the Preamble.[23] This difference in approach is all the more noteworthy as the two clauses are identical. There appears to be a distinction in the Commission's approach to EU criminal justice in general and to pre-emptive counter-terrorism in particular.

The final, but ever-present example of power as a generator of 'truth' is the constant assertions of the necessity and effectiveness of the measures adopted. The practice of policy-laundering can be identified in relation to the Framework Decision on Combating Terrorism (whereby overlapping definitions of terrorism are deployed in international and subsequently national law), the anti-money-laundering and counter-terrorist finance measures (where soft law rules are incorporated into binding legislation) and the surveillance regimes (where EU action followed domestic initiatives by various states). In none of these cases has the effectiveness of the measures been proven: at best it has been assumed or simply

---

[22] Commission (EC), 'Report from the Commission based on Article 11 of the Council Framework Decision of 13 June 2002 on combating terrorism' COM (2004) 409, Brussels, 8 June 2004.

[23] Commission (EC), 'Report from the Commission on the implementation since 2005 of the Council Framework Decision of 13 June 2002 on the European arrest warrant and the surrender procedures between Member States' COM (2007) 407 final, Brussels, 11 July 2007.

asserted and at worst the idea of proving effectiveness has been rejected for fear of interfering with operational secrecy. Thus, the 'truth' used to justify these measures is little more than the exercise of power by state and private agents. Truth is 'a thing of this world: it is produced only by virtue of multiple forms of constraint'.[24] This is particularly problematic when the essential part of any justification for infringing upon human rights is whether the measures are necessary in a democratic society.

B. The Dispersal of Power

The various institutions that affect EU counter-terrorism were detailed in Table 1, including national organs of government, EU institutions, international organisations and private actors. The principal difficulty with dispersed power is that it is much more difficult to hold to account. The attempts by those on the UN sanctions list to achieve delisting, or those who wish to access and correct PNR data or TFTP data held by US authorities is clear evidence of this.[25] Some states have been able to use counter-terrorism co-operation to pursue their own policy objectives. For example, the use of PNR and TFTP data retention schemes and the proliferation of targeted asset-freezing sanctions since 11 September 2001 can be traced to the Bush administration. In a similar vein the criminalisation of 'incitement' offences in relation to terrorism was originally a UK policy goal.[26]

Indeed, one of the lessons learned when reading the Commission's evaluation reports on the implementation of the Framework Decision on Combating Terrorism and the Framework Decision on the EAW is the endurance of state power within the EU. Just as some states have been successful in using the EU and other supra- and international fora for the pursuit of domestic legislative goals (eg through policy-laundering), so too have Member States that have agreed measures at European level altered their provision when transposing them into national law. Recent attempts by Germany to curtail the effect of the breadth of the 32 offences listed in the Framework Decisions on the EAW and EEW is clear evidence of this, as is the failure (or refusal) of several Member States to correctly transpose several of the provisions of the Framework Decision on Combating Terrorism.[27]

Indeed, faced with the use of the EU to further certain Member States' agendas, it is worth considering if it is possible to articulate a specifically 'EU' counter-terrorism strategy at all. Eeckhout suggests that the EU is simply a tool of the

---

[24] M Foucault, 'Truth and Power' in C Gordon (ed), *Power/Knowledge: Selected Interviews and Other Writings 1972–77* (Harlow, Longman, 1980) 131.

[25] Joined Cases C-402/05 P & C-415/05 P, *Yassin Abdullah Kadi, Al Barakaat International Foundation v Council of the European Union*, [2008] ECR I-6351; For details of the difficulty in accessing PNR data, see: www.statewatch.org/pnrobservatory.htm, last accessed 14 September 2011.

[26] 'Blair to ask UN for crackdown on incitement', *Guardian* (12 September 2005).

[27] Commission (EC), n 22 and n 23 above.

Member States and other actors in this policy sphere.[28] Whether the merging of the first and third pillars of the EU by the Lisbon Treaty and the resulting increase in power for the supranational institutions will allow a more 'European' counter-terrorism strategy to be formulated remains to be seen. In the interim, the difficulty of holding dispersed power to account remains a problem. This problem is particularly acute when power is exercised through new techniques and apparatuses which avoid many of the protections of traditional criminal justice.

C. The Emphasis on Control

The final aspect of pre-emptive counter-terrorism considered here is the means by which power is actually exercised on individuals. The tendency towards control and incapacitation is a signature of both the risk society and pre-emptive counter-terrorism. Rather than seek to arrest, prosecute and convict criminals the pre-emptive approach seeks to identify those who might commit crimes, such as terrorism, in the future and remove their ability to do so. Examples of incapacitation have been encountered throughout this study of EU counter-terrorism, from the overt (targeted asset-freezing sanctions) to the more covert (financial, telecommunications and travel surveillance).

It is useful to begin with covert incapacitation. The reduction of the individual to an 'object' to be acted upon was encountered in the evolution from ordinary criminal justice, through the risk society, and on into the pre-emptive approach. Preventing the individual from being an autonomous actor in the criminal justice process runs counter to the rule of law. When this approach is pursued through blanket surveillance, it affects not just those in the criminal justice system but the entire population. Nonetheless, this is one of the means by which modern criminal justice, and pre-emptive counter-terrorism in particular, operates. The effect on the right to privacy and freedom of expression evidences the spread of counter-terrorism action outside the strict confines of the criminal justice system. The ostensible targets of the Framework Decision on Combating Terrorism, the Data Retention Directive, the Anti-Money-Laundering Directives, and the PNR and TFTP Agreements are those who incite, finance, support and carry out acts of terrorism. However, the entire population is affected by the legislation put in place for this purpose. It is significant that the substantive rights that are arguably most affected by this counter-terrorism are freedom of expression and association and the right to privacy. By shrinking the private space available in which to develop thoughts of resistance (eg through restricting the literature available in libraries or over the internet) and limiting the ability to express extreme political views, the pre-emptive regime has furthered its self-preservation. It is in this way that

---

[28] P Eeckhout, Presentation at the European University Institute, Florence, 30–31 May 2009.

the actual exercise of force becomes unnecessary; the population is controlled by a mode of governance that diminishes the scope for political dissent.

Nonetheless, coercive power is also actually exercised through overt incapacitation: the targeted asset-freezing sanctions. This overt incapacitation can be a tool for controlling the 'suspect communities'. The use of the counter-terrorism law to identify certain persons as political outsiders—those with 'extremist' views or simply vulnerable migrants—has been discussed throughout this book. Though these powers are quite draconian, they go largely unscrutinised in public debate. The use of certain techniques of power is accepted by liberal democracies due to their selective application. The same problem has been identified by opponents of the 'liberty versus security' balancing metaphor that has been much discussed in the 'war on terror'. Marks and Clapham describe the balancing act as an anti-democratic illusion. Those who offer to curb their liberty for a perceived increase in security are rarely those who actually bear the burden of the restrictive measures.[29] So too it is with the pre-emptive counter-terrorism.

Perhaps most disturbing about this counter-terrorism is its potential permanence. The attempt by the Bush administration to declare a state of exception provoked opposition. For example, successive US Supreme Court judgments undermined the efforts to place Guantánamo Bay detainees beyond the reach of the law.[30] Furthermore, popular and political opposition has led to an official policy of closing the facility entirely.[31] Thus the state of exception may be ended. As many of the instruments of pre-emptive counter-terrorism use less overt and more insidious systems of control they are more difficult to oppose.

---

[29] S Marks and A Clapham, *International Human Rights Lexicon* (Oxford, Oxford University Press, 2005) p 356.

[30] See in particular: *Boumediene v Bush* 553 US_ (2008).

[31] CNN, 'Obama to order Guantanamo Bay prison closed', available: edition.cnn.com/2009/POLITICS/01/ 12/obama.gitmo/index.html, last accessed 14 September 2011.

Epilogue

EU Counter-Terrorism in a post-'War on Terror' World

> Liberty lies in the hearts of men and women; when it dies there, no
> constitution, no law, no court can even do much to help it. While it lies
> there it needs no constitution, no law, no court to save it.[1]

THE EU RULE of law has been evaded and eroded in recent years. Though European and domestic judiciaries have attempted to mitigate the effects of EU counter-terrorism action, their efforts have been of limited effect in the face of the overwhelming political will to act pre-emptively. That political will is particularly potent when pursued through the EU—where Member State governments have heightened powers and benefit from reduced public scrutiny. The result has been the reshaping of the EU legal order at the cost of human rights and the rule of law. However, if the early years after the 2001 attacks were characterised by the failure of legal and democratic institutions to check the excesses of executive action then the tale of more recent years has been of the resilience of human rights and the rule of law.[2] David Cole, a critic of both the Bush and Obama administration's counter-terrorism action, commented on the tenth anniversary of the attacks that 'one of the most important lessons of the past decade may be that the rule of law, seemingly so vulnerable in the attacks' aftermath, proved far more resilient than many would have predicted'.[3] As we enter the second decade since the September 11 attacks we are entering a post-'war on terror' world wherein governments acknowledge the need for reform but remain slow to act. Reluctant reform may simply be an exercise in refining the tools of law enforcement. Nevertheless, with the coming into force of the Lisbon Treaty and the adoption of the Stockholm Programme we may be at a point where a

---

[1] Former US Judge Learned Hand, quoted in D Cole, 'After September 11 2001: What We Still Don't Know', *New York Review of Books* (29 September 2011).

[2] For a good overview of the post-September 11, 2001 landscape see: KL Scheppele, 'The Migration of Anti-Constitutional Ideas: The Post-9/11 Globalization of Public Law and the International State of Emergency' in S Choudhry (ed), *The Migration of Constitutional Ideas* (Oxford, Oxford University Press, 2006). For a recent discussion of the resilience of human rights law see F de Londras, *Detention in the 'War on Terror': Can Human Rights Fight Back?* (Cambridge, Cambridge University Press, 2011).

[3] Cole, n 1 above.

rational debate can be carried out. The debate will have to consider the appropriate relationship between EU action in counter-terrorism, the EU's commitment to principles such as the rule of law and the developing EU criminal justice system.

I. RESISTANCE TO PRE-EMPTIVE COUNTER-TERRORISM

A counter-narrative to the pre-emptive counter-terrorism might be imagined as emanating from the fundamental principles that are the foundation of EU law and in particular the rule of law. Points of exercise of power may also provide points of resistance.[4] This resistance has been seen in various forms in recent years. In academia, the development of 'terrorology', a purported science of terrorism, has prompted the development of a rival field of critical terrorism studies.[5] Individuals dissatisfied with increasing surveillance of public and private space have developed practices of *sousveillance*—for example, taking video footage of police officers at public protests to document abuses of power.[6] In the EU constitutional system resistance to the pre-emptive counter-terrorism may be judicial, legislative or political.

A. Judicial Resistance

Within the context of the legal system, resistance is most likely to come from the courts of Europe: national constitutional courts, the ECJ and ECtHR. There is already some evidence of this approach. While the *Kadi* line of cases is the most obvious example there are also more subtle examples.[7] For instance, several of the measures considered in this book have the relevant safeguards in the Preamble of the measure rather than in the operative text. This is most noteworthy in relation to the Framework Decision on Combating Terrorism but it is also the Anti-Money-Laundering Directives. Such an approach is problematic as the Preamble is not legally binding, and may lead to transposing legislation failing to put in place safeguards against the more intrusive aspects of the law. However, the problem may be solved if domestic and European courts take the approach of Advocate General Maduro in the legal privilege case. There, the Advocate General noted that so long as the operative part of the text that applied to the legal profession was read in conjunction with the seventeenth recital to the Preamble (which referred

---

[4] D Lacombe, 'Reforming Foucault: A Critique of the Social Control Thesis' (1996) 47 *The British Journal of Sociology* 332.

[5] R Jackson, M Breen Smyth and J Gunning, *Critical Terrorism Studies: A New Research Agenda* (Abingdon, Routledge, 2009).

[6] S Mann, J Nolan and B Wellman, 'Sousveillance: Inventing and Using Wearable Computing Devices for Data Collection in Surveillance Environments' (2003) 1 *Surveillance and Society* 331.

[7] See, most recently, Joined Cases C-584/10 P, C-593/10 P & C-595/10 P OJ C 72 (5 March 2011).

to protection of legal privilege) then the directive could be considered lawful.[8] In this manner, courts can harness the text in the Preamble and use it to mitigate the worst effects of the operative clauses.

There is further scope for such resistance in relation to targeted sanctions. The distinction between criminal and non-criminal law and the related sanctions has been a recurring theme throughout this study. It was established at the outset that the definitions of 'criminal charge' and 'criminal penalty' under the ECHR and EU law are somewhat formalistic and as such that pre-emptive measures such as the targeted sanctions may evade the higher human rights protections that apply in criminal law cases. Using the adoption of pre-emptive counter-terrorism instruments as an opportunity to reconsider the rather formalistic tests would allow the European courts to link the higher standards of protection to the degree of interference with individual rights instead of formalistic notions of what constitutes a 'criminal' charge or penalty. It is entirely rational that the evolution of tools of state power should be matched by evolution of the safeguards on that power.

Unfortunately, despite the courts' laudable efforts to date judicial resistance has had limited success on this front. While the case law has steadily asserted the need to respect the rule of law, that resistance has proven of limited effect in terms of actually altering the factual situation of those targeted. Indeed, effective relief has been achieved largely through the political process: Mr Yusuf was delisted only following a long diplomatic campaign by the Swedish government. The delisting of OMPI also owed as much to politics as it did to legal remedies. On occasion upholding one aspect of the rule of law can have unintended consequences. Thus, when the ECJ annulled the First PNR Agreement, finding that the EU was not competent to adopt the agreement under the first pillar, the result was two subsequent agreements that worsened rather than improved protection for individuals. As such, one lesson from EU counter-terrorism is the limit of the rule of law in the face of determined political power. In instances where the legal system itself is being subverted it may be that resistance is instead manifested outside that system through constitutional politics.

B. Resistance by Legislatures

While courts can use various techniques of interpretation and, if necessary, annulment to curb counter-terrorism action a vigilant legislature can prevent bad policy from becoming law. Within the EU legislature, given the strong position of Member State governments in the Council it falls to the European Parliament to resist executive overreach. Thus, one might argue, if the Parliament's role in promulgating (say) the Framework Decision on Combating Terrorism was one of

---

[8] Opinion of Advocate General Maduro in C-305/05 *Ordre de barreaux francophones et germanophone, Ordre francais des avocats du barreau de Bruxelles, Ordre dex barreaux flamands, Ordre néerlandais des avocats du barreau de Bruxelles v Conseil des Ministres* [2007] ECR I-5305.

co-legislator rather than just being consulted, the measure may have been more respectful of the rule of law. The Parliament's opinions and reports have certainly urged the Council and Commission to be mindful of constitutional principles. However, this analysis may be too simplistic and may place too much faith in the legislature. They too are political actors and are subject to political pressure—as demonstrated by the effectiveness of UK's pressure on the European Parliament to agree to the Data Retention Directive.[9] The recent history of immigration legislation also evidences this point.[10] Acosta notes that the European Parliament approved the negotiated text for the Returns Directive at first reading without tabling a single amendment. This is significant as the directive is the first immigration measure to be adopted under co-decision.[11] As a result, the Parliament has been subjected to much criticism for abandoning what was previously described as a 'migrant-friendly approach'.[12] Acosta concludes that the example presents 'a dangerous signal for the future of the co-decision process'.[13] If the Returns Directive offers any insight into how the Parliament operates as a co-legislator now the first and third pillars have been merged by the Lisbon Treaty, then any optimism for more rule of law-compliant counter-terrorism legislation must be dampened. A more recent and even more pertinent example may bear out Acosta's warning: despite its concerns about the operation of the TFTP system the Parliament consented to the TFTP-II Agreement—though not before extracting concessions from the Council.

C. Popular Political Resistance

In the face of limited success within the legal and parliamentary processes, it may be that effective resistance to pre-emptive counter-terrorism comes from outside the legal system. In this regard, it is worth recalling Habermas and Derrida's call for a European public voice to counterbalance that of the US.[14] Consensual politics may 'serve either as a regulatory principle, or better yet as a critical principle with respect to other political forms'.[15] Thus, in light of the broad effect of post-September 11 counter-terrorism, it may be that the only effective resistance is popular political resistance. There is not the space here to conduct a critique of the

---

[9] *Euractiv.com* 'Data Retention: Parliament caves in to Council pressure', 14 December 2005.
[10] D Acosta, 'The Good, the Bad and the Ugly in EU Migration Law: Is the European Parliament Becoming Bad and Ugly? (The Adoption of Directive 2008/15: The Returns Directive)' (2009) *European Journal of Migration and Law* 19.
[11] Ibid.
[12] Ibid, p 20.
[13] Ibid, p 39.
[14] J Habermas, 'February 15, or: What Binds Europeans' in *The Divided West* (Cambridge, Polity Press, 2006).
[15] M Foucault, 'Politics and Ethics: An Interview' in P Rabinow (ed), *The Foucault Reader* (London, Penguin, 1991) 378.

(absence of a) European public sphere.[16] However, it is not unreasonable to suggest that greater awareness of EU counter-terrorism action might lead to greater public pressure on Member State governments and in turn on the institutions of the EU. The obvious example in this respect is the opposition, in particular in Germany, to the Data Retention Directive. The case was brought before the German Federal Constitutional Court on Germany's implementation of the directive by 24,000 citizens. Thus, the legal resistance was merely the tip of a sword swung by a mix of the citizenry, civil society and parliamentarians. If the inevitable consequence of pre-emptive counter-terrorism is to shrink the space for political contest—to pursue a 'militant democracy'[17]—then it is only through opening up that space that resistance can be effective. This resistance may then provide the means to articulate the fundamental values of the EU legal system: 'liberty, democracy, respect for human rights and fundamental freedoms, and the rule of law, principles which are common to the Member States'.[18] In the absence of a vibrant European public sphere in which to develop that discourse, those values remain solely subject to interpretation by the Member State governments and EU institutions—to the detriment of the legal system itself and those subject to it.

II. THE LISBON TREATY AND THE STOCKHOLM PROGRAMME

In December 2009 the EU witnessed the coming into force of the Lisbon Treaty and agreement on the Stockholm Programme which sets out (amongst other matters) the EU's priorities in the area of criminal justice co-operation for the coming years. Both the Treaty and the Programme will have implications for criminal justice co-operation and counter-terrorism. The Lisbon Treaty provides new competences in the field of criminal justice and shifts Justice and Home Affairs from the intergovernmental processes of the former third pillar into the realm of supranational governance.[19] In addition, an explicit legal basis has been provided for the targeted sanctions systems deployed against suspected terrorists. Nevertheless, as the *Parliament v Council* case before the ECJ demonstrates, there remains uncertainty over the appropriate EU powers for counter-terrorism.[20]

The Stockholm Programme is the latest in the area of freedom, security and justice and succeeds the Tampere Programme and the Hague Programme. It claims its focus is 'on the interests and needs of citizens. The challenge will be to ensure respect for fundamental freedoms and integrity while guaranteeing

---

[16] See generally: JHH Weiler, *The Constitution of Europe: 'Do the New Clothes Have an Emperor?' and Other Essays on European Integration* (Cambridge, Cambridge University Press, 1999).

[17] W Sadurski (ed), *Political Rights Under Stress in 21st Century Europe* (Oxford, Oxford University Press, 2006).

[18] Art 6 TEU.

[19] Art 83 TFEU.

[20] Case C-130/10 *European Parliament v Council of the European Union* OJ 2010 C 134.

security in Europe'.[21] The Stockholm Programme sets out an ambitious set of proposals in relation to criminal law and criminal justice. The legislative priorities to be implemented under the programme have been clarified by an Action Plan which makes clear that the volume of EU criminal law is set to increase in the coming years. The Stockholm Programme will be pursued on the basis of the new constitutional arrangements brought into place by the Lisbon Treaty. The programme is likely to have implications for EU counter-terrorism. It is through an accident of history, or more accurately the designs of nineteen hijackers, that counter-terrorism has proven to be the focal point for the development of the EU's role in criminal justice. This has been an unfortunate mode of development—for counter-terrorism has proven time and again in jurisdictions the world over to have a corrosive effect on criminal justice.[22] Developments in this field tend to be reactive: the establishment of the Counter-Terrorism Co-ordinator was a reaction to the Madrid bombings and agreement on the Data Retention Directive came in the wake of the London bombings. The task of constructing a European criminal law and criminal justice is not one that should be pursued in haste simply so as to be seen to be acting against the threat of violence. A reactionary approach such as the one observable in the aftermath of September 11 will almost inevitably be enforcement-led and undermine principles such as the rule of law in the name of protecting security.

EU criminal justice has been marked by an emphasis on enforcement. It is an example of Herbert Packer's classic 'crime control' model of criminal justice.[23] In the future, EU counter-terrorism may become subsumed in the broader, growing, policy field of EU criminal justice. It is likely, at the very least, to remain a key site for discussion of the problems for the nascent multi-level criminal justice system. The European Arrest Warrant could be a positive example of EU co-operation if there was the necessary mutual trust, minimum standards of protection, and proportionate use by law enforcement authorities. Instead it is seen as EU over-reaching—a consequence perhaps of its hasty adoption in the wake of the September 11 attacks. Though serious concerns remain relating to the Warrant's operation these pertain to the development of an EU criminal justice system and the establishment of appropriate safeguards in that context. A review is envisaged by the Stockholm Programme and any reform will be indicative of the future of EU counter-terrorism in particular and EU criminal justice in general. It will help to determine whether EU counter-terrorism can indeed comply with 'the rule of law, without which, in the long run, no democratic society can truly prosper'.[24]

---

[21] Council of the European Union, The Stockholm Programme: an open and secure europe serving and protecting the citizens, Brussels, 2 December 2009, p 3.

[22] For an enlightened discussion see K Roach, 'The Criminal Law and Terrorism' in V Ramraj, M Hor and K Roach, *Global Anti-Terrorism Law and Policy* (Cambridge, Cambridge University Press, 2005).

[23] H Packer, *The Limits of the Criminal Sanction* (Stanford, Stanford University Press, 1968).

[24] Opinion of Advocate General Poiares Maduro in Joined Cases C-402/05 P & C-415/05 P *Yassin Abdullah Kadi, Al Barakaat International Foundation v Council of the European Union* [2008] ECR I-6351.

III. CONCLUSION: WHERE LIES THE RULE OF LAW?

Since the September 11 attacks in New York and Washington the EU has sought to develop its role in counter-terrorism action. The instruments discussed in this book represent the key legislative aspects of the pre-emptive approach to counter-terrorism that has evolved in the EU since that day. Pre-emptive counter-terrorism action has had a detrimental effect on the rule of law in the EU. In terms of the rule of law's constitutive role, the pressure on the EU to agree on counter-terrorism action has caused greater political compromises in drafting legislation and therefore provided scope for diverging implementation. Divergence is a particular feature of framework decisions where limitations on the power of the European Commission and ECJ prevent transposition from being effectively monitored. The action taken has also caused significant difficulties in relation to the principle of conferred competences, with the European courts struggling to find legal bases for some measures and offering inconsistent decisions in relation to others. Though EU pre-emption has empowered a wide range of public and private actors, EU action also evidences the endurance of state power. Some EU Member States such as the United Kingdom have used the September 11 attacks to pursue a vigorous counter-terrorism agenda. Others, such as Germany, appear to be more reticent and have negotiated declarations and controlled transposition to prevent the worst aspects of counter-terrorism action from undermining their legal systems. In relation to the rule of law's safeguarding role, the pre-emptive approach to counter-terrorism has both evaded and eroded the rights of those targeted. Some measures, such as asset-freezing sanctions, evade criminal justice principles of legality and fair trial rights while subjecting individuals to severely coercive controls. Other measures, including the Framework Decision on Combating Terrorism, Anti-Money-Laundering Directives and surveillance measures infringe upon the right to privacy and to freedom of expression and association. The restriction of rights curtails political speech and discourages dissent. Perhaps the strongest conclusion that can be drawn from the analysis is the limit of the rule of law. As the ongoing targeted sanctions saga makes clear, when political actors subvert the legal system, courts can struggle to reassert fundamental principles. These principles, such as the rule of law, are just as strong as the support they receive from political institutions and the public in general. In the end the rule of law, like liberty, might be found in the hearts of Europe's men and women.

Bibliography

Ackerman, B, 'This is Not a War' (2004) 113 *Yale Law Journal* 1870.

Acosta, D, 'The Good, the Bad and the Ugly in EU Migration Law: Is the European Parliament Becoming Bad and Ugly? (The Adoption of Directive 2008/15: The Returns Directive)' (2009) *European Journal of Migration and Law* 19.

Aldhouse, F, 'Comment: SWIFT and the new EU–US data transfer agreement' (2010) 7 *Data Protection Law and Policy*.

Aldrich, RJ, 'Transatlantic Intelligence and Security Co-operation' (2004) 80 *International Affairs* 731.

Alegre, S and Leaf, M, *European Arrest Warrant: A Solution Ahead of its Time?* (London, JUSTICE, 2003).

Alexander, K, Dhumale, R and Eatwell, J, *Global Governance of Financial Systems: The International Regulation of Systemic Risk* (New York, Oxford University Press, 2006).

Alter, K, *Establishing the Supremacy of European Law: The Making of an International Rule of Law in Europe* (Oxford, Oxford University Press, 2001).

Alvarez, JE, 'Hegemonic International Law Revisited' (2003) 97 *American Journal of International Law* 873.

Amoore, L, 'Risk before Justice: When the Law Contests its own Suspension' (2008) 21 *Leiden Journal of International Law* 847.

—— and Goede, M de, 'Governance, Risk and Dataveillance in the War on Terror' (2005) 43 *Crime, Law and Social Change* 149.

—— and —— *Risk and the War on Terror* (London, Routledge, 2008).

Anderson, D, Centre of European Law Annual Conference, King's College London, 10 March 2006.

—— and CC Murphy, 'The Charter of Fundamental Rights' in A Biondi, P Eeckhout and S Ripley, *EU Law after the Lisbon Treaty* (Oxford, Oxford University Press, 2011).

Ashworth, A, 'Criminal Law, Human Rights and Preventative Justice' in B McSherry, A Norrie and S Bronitt (eds), *Regulating Deviance: The Redirection of Criminalisation and the Futures of Criminal Law* (Oxford, Hart Publishing, 2009).

—— 'Four Threats to the Presumption of Innocence' (2006) 10 *International Journal of Evidence and Proof* 241.

Baker, E and Harding, C, 'From Past Imperfect to Future Perfect? A Longitudinal Study of the Third Pillar' (2009) 34 *European Law Review* 25.

Barber, N, 'Must Legalistic Conceptions of the Rule of Law Have a Social Dimension' (2004) 17 *Ratio Juris* 474.

Beck, U, *Risk Society: Towards a New Modernity* (London, Sage Publications, 1992).

Belfiore, R, 'Movement of Evidence in the EU: The Present Scenario and Possible Future Developments' (2009) 17 *European Journal of Crime, Criminal Law and Criminal Justice* 1.

Benyon, J, 'Policing the European Union: The Changing Basis of Co-operation on Law Enforcement' (1994) 70 *International Affairs* 497.

Bingham, T, *The Rule of Law* (London, Allen Lane, 2010).

Blakeney, S, 'The Data Retention Directive: Combating Terrorism or Invading Privacy?' (2007) *Computer and Telecommunications Law Review* 153.

Bobbit, P, *The Shield of Achilles: War, Peace and the Course of History* (London, Penguin, 2003).

—— *Terror and Consent: The Wars for the Twenty-First Century* (London, Allen Lane, 2008).

Bogdandy, A von, 'Constitutional Principles' in A von Bogdandy and J Bast (eds), *Principles of European Constitutional Law*, 1st edn (Oxford, Hart Publishing, 2006).

—— *Doctrine of Principles*, Jean Monnet Working Paper 9/03 (New York, NYU School of Law, 2003).

—— 'The European Union as a Human Rights Organisation? Human Rights and the Core of the European Union' (2000) 37 *Common Market Law Review* 1307.

—— 'Founding Principles' in A von Bogdandy and J Bast (eds), *Principles of European Constitutional Law*, rev 2nd edn (Oxford, Hart Publishing, 2009).

Borradori, G (ed), *Philosophy in a Time of Terror: Dialogues with Jürgen Habermas and Jacques Derrida* (Chicago, University of Chicago Press, 2003).

Bossong, R, 'The Action Plan on Combating Terrorism: A Flawed Instrument of EU Security Governance' (2008) 46 *Journal of Common Market Studies* 27.

Boulden, J, 'The Security Council and Terrorism' in V Lowe, A Roberts, J Welsh and D Zaum (eds), *The United Nations Security Council and War: The Evolution of Thought and Practice since 1945* (Oxford, Oxford University Press, 2008).

Bowling, B, Marks, A and Murphy, CC, 'Crime Control Technologies: Towards an Analytical Framework and Research Agenda' in R Brownsword and K Yeung (eds), *Regulating Technologies* (Oxford, Hart Publishing, 2008).

Boyle, K, Hadden, T and Hillyard, P, *Law and State: The Case of Northern Ireland* (Massachusetts, University of Massachusetts Press, 1975).

Bradley, AW and Ewing, KD, *Constitutional and Administrative Law*, 14th edn (London, Longman, 2008).

Breen Smyth, M, Gunning, J, Jackson, R, Kassimeris, G and Robinson, P, 'Critical Terrorism Studies: An Introduction' (2008) 1 *Critical Studies on Terrorism* 1.

Breyer, P, 'Telecommunications Data Retention and Human Rights: The Compatibility of Blanket Traffic Data Retention with the ECHR' (2005) 11 *European Law Journal* 365.

Brownlee, I, 'New Labour: New Penology? Punitive Rhetoric and the Limits of Managerialism in Criminal Justice Policy' (1998) 25 *Journal of Law and Society* 313.

Bunyan, T, *The EU's Police Chief Task Force (PCTF) and Police Chiefs Committee* (London, StateWatch, 2006).

—— 'Trevi, Europol and the European State', in *Statewatching the new Europe* (London, StateWatch, 1993).

Bures, O, 'EU Counterterrorism Policy: A Paper Tiger?' (2006) 18 *Terrorism and Political Violence* 57.

—— 'EU's Fight against Terrorist Finances: Internal Shortcomings and Unsuitable External Models' (2010) 22 *Terrorism and Political Violence* 418.

Burke, E, *Letters on a Regicide Peace* (1796).

Cameron, I, 'UN Targeted Sanctions, Legal Safeguards and the European Convention on Human Rights' (2003) 72 *Nordic Journal of International Law* 159.

Cassese, A, 'The multifaceted criminal notion of terrorism in international law' (2006) *Journal of International Criminal Justice* 933.

Chadwick, E, 'The 2005 Terrorism Convention: A Flexible Step Too Far?' (2007) 16 *Nottingham Law Journal* 29.

Chalmers, D, 'Political Rights and Political Reason in the European Union in Times of Stress', in W Sadurski (ed), *Political Rights under Stress in 21st Century Europe* (Oxford, Oxford University Press, 2006).

Chinkin, C, 'The Challenge of Soft Law: Development and Change in International Law' (1989) 38 *International and Comparative Law Quarterly* 850.

Chomsky, N, 'International Terrorism: Image and Reality' in A George (ed), *Western State Terrorism* (Oxford, Polity Press, 1991).

Cole, D, 'After September 11 2001: What We Still Don't Know', *New York Review of Books* (29 September 2011).

—— 'Closing Guantánamo: The Problem of Preventive Detention', *Boston Review* (January/February 2009), available: www.bostonreview.net/BR34.1/cole.php.

—— *Enemy Aliens* (New York, The New Press, 2003).

—— 'Terror Financing, Guilt by Association and the Paradigm of Prevention in the "War on Terror"' in A Bianchi and A Keller (eds), *Counterterrorism: Democracy's Challenge* (Oxford, Hart Publishing, 2008).

—— and Lobel, J, *Less Safe, Less Free: Why America is Losing the War on Terror* (New York, The New Press, 2007).

Comella, VF, 'Freedom of Expression in Political Contexts: Some Reflections on the Case-Law of the European Court of Human Rights' in W Sadurski (ed), *Political Rights Under Stress in 21st Century Europe* (Oxford, Oxford University Press, 2006).

Connorton, PM, 'Tracking Terrorist Financing Through SWIFT: When U.S. Subpoenas and Foreign Privacy Law Collide' (2007) 76 *Fordham Law Review* 101.

Costa, P and Zola, D, eds, *The Rule of Law: History, Theory and Criticism* (Netherlands, Springer, 2010).

Coutts, S, 'The Lisbon Treaty and the Area of Freedom, Security and Justice as an Area of Legal Integration', Presentation to King's College London Centre of European Law, 10 June 2011 (copy with author).

Craig, P, 'Formal and Substantive Conceptions of the Rule of Law' (1997) *Public Law* 467.

—— *The Lisbon Treaty: Law, Politics and Treaty Reform* (Oxford, Oxford University Press, 2010).

Curtin, D, *Executive Power of the European Union: Law, Practices and the Living Constitution* (Oxford, Oxford University Press, 2009).

Davidson, R, 'A Sledgehammer to Crack a Nut? Should There be a Bar of Triviality in European Arrest Warrant Cases?' (2009) (1) *Criminal Law Review* 31.

De Búrca, G, 'The EU, the European Court of Justice and the International Legal Order after *Kadi*' (2010) 51 *Harvard International Law Journal* 1.

De Goede *see* Goede, M de.

de Hert, P, 'Division of Competencies between National and European Levels with regard to Justice and Home Affairs' in J Apap (ed), *Justice and Home Affairs in the EU: Liberty and Security Issues after Enlargement* (Cheltenham, Edward Elgar Publishing, c2004).

—— and Papakonstantinou, V, 'The EU PNR Framework Decision Proposal: Towards Completion of the PNR Processing Scene in Europe' (2010) 26 *Computer Law and Security Review* 368.

de Londras, F, *Detention in the 'War on Terror': Can Human Rights Fight Back?* (Cambridge, Cambridge University Press, 2011).

de Londras, F and Davis, F, 'Controlling the Executive in Times of Terrorism: Competing Perspectives on Effective Oversight Mechanisms' (2010) 30 *Oxford Journal of Legal Studies* 19.

Deflem, M, 'Europol and the Policing of International Terrorism: Counter-Terrorism in a Global Perspective' (2006) 23 *Justice Quarterly* 336.

Den Boer, M and Monar, J, 'Keynote Article: 11 September and the Challenge of Global Terrorism to the EU as a Security Actor', in G Edwards and G Wiessala (eds), *The European Union: Annual Review of the EU 2001/2002* (Oxford, Blackwell, 2002).

Den Boer, M, Hillebrand, C and Nolke, A, 'Legitimacy under Pressure: The European Web of Counter-Terrorism Networks' (2008) 46 *Journal of Common Market Studies* 101.

Denza, E, *The Intergovernmental Pillars of the European Union* (Oxford, Oxford University Press, 2002).

DeSimone, C, 'Pitting Karlsruhe Against Luxembourg? German Data Protection and the Contested Implementation of the EU Data Retention Directive' (2010) 11 *German Law Journal* 291.

Donohue, LK, *The Cost of Counterterrorism: Power, Politics, and Liberty* (Cambridge, Cambridge University Press, 2008).

Douglas-Scott, S, *Constitutional Law of the European Union* (Harlow, Longman, 2002).

—— 'The Rule of Law in the European Union: Putting the Security in the "Area of Freedom, Security and Justice"' (2004) 29 *European Law Review* 219.

—— 'A Tale of Two Courts: Luxembourg, Strasbourg and the Growing European Human Rights Acquis' (2006) 43 *Common Market Law Review* 619.

Dubois, D, 'The Attacks of 11 September: EU–US Co-operation Against Terrorism in the Field of Justice and Home Affairs' (2002) 7 *European Foreign Affairs Review* 317.

Dumitriu, E, 'The EU's Definition of Terrorism: The Council Framework Decision on Combating Terrorism' (2004) 5 *German Law Journal* 585.

Dworkin, R, *Law's Empire* (Harvard, Harvard University Press, 1986).

Dyzenhaus, D, (ed), *Recrafting the Rule of Law: The Limits of Legal Order* (Oxford, Hart Publishing, 1999).

Eagleton, T, *Holy Terror* (Oxford, Oxford University Press, 2005).

Eckes, C, *EU Counter-Terrorist Policies and Fundamental Rights: The Case of Individual Sanctions* (Oxford, Oxford University Press, 2009).

—— 'Judicial Review of European Anti-Terrorism Measures: The *Yusuf* and *Kadi* Judgments of the Court of First Instance' (2008) 14 *European Law Journal* 74.

Eeckhout, P, 'Community Terrorism Listings, Fundamental Rights, and UN Security Council Resolutions. In Search of the Right Fit' (2007) *European Constitutional Law Review* 183.

—— *EU External Relations Law* Second edn (Oxford, Oxford University Press, 2011).

—— 'Kadi and Al Barakaat: Luxembourg is not Texas—or Washington DC' *EJIL: Talk!* (25 February 2009).

—— Presentation at the European University Institute, Florence, 30–31 May 2009.

—— and Tridimas, T (eds), *Yearbook of European Law* (Oxford, Oxford University Press, 2009).

Ericson, R, *Crime in an Insecure World* (Cambridge, Polity Press, 2007).

—— 'The State of Preemption: Managing Terrorism Through Counter Law' in L Amoore and M De Goede (eds), *Risk and the War on Terror* (Abingdon, Routledge, 2008).

—— and Haggerty, KD, *Policing the Risk Society* (Oxford, Clarendon Press, 1997).

Ewing, KD and Tham, JC, 'The Continuing Futility of the Human Rights Act' (2008) *Public Law* 668.

Fabbrini, F, 'The Role of the Judiciary in Times of Emergency: Judicial Review of Counter-terrorism Measures in the United States Supreme Court and the European Court of Justice' in P Eeckhout and T Tridimas (eds), *Yearbook of European Law* (Oxford, Oxford University Press, 2009).

Feeley, M and Simon, J, 'Actuarial Justice: The Emerging New Criminal Law', in D Nelken (ed), *The Futures of Criminology* (London, Sage Publishing, 1994).

—— and —— 'The New Penology: Notes on the Emerging Strategy of Corrections and Its Implications' (1992) 30 *Criminology* 449.

Fekete, L, 'Anti-Terrorism and Civil Liberties: Country Summaries' *European Race Bulletin* (London, Institute of Race Relations, Autumn 2007).

—— 'Anti-terrorism and Human Rights' (2004) 47 *European Race Bulletin*.

Floud, J and Young, W, *Dangerousness and Criminal Justice* (London, Heinemann, 1981).

Flynn, EJ, 'The Security Council's Counter-Terrorism Committee and Human Rights' (2007) *Human Rights Law Review* 371.

Foucault, M, *Discipline and Punish: The Birth of the Prison*, new edn (London, Penguin, 1991).

—— 'Politics and Ethics: An Interview' in Rabinow (ed), *The Foucault Reader* (London, Penguin, 1991).

—— 'Truth and Power' in C Gordon (ed), *Power/Knowledge: Selected Interviews and Other Writings 1972–77* (Harlow, Longman, 1980).

Freestone, D, 'The EEC Treaty and Common Action on Terrorism' (1984) 4 *Yearbook of European Law* 207.

Gaja, G, 'Accession to the ECHR' in A Biondi, P Eeckhout and S Ripley, *EU Law after the Lisbon Treaty* (Oxford, Oxford University Press, 2011).

Gallie, WB, 'Essentially Contested Concepts' (1956) 56 *Proceedings of the Aristotelian Society* 167.

Gardella, A, 'The Fight Against the Financing of Terrorism between Judicial and Regulatory Co-operation' in A. Bianchi (ed), *Enforcing International Law Norms Against Terrorism* (Oxford, Hart Publishing, 2004).

Garland, D, *The Culture of Control: Crime and Social Order in Contemporary Society* (Chicago, The University of Chicago Press, 2001).

Gearty, C, 'Can Human Rights Survive? A Symposium on the 2005 Hamlyn Lectures' (2007) *Public Law* 209.

—— *The Future of Terrorism* (London, Phoenix, 1997).

—— 'Terrorism and Human Rights' (2007) 42 *Government and Opposition* 340.

—— 'Terrorism and Morality' (2003) *European Human Rights Law Review* 377.

—— *Principles of Human Rights Adjudication* (Oxford, Oxford University Press, 2003).

Gilmore, G and Rijpma, J, 'Joined Cases C-317/04 and C-318/04, *European Parliament* v. *Council and Commission*, Judgment of the Grand Chamber of 30 May 2006, [2006] ECR I-4721' (2007) 44 *Common Market Law Review* 1081.

Gilmore, WC, *Dirty Money: The evolution of international measures to counter money laundering and the financing of terrorism* 3rd edn (Strasbourg, Council of Europe Publishing, 2004).

Goede, M de, 'Beyond Risk: Premediation and the Post-9/11 Security Imagination' (2008) 39 *Security Dialogue* 155.

Goede, M de, 'The Politics of Preemption and the War on Terror in Europe' (2008) 14 *European Journal of International Relations* 161.

Greenberg, K, *The Least Worst Place: How Guantanamo Became the World's Most Notorious Prison* (Oxford, Oxford University Press, 2009).

—— and Dratel, J, (eds), *The Torture Papers: The Road to Abu Ghraib* (Cambridge, Cambridge University Press, 2005).

Greer, S, *The European Convention on Human Rights: Achievements, Problems and Prospects* (Cambridge, Cambridge University Press, 2006).

Habermas, J, 'February 15, or: What Binds Europeans' in *The Divided West* (Cambridge, Polity Press, 2006).

Hallstein, W, *Die Europäishe Gemeinschaft*, 5th edn (Düsseldorf, Econ, 1979).

Heaney, S, 'Anything Can Happen: After Horace, Odes, I, 34', District and Circle (London, Faber, 2006).

Heng, Y-K and McDonagh, K, *Risk, Global Governance and Security: The Other War on Terror* (London, Routledge, 2009).

Herlin-Karnell, E, 'European Arrest Warrant Cases and the Principles of Non-Discrimination and EU Citizenship' (2010) 73 *Modern Law Review* 824.

Heyvaert, V, 'Facing the Consequences of the Precautionary Principle in European Community Law' (2006) 31 *European Law Review* 185.

Hijmans, H and Scirocco, A, 'Shortcomings in EU Data Protection in the Third and The Second Pillars. Can the Lisbon Treaty be Expected to Help?' (2009) 46 *Common Market Law Review* 1485.

Hillyard, P, *Suspect Community: People's Experience of the Prevention of Terrorism Acts in Britain* (London, Pluto Press, 1993).

Hoffmann, B, *Inside Terrorism*, rev and expanded edn (Columbia, Columbia University Press, 2006).

Hornung, G and Schnabel, C, 'Data Protection in Germany. I: The Population Census Decision and the Right to Informational Self-Determination' (2009) 25 *Computer Law and Security Review* 84.

—— and —— 'Data Protection in Germany. II: Recent Decisions on Online-Searching of Computers, Automatic Number Plate Recognition and Data Retention' (2009) 25 *Computer Law and Security Review* 115.

Human Rights Watch, *Pre-empting Justice: Counter-Terrorism Laws and Procedures in France* (Paris, Human Rights Watch, 2008).

Hunt, A, 'The Council of Europe Convention on the Prevention of Terrorism' (2006) 12 *European Public Law* 603.

Husabø, EJ, *Fighting Terrorism through Multilevel Criminal Legislation: Security Council Resolution 1373, the EU Framework Decision on Combating Terrorism and Their Implementation in Nordic, Dutch and German Criminal Law* (Leiden, Martinus Nijhoff Publishers, 2009).

Hutchinson, AC and Monahan, P (eds), *The Rule of Law: Ideal or Ideology* (Toronto, Carswell, 1987).

Jackson, R, 'An Analysis of EU Counterterrorism Discourse post-September 11' (2007) 20 *Cambridge Review of International Affairs* 233.

—— Breen Smyth, M and Gunning, J, *Critical Terrorism Studies: A New Research Agenda* (Abingdon, Routledge, 2009).

Jacobs, FG, *The Sovereignty of Law: The European Way* (Cambridge, Cambridge University Press, 2007).

Jenkins, D, 'The Closure of Guantanamo Bay: What Next for the Detainees?' (2010) *Public Law* 46.

Kennedy, D, *Of War and Law* (Princeton, Princeton University Press, 2006).

Kessler, O, 'Is Risk Changing the Politics of Legal Argumentation?' (2008) 21 *Leiden Journal of International Law* 863.

Khoury, A, 'Is it Time for an EU Definition of the Precautionary Principle?' (2010) 21 *King's Law Journal* 133.

Koh, J, *Suppressing Terrorist Financing and Money Laundering* (New York, Springer, 2006).

Komárek, J, 'European Constitutionalism and the European Arrest Warrant: In Search of the Limits of "Contrapunctual Principles"' (2007) 44 *Common Market Law Review* 9.

Kundnani, A, *Spooked! How Not to Prevent Violent Extremism* (London, Institute of Race Relations, 2010).

Lacombe, D, 'Reforming Foucault: A Critique of the Social Control Thesis' (1996) 47 *The British Journal of Sociology* 332.

Ladeur, K, 'The Introduction of the Precautionary Principle into EU Law: A Pyrrhic Victory for Environmental and Public Health Law? Decision-Making Under Conditions of Complexity in Multi-level Political Systems' (2003) 40 *Common Market Law Review* 1455.

Lander, S, 'International Intelligence Co-operation: An Inside Perspective' (2004) 17 *Cambridge Review of International Affairs* 481.

Lazowski, A, 'Half Full and Half Empty Glass: The Application of EU Law in Poland (2004–2010)' (2011) 48 *Common Market Law Review* 503.

Leczykiewicz, D, 'Constitutional Conflicts and the Third Pillar' (2008) 33 *European Law Review* 230.

Levi, M, 'Combating the Financing of Terrorism: A History and Assessment of the Control of "Threat Finance"' (2010) 50 *British Journal of Criminology* 650.

—— and Wall, D, 'Technologies, security and privacy in the post 9/11 European Information Society' (2004) 31 *Journal of Law and Society* 194.

Lööf, R, 'Obtaining, adducing and contesting evidence from abroad: a defence perspective on cross-border evidence' (2011) (1) *Criminal Law Review* 40.

Lugna, L, 'Insitutional Framework of the European Union Counter-Terrorism Policy Setting' (2006) 8 *Baltic Security and Defence Review* 101.

Maduro, M, 'So Close and Yet So Far: The Paradoxes of Mutual Recognition' (2007) 14 *Journal of European Public Policy* 814.

—— *We the Court: The European Court of Justice and the European Economic Constitution* (Oxford, Hart Publishing, 1998).

Mann, S, Nolan, J and Wellman, B, 'Sousveillance: Inventing and Using Wearable Computing Devices for Data Collection in Surveillance Environments' (2003) 1 *Surveillance and Society* 331.

Marks, S, 'Comment on a Paper by Joseph Raz: Human Rights in the New World Order' *ISCI Working Paper 2/2010*, available: www.statecrime.org.

—— and Clapham, A, *International Human Rights Lexicon* (Oxford, Oxford University Press, 2005).

Marmor, A, 'The Rule of Law and its Limits' (2004) 23 *Law and Philosophy* 1.

Marques da Silva, S, 'The TFTP Agreements: A Legal and Contextual Analysis', King's College London LLM Dissertation 2011 (copy with author).

—— and Murphy, CC, 'Proscription of Organisations in UK Counter-Terrorism Law' in Cameron (ed), *Legal Aspects of EU Sanctions* (Mortsel, Intersentia, 2012).

Mathiesen, T, 'On the Globalisation of Control: Towards an Integrated Surveillance System in Europe' in P Green and A Rutherford (eds), *Criminal Policy in Transition* (Oxford, Hart Publishing, 2000).

Matua, M, 'Terrorism and Human Rights: Power, Culture, and Subordination' (2002) 8 *Buffalo Human Rights Law Review* 1.

McCulloch, J and Carlton, B, 'Preempting Justice: Suppression of Financing of Terrorism and the "War on Terror"' (2005–2006) 17 *Current Issues in Criminal Justice* 397.

McCulloch, J and Pickering, S, 'Pre-crime and Counter-terrorism: Imagining Future Crime in the "War on Terror"' (2009) 49 *British Journal of Criminology* 628.

—— and —— 'Suppressing the Financing of Terrorism: Proliferating State Crime, Eroding Censure and Extending Neo-Colonialism' (2005) 45 *British Journal of Criminology* 470.

McKittrick, D and McVea, D, *Making Sense of the Troubles* (London, Penguin, 2001).

Mitchell, PR and Schoeffel, J, (eds), *Understanding Power: The Indispensible Chomsky* (New York, The New Press, 2002).

Mitsilegas, V, *EU Criminal Law* (Oxford, Hart Publishing, 2009).

—— 'The Transformation of Border Controls in an Era of Security: UK and EU Systems Converging?' (2010) 24 *Journal of Immigration Asylum and Nationality Law* 233.

—— and Gilmore, B, 'The EU Legislative Framework Against Money Laundering and Terrorist Finance: A Critical Analysis in the Light of Evolving Global Standards' (2007) 56 *International and Comparative Law Quarterly* 119.

Monar, J, 'Common Threat and Common Response? The European Union's Counter-Terrorism Strategy and its Problems' (2007) 42 *Government and Opposition* 292.

—— 'Editorial Comment: The Rejection of the EU–US SWIFT Interim Agreement by the European Parliament: A Historic Vote and Its Implications' (2010) 15 *European Foreign Affairs Review* 143.

—— 'The EU's Approach post-September 11: Global Terrorism as a Multidimensional Law Enforcement Challenge' (2007) 20 *Cambridge Review of International Affairs* 267.

Möstl, M, 'Preconditions of Mutual Recognition' (2010) 47 *Common Market Law Review* 405–436.

Muller, WH, Kälin, CH and Goldsworth, JG (eds), *Anti-Money Laundering: International Law and Practice* (West Sussex, John Wiley & Sons Ltd, 2007).

Murphy, CC, '*Ayadi v Council*: Competence and Justice in the "War on Terrorism"' (2007) 29 *Dublin University Law Journal* 426.

—— 'Fundamental Rights and Security: The Difficult Position of the European Judiciary' (2010) 16 *European Public Law* 289.

—— 'The Principle of Legality in Criminal Law under the ECHR' (2010) *European Human Rights Law Review* 192.

—— 'Questioning *Yusef*: Quis custodiet ipsos custodes?' (2006) *University College Dublin Law Review* 109.

Naert, F and Wouters, J, 'Of Arrest Warrants, Terrorist Offences and Extradition Deals: an Appraisal of the EU'S Main Criminal Law Measures Against Terrorism after "11 September"' (2004) 41 *Common Market Law Review* 909.

National Commission on Terrorist Attacks Upon the United States, *The 9/11 Commission Report: Final Report of the National Commission on Terrorist Attacks Upon the United States* (New York, WH Norton & Co, 2004).

Neumann, F, *The Rule of Law: Political Theory and the Legal System in Modern Society* (Leamington Spa, Berg Publishers, 1986).

Neumann, M, *The Rule of Law: Politicizing Ethics* (Aldershot, Ashgate Publishing, 2002).

Nohlen, N, 'Germany: The European Arrest Warrant case' (2008) 6(1) *International Journal of Constitutional Law* 153.

Norrie, A, 'Citizenship, Authoritarianism and the Changing Shape of the Criminal Law' in B McSherry, A Norrie and S Bronitt (eds), *Regulating Deviance: The Redirection of Criminalisation and the Futures of Criminal Law* (Oxford, Hart Publishing, 2009).

Nuotio, K, 'Terrorism as a Catalyst for the Emergence, Harmonisation and Reform of Criminal Law' (2006) 4 *Journal of International Criminal Justice* 998.

Packer, H, *The Limits of the Criminal Sanction* (Stanford, Stanford University Press, 1968).

Papakonstantinou, V and de Hert, 'The PNR Agreement and Transatlantic Anti-Terrorism Co-operation: No Firm Human Rights Framework on Either Side of the Atlantic' (2009) 46 *Common Market Law Review* 885.

Passas, N, 'Setting Global CFT Standards: a Critique and Suggestions' (2006) 9 *Journal of Money Laundering Control* 281.

Pech, L, *The Rule of Law as a Constitutional Principle of the European Union*, Jean Monnet Working Paper 04/09 (New York, NYU School of Law, 2009).

Peers, S, 'Current Developments: EC Law II. Justice and Home Affairs' (2000) 49 *International and Comparative Law Quarterly* 222.

—— *EU Justice and Home Affairs Law*, 2nd edn (Oxford, Oxford University Press, 2006).

—— *EU Justice and Home Affairs Law*, 3rd edn (Oxford, Oxford University Press, 2011).

—— 'EU Responses to Terrorism' (2003) 52 *International and Comparative Law Quarterly* 227.

—— 'Mutual Recognition and Criminal Law in the European Union: Has the Council Got it Wrong?' (2004) 41 *Common Market Law Review* 5.

Peirce, G, 'Was It Like This for the Irish?' (2008) 30(7) *London Review of Books* 3.

Peterson, J, 'Europe, America and 11 September' (2002) 13 *Irish Studies in International Affairs* 1.

Pfisterer, V, 'The Second SWIFT Agreement Between the European Union and the United States of America: An Overview' (2010) 11 *German Law Journal* 1173.

Pieth, M, 'Criminalizing the Financing of Terrorism' (2006) *Journal of International Criminal Justice* 1074.

Plachta, M, 'European Arrest Warrant: revolution in extradition?' (2003) 11 *European Journal of Crime, Criminal Law and Criminal Justice* 178.

Poole, S, *Unspeak* (London, Little Brown, 2006).

Rackow, P and Birr, C, 'Recent Developments in Legal Assistance in Criminal Matters' (2010) 2 *Goettingen Journal of International Law* 1087.

Ramage, S, '2008 amendments of the Proceeds of Crime Act 2002 and Other Legislation that Combats Terrorist Financing' (2008) *Criminal Lawyer* 1.

Rasmussen, DR, 'Is International Travel *Per Se* Suspicion of Terrorism? The Dispute Between the United States and European Union over Passenger Name Record Data Transfers' (2008) 26 *Wisconsin International Law Journal* 551.

Raz, J, *The Authority of Law* (Oxford, Oxford University Press, 1979).

—— 'The Rule of Law and its Virtue' (1977) 93 *Law Quarterly Review* 195.

Richardson, L, *What Terrorists Want: Understanding the Terrorist Threat* (London, John Murray, 2006).

Rijken, C, 'Re-balancing Security and Justice: Protection of Fundamental Rights in Police and Judicial Cooperation in Criminal Matters' (2010) 47 *Common Market Law Review* 1455.

Roach, K, 'The Criminal Law and Terrorism' in VV Ramraj, M Hor and K Roach (eds), *Global Anti-Terrorism Law and Policy* (Cambridge, Cambridge University Press, 2005).

Rockmore, T, Margolis, J and Marsoobian, AT (eds), *The Philosophical Challenge of September 11* (London, Wiley-Blackwell, 2004).

Rosand, E, 'The UN-led Multilateral Institutional Response to Jihadist Terrorism: is a Global Counterterrorism Body Needed?' (2006) *Journal of Conflict and Security Law* 399.

Rose, J, 'The Rule of Law in the Western World: An Overview' (2004) 35 *Journal of Social Philosophy* 457.

Sadurski, W (ed), *Political Rights Under Stress in 21st Century Europe* (Oxford, Oxford University Press, 2006).

Sagemann, M, *Understanding Terror Networks* (Philadelphia, University of Pennsylvania Press, 2004).

Sands, P, *Lawless World: Making and Breaking Global Rules* (London, Penguin, 2006).

Sanfrutos-Cano, E, 'The End of the Pillars? A Single EU Legal Order after Lisbon' in CC Murphy and P Green (eds), *Law and Outsiders: Norms, Processes and 'Othering' in the 21st Century* (Oxford, Hart Publishing, 2011).

Saul, B, *Defining Terrorism in International Law* (Oxford, Oxford University Press, 2006).

—— 'International Terrorism as a European Crime: the Policy Rationale for Criminalization' (2003) 11 *European Journal of Crime, Criminal Law and Criminal Justice* 323.

—— 'The Legal Response of the League of Nations to Terrorism' (2006) *Journal of International Criminal Justice* 78.

Scheinin, M, 'Is the ECJ Ruling in *Kadi* Incompatible with International Law?' in P Eeckhout and T Tridimas (eds), *Yearbook of European Law* (Oxford, Oxford University Press, 2009).

Scheppele, KL, 'The Migration of Anti-Constitutional Ideas: The Post-9/11 Globalization of *Public Law* and the International State of Emergency' in S Choudhry (ed), *The Migration of Constitutional Ideas* (Oxford, Oxford University Press, 2006).

Schmid, AP, 'Terrorism: The Definitional Problem' (2004) 36 *Case Western Reserve Journal of International Law* 375.

Schmitt, C, *The Concept of the Political* (Chicago, Chicago University Press, 2007).

—— *Political Theology: Four Chapters on the Concept of Sovereignty* (Chicago, University of Chicago Press, 2006).

Scraton, P (ed), *Beyond September 11: An Anthology of Dissent* (London, Pluto Press, 2002).

Shaughnessy, P, 'The New EU Money-Laundering Directive: Lawyers As Gate-Keepers and Whistle-Blowers' (2002–2003) 34*Law and Policy in International Business* 25.

Shaw, CJ, 'Worldwide War on Terrorist Finance' (2007) *Journal of International Banking Law and Regulation* 469.

Silver, E and Miller, LL, 'A Cautionary Note on the Use of Actuarial Risk Assessment Tools for Social Control' (2002) 48 *Crime Delinquency* 138.

Simons, GL, *The Scourging of Iraq: Sanctions Law and Natural Justice* (London, Macmillan, 1996).

Skhlar, J, 'Political Theory and the Rule of Law' in AC Hutchinson and P Monahan (eds), *The Rule of Law: Ideal or Ideology* (Toronto, Carswell, 1987).

Sofaer, AD, 'On the Necessity of Pre-emption' (2003) 14 *European Journal of International Law* 209.

Sottiaux, S, '*Leroy v France:* Apology of Terrorism and the Malaise of the European Court of Human Rights' Free Speech Jurisprudence' (2009) *European Human Rights Law Review* 415.

—— *Terrorism and the Limitation of Human Rights: The ECHR and the US Constitution* (Oxford, Hart Publishing, 2008).

Spencer, JR, 'The Problems of Trans-border Evidence and European Initiatives to Resolve Them' (2007) 9 *Cambridge Yearbook of European Legal Studies* 477.

Steele, J, *Risks and Legal Theory* (Oxford, Hart Publishing, 2004).

Steinhardt, B, 'Problem of Policy Laundering', American Civil Liberties Union, 13 August 2004.

Sterba, JP (ed), *Terrorism and International Justice* (Oxford, Oxford University Press, 2003).

Sullivan, G and Hayes, B, *Blacklisted: Targeted Sanctions, Preemptive Security and Fundamental Rights* (Berlin, European Centre for Constitutional and Human Rights, 2011).

Sunstein, C, *Laws of Fear: Beyond the Precautionary Principle* (Cambridge, Cambridge University Press, 2005).

Suskind, R, *The One Percent Doctrine: Deep Inside America's Pursuit of its Enemies since 9/11* (New York, Simon & Schuster, 2006).

Symeonidou-Kastanidou, E, 'Defining Terrorism' (2004) 12 *European Journal of Crime, Criminal Law and Criminal Justice* 14.

Tamanaha, BZ, *On the Rule of Law: History, Politics, Theory* (Cambridge, Cambridge University Press, 2006).

Thorny, J-F, 'Processing Financial Information in Money Laundering Matters: The Financial Intelligence Units' (1996) 4 *European Journal of Crime, Criminal Law and Criminal Justice* 257.

Timmermans, C, 'The European Court of Justice as a Human Rights Court?' Annual Lecture, Centre of European Law, King's College London, 6 May 2010.

Tomkins, A, 'Legislating Against Terror: The Anti-terrorism, Crime and Security Act 2001' (2002) *Public Law* 205.

Tomuschat, C, 'Case T-306/01, *Ahmed Ali Yusuf and Al Barakaat International Foundation v Council and Commission*; Case T-315/01, *Yassin Abdullah Kadi v Council and Commission*' (2006) 43 *Common Market Law Review* 537.

Trechsel, S, *Human Rights in Criminal Proceedings* (Oxford, Oxford University Press, 2005).

Tridimas, T, 'Economic Sanctions, Procedural Rights and Judicial Scrutiny: Post-Kadi Developments' (2010) *Cambridge Yearbook of European Legal Studies* 455.

—— *The General Principles of EU Law*, 2nd edn (Oxford, Oxford University Press, 2007).

—— 'Terrorism and the ECJ: Empowerment and Democracy in the EC Legal Order' *Queen Mary School of Law Legal Studies Research Paper* No 12/2009.

Trubek, DM, Cottrell, P and Nance, M, '"Soft Law", "Hard Law," and European Integration: Toward a Theory of Hybridity', *Jean Monnet Working Paper 02/05* (New York, NYU School of Law, 2005).

Türk, AH, *The Concept of Legislation in European Community Law: A Comparative Perspective* (Netherlands, Kluwer Law International, 2006).

Türk, V, 'Forced Migration and Security' (2003) 15 *International Journal of Refugee Law* 113.

Tzanou, M and El-Droubi, S, 'Case T-318/01, *Omar Mohommad Othman* v. *Council of the European Union and Commission of the European Communities*, Judgment of the Court of First Instance of 11 June 2009 (Seventh Chamber), not yet reported.' (2010) 47 *Common Market Law Review* 1233.

VanWasshnova, MR, 'Data Protection Conflicts Between the United States and the European Union in the War on Terror: Lessons Learned from the Existing System of Financial Information Exchange' (2006–2008) 29 *Case Western Reserve Journal of International Law* 827.

Vilasau, M, 'Traffic Data Retention v Data Protection: The New European Framework' (2007) *Computer and Telecommunications Law Review* 52.

Vogel, J and Spencer, JR, 'Proportionality and the European Arrest Warrant' (2010)(6) *Criminal Law Review* 47.

Von Bogdandy, A *see* Bogdandy, A von.

Walker, C, *Blackstone's Guide to the Anti-Terrorism Legislation*, 2nd edn (Oxford, Oxford University Press, 2009).

—— 'The Legal Definition of "Terrorism" in United Kingdom Law and Beyond' (2007) *Public Law* 331.

—— *Terrorism and the Law* (Oxford, Oxford University Press, 2011).

—— 'The Threat of Terrorism and the Fate of Control Orders' (2010) *Public Law* 4.

Walker, N, 'Unscientific, Unwise, Unprofitable or Unjust? The Anti-Protectionist Arguments' (1982) 22 *British Journal of Criminology* 276.

Walsh, D, 'Parliamentary Scrutiny of EU Criminal Law in Ireland' (2006) 31 *European Law Review* 48.

Warren, SD and Brandeis, LD, 'The Right to Privacy' (1890) 4 *Harvard Law Review* 193.

Weber, L and Bowling, B, 'Valiant Beggars and Global Vagabonds: Select, Eject, Immobilize' (2008) 12 *Theoretical Criminology* 355.

Weber, M, *Politics as a Vocation*, Lecture to Munich University, January 1919.

Weiler, JHH, *The Constitution of Europe: 'Do the New Clothes Have an Emperor?' and Other Essays on European Integration* (Cambridge, Cambridge University Press, 1999).

Whitman, JQ, 'The Two Western Cultures of Privacy: Dignity Versus Liberty' (2004) 113 *Yale Law Journal* 1151.

Wood, MC, 'The European Convention on the Suppression of Terrorism' (1981) *Yearbook of European Law* 307.

Woodley, M (ed), *Osborn's Concise Law Dictionary*, 10th edn (London, Sweet & Maxwell, 2005).

Zedner, L, 'Fixing the Future? The Pre-emption Turn in Criminal Justice' in B McSherry, A Norrie and S Bronitt (eds), *Regulating Deviance: The Redirection of Criminalisation and the Futures of Criminal Law* (Oxford, Hart Publishing, 2009).

—— 'Pre-Crime and post-Criminology?' (2007) 11 *Theoretical Criminology* 261.

Index